Centre for the Study of
Human Rights

INTERNET PRIVACY RIGHTS

Internet Privacy Rights analyses the current threats to our online autonomy and privacy, and proposes a new model for the gathering, retention and use of personal data. Key to the model is the development of specific privacy rights: a right to roam the internet with privacy, a right to monitor the monitors, a right to delete personal data, and a right to create, assert and protect an online identity. These rights could help in the formulation of more effective and appropriate legislation, and shape more privacy-friendly business models. The conclusion examines how the internet might look with these rights in place and whether such an internet could be sustainable from both a governmental and a business perspective.

PAUL BERNAL is a lecturer in information technology, intellectual property and media law at the University of East Anglia Law School, where his research centres around privacy and human rights, particularly on the internet.

CAMBRIDGE INTELLECTUAL PROPERTY AND INFORMATION LAW

As its economic potential has rapidly expanded, intellectual property has become a subject of front-rank legal importance. *Cambridge Intellectual Property and Information Law* is a series of monograph studies of major current issues in intellectual property. Each volume contains a mix of international, European, comparative and national law, making this a highly significant series for practitioners, judges and academic researchers in many countries.

Series editors
Lionel Bently
Herchel Smith Professor of Intellectual Property Law, University of Cambridge
William R. Cornish
Emeritus Herchel Smith Professor of Intellectual Property Law,
University of Cambridge

Advisory editors
François Dessemontet, Professor of Law, University of Lausanne
Paul Goldstein, Professor of Law, Stanford University
The Rt Hon. Sir Robin Jacob, Hugh Laddie Professor of Intellectual Property,
University College, London

A list of books in the series can be found at the end of this volume.

INTERNET PRIVACY RIGHTS

Rights to Protect Autonomy

PAUL BERNAL

CAMBRIDGE
UNIVERSITY PRESS

CAMBRIDGE
UNIVERSITY PRESS

University Printing House, Cambridge CB2 8BS, United Kingdom

Published in the United States of America by Cambridge University Press, New York

Cambridge University Press is part of the University of Cambridge.

It furthers the University's mission by disseminating knowledge in the pursuit of education, learning and research at the highest international levels of excellence.

www.cambridge.org
Information on this title: www.cambridge.org/9781107042735

First published 2014

Printed in the United Kingdom by Clays, St Ives plc

A catalogue record for this publication is available from the British Library

Library of Congress Cataloguing in Publication data
Bernal, Paul, 1964–
Internet privacy rights : rights to protect autonomy / Paul Bernal.
p.   cm. – (Cambridge intellectual property and information law ; 24)
Includes bibliographical references and index.
ISBN 978-1-107-04273-5 (hardback)
1. Data protection–Law and legislation.   2. Computer security–Law and legislation.
3. Internet–Security measures.   4. Internet–Safety measures.   5. Privacy,
Right of.   I. Title.
K3264.C65B49   2014
323.44′8–dc23
2013045717

ISBN 978-1-107-04273-5 Hardback

CONTENTS

Privacy on the internet has never mattered more. The internet is now part of almost every aspect of our lives, from the personal and intimate to the professional, from our finances to our leisure, from our interactions with each other to our interactions with our governments. It is no longer something optional, something that we can avoid: if we want to live full lives, to participate in society, to take advantage of all our opportunities, we need the internet.

What happens to us on the internet impacts upon our autonomy – our freedom to act, our freedom to decide for ourselves how we live our lives – and not just our autonomy online but our autonomy in the 'real', offline world. Part of this impact arises from the way that our privacy is infringed upon, directly and indirectly, intentionally and unintentionally, by a wide variety of people, companies and government agencies. People are increasingly becoming aware of these problems: internet privacy issues, once of interest to only those loosely described as geeks and nerds, are now headline news all around the world. Internet privacy not only matters, but it is beginning to be seen to matter.

It has been argued that privacy is 'dead', that privacy is 'outdated' and even that privacy is in itself damaging and that we should embrace transparency and openness in its place. These arguments are not trivial or simplistic, and there is evidence to support all of them, but ultimately they are fundamentally flawed. If we want autonomy, if we want freedom, we need privacy to protect it. We need privacy *rights*.

This book presents a linked set of internet privacy rights – rights that, sometimes even without knowing it, people are already starting to claim. These are not 'legal' rights in a precise and enforceable sense, but something more akin to natural rights. They reflect the rights that people *believe* that they have, that people *need* to have in order to function freely on the internet. What these rights are, why they are appropriate and how they could help people and help shape the internet into a more privacy-friendly form in the future is the main purpose of *Internet Privacy Rights*.

Some people express concern primarily against invasions of privacy by the likes of Google and Facebook, some by government agencies such as the US National Security Agency (NSA) and the UK's Government Communications Headquarters (GCHQ) – particularly in the light of the PRISM, Tempora and related revelations of 2013 – while others seem worried most by criminal scammers and identity thieves. Which of these groups is right? In different ways, each of them has very legitimate concerns, but they cannot be considered separately. The relationships between businesses and governments are complex and intertwined, and criminals and scammers can feed off both. Data gathered by businesses can be accessed and used by government agencies, or hacked or stolen by criminals. Business models based on privacy invasions can be legitimised by governments against the interests of individuals as a result of lobbying, or from the tacit understanding that both businesses and governments can benefit from having more and more information about us.

This is where the rights presented here come in: they can help people to fight their corner. Rights provide a language for people to use, a way to express themselves in the face of what often seems to be the overwhelming power of both the corporate and the security lobbies.

Internet Privacy Rights starts with a theoretical analysis of both privacy and autonomy, and how they apply in the current, substantially commercial form of the internet. It sets out a model – the *Symbiotic Web* – to explain the current, principally commercial way that the internet functions, with individuals dependent on free or discounted services and businesses relying on their ability to gather and use our personal data. This symbiosis is currently essentially beneficial to both individuals and businesses, but there are significant risks attached. Those risks are both analysed theoretically and illustrated through case studies of situations familiar to most people from their everyday experience on the internet. Some of the most common activities on the internet are examined: the use of search engines, the way that behavioural advertising works and so on. The rights suggested in *Internet Privacy Rights* emerge from these case studies: in part as a solution to the problems encountered and in part as a reflection of the way that people, in practice, have responded to those problems.

A number of concepts are introduced in this book: the aforementioned model, the *Symbiotic Web*; *Collaborative Consent*, a new way to look at how to deal with the thorny issue of consent in the online context; *Autonomy by Design*, taking privacy by design a stage further; *Disclosure Minimisation*, a privacy-friendly way of looking at the assertion and verification of identity; and *Surveillance Minimisation*, addressing the rising issue of government surveillance of the internet. Each of these concepts addresses potentially critical issues that arise from an examination of how the internet currently functions: *Internet Privacy Rights* looks at the internet from both a conceptual and a pragmatic perspective.

This book is a development of the work that I undertook for my PhD thesis at the London School of Economics, and some of the ideas in this book have previously been published (Bernal, 2010a, 2010b, 2011a, 2011b). I should like to thank the LSE and the Arts and Humanities Research Council who provided the funding for the research, and in particular my two excellent PhD supervisors Professor Conor Gearty and Professor Andrew Murray. The central premise of this book joins their two fields – human rights and internet law – and without their expertise, encouragement and support this book would never have been written. I should also like to thank Professor Alastair Mullis whose support at the UEA was invaluable, and my other excellent colleagues at the UEA Law School. Most of all, I would like to thank my daughter Alice for keeping me grounded and reminding me what really matters, and my wife Corina for emotional support, vital assistance with editing and proofreading, and much, much more.

The internet world – particularly insofar as it concerns privacy – is in a state of flux. At the time of writing, that world was still reeling from Edward Snowden's whistle-blowing over PRISM, surveillance and censorship laws and rules were being implemented or contemplated all over the world, and Europe was in the throes of an almost tortuous reform process over data protection. Predicting the future is, as a consequence, fraught with danger. I am not what Morozov might describe as a cyber-utopian, but neither am I a full-fledged 'cyberdystopian', seeing the internet either now or in the future primarily as a tool for authoritarianism and control. The research into internet privacy that is the background to this book reveals a great many problems, some of which seem almost to be insurmountable, but it also reveals some progress, both in practice, with 'victories' for those supporting privacy, and also a significant improvement in awareness of privacy issues. The internet is not, by any stretch of the imagination, 'privacy-friendly' at present – but that does not mean that it is impossible for it to become, at least in some ways, more privacy-friendly.

I believe an improvement might be possible. Whether it will happen is another question entirely. It is very hard to tell, and there are signs in both positive and negative directions. In some ways I suspect a more privacy-friendly internet is inevitable – the more we know, the more we seem to care, and ultimately companies and governments have to take account of that. At the moment, however, that seems to be a very long way away, but it is of great importance for anyone interested in autonomy and freedom, and not just on the internet.

Internet privacy rights

1   Introduction

Privacy on the internet has gone from being a subject of interest only to what might loosely be described as 'geeks' and 'nerds' to something that is of relevance to almost everyone. The internet is huge business. Facebook has more than a billion users worldwide.[1] Apple, whose products are almost all internet based – the 'i' in 'iMac', which led to the 'i' in iPod, iPhone and iPad, originally stood for 'internet'[2] – and Google are two of the world's three biggest corporations.[3] For all of these organisations, privacy has become increasingly important. Data breaches have started to become front-page news. Privacy policies and practices are now taken far more seriously; whenever Mark Zuckerberg announces a new product or service for Facebook, he makes privacy one of the key things that he talks about.[4] The authorities, too, are taking privacy more seriously: in the United States, for example, Google and Facebook have been made subject to Federal Trade Commission (FTC) privacy audits for twenty years, and Twitter for ten.[5]

Why has privacy become such a big issue? Do we need a new approach to understanding it? These are questions that have been coming more and more to the fore. Amongst other things, this book attempts to explain

---

[1] Facebook passed 1 billion active users in October 2012: see their press release at http://newsroom.fb.com/News/457/One-Billion-People-on-Facebook.

[2] When Steve Jobs first introduced the iMac in 1998, he said 'iMac comes from the marriage of the excitement of the Internet with the simplicity of Macintosh'.

[3] See for example http://online.wsj.com/article/SB10001424127887323539804578264024260588396.html. In January 2013, in terms of market capitalisation Apple was the second largest and Google the third largest corporation in the world.

[4] When launching Graph Search in January 2013, Zuckerberg said 'We've built Graph Search from the start with privacy in mind, and it respects the privacy and audience of each piece of content on Facebook.' See http://newsroom.fb.com/News/562/Introducing-Graph-Search-Beta.

[5] For Facebook see www.ftc.gov/opa/2011/11/privacysettlement.shtm, for Google see www.ftc.gov/opa/2011/10/buzz.shtm, for Twitter see www.ftc.gov/opa/2011/03/twitter.shtm.

why and to suggest a way forward. The key to that approach is an understanding that the key reason that privacy has become important is that privacy matters to people, at least in part, because people care about their autonomy, and privacy is a crucial protector of autonomy.

When people care about something, ultimately that finds its way into how businesses react, and how governments react. That is why both businesses and governments are beginning to take privacy seriously. As the case studies in this book reveal, however, that process is taking a long time, and there has been a lot of pain and misunderstanding along the way. The ideas presented in this book are intended to help to reduce that time, and to minimise the pain and misunderstanding. The starting point to that is to have a better understanding of the role that the internet plays in people's lives. From there we can start to understand what people expect from the internet, and what they believe their *rights* should be while they operate on the internet.

1.1   The internet in contemporary life

For most people in what might loosely be described as the developed world the internet can no longer be considered an optional extra, but an intrinsic part of life in a modern, developed society. Significant aspects of life take place on the internet. Interactions with government, for example, are becoming increasingly electronic, not only in terms of access to information but more directly and interactively: the completion of tax returns, access to health services,[6] interaction with local government, and much more. Indeed, the UK government is moving to a 'digital by default' policy.[7] The digital economy has already become a significant part of the economy as a whole, and this is increasing all the time. In the UK, it is predicted that by 2016, 23 per cent of all purchases in this country will be made online.[8] It is increasingly the case that people who are not able to access products and services online are at a significant disadvantage, being unable to take advantages of discounts for insurance,[9] better interest rates

---

[6] See www.nhsdirect.nhs.uk/. NHS Direct is suggested as the first port of call for health problems in the UK.

[7] See http://digital.cabinetoffice.gov.uk/about/ – Digital by Default is central to the UK government digital strategy.

[8] See www.bcgperspectives.com/content/articles/media_entertainment_strategic_planning_4_2_trillion_opportunity_internet_economy_g20/.

[9] Aviva insurance, for example, in February 2012, was offering a 20 per cent discount for online applications for car insurance. See www.aviva.co.uk/car-insurance/.

on savings,[10] and having tighter deadlines for the submission of information, for example.[11] Moreover, there are some very useful services that are only available online, such as price comparison sites for insurance and other financial services.[12] Shopping has been revolutionised, from specialised online services such as Amazon and auction sites such as eBay to the online versions of existing supermarkets, allowing ordering online and delivery to your home.[13]

All this is without considering the most direct, 'traditional' uses of the internet, as an unparalleled source of information, for educational or recreational purposes, as an increasingly important news source,[14] or simply to discover practical information such as the location and opening hours of shops, events and so forth.

Perhaps even more important is not the extent to which a capacity to use the internet is now required but the reality of how much it is used in practice. The numerous sites and services noted above are only a small part of what has become a significant element of life. There are many others that have become part of the social fabric for a large section of society. Social networking sites are just one example. They cannot generally be said to be either practically necessary or economically advantageous but they are used, extensively and increasingly, and not just by young people. The same can be said of a whole range of other services, from message boards and blogs to media services such as YouTube.

Further, the internet is no longer something that is only to be accessed through computers. More and more devices can and do use or provide a connection to the internet, from smartphones and tablet devices to Blu-ray players, TV receivers, game machines and digital cameras. This trend appears certain to increase, and increase rapidly,

---

[10] Most UK banks offer 'e-savings' accounts or equivalents, only accessible online, offering better interest rates or other advantages.

[11] UK tax returns submitted on paper, for example, are required to be submitted by 31 October each year, while online submissions are allowed until 31 January the following year. See www.hmrc.gov.uk/sa/deadlines-penalties.htm.

[12] E.g. www.gocompare.com/, www.confused.com/, www.comparethemarket.com/.

[13] See www.amazon.com or www.amazon.co.uk, www.ebay.com and, for example, www.sainsburys.co.uk/home or www.tesco.com/ for online stores of supermarkets.

[14] In the 2008 US election, for example, the Internet was one of the most important sources of news for voters, particularly for young people. Pew Internet Research reported that '42% of those ages 18 to 29 say they regularly learn about the campaign from the internet, the highest percentage for any news source'. See http://people-press.org/report/384/internets-broader-role-in-campaign-2008.

as the advantages of using internet connections for all kinds of devices become more apparent, and more innovative ideas such as Google's Glass[15] are developed.

The ultimate implication of this is that living without using the internet places people at a significant disadvantage in many different ways, including socially, culturally, democratically and financially. The concept of a 'digital divide', or more accurately 'digital divides',[16] between those who have the skills and opportunities to take advantage of digital services and those who don't, has been discussed since the 1990s – see for example the work of Norris (2001) and Mossberger (Mossberger *et al.*, 2003). The nature of the relevant divides has changed considerably over the last decade, as the role that the internet plays in society has become more significant, as outlined above, and access to it has become the norm rather than the exception. The disadvantages to those who do not have internet access are continuing to grow both in scale and breadth, which is one of the reasons why there are increasing calls to consider access to the internet a 'right'.

The idea of internet access as a basic human right has been put forward by many, and according to a large survey by the BBC World Service, nearly 80 per cent of people around the world believe that it should be.[17] In Estonia,[18] France[19] and Greece,[20] for example, internet access has already been made a constitutional right, while in Finland this right has become

---

[15]   Google Glass is a headset designed to be worn like glasses, 'reading' what you see and providing a 'heads-up display' of relevant data before your eyes. See www.google.com/glass/start/.

[16]   Divides between rich and poor nations, between the rich and the poor within nations, between the better and worse educated, between the urban and the rural, divides based on gender, disability, race and more – there are many possible reasons for what might be termed digital disadvantage. Mossberger also identifies different aspects of the divides – what she terms the 'access divide', the 'skills divide', the 'economic opportunity divide' and the 'democratic divide', paralleling some of the discussion in this chapter. See Mossberger, Tolbert and Stansbury (2003, particularly p. 9).

[17]   http://news.bbc.co.uk/1/shared/bsp/hi/pdfs/08_03_10_BBC_internet_poll.pdf. The survey included more than 27,000 people in twenty-six countries.

[18]   See http://news.bbc.co.uk/1/hi/world/europe/3603943.stm.

[19]   See for example www.dailymail.co.uk/news/worldnews/article-1192359/Internet-access-fundamental-human-right-rules-French-court.html?ITO=1490.

[20]   Article 5A, paragraph 2 of the Constitution of Greece states that 'All persons are entitled to participate in the Information Society. Facilitation of access to electronically handled information, as well as of the production, exchange and diffusion thereof constitutes an obligation of the State.' See for example www.unhcr.org/refworld/docid/4c52794f2.html.

legally enforceable.[21] The EU Telecoms Reform Package agreed in 2009 supports high-speed access for 'all citizens' throughout the EU.[22]

In the UK, surveys suggest the same. In 2009, a survey for the Communications Consumer Panel showed that '84 per cent of people agreed that it should be possible for everyone in the UK to have broadband at home, regardless of where they live. Many people already see broadband as essential and even more believe that soon it will be essential for everyone.' As Communications Consumer Panel Chair Anna Bradley put it:

> The tipping point will be when broadband does not just provide an advantage to people who have it, but disadvantages people who do not. Interestingly some people already feel disadvantaged: those who live in not-spots and those who have school-age children but do not have broadband at home.[23]

The idea that internet access could be a human right is debatable. Vint Cerf, for example, one of the 'fathers of the internet', has suggested that it is not.[24] The nature and scale of the discussion over this issue, however, and the reality of the way that the internet is used in practice do suggest that at the very least an inability to access the internet puts people at a significant disadvantage. To be able to participate fully in contemporary life, people need internet access, and so to participate freely in that life, people need the opportunity to act freely on the internet.

1.2 Data and the internet

The internet offers hitherto unheard-of opportunities to gather, analyse, use and store personal data, and it has become the focus of efforts to do all of this.[25] The case studies in Chapters 5 to 7 reveal just some of the ways in which this is already happening, and give at least some idea of how this could develop into the future.

---

[21] See for example www.bbc.co.uk/news/10461048. Finland not only made internet access a legal right, but specified a minimum speed of access of 1Mbps.

[22] See http://europa.eu/rapid/pressReleasesAction.do?reference=MEMO/09/491.

[23] www.communicationsconsumerpanel.org.uk/press-releases/press-releases/post/173-soon-it-will-be-essential-for-everyone-to-have-broadband.

[24] See for example www.nytimes.com/2012/01/05/opinion/internet-access-is-not-a-human-right.html?_r=0.

[25] Each of Cate's four principles for data growth, set out in Cate (1997, pp. 13–16), applies directly to the Internet. His fourth principle in particular refers to the impact of computer networks.

The nature of the internet makes manipulation of the lives of individuals through the use of personal data particularly easy. The ways in which this can work are analysed throughout the book and specifically in Chapter 3, where a model describing the current functions of the internet is set out, and its implications explored, including some of the direct and indirect ways that individuals' autonomy can be threatened. This model, the Symbiotic Web, suggests that there is a symbiotic relationship between the individuals who use the internet, and are reliant on 'free' sites and services, and the businesses that provide those services and which have built business models dependent on their ability to gather and process personal data from those individuals.

It is becoming increasingly difficult to separate 'online' and 'offline' data. As the internet becomes more and more integrated into 'real' life, online and offline data become commixed. To take one example, one of the largest types of data gathered in the 'real' world is that gathered by supermarkets for their loyalty schemes, such as the Tesco Clubcard and the Nectar service operated by Sainsbury's, BP and others. Though initially this data is gathered and used in relation to 'real-world' shopping, it now includes the shopping done online, and it is held in such a way that it can be accessed online and used online. The data itself has become online data.

Even data held by corporations or government departments on 'private' computers or networks is also becoming part of the 'online' world, as those networks are using 'public' infrastructure or running on 'virtual private networks' on the internet, with the same computers being used to gather, hold and access the data that are also used to access the internet. Separation and isolation of computers from the internet is increasingly uncommon and likely to become more so. Added to that, data gathered offline may be (and is likely to increasingly be) integrated and aggregated with other data, much of which is gathered online, and the results are then stored and used online.

The concepts of an 'internet of things' and 'augmented reality' take the integration between the online and offline worlds further steps forward. The 'internet of things' refers to the way that more and more 'real' objects have an online 'presence' through chips (and particularly RFID chips) built into them, allowing them to be mapped, tracked, inventoried and so forth,[26]

---

[26] The term 'internet of things' may have been coined by Kevin Ashton in 1999, though it is now of common usage. See Ashton's article in *RFID Journal* in 2009 'That "Internet of Things" Thing', accessible at www.rfidjournal.com/article/view/4986.

while 'augmented reality' refers to the use of digital information to supplement 'real' information in heads-up displays in aeroplanes and cars, providing assistance for pilots and drivers, or in mapping applications for smartphones, for example. The use of augmented reality in smartphones in particular – taking advantage of the geo-location systems built into such phones – is already relatively widespread.[27] With the increasing prevalence of smartphones, augmented reality might be expected to become more common. Google Glass takes this to the next logical stage, with the possibility of an always-on camera, always-on geo-location and a constant stream of data in both directions, integrating pretty much your entire life with the internet.

Finally, the internet introduces new levels of vulnerability and new ways in which private data, once it has been gathered, stolen or otherwise acquired, appropriately or inappropriately, may be loosed upon the world. The most graphic examples of this involve leaks such as those performed by WikiLeaks, but there are many more insidious and less dramatic ways in which this happens. This is an issue that is not going to disappear: quite the opposite, it can only be expected to grow.

1.3   Underlying questions and a paradigm shift

One of the underlying questions in this book is how 'public' is the internet? Should the internet, or some significant part of it, be considered a 'public space' and if so, what does that imply? If the answer to this question is 'yes', as this book contends, then the implications are considerable, not just for the rights of individuals as they browse the web or use internet-based services, but for the obligations of those providing or hosting websites or offering internet-based services.

How 'public' the internet should be considered is a complex question, and one that cannot easily be answered using what might be termed 'old-style' rules. It raises numerous issues: what is cyberspace, and what is the internet? Is it simply a collection of connected private spaces, each owned and governed by the people who run the websites concerned? In practice, the vast majority of the internet is owned and run privately. So should the web be considered something effectively private, with browsers having to follow whatever rules the web owner sets, particularly in terms of privacy? Or is it a public space, and governed by public rules, public

---

[27] By June 2013 the number of augmented reality apps available through the iTunes Store was in the thousands.

norms and so forth, with people having an expectation that they should have certain rights, and that those rights will be respected as they browse the internet?

The implication of the suggestion that the internet is now an intrinsic part of contemporary life is that it should, in certain ways, be considered public, and that people who use it should be able to rely on their rights being respected. This is already true to an extent in terms of commerce – commercial law including contract law applies to commercial transactions that take place over the internet – and issues such as copyright, defamation, pornography and so forth. Though there are complications, jurisdictional issues and so forth, the principles in all these areas are clear. Despite the declarations of independence of cyberspace from Barlow onwards,[28] law has been applied to online life, with varying degrees of success, in many different ways.

This leads to the conclusion that we must consider the internet to be to a significant extent a public space and that rights are applied to the internet as a consequence. If we as people have the *need* to use the internet, and the *right* to use the internet, we should have appropriate protections and rights *when* we use the internet.

This brings up the question of which parts of the internet should be considered public and which private, and hence what kinds of right (and in particular what degree of privacy) someone using those parts can reasonably expect. The principle answer, this book suggests, is that the default position, the assumption, should be that everywhere on the internet should be considered public unless there is a compelling reason to the contrary.

A second underlying question concerns the personal data itself: to what extent is personal data 'ours'? And, behind that question is the question of what actually counts as 'personal' data. Opinion, law and practice produce a wide variety of potential answers to both of these questions. In countries such as the United States few forms of data are considered personal enough that an individual has any rights over them at all, while the data protection regimes in Europe effectively consider any data that can be directly linked to an individual as 'personal'. The issue of what rights an individual has concerning data held 'about' them is another central

---

[28] Barlow's famous 'Declaration of the Independence of Cyberspace', found at https://projects.eff.org/~barlow/Declaration-Final.html, was made in 1996, but there have been similar claims made subsequently over the years, right up to the claims by the hacker group Anonymous in 2010. See www.youtube.com/watch?v=gbqC8BnvVHQ.

theme, and one of the conclusions drawn is that more rights are needed in order to give individuals more control, and hence more autonomy.

If the answers to these underlying questions are as suggested, what is required is a paradigm shift in attitudes to privacy on the internet, and to data privacy in general. In a private place, individuals control their own 'privacy settings', while in a public place individuals do not, and hence require protection through privacy rights.[29] The default position needs to shift from one where privacy is the exception to one where privacy is the general rule. Surveillance on the net should not be *assumed* to be acceptable, and neither should the gathering, processing or holding of personal data. At present, unless an objection is made, it appears that surveillance can and does happen, without the knowledge or consent of the individual, and that data can be and is gathered, processed and held, similarly without the knowledge or consent of the individual. The opposite needs to become the case: those who want to monitor people and those who desire to gather, use or hold data about people should need to justify that monitoring, that data gathering, use or holding. If they cannot justify it, or if their justification is inadequate or inappropriate, they should not be able to perform that monitoring or data gathering, and they should not be able to use or hold that data. The privacy rights suggested here are designed to support and enable that paradigm shift.

1.4   Autonomy as the prime concern

This book takes an essentially liberal perspective that takes autonomy as its prime concern. What is meant by autonomy in the context of this book is examined in depth in Chapter 2, but the essence is relatively simple. The approach is drawn primarily from Raz's conception of autonomy, describing an autonomous person as one who 'is a (part) author of his own life' (Raz, 1986, p. 369). It is an approach that sees autonomy as a 'constituent element of the good life' (Raz, 1986, p. 408). The rights set out flow directly from this idea of autonomy: they arise from autonomy and if brought into play they support, protect and help preserve autonomy.

Though the issue of privacy is central, it is privacy as a protector of autonomy rather than privacy per se that is of prime concern. As already

---

[29]   Cases such as *Campbell* v. *Mirror Group Newspapers Ltd* [2004] UKHL 22, *Von Hannover* v. *Germany* [2004] ECHR 294 and *Mosley* v. *News Group Newspapers* [2008] EWHC 1777 (QB) have centred around what expectations of privacy are appropriate in private or public spaces.

noted, it is particularly true that in the digital world privacy is crucial to protect autonomy. As Nissenbaum puts it:

> Widespread surveillance and the aggregation and analysis of information enhance the range of influence that powerful actors, such as government agencies, marketers, and potential employees, can have in shaping people's choices and actions. (Nissenbaum, 2010, p. 83)

Nissenbaum's analysis categorises the relationship between privacy and autonomy in the digital context in three ways. Firstly, that privacy can itself be considered an aspect of autonomy: autonomy over one's personal information. Secondly, that as privacy frees us from the 'stultifying effects of scrutiny and approbation (or disapprobation)', it contributes to an environment that supports the 'development and exercise of autonomy and freedom in thought and action' (Nissenbaum, 2010, p. 83). This can be looked on as a converse to the panopticon effect: if we don't feel ourselves to be under the constant risk of observation we will feel more able to think and act freely. Thirdly, and most directly for the purposes of this book, that without privacy our ability both to make effective choices and crucially to follow them through can be curtailed (Nissenbaum, 2010, pp. 82–3). The nature of the manipulations possible can be both in terms of the choices suggested and offered, and the information provided in order to aid in making those choices.

1.5   Privacy per se?

The existence and nature of any 'right to privacy' is a subject that is much discussed, and as the digital world becomes more significant it is likely to be discussed even more. The difficulties in pinning down the definition of privacy are discussed in Chapter 2, but they are not of a key, central concern here. Nonetheless, the conclusions and suggestions of this book could, indeed *would*, have a significant effect on privacy in many ways, as well as providing more autonomy for individuals, but these can be considered as side effects or peripheral benefits rather than the main intention.

Privacy and autonomy go hand in hand in protecting and supporting many 'human rights', as we currently consider them. Most directly, such rights are often called 'civil liberties' – freedom of association, freedom of expression, freedom of assembly, freedom of religion and so forth – but they also embrace other important rights including social, cultural and economic rights. The last of these is one that demonstrates some of the most insidious problems on the internet: without appropriate privacy it can be possible for people to be economically disadvantaged and discriminated against, with services made unavailable for some or priced differently for others based on private and personal information about those individuals.

1.6   Symbiotic regulation and the Symbiotic Web

Murray's concept of symbiotic regulation[30] can help to explain the way in which the rights set out here can come into effect. Symbiotic regulation starts by understanding the significant and active role played by the community in responding to regulatory actions. Further, it suggests that by mapping the relationships between the regulated parties, a desired regulatory result may be brought about through the harnessing of those relationships. The theory of symbiotic regulation is particularly suited to the digital environment and, as will be shown, applies directly to the examples set out in later chapters. Understanding the role that the community can play – and has already played – in the ways that regulation functions in the online world is of crucial importance: the symbiotic regulation model clarifies that role as well as suggesting effective routes for future regulatory approaches.

Building on this, an underlying theory of how the current, substantially commercial state of the internet functions will be put forward: the Symbiotic Web. This theory underpins the analysis not only of the case studies used but the conclusions that are drawn from them. Essentially, it suggests that a form of symbiosis has developed on the web. Individuals and commercial enterprises are mutually dependent: enterprises have built business models reliant on a currency of personal data, while individuals depend on free access to many services, from search engines, email systems and social networking sites to media services such as YouTube. These 'free' services use personal data as their way of generating revenues through targeted advertising, profile building and the direct sale of personal data.

The symbiosis is essentially benign and lies behind many positive developments on the internet. It benefits both the users and the businesses that provide services through the internet. Nevertheless, there are significant risks associated with this symbiotic nature that need to be addressed. In essence, the problems lie in the way that the symbiosis can drive an even greater tendency to gather personal data than before,

---

[30]   As set out in Chapter 8 of Murray (2006).

and then pressurise those who hold data to find ways to use it, ways that are potentially not merely non-consensual but harmful. Further, significantly from the perspective of autonomy, techniques are developing for targeting and 'tailoring' both content and links to individuals, often without their knowledge, understanding or consent. This in turn can lead to control over (and potentially automatic selection of) the choices made for individuals, material displayed for individuals and so forth, and potentially the opening up of opportunities for such pernicious practices as price discrimination and even racial, religious or gender-based access to particular websites. The evidence for the emergence of this kind of practice is becoming more compelling, and more and more variants of it are likely to develop.

The terms symbiotic regulation and Symbiotic Web are not coincidentally similar: rather, they both reflect the complexity and nature of the internet, the intertwined relationships between individuals, businesses, governments and others, between the hardware, software and services, and so forth. It should be noted, however, that the current situation is not something that is separate and unrelated from what has gone on before, but is a modern (and current) illustration of long-standing tensions that have always existed: those between privacy, security and economics on the one hand, and between individuals, governments and businesses on the other.

2   Privacy and autonomy on the internet

As the internet has become increasing integrated into our lives, our autonomy online has become more and more significant. The extent to which our online activities are 'free' is in many ways a reflection of the extent to which our offline lives are free, and the two are becoming inextricably linked. Where our online activities are restricted, controlled or unduly influenced, the result can be that our 'real-life' activities are restricted, controlled and unduly influenced. This is why online autonomy matters and why online privacy, a key protector of online autonomy, matters. This is not just about the internet, it is about our lives as a whole.

2.1   Threats to autonomy on the internet

Autonomy online can be threatened in a number of different ways. The case studies in the substantive chapters have been chosen directly with those threats in mind; and the privacy rights suggested arise as responses to those threats. Just as everything else in the online world is constantly developing in often unpredictable ways, the potential threats to autonomy are developing, and new threats are emerging all the time. As a consequence, what is discussed here is far from an exhaustive list.

The first threat examined relates to our navigation of the internet and search engines in particular. Though their role may not be as all-encompassing now as it has been, search engines still represent the most important tool that people have to find things on the internet, and the results of a search, and the way that this search is displayed, have a huge influence over which links people follow, which websites they visit. Conversely, search results can make other links less likely to be followed, or even completely concealed. As these search results become increasingly personalised or tailored to individuals, the impact upon autonomy can become more direct. Can people trust their search results? Can they find what they want to find, rather than what the search engines want them to find? The idea of personalisation is a key feature of the current internet and it has distinct advantages in many ways. It also, however, has risks, risks that relate directly to autonomy. Those risks need to be understood and addressed.

The second threat examined relates to tracking and monitoring, and in particular the kind of behavioural tracking and targeting that is becoming prevalent in the online advertising industry. Though it initially relates to what might be seen as a relatively harmless activity – advertising – the implications are far broader and more significant. Techniques developed to profile, target and predict interests and activities developed for advertising can be applied in other fields: the impact in terms of politics is perhaps the most obvious and potentially pernicious.

That leads directly to the third key threat: the threat that arises from the whole idea of profiling and its related processes. This builds on both of the previous threats: profiles are built up from such things as search logs and behavioural tracking amongst others. Profiling can have an impact on autonomy both when it is overly accurate (stories about people's sexuality or pregnancy being 'outed' by profiling are not just apocryphal) and when it is inaccurate, and inappropriate decisions are made on its basis. Profiles can potentially be built up and used for almost any purpose and can potentially be used automatically and invisibly as well as consciously and deliberately. If we are to protect autonomy, we need to be more aware of how the profiling takes place, and be better able to at least influence what happens to these profiles and how and when they are used.

There are of course other threats to autonomy online. Some are specific to particular services (e.g. social networking systems), some specific to particular data types (e.g. geo-location data). These and many others will be touched on; the breadth and variety of threats that exist are growing all the time. The responses and approaches taken to address them need to be flexible and adaptable if they are to be effective.

2.2   Competing interests: individuals, governments, businesses

Underlying all these threats is an environment where there are conflicting and competing interests and where the interests of individuals can find themselves squeezed. The priorities of individuals, governments and businesses are different, and though interests can and do coincide on many points (all three benefit from prosperity and security, for example) they do not always match, and where they don't it can be hard for individuals to 'fight their corner'.

In very broad-brush terms, governments have an interest in security and stability that can at times override individuals' desires and needs for privacy and autonomy. Businesses, on the other hand, have only one ultimate interest: making money. Both businesses and governments can support those interests by gathering more and more data and by knowing more and more about people and people's activities, interests and so forth. Those interests are legitimate and are not in principle in conflict with individuals' rights and needs. Individuals have a strong interest in (indeed a need for) the security provided by government and the prosperity provided by a thriving business sector, but there is often tension that can and does spill over into genuine conflict. Where businesses or governments go too far, individuals can and do suffer, and also sometimes rebel. The story of Phorm, discussed in depth in Chapter 6, should be a salutary tale for both governments and businesses about the need to find the appropriate balance and the need to respect the interests – the rights – of individuals.

That is the key reason for the idea of internet privacy rights put forward here. By articulating these rights, not only can individuals be helped in expressing their concerns and putting forward their case for privacy, but both businesses and governments can avoid going too far in the first place. If they understand what people want and expect, what people consider their rights, they are less likely to ride roughshod over them. Governments should be less likely to draft inappropriate laws, businesses should be less likely to design inappropriate business models. At the moment, at least on the surface, it appears that peoples' desires and needs for privacy and autonomy are barely understood, let alone taken seriously. That needs to change.

2.3   Privacy as a protection for autonomy

The relationship between privacy and autonomy will be explored more in the next chapter. The key, however, needs to be understood from the outset. Privacy is at least in some ways about control over how much is known about us by whom. In the online world, where decisions are made on the basis of information – of data – that aspect of privacy becomes particularly significant. To protect our autonomy, to have influence over what happens to us online, over what we see online, over what decisions are made about us and for us, we need to have protection over our data online. That means protection over how data is gathered about us, how that data is used, who can hold that data and so forth. The approach suggested here is that we have a right to this protection, and that in turn is the basis for the primary proposal of this book: internet privacy rights.

3   Internet privacy rights

The approach taken here is rights-based: what is meant by a rights-based approach, how it differs from current practice, whether such an approach would be effective and precisely what rights should be used are all central to the theme. The rights themselves are described in more depth below, as is the role that rights could play and the impact that they could have on individuals, on businesses and on governments. These rights are not intended as purely legal rights; indeed, they are not rights that could simply and easily be expressed as directly enforceable laws. Instead, they represent principles that could be reflected in laws, and understood as a basis of laws.

One key suggestion is that the rights identified here – a right to roam the internet with privacy, a right to monitor those monitoring us, a right to delete personal data and a right to an online identity – *are* rights in a philosophical sense. Connected to this idea is the suggestion that they represent the real wishes, desires and understanding of the people concerned; they reflect what people *consider* to be their rights. Finally, and most importantly, they could, from a practical perspective, have a significant and positive impact upon people's autonomy.

3.1   A right to roam the internet with privacy

The first suggested right is a right to roam the internet with privacy. When we browse the web, when we search for information and for things to do, see or buy, we should have a reasonable expectation of privacy – and that privacy should be the default. The exploration of what is meant by *roam* and by *privacy* will begin in Chapter 5, where navigation of the internet is the theme and search engines the focus. The role of search engines, and Google in particular, has been key to the development of the internet in its current, substantially commercial form. It has also been key to the role that personal, private data has played in that development.

Suggesting such a right is a radical suggestion. It challenges the way that Google and others have been operating over recent years, but it matches both the expectations and the needs of people using the internet. It also starts the process of bringing the operators of services such as Google into a position where they have to be more direct and open with their customers: if we have the right to roam with privacy, they will need to convince us that we should not take up that right. If they need us to consent to be tracked and monitored, to have our data gathered, they will need to persuade us that being tracked and monitored, and having our data gathered, is actually something that will benefit us. A key starting point in that process would be to ensure that it actually *does* benefit us, rather than just benefit their business, so a right such as this could encourage the development of models more directly to the benefit of all of us.

The right to roam with privacy would have a much broader application than just for search engines: it would apply for all internet navigation. It would have direct implications for Internet Service Providers (ISPs), for example, impacting upon their ability to gather clickstream data. It could potentially have implications for any operator of any services online, as will be discussed when the Symbiotic Web model is detailed. A vast array of those operating services online now gather and use data about those who visit their sites or use their services. The primary implication, however, is quite simple and direct: the default position should be one of privacy.

The right to roam with privacy could conflict directly with many current government practices, most directly internet surveillance and data retention. That tension is inevitable: at present, the general approach to internet surveillance and data gathering is essentially at odds with privacy. It relies on the idea that data should be gathered and held on a blanket basis, regardless of guilt or innocence or even suspicion. This tension must be understood and addressed but it should not be assumed that either side of the argument should automatically 'win'. The cause of security cannot automatically trump the cause of privacy, but neither can the converse be assumed. Ultimately this is a question of balance and one that is central to some of the key arguments over internet privacy.

It is important to understand that there is a difference between privacy and anonymity. This difference is of particular relevance to activities on the internet. The two are closely linked: both, indeed, can be viewed as aspects of identity protection. This is an area explored in Chapter 9, where the issue of online identity is examined in some depth. It is of specific relevance when considering the right to roam the internet with privacy: the right suggested here is not 'carte blanche' to operate without checks and balances, without accountability and without consequences for your actions.

3.2   A right to monitor those who monitor us

The second right set out here – a right that directly complements the right to roam with privacy – is a right to monitor those who monitor us. Even if we are accorded a right to roam with privacy, there are times when we will be monitored and times when we will want to be monitored. The former will occur in general because that monitoring is necessary for some reason, the latter because that monitoring is beneficial to us. That latter is particularly important to understand. From the perspective of privacy it might sometimes appear that all monitoring and tracking is somehow negative, intrusive and to be avoided. In practice, as the theory of the Symbiotic Web implies, it can often be beneficial. It can be good to be profiled, to have information tailored to you, to be given appropriate and helpful links and suggestions. The key, particularly from the perspective of autonomy, is that this kind of tracking and monitoring needs to be done on terms that we can understand and that we consent to. That, then, implies a right to monitor those who monitor us. We have the right to know when we are being tracked, by whom and what that tracking is being used for.

Monitoring the monitors means more than just knowing what data they are gathering. As the case study of Phorm in Chapter 6 reveals, a focus on the data can potentially be sidestepped. It means that being watched, even without data being held, is something that we should know about and be entitled to object to. As the technology develops, the ability to gather and use data instantaneously, without holding it in a 'personal' form, is only likely to increase and become more important. There are some serious benefits to that kind of approach – it matches with the important principle of data minimisation – but it should not be used as a way of sidestepping the rights of people to know that they are being watched.

Underlying the right to monitor the monitors is the related and newly introduced concept of 'collaborative consent': that consent should be treated as a collaborative, interactive and dynamic process rather than as a one-off, binary, superficial and almost irrelevant issue, as it often seems to have become in current practice on the internet.

3.3   A right to delete personal data

The third right set out in this book is a right to delete personal data. This directly addresses the second of the underlying questions discussed in 1.3 above: the extent to which personal data should be considered 'ours'. It is a subject of great contention and significant debate, and the often vitriolic disputes about the idea of the 'right to be forgotten' hinge upon very different attitudes that have prevailed about this issue. Who has rights over data? Those who gather the data, those who hold the data, those who 'express' the data – or those to whom the data relates? All of them? The right to delete as put forward in this book is qualitatively different from the idea of a 'right to be forgotten': more pragmatic, more balanced, more direct, more transparent and more limited, and less in conflict with the key right to free expression.

The essence of the right to delete personal data is a simple one: that the default position should be that people are able to have their personal data deleted. Specifically, rather than making the person who wishes their data to be deleted justify that deletion, those wishing to continue to hold that data should need to justify that holding. Like all the rights set out here, the right to delete is not an absolute right, but one held in balance with other rights – and those rights should prevail in certain circumstances. Broadly speaking, there are six categories:

- paternalistic reasons (for the good of the individual);
- communitarian reasons (for the good of the community);
- administrative or economic reasons (including tax records, electoral rolls etc);
- archival reasons (which would include journalistic records as well as historical archives);
- free expression reasons (which would cover expressed rather than held data, and help maintain the balance between rights); and
- security reasons (for national security or crime prevention).

How these 'exemptions' to the right to delete might work out in practice, and how they address the legitimate objections that some have to the idea of a right to be forgotten, is discussed in detail in Chapter 7. The right to delete is not intended to be something that allows or supports censorship or the rewriting of history: rather, it is intended to provide individuals with more control over what is held about them, as well as an encouragement to businesses and governments to be more appropriately 'efficient' in how they hold data. If they know that data could be deleted, they know that business models reliant on the holding of personal data against the will of the individuals concerned will be vulnerable, appropriately so.

3.4   A right to an online identity

The fourth right to be suggested in this book is a right to an online identity. This is intended as a three-pronged right: a right to *create* an online identity, a right to *assert* that online identity and a right to *protect* that online identity. The relationships between privacy, identity and autonomy are complex, subtle and ever evolving. Many of the ways that the internet is used require some kind of identity to be used, whether it is an identity on a social networking system, a method of accessing online bank accounts or a username to play a game.

How much that identity reveals about the real person behind it is a question that relates to both privacy and autonomy, and it should, in general, be the right of the individual to determine. In some places and in some situations the links between online and offline identities need to be made clear and explicit, but those situations are rarer than many of those operating businesses suggest. In particular, an internet where a 'real names' policy is the norm is one where people's privacy and autonomy are unnecessarily compromised. The paradigm shift in attitudes that is one of the overall messages of this book applies very directly here: a requirement for 'real names' should be the exception rather than the rule.

Further to that, the amount of information that a person needs to reveal in order to access a service or system should, in general, be minimised. This idea – disclosure minimisation – parallels the concept of data minimisation, a key aspect of the data protection regime and a crucial part of data privacy on the internet.

4   The impact of internet privacy rights

The tension between individuals, businesses and governments over privacy on the internet is of critical importance: the primary role of the privacy rights set out here is to help clarify and moderate that tension.

Understanding these rights can help all three parties: it is not the contention of this book that either governments or businesses are seen as 'enemies' of individuals, or that rights should be seen primarily as 'protection' for those individuals from these 'enemies'. That kind of enmity can often seem to be the initial and immediate effect of the rights, but the ultimate result should be very much the opposite. Rights should help all three groups to find more appropriate, effective, balanced and supportive relationships with each other.

4.1   The impact on individuals

Rights, in the sense that they are intended here, exist in the first instance to help individuals. They work on a number of levels, but perhaps the most important is to help to clarify to individuals what they should be able to expect from those providing services online, from businesses, from governments and others. The central idea in this context is that the rights presented match with the rights that people believe they should have, and that are appropriate for the situation. These are not rights granted from above or imposed through law, but rights that emerge as a consequence of the nature of online activities.

If people find that their rights are reflected in reality – in online reality – their trust in that online reality can grow and their willingness to use the internet freely can grow. Conversely, where people find their rights are being infringed, coherent internet privacy rights help them to understand that and to start to do something about it. It can give them a language to use to articulate their objections to that infringement. It can help them to mobilise, to protest against inappropriate laws, to negotiate with corporations, to make better choices between competing providers, to advocate for better services and so on. The language of rights has a long and proud history in this way. Internet privacy rights could continue that history.

4.2   The impact on governments

Governments have a complex position in relation to privacy on the internet, one which they often seem to find very hard to negotiate. Indeed, it often seems as though governments get digital policies of all kinds wrong much more often than they get it right. In relation to privacy, they have two very different roles. On the one hand, certain arms of government have a tendency, and indeed a need, to 'invade' the privacy of their citizens. Sometimes this is for appropriate and legitimate reasons, but sometimes it goes beyond what would be appropriate: the revelations over PRISM, for example, seem to demonstrate that.[31] A proper understanding of individuals' privacy rights could help them to better find a balance and to draft more appropriate laws and enforce them more proportionately. It might require a targeted rather than universal approach to internet surveillance – 'surveillance minimisation',[32] mirroring data minimisation and 'disclosure minimisation' – or stricter rules about the holding of data on people who are innocent of crime, or who are 'suspects' in a loose rather than a specific sense.

On the other hand, governments have a key role in mediating between individuals and businesses, and in ensuring that businesses are able to innovate and thrive, and compete in the world, while protecting individuals against the excesses of businesses. A proper understanding of internet privacy rights could help them in this role also, helping them to know when and how to set appropriate rules for business in relation to privacy. In practice there appears to be a distinct tendency of governments to place the interests of business ahead of those of individuals – as the Phorm saga demonstrates graphically,[33] with distinctly negative consequences for the government concerned. This needs to change, and internet privacy rights could play a part in making that happen.

4.3   The impact on businesses

It may appear on the surface as though the rights envisaged here would be a 'restriction' on businesses – and privacy advocates often seem to be seen as 'enemies' of businesses – but it is contended that ultimately the opposite is true. Privacy, particularly in its aspect as a protector of autonomy, is something that people want and expect. When it is invaded, when people's autonomy is overly restricted, people react and dislike it. One common thread of the case studies throughout this book is that it appears that the more people know about how, when and where their privacy has been invaded, the more they want to protect that privacy. In the end, businesses need to understand this if they are to meet consumer wishes.

A proper understanding of what people consider to be their rights could help businesses to meet those consumer wishes. They should be able to build better, more appropriate, more sustainable business models

---

[31] The PRISM revelations, from June 2013, are discussed in Chapters 3, 4 and 7.
[32] The concept of surveillance minimisation is discussed in Chapter 10, Section 2.4.
[33] See Chapter 6.

that match people's long-term needs and wishes. The importance of this cannot be overstressed: business models are crucial. As the model of the Symbiotic Web suggests, some of the most important factors in the development of the internet over recent years have been the business models of Google, Facebook and their competitors. How the internet of the future is shaped will depend in a similar way on the business models of that future: if 'privacy-friendly' business models emerge, a privacy-friendly internet will become much more possible.

Many businesses will resist change, particularly when that change challenges an existing business model. The case studies used here demonstrate that graphically, from Google's resistance to the Article 29 Working Party's insistence on reduced data retention periods, to the online advertising industry's opposition to an effective form of 'Do Not Track'. Some businesses will undoubtedly suffer if privacy becomes more of a norm, but that should not be considered to be necessarily bad. Businesses do change as technology, habits, priorities and people's understanding change. Some do not survive those changes, quite rightly so if their businesses do not match the needs, the *rights* of the people. If a business can only function with excessive and non-consensual invasions of people's privacy, it should not survive.

If businesses do want to use our personal data, or do want to monitor and track us, they should do it transparently and consensually. The pressure should be on businesses to explain why they are monitoring us and how that monitoring benefits us. For some it is unlikely to be easy, but it is a challenge that businesses will increasingly have to face.

5   A privacy-friendly future?

How those business models might develop is a key question. 'Privacy-friendly' businesses are an essential part of any privacy-friendly future for the internet. The shape that they might take is one of the subjects of the final chapter of this book. One of the more potentially contentious suggestions here is that privacy-friendly businesses are not just possible, but inevitable. How soon they emerge, and how much pain there is on the way, is far less certain.

Part of the evolution of a privacy-friendly internet is the development of privacy-friendly technology: this kind of technology is already being created. Search engines such as DuckDuckGo[34] and StartPage,[35]

---

[34] https://duckduckgo.com.   [35] https://startpage.com.

tools for monitoring and blocking tracking such as Ghostery[36] and DoNotTrackMe,[37] and Virtual Private Network (VPN) systems such as HideMyAss[38] have all emerged in response to what are perceived as privacy-invasive practices on the internet. What is more, their development and use seems to be increasing, fostered by the often tacit understanding of the kind of rights proposed here. More explicit, coherent and consistent rights could help support this development.

The emergence of these privacy-friendly systems and services is part of what can be seen as a 'creative tension' over privacy. That is, where privacy-invasive tactics or technologies develop, they inspire the development of privacy-protective tactics or technologies and vice-versa. The result can often be positive. New and better services and systems emerge, and better understandings of what is acceptable and what is not become clear. That is part of the nature of what is set out here as the Symbiotic Web. It is in general a mutually beneficial symbiosis, a creative and supportive symbiosis.

The extent to which a privacy-friendly future is possible in reality is hard to determine. Though there are many trends against privacy on the internet, from the current trend within governments towards increased internet surveillance[39] to the unabated enthusiasm for behavioural tracking and targeting of the online advertising industry,[40] there are also a few more positive signs, not least the way in which privacy has gone from being a minor and academic subject only a few years ago to a regular subject of headline news. As the case studies here will reveal, some minor (and some not so minor) skirmishes have been won by those in favour of privacy, and the overall battle, if battle it is, has not yet been lost.

What this privacy-friendly internet would look like is the subject of the final chapter of this book. The vision is one where privacy is the norm, and where the extremes of complete transparency (where identity and all information is fixed and visible) and complete opacity (where people operate with absolute anonymity) are very much the exception. This would match with what many people feel is right in the real world, where we are not required to have our identity and all our personal details on display for anyone to look at any time, but where we can be asked for information by appropriately authorised people at appropriate times and for appropriate reasons.

Internet privacy rights are intended as a tool to help to bring about this kind of privacy-friendly future for the internet.

---

[36] www.ghostery.com.   [37] www.abine.com/dntdetail.php.
[38] www.hidemyass.com/vpn/.   [39] See Chapters 4 and 7.   [40] See Chapter 6.

2

Privacy, autonomy and the internet

1 Autonomy

The rights postulated here are intended specifically as rights to support and protect autonomy, so it is important to establish both what autonomy means and why it matters. The starting point is to look at the meaning of autonomy, first from a philosophical perspective and then from a practical perspective in the society that exists today, building to a broad conception of autonomy, one not purely rational or individualistic.

1.1 A broad definition of autonomy

In *The Morality of Freedom* Joseph Raz sets out his conception of autonomy:

> The autonomous person is a (part) author of his own life. The ideal of personal autonomy is the vision of people controlling, to some degree, their own destiny, fashioning it through successive decisions throughout their lives. (Raz, 1986, p. 369)

For the purposes of this book, this can be considered the starting point for a definition of autonomy. The kind of autonomy being put forward here follows Raz in learning from the Rawls' conception of autonomy as the capacity for people to 'decide upon, to revise, and rationally to pursue a conception of the good' (Rawls and Freeman, 1999, p. 365), but the idea of being an 'author' of your own life can be seen as broader and less rigid than that proposed by Rawls. It also makes the concept of autonomy effectively of value in its own right. As Raz puts it, 'Autonomy is a constituent element of the good life' (Raz, 1986, p. 408). That is, according to this view, without autonomy a good life is not possible: this view is fundamental to the ideas presented here.

The way that the rights presented here might be implemented also follows Raz over Rawls in terms of the degree to which it is viewed as appropriate for governments to intervene in order to protect people's autonomy, the ultimate purpose of the rights suggested. There is a clear role for government in implementing and supporting those rights. In the words of Raz:

> The doctrine of autonomy-based freedom is not inimical to political authority. On the contrary, it looks to governments to take positive action to enhance the freedom of their subjects. (Raz, 1986, p. 427)

Autonomy must allow choice, it must allow changes to be made continually, and it must allow choices to come into action in reality as well as in theory. To be autonomous, therefore, meaningful choices have to be present and one needs to be given the opportunity to make those choices, appropriately informed and free from coercion, restraint, or excessive or undue influence. This means not only that choices must be available, but that these choices must be meaningful. Contrast the dystopian vision of Orwell's *1984* where there are almost no choices at all with that of Huxley's *Brave New World* in which there are a plethora of choices, all of them effectively meaningless.

Accordingly, for autonomy to function it is necessary to ensure that choice exists, that there is an opportunity to exercise choice and, often more to the point in our modern, seemingly choice-filled society, that these opportunities are appropriately informed and free from coercion, restraint, and excessive or undue influence. In many current situations those who would control people, who would restrict people's autonomy, are often far too subtle to use obvious coercion or restraint, but their ability to influence and persuade is remarkable and appears to be growing, and their methods of limiting and controlling the choices available to others are becoming ever more sophisticated. Freedom from manipulation is as important in this context as freedom from coercion. As Raz puts it:

> Manipulating people, for example, interferes with their autonomy, and does so in much the same way and to the same degree, as coercing them. Resort to manipulation should be subject to the same condition as resort to coercion. (Raz, 1986, p. 420)

When looked at in the context of the digital world, this matches closely with Nissembaum's description of the world of 'pervasive monitoring, data aggregation, unconstrained publication, profiling and segmentation':

> the manipulation that deprives us of autonomy is more subtle than the world in which lifestyle choices are punished and explicitly blocked.[1]

---

[1] Nissenbaum (2010, p. 83). The world that Nissenbaum describes draws from the work of Gandy (1993).

Protecting people from this kind of manipulation is one of the prime functions of the rights set out here.

It is important to differentiate between capacity and opportunity. Capacity is essentially a biological question, clearly present in most adult humans, clearly absent in inanimate objects, and debatable at the margins – children, animals, the mentally ill, people in persistent vegetative states and so forth.[2] These marginal cases are not central to the issue here. This book principally concerns the mainstream, namely mentally functional adults in ordinary society, generally those with the capacity to use computers and the internet. Those on the margins may still have a need for some kinds of special protection in relation to privacy and personal data precisely because they either do not or might not pass the *capacity* test for autonomy. They may benefit from some of the envisaged rights; the personal data of many of the persons within many of these categories requires specifically tailored protection, and the impact of the introduction of the kinds of right envisaged here might well provide or enable that kind of protection.

What is central to the ideas examined here is not capacity but the opportunity aspect of autonomy, and one of the conclusions is that if someone possesses the *capacity* then they should be allowed the *opportunity* for autonomy. The concept of autonomy is understood broadly, beyond the purely individualistic and rationalistic form, in two specific ways in particular, both of which emerge from the theories of Raz:

1. Firstly, autonomy is taken to include a 'freedom to be irrational'. Autonomy as it is commonly discussed can appear cold, based only on 'rational decision-making',[3] when people in real life often make their decisions emotionally, or based on tastes or instincts rather than values or logic. Raz's broad definition of an autonomous person as 'author' of their own life allows for that freedom. Conversely, again following Raz as noted above, autonomy should mean freedom not only from coercion but also from undue influence, unfair or excessive persuasion (which may also be based on emotions and tastes rather than values or logic) and so forth.[4] This kind of manipulation can interfere with autonomy in another qualitatively different way, ultimately resulting in alienation. As Raz puts it:

---

[2] For work in some of these areas see for example Jackson (2001) and Cochrane (2007).
[3] Cf. Rawls' description noted earlier, 'and rationally to pursue a conception of the good', in Rawls and Freeman (1999, p. 365).
[4] See for example in the context of advertising Crisp (1987).

A person who feels driven by forces which he disowns but cannot control, who hates or detests the desires which motivate him or the aims that he is pursuing, does not lead an autonomous life. His life is not his own. He is thoroughly alienated from it.

2. Secondly, the concept of autonomy considers people not only as individuals, but also in a social context: autonomy should include the opportunity to function fully in all the key aspects of society, without undue restriction, discrimination and the like. This might best be described as a form of 'social freedom'. As society develops in new ways, autonomy 'expands' to include these new aspects of society. In particular, as will be discussed in depth below, in the digital age this means that autonomy must include the opportunity to function fully in the online world, as well as in the 'offline world'. Again this draws on Raz. Throughout his work Raz envisages individuals very much in the social context, and takes into account the needs of individuals for society – and that particular features of society naturally benefit the individual:

It is a public good, and inherently so, that this society is a tolerant society, that it is an educated society, that it is infused with a sense of respect for human beings, etc. Living in a society with these characteristics is generally of benefit to individuals. (Raz, 1986, p. 199)

Autonomy set out in this way, incorporating these two aspects, has advantages in this context. Firstly, it begins to address the feminist and communitarian critiques of autonomy and privacy, which will be discussed later in this chapter, allowing autonomy to become something stronger and more rounded as a result. Secondly, it takes into account the nature of the real problems found in this field. Many of the ways in which autonomy is threatened on the internet are connected with the ways that people are able to function in a social context; the methods used are often based on persuasion and emotion. In particular, practices are arising through advertising techniques that by their nature have a tendency to use psychological rather than coercive tactics. This is a theme that runs through many different parts of this book, but in particular in Chapter 3, which sets out the model of the Symbiotic Web, and Chapter 6, which looks at what is known as 'behavioural targeting', perhaps the most significant recent manifestation of this kind of technique.

The internet, in its current form, is a social medium. It provides a basis for communication in many forms, from email and online chat to VoIP telephony and video conferencing. It allows collaborative work on a hitherto unimaginable scale: Wikipedia is the best-known example, but there are vast numbers of others. It allows sharing of creative work via services such as YouTube and through systems such as MySpace, Instagram, Pinterest and so forth. Perhaps most significant of all is the social networking service – at the time of writing, Facebook had more than a billion users, Twitter more than half a billion. Some of the most valued data held about individuals is what might be described as 'social data', who people know, who they communicate with and how. All these together mean that something that affects individuals' behaviour on the internet invariably has a social as well as an individual impact, and that manipulation of an individual's behaviour often happens in a social context, from pressure to join and participate in a social network such as Facebook onwards. Autonomy, in the current context, must take this into account.

This extended form of autonomy follows Raz beyond the Rawlsian conception, but it is consistent with the essential meaning of the word ('self-government')[5] and arguably more so than the 'purer' Rawlsian form, which in many ways bears less resemblance to the way that people both behave and wish to behave in the real world. Few people wish to live separately from society and to follow purely rational thoughts. The ways that people 'govern' themselves include emotion (few would wish to live without love, for example) and operate in a social context (hermits and recluses exist, but are very much a rarity) so 'self-government' both does and should include both those expansions.

1.2   Legal philosophy

In legal philosophy there are two main theories about rights, the 'will theory' and the 'interests' theory. Rather than arguing that one or other of these theories is to be preferred, it is suggested that adherents of both would support the central importance of autonomy, and of its close connection to human rights. Whichever of the theories is followed, whether or not a person believes in natural rights or is a positivist, or if a simply pragmatic approach is followed, from a liberal perspective, autonomy remains central, and rights can and do exist to support it.

---

[5] Dictionary definitions of autonomy centre around this concept. Merriam-Webster's Dictionary of Law, for example, defines autonomy as 'the quality or state of being self-governing; especially: the right of self-government', (see http://dictionary.reference.com/browse/autonomy).

Taking the will theory first, the situation is relatively straightforward: the importance of autonomy is essentially a presupposition of the whole theory, since it rests on the importance of people's choices, and autonomy is a requirement for valid, meaningful choices to exist. It may be expressed in a number of different ways – Hart (1955), for example, talks about all rights as being effectively reducible to the 'equal right of all men to be free' – but it ultimately amounts to substantially the same thing.[6]

For those who follow the interests theory the situation is a little more complex. It can be argued that there is a right to autonomy, since there is a clear interest in autonomy for the vast majority of humanity. There are potential objections to this contention, principally concerning the broadness of the concept of autonomy. Raz, for example, considers that the suggestion that there is a right to autonomy could fail since it would need to impose too many duties on too many people, but in practice he takes autonomy even more seriously, considering it a 'moral ideal' and joining the will theorists in considering it a suitable basis for rights rather than a right in itself.

For our purposes it is sufficient to say that from both legal philosophical perspectives autonomy can be seen as a strong basis for rights for the main body of humanity under consideration.

1.3   Historical, natural rights and positivist perspectives

Given this, it is not surprising that autonomy and its related concepts have historically taken a central place in human rights documents, albeit often not explicitly referred to under this label. Thomas Paine, for example, in his *Rights of Man*, considered 'natural rights' to include 'all those rights *of acting as an individual* for his own comfort and happiness' (Paine and Burke, 1791, p. 34), i.e. all those rights that support an individual's autonomy. Not only believers and supporters of 'natural rights' took autonomy seriously: Bentham, one of the staunchest and most effective opponents of the very idea of natural rights, considered that one of the functions of the law was to allow individuals to form and pursue their own conception of wellbeing,[7] something close to the Rawls/Raz

---

[6] Another will theorist, Gewirth, expressed it more directly: 'All the human rights, those of well-being as well as of freedom, have as their aim that each person have rational autonomy in the sense of being a self-controlling, self-developing agent who can relate to other persons on a basis of mutual respect and cooperation, in contrast to being a dependent, passive recipient of the agency of others' (Gewirth, 1982, p.5).

[7] See for example Kelly, 1990 (particularly pp.102–3).

definition used earlier. In a manner that draws parallels with the current disagreements between will and interest theorists, Bentham and Paine disagreed deeply about the existence and effectiveness of 'natural rights', but they both thought autonomy of the most fundamental importance. For J. S. Mill, the significance of autonomy was even clearer; indeed, autonomy could be said to be the most important aspect of his political philosophy.[8]

More recently, the approach adopted in the plethora of human rights conventions and declarations that has emerged since the Second World War has followed a similar pattern, supporting autonomy as an underlying concept upon which to base detailed, substantive rights. In the Universal Declaration of Human Rights (UDHR), for example, articles refer to human beings being 'born free' and 'endowed with reason and conscience',[9] and that everyone has a 'right to liberty'[10] in a general and undefined way, before going on to talk about specifics.

Conversely, the European Convention for the Protection of Human Rights and Fundamental Freedoms (better known as the European Convention on Human Rights or ECHR) makes no mention of anything directly resembling autonomy, but includes specific rights that are closely connected to it, such as respect for family and private life,[11] freedom of thought, conscience and religion,[12] expression,[13] and assembly and association.[14] It is into this spectrum of rights that the proposed right governing internet privacy is intended to fit. Indeed, as will be shown, the proposed right helps support not just the rights of individuals to online privacy, but to online freedom of expression, online assembly and association, and so forth.

Taking this approach a step further, one way to look at this issue is to consider autonomy as an aspect of freedom. Indeed, it is difficult to frame a conception of freedom that does not include some degree of autonomy. As a consequence, if rights supportive of freedom are posited, then so must these rights also be supportive of autonomy. Without autonomy, people are not really free.

Further, there is little doubting the power of human rights in today's world, whether one believes human rights spring from the most solid of foundations (religious or otherwise), or are often born, at least in part and unashamedly, from emotion and sentimentality (as Rorty, 1993 appears

---

[8] See Mill and Himmelfarb, 1982, as well as much of the subsequent study of Mill's philosophy.
[9] UDHR, Article 1.   [10] UDHR, Article 3.   [11] ECHR, Article 8.
[12] ECHR, Article 9.   [13] ECHR, Article 10.   [14] ECHR, Article 11.

to suggest), or do not really exist at all (as MacIntyre contends).[15] They appear to be, as Klug (2000) puts it, an idea whose time has come. On its own this is a pragmatic reason for using the rights-based approach, provided that the importance of autonomy is accepted as within it.

It is not suggested here that such pragmatism should be relied upon, or that any particular school of legal philosophy be followed. Instead, it is posited that whether it is looked at from a philosophical, historical, positivist, instinctive or pragmatic perspective, for the vast majority of humanity – and certainly those under consideration here – autonomy is an appropriate basis for establishing human rights. It may be the most appropriate basis possible if a liberal, democratic stance is taken.

1.4   Limitations to autonomy

This form of autonomy is not absolute and is compromised, limited and restricted in many ways. Keeping the balance between the needs and wishes of individuals and the requirements of governments and communities (and indeed the needs and wishes of other individuals) means that individual freedom (and therefore individual autonomy) cannot be unrestricted. The key question is which restrictions are to be considered acceptable – or even necessary – and which of them are to be rejected. Essentially, a restriction to autonomy can be viewed as acceptable, appropriate or necessary if the benefits that arise as a result of that restriction are of sufficient importance, such as when the restrictions protect the rights of others or protect the nation or community, the criminal law being perhaps the most obvious example of this.[16] As noted above, the 'Razian' understanding of autonomy used in this book also allows for, and indeed requires, intervention by governments in support of autonomy.

Many of the restrictions or threats to autonomy that result from deficiencies in informational privacy, on the other hand, are unacceptable because:

- they are often covert and based on information asymmetry;
- they can be discriminatory and reinforce existing and pernicious imbalances of power;

---

[15] In MacIntyre, 1981 (p. 67) he famously suggests: 'There are no [human] rights, and belief in them is one with belief in unicorns and witches.'

[16] For example, see Raz's work on the relationship between authority and autonomy, particularly in chapters 2–4 of Raz, 1986.

- they have a real and increasing effect on both real lives and online activities; and
- they tend to be open-ended in scope, and to be increasing in significance as people's reliance on data and in particular online activity for societal functions increases.

Crucially from the perspective of the justifiability of limitations, the compensating 'goods' (most directly financial benefits to businesses and, more debatably, security benefits to governments) are insufficient to make the loss of autonomy acceptable, however generous the breadth of such limitations. Moreover, these 'goods' are not even as 'good' as they appear to be. Specifically, the underlying theory set out in Chapter 3, the Symbiotic Web, concerning the mutual dependence of businesses and individuals in the current state of the internet ultimately suggests that unless businesses find ways to be more open, direct and cooperative with their customers and potential customers, the economic benefits they enjoy from the internet will be short-lived.

What is more, the threats to autonomy posed by current practices compromise key human rights, most directly 'civil liberties' such as freedoms of assembly, association, thought and religion, but also other rights, including social, cultural and economic rights. Those direct threats also need to be taken seriously, for they have an impact not only upon 'online' lives, but also upon the 'real' lives of increasing numbers of people throughout the world.

2   Privacy

As has already been discussed, privacy per se is not central to the ideas put forward in this book. Nonetheless, it is important to assess its significance and ascertain at least some of the issues that surround it.

2.1   The challenge of capturing the character of privacy

Perhaps the most important of these issues is how difficult it is even to capture the character of the concept of privacy. It is far from easy. As Solove (2011, p. 24) puts it:

> What is 'privacy'? Most attempts to understand privacy do so by attempting to locate the essence of privacy – its core characteristics or the common denominator that links together the various things we classify under the rubric of 'privacy'. Privacy, however, is too complex a concept to be

reduced to a singular essence. It is a plurality of different things that do not share one element in common but that nevertheless bear a resemblance to each other.

There have been many such attempts, from the seminal work 'The Right to Privacy' by Warren and Brandeis (1890) onwards. Warren and Brandeis described privacy as the right to be let alone: it is a description that is attractive in its simplicity but misses out a great deal of the complexity and multifaceted nature of the concept. Others have tried to improve or modify that definition over the years: such an attempt will not be made in this book. Indeed, such an attempt may be counterproductive. As Nissenbaum (2010, p. 2) puts it:

> Believing that one must define or provide an account of privacy before one can systematically address critical challenges can thwart further progress.

This is particularly true when the online world is taken into account: the nature of privacy and in particular of challenges to privacy are fluid and fast developing. Attempts to fix a definition of privacy are likely to become outdated very fast and hard to relate to a new situation.

2.2 Privacy as a fundamental or an instrumental right

Related to this is the question of whether privacy is a fundamental or an instrumental right. That is, do we have a right to privacy in an absolute sense, as, for example, an aspect of human dignity? Alternatively, is privacy only a right in an instrumental sense, as something that protects other more fundamental rights, such as a right to a family life, or to freedom of thought, of expression, of association or assembly?

This again has been a matter of significant debate that impinges on many of the issues discussed in this book. If privacy is an absolute and fundamental right, for example, how can people consider that privacy is 'dead'?[17] Similarly, if privacy is an instrumental right, how can it be 'dead'? However, for the purposes of this book it is not a question that needs to be answered. Privacy, here, is considered primarily in an instrumental sense – as a protector and supporter of autonomy – without denying the idea that a right to privacy could be considered an absolute and fundamental right.

---

[17] The idea that privacy is 'dead' is part of what is described here as the 'transparency critique': see Section 4.5 below.

2.3   Informational privacy and internet privacy

The relationship between personal privacy and what can be described as 'informational' privacy is another area of complexity and contention. There are many questions that can be asked about it. To what degree is 'our' privacy vested in the privacy of information held about us? Further, what kind of information should be considered 'private'? Is there a difference between 'personal' information and 'private' information?

None of these questions are easily answered, and the shift from analogue to digital information, particularly since the growth of the internet, has made them even more difficult to answer. Borders have become more and more blurred and, indeed, are constantly shifting. Nissenbaum is right to suggest that privacy should be considered contextually: the extent to which the flow of information matters depends on the context. That context includes not just who has access to information but when, how, what it might be used for and so forth. It is also subject to immediate and radical change: a piece of information that in one moment appears innocuous can in another be of the greatest sensitivity and importance. As the various examples used throughout this book will illustrate, the developing techniques of data mining, data aggregation, profiling and so forth make this particularly relevant and likely to become more so.

The implications of this are significant. Setting hard-and-fast laws about data types and so on becomes much harder, and much less likely to be successful. Medical data, for example, might be considered of the most sensitive kind: shopping data much less so. If, however, shopping data reveals that an individual buys sugar-free chocolate, and profilers can deduce from that that there is a high probability that the individual is a diabetic, then the shopping data suddenly becomes highly sensitive. This does not necessarily mean that all data, whatever its nature, should be treated as highly personal and private, but it does mean that we need to be more careful about assuming that mundane or seemingly innocuous data needs little or no protection.

Further, when considering online interaction, ultimately everything is data. It might be considered that a person only 'exists' online in terms of data. The link between an individual and 'their' data is a crucial issue when considering online privacy and of particular significance when considering the nature of online identity.[18]

---

[18] Online identity is the subject of Chapter 9.

2.4   Privacy and control

As the extensive analysis of Solove and others has made abundantly clear, privacy is not really about 'hiding' information. A much better way to look at it is to consider privacy as being about control. As Nissenbaum puts it:

> [W]hat people care most about is not simply *restricting* the flow of information but ensuring that it flows *appropriately*. (Nissenbaum, 2010, p. 2. Emphasis supplied)

At a basic level people want to control, at least to a degree, what kind of information about them is released to whom. People will tell very different things to their parents than to their partners, to their employers or to their children. It is not that this control is complete – indeed, in the field of privacy very little is complete or absolute – but that some degree of control is both desirable and appropriate. If privacy is considered in relation to autonomy, this is doubly relevant: we want autonomy over what information is available to whom both for its own sake and for its implications for other aspects of our autonomy.

2.5   How the internet has challenged privacy

The development of the internet has had huge and complex implications for privacy: it is not just about the amount of data that is gathered, nor just about how that data might be used, but about the very nature of the data gathered. It is about how much of our lives we spend on the internet – and how integrated our online and offline worlds have become.

Chapter 1 began the process of examining the role that the internet has in contemporary life but it is worth reiterating because that role is becoming more and more significant. In particular, the way that it involves privacy should not be understated. It is difficult to conceive of a single element of our lives that has not been touched by the internet in some way, and that in itself has implications for privacy. If privacy is about the control and context of information flows, and flows of data on the internet encompass almost every element of our lives, the potential impact of the development of the internet upon our privacy is deeply significant. Indeed, it is fundamental. The internet, and the role that it plays (and will continue to play) in our lives challenges almost every aspect of our privacy.

3   Autonomy and consent

Another recurrent theme in the field of internet privacy and autonomy is consent. The relationship between autonomy and consent is one that is often misunderstood, and the ways that consent is treated on the internet (sometimes sidestepped, sometimes ignored, sometimes made so complex it becomes irrelevant, and all too often ridden roughshod over) can make that relationship even more confusing than it is inherently.

3.1   The complexity of consent on the internet

Consent is a more complex issue than it seems – it is not simply a matter of getting a user's consent before doing something. The Data Protection Directive[19] talks about 'express, informed consent', and all three of those words need to be considered carefully. Moreover, there are some things that it should simply not be possible to consent to, where it may be deemed that if someone appears to consent to it, then either they cannot have been properly informed or something must have prevented them from making an appropriate decision, whether it is duress, lack of mental capacity or something similarly significant.

It is crucial that the issue of consent is understood better and engaged with directly. At present, it is an issue that is often either avoided or treated in such way as to make is mere legal form rather than having any real connection with what would be understood in any 'real-world' sense as 'consent'. On the internet, and indeed when dealing with computer software in general, the kind of consent generally gained is by a user scrolling down a long page of writing that they do not read and then clicking 'OK' at the end to confirm that they have 'read and understood' the terms and conditions. The information thus presented (but rarely read)[20] is deemed to make the consent 'informed', while the clicking of OK is deemed to make it 'express'. This 'click-wrap consent' has been generally found to be legally acceptable[21] – but if autonomy is taken at all seriously it is close to meaningless.

---

[19] Directive 95/46/EC – discussed in more depth in Chapter 4

[20] A dramatic example of this was demonstrated by the April Fool's joke played by the games company Gamestation who changed their terms and conditions to include a term through which customers gave the company their immortal souls. Nearly ninety per cent of them did so, even though they were given a gift of a £5 voucher if they chose to opt out. See for example http://blogs.telegraph.co.uk/technology/shanerichmond/100004946/gamestation-collects-customers-souls-in-april-fools-gag/.

[21] For example in *ProCD* v. *Zeidenberg*, 86 F.3d 1447 (7th Cir. 1996), *Specht* v. *Netscape Communications Corp.*, 150 F.Supp.2d 585 (S.D.N.Y. 2001) and *Hotmail Corp.* v. *Van$ Money Pie*, No. 98–20064, 1998 WL 388389 (N.D. Cal. Apr. 16, 1998).

'Browse-wrap' consent, whereby following links is deemed to mean that a user has consented to terms and conditions, is less legally compelling than click-wrap consent. Even so, Google and others use it, though their use of it has come under criticism from the Article 29 Working Party amongst others.[22] In the Working Party's view, where search engines are concerned, ordinary, anonymous users cannot be considered to have given consent, and the 'de facto contractual relationship' when using a search engine in its usual form 'does not meet the strict limitation of necessity as required in the Directive'.[23] Moreover, it is even less understood by users, and hence of more concern in respect of autonomy.

Many internet providers stretch the consent issue even further, setting their terms and conditions so that by 'signing in' to one service, a user consents to having his or her data gathered and aggregated for other services provided by the same company. If a user signs in to Gmail, for example, and then subsequently uses any of the other Google services (from Google Search to Google Maps etc.), then data is gathered about what is searched for or any places examined in Google Maps, and aggregated with the data record of the individual signed in to Gmail. As Google puts it in its privacy policy:

> We may combine personal information from one service with information, including personal information, from other Google services – for example to make it easier to share things with people you know.[24]

Whether this policy is legal or not under European Law is currently under investigation.[25] It is worth noting that Google does not define precisely which services it is talking about and not all 'Google services' are labelled with the Google name, YouTube.com being the most obvious example. If you are signed in to Gmail, does that mean that you have effectively consented to having your YouTube.com activities monitored and aggregated with your Gmail data? A further question is whether people understand the linkages between the different services, even if they all bear the same labels. Are they aware that by signing in to Gmail they are giving Google the legal green light to gather data from all of their services? What is true of Google is likely to be equally true of the other big internet companies such as Yahoo!, Microsoft and Facebook, all of whom have a raft of different services with the capability to monitor and gather different kinds of

---

[22] See Chapter 5, Section 2.   [23] See Working Party Opinion 148, p. 17.
[24] www.google.com/policies/privacy/.   [25] See Chapter 5, Section 3.

information, under current law, seemingly entirely legally if consent has been given through sign-in to just one of their services.

The main issue, therefore, is not what kind of consent is currently legal but how we should consider using law to make sure that legal consent more closely resembles 'real' consent, in the sense that it relates to having made an informed, autonomous decision.

3.2   The power of the default – and opt-in or opt-out

Defaults are very powerful: many users accept what they are given, others don't even know that they have any choice. As will be noted in the discussion of the Do Not Track initiative,[26] there have been significant conflicts over the default settings in that context, primarily because both sides of the debate know that what is set as a default can often make more difference than the options that are actually offered.

Closely related to the question of what the default should be is the question of when consent can be 'assumed': the default setting should be what people can be 'assumed' to accept. From a legal perspective, the determining factor is generally whether assuming consent is 'reasonable'. In the Regulation of Investigatory Powers Act 2000 (RIPA)[27] interception of communications can be lawful if there are 'reasonable grounds' to assume the communicators' consent.[28] The question, therefore, becomes what is 'reasonable'? At the very least, it is clearly unreasonable to assume that someone will consent to things that most members of a society reject. Where there is doubt, further questions must be asked and further information sought before consent may be assumed. While doubt exists, consent cannot be assumed, particularly in a business context.

There is one kind of exception to this, but it is an argument that is both highly contentious and could only apply in very unusual circumstances. It can be argued that there are situations where the needs of society as a whole outweigh the rights of individuals to choose. One specific example is the suggestion that organ donation should be opt-out rather than opt-in. Could society's need for organs for medical purposes outweigh the need for each individual to make an active choice? The choice would only come into play once the individual is dead, and the most common reason to refuse donating one's organs is a strong, positive and often religious objection, one that could be actively exercised within an 'opt-out' system. In July 2013, Wales became the first country in the United Kingdom to

---

[26] See Chapter 6.   [27] See Chapter 4, Section 3.   [28] RIPA Section 3(1).

make organ donation opt-out, though the vote was not without controversy, with opposition from religious groups and the Conservative opposition.[29] Another is the idea that vaccination against certain diseases should
be compulsory rather than optional, as it functions properly if the vast
majority of people are vaccinated. For something like this to apply, the
benefit to society must be overwhelmingly clear, and society must in some
way consent as a whole. In a democratic society that might be through
the decisions of government, or through obligations under international
treaties – there are things that, even if the majority of individual members
of a society would like them, international obligations might prevent. One
of the clearest examples in the UK could be the use of the death penalty.[30]

Is the benefit to society of the existence of a slickly functional and profitable internet business sector so clear and overwhelming that it should
override the individual's right to choose? There may be some who would
argue this, but it is an argument that is hard to sustain if privacy is taken
seriously, and moreover that kind of decision would need to be made at
the highest political level.

As well as determining whether consent can be assumed or needs to be
individually sought, 'societal consent' should determine whether a system or service needs 'opt-in' or 'opt-out' consent. If it is 'normal' in a society for something to be acceptable, then using an opt-out consent system
could potentially be adequate, but if it is normal in a society for something to be unacceptable, then an 'opt-in' system is crucial. If a paradigm
shift in favour of privacy is to be followed, where there is any doubt about
whether something is acceptable or unacceptable, the rights of the individual should have the benefit of the doubt, and only an 'opt-in' system
should be possible.

3.3   Is consent a red herring?

Google's Global Privacy Counsel, Peter Fleischer, speaking at the
Computers, Privacy and Data Protection Conference in Brussels in
January 2010, suggested that the question of 'opt-out, opt-in' in relation
to behavioural tracking is a bit of a red herring, for two reasons. Firstly,
because even opting in is often not very meaningful, as people just scroll

[29] See for example www.bbc.co.uk/news/uk-wales-politics-23143236.
[30] It is difficult to gauge levels of support for the reintroduction of the death penalty, but
      over recent years it has appeared that a majority may support it. See for example www.
      lawgazette.co.uk/blogs/blogs/news-blogs/bringing-back-death-penalty.

and click, without understanding, and secondly, because you cannot expect one company (in his case Google) to take the opt-in route unilaterally, as it would be shooting itself in the foot. The second objection would be easily bypassed by a legal requirement for opt-in rather than opt-out consent. The first objection is a much more important one, but the consequence of it is not that the idea of opt-in should be abandoned, but that a way needs to be found for opting in (and indeed all forms of consent) to become more meaningful. If that way can be found, then the objection just melts away.

Fleischer's argument, however, is one that is taken very seriously by many people, particularly within what can loosely be described as the internet industry, and not just in terms of opt-in v. opt-out but also in terms of consent for processing of personal data as a whole.[31] The suggestion is that consent is an effectively meaningless process, at best satisfying the letter of the law and ultimately not providing any real benefit to the people who use the internet. All that requiring consent does is get in the way of things that can be beneficial, delaying or blocking innovation, annoying people, and not doing anything useful in terms of autonomy and privacy. When practical experience on the internet is examined, there does seem to be a case to answer. The 'cookie warnings' required by the 'Cookies Directive'[32] do not seem to have been particularly effective and for many people are extremely annoying.[33] Does that mean that the whole idea of consent should be abandoned? If autonomy is considered important, it cannot be. Instead, more radical solutions must be considered.

3.4   Collaborative consent: consent as a process and a dialogue

One possible solution is the idea of collaborative consent.[34] It starts from taking the idea of 'informed' consent seriously. There are two very different ways to look at the idea of informed consent: does 'informed' just mean that information has to be given, or does it mean that an 'informed

---

[31] See for example Tene and Wolf, 2013. Tene and Wolf effectively argue that the burden of a general requirement for explicit consent outweighs its benefits. The Future of Privacy Forum is a 'Washington DC-based Think Tank' that receives funding from, amongst others, many internet companies, such as Amazon, Apple, Facebook, Google and Yahoo! See www.futureofprivacy.org/about/supporters/.

[32] See Chapter 4, Section 2.

[33] See for example http://nocookielaw.com, a website specifically dedicated to the way that the cookie warnings and the Cookie Directive have caused disruption and annoyance.

[34] The concept of collaborative consent was introduced in Bernal, 2010a, where a more detailed description may be found.

decision' needs to be enabled, a decision where the information has not only been given but has been understood. The former, where information is given, is what generally happens on the internet: the information that users scroll down without reading before clicking 'OK' can be said to have been given, but it is rarely read, let alone understood. The latter, where information is not only given but understood, and a genuinely informed decision is enabled, is what those interested in autonomy would demand.

In the field of medical law the concept of informed consent has been investigated in depth. Harvey Teff introduced a concept he called 'collaborative autonomy' to find a way through the maze of ethical and medical problems surrounding the need for and meaning of 'informed consent'. In it, Teff suggests a process of communication, a dialogue, through which more complex issues are discussed until they are understood, and as the situation develops and the patient's understanding and views develop, the decision as to whether to continue with treatment or change direction can be made in a manner that is both better informed and more flexible. As he puts it:

> What many patients seek is sufficient understanding to reach an 'informed' decision in the fuller sense of the term; this can seldom be achieved without the kind of dialogue, and the kind of relationship, to which the collaborative model of medical practice alone aspires. (Teff, 1994, p. 198)

Though the issues involved in medical consent are qualitatively different to those on the internet, there are similarities, and a similarly collaborative model is possible. The idea that consent should be a dialogue, a process rather than a one-off decision based on fixed, provided information can be taken a step further, for what is often being consented to is a continuing process rather than a single discrete event, and that places particular demands on consent. Moreover, the internet itself is a communications medium, and one that lends itself ideally to communicative processes.

The unparalleled communications opportunities presented by the internet can be harnessed to produce a different kind of consent that allows informed decisions and a real opportunity for those decisions to be expressed. Using the communicative potential of the internet can allow consent to become much more of a collaboration between those gathering data or monitoring users and the users themselves.

The starting point is to ensure that contracts, Terms and Conditions, End User Licence Agreements and so forth, are written in plain, understandable language, using agreed and standardised terms for certain forms of activity. These contracts would be designed as much to inform the user – to communicate – as to satisfy legal obligations. The Code of Practice for Privacy Notices issued by the Information Commissioner's Office (ICO)[35] gives clues as to how this might work. Both the privacy notices themselves and the code of practice concerning them are intended to be communicative and to begin the process of using the communications opportunities of the internet in a positive way. As the ICO puts it:

> It's a lot easier to actively communicate a privacy notice in an online context than in a 'bricks and mortar' one. You should make full use of the technology available to you to promote transparency and fairness.[36]

Collaborative consent would take this a step further, using the online context not just to communicate such things as privacy notices, but to include the whole consent process. The provider of a service would engage in a direct dialogue with the user, telling that user all the relevant information as it happens, alerting the user to important changes as they happen, and needing direct responses before taking any action. This dialogue would be supported by further, backup information – in particular, information about what data is being gathered (and has been gathered) and how it is being used – taking the Data Protection 'access' principle into the interactive age.

Collaborative consent could be a key enabler for the 'right to monitor the monitors'. If those who are monitoring and targeting people require continued consent from those being monitored and targeted, then they will need to communicate the benefits for those who are being monitored and targeted. In order to communicate those benefits, they first need to ensure that benefits really exist and hence that the symbiosis is beneficial rather than parasitical.

4   Autonomy, privacy, challenges and criticisms

The approach taken here is essentially liberal, democratic and rights-based. What are being suggested here in terms of rights (including the related and supporting concepts of collaborative consent and autonomy by design[37]) are intended to support the idea of giving individuals more autonomy both in their lives online and in the 'real' world – but neither

---

[35] Downloadable from www.ico.gov.uk/for_organisations/topic_specific_guides/privacy_notices.aspx.
[36] ICO Privacy Notices Code of Practice, p. 9.   [37] See Chapter 8, Section 2.

autonomy itself nor the idea of privacy, and in particular informational privacy on the internet, are ideas that are universally accepted as having central (let alone fundamental) importance. There are criticisms both of the concept of autonomy and of its specific application here. The most important of them are set out in this section, together with a preliminary indication of how they will be addressed. It should be noted that while these critiques fuel approaches to exceptions to autonomy-based rights that are very broad, they do not undermine rights-talk in today's society. Rather they make this talk more porous and vulnerable to sanctioned exception and hence less effective in real terms.

The primary challenges and critiques can be broadly divided into five: two essentially pragmatic challenges, security and economic challenges, based on specific issues concerning the internet, and three theoretical critiques, the communitarian, feminist and transparency critiques, which, though of general application, have a particular relevance to the field under scrutiny too. These challenges and critiques are related and overlapping, both from a theoretical and a practical perspective. The security and economic challenges, in particular, can both be viewed from a communitarian perspective: maintaining security and prioritising business success over individual privacy and autonomy can both be seen as communitarian and even utilitarian goals. All five critiques and challenges question priorities and motives, and all five have strong arguments and powerful supporters.

4.1   The security challenge

The essence of the security challenge is that it suggests that excessive rights to privacy tend to protect the criminal and terrorist and, ultimately, that autonomy is less important than security. This is played out in a number of ways.

First of all, the internet can be seen as a 'tool for terrorists', for example to spread their 'hate speech'. The 2010 case of Roshonara Choudhry, the young woman who stabbed her MP, Stephen Timms, at his surgery in East London, is a prime example. According to reports, she had been 'radicalised' by watching video 'sermons' by Anwar al-Awlaki, a radical Muslim cleric, on YouTube.[38] Moreover, many of the tools that have made the internet such a success – near-instant, worldwide communications, the apparent opportunity for anonymity, relative cheapness and so

---

[38]   See for example www.bbc.co.uk/news/uk-11686764.

forth – make it ideally suited for small, mobile and geographically spread organisations to function.

The general approach to security matters, particularly evident in the concept of 'data retention',[39] is to make surveillance as general as possible, and gather as much data as possible, with the idea that by sifting through all that data it will be possible to find what is needed to catch terrorists and other threats to security. Surveillance should, under these terms, be universal, with no exceptions. However, it will be suggested in this book that the idea of general surveillance and universal data gathering should not be accepted,[40] and that there are other possible approaches. Specific solutions to some of the particular problems in security that do not impinge so directly on general privacy will be suggested, together with a new approach to surveillance: 'surveillance minimisation'.[41] It is difficult, however, to make an entirely convincing case for privacy in the security field, as the security forces are not, for understandable reasons, willing to provide complete information either as to their methods of countering terrorism or as to how successful particular tactics have proven to be. Privacy advocates, as a consequence, cannot point to evidence to suggest, let alone prove, that the idea of general data retention or universal surveillance is ineffective or inefficient in the field of counterterrorism. It is equally true that those in favour of such tactics cannot prove that they are effective, but they can argue that the risks involved are sufficient to warrant the tactics.

However, as Gearty puts it, 'In taming counter-terrorism law human rights has the chance to renew its soul',[42] addressing the security challenge over data and surveillance on the internet is a prime example of what is required. The presumption of innocence, making surveillance, data collection and its equivalents the exception – and an exception that must be justified – rather than the rule (the paradigm shift suggested in Chapter 1) is a key element of that. There are parallels here with the transparency critiques below and in particular with responses to the suggestion 'if

---

[39] Discussed in Chapter 4, Section 3, and central to the case study in Chapter 5, Section 2.

[40] This suggestion is supported by the ruling in *Liberty* v. *UK* [2008] 48 EHRR 1, where the European Court of Human Rights held that the broadness and lack of clarity of the rights of government agencies to intercept communications set out by the Interception of Communications Act 1985 led to a breach of Article 8 of the European Convention on Human Rights (ECHR).

[41] See Chapter 10, Section 2.

[42] The sixth point of his 'Manifesto', which makes up the central part of the collaborative web project 'The Rights' Future', at http://therightsfuture.com/manifesto/.

you've got nothing to hide, you've got nothing to fear' so often deployed by 'security advocates' in favour of what amounts to general internet surveillance. As Solove argues,[43] this 'reason' has many flaws, some fatal when looked at closely with anything resembling a liberal standpoint: this is something dealt with in more detail below when looking at transparency critiques, but it remains an issue that needs to be addressed.

4.2   The economic challenge

The essence of the economic challenge is that excessive support for privacy reduces business opportunities, and the niceties of individual autonomy are less important than a thriving economy. From another angle it can be argued that it may be impossible to overcome the power and momentum of business in this field.

It is a central contention of the theories put forward here that the economic benefits of abuses of privacy and autonomy are short term. For long-term and sustainable economic benefits, a positive relationship between the needs and desires of individuals must be held in balance, which, ultimately, means more respect for the privacy and autonomy of those individuals. The model of the Symbiotic Web and the outcomes of the case studies in Chapters 5 to 7 suggest that where these needs are not respected, businesses are likely to suffer or even fail.

The economic challenge remains a crucial challenge to the whole concept of privacy. Businesses are the key drivers in the development of both the technology and the reality of the internet and, particularly in the current climate, it is very difficult to persuade businesses to change their methods for a perceived and potentially highly debatable long-term future benefit. Moreover, businesses are unlikely to be persuaded by any kind of moral or philosophical argument – they will respond only to the demands of law, of finance or of their customers. That is what underlies the symbiotic regulation approach: to work through precisely those mechanisms, the relationships between businesses and their customers, their competitors and so forth. It is crucial, however, that the rights envisaged here are not intended to override the freedoms that businesses require in order to thrive. Rather, the competing rights and freedoms must be kept in balance. It is through that balance that the beneficial aspects of the web symbiosis is maintained and supported.

---

[43]   Particularly in his article Solove, 2007.

4.3   The communitarian critique

The communitarian critique suggests that privacy and individual autonomy prioritise the individual over the community and in some ways misunderstand the essentially social nature of humanity.[44] Privacy, according to this account, provides excessive benefits to individuals and often to individuals with little need or right to such benefits. The way that privacy law has often focussed on cases of celebrities, politicians and sports stars is just part of how this plays out.

Communitarian critiques are addressed partly through the breadth of the definition of autonomy being used, as noted above, and by considering rights to both autonomy and privacy only in balance with the needs of society. It is a delicate balance, and one that requires constant monitoring and rebalancing. However, there is another factor that comes into play here: a consideration of how privacy, anonymity and autonomy can play key parts in protecting the functioning of communities on the internet. Indeed, the ability of individuals to fulfil their roles in a community is one of the things that the rights proposed are specifically designed to protect, and a fracturing of online communities is one of the specific dangers discussed in this book, a risk inherent in the current system as it is developing, as set out in the model of the Symbiotic Web.

The communitarian critique has, in some forms, a close relationship with the security challenge. Certainly the Chinese government would make use of both arguments in favour of their approach to internet surveillance and control. They do what they do, they say, both to ensure security and to support the coherence and stability of their community.[45] From a political standpoint, once more it is a question of where the balance is placed and what the overall result of policies produces.

---

[44] See for example Charles Taylor, who describes individualism as the first 'source of worry', in relation to the 'malaises of modernity'. Taylor, recalling Alexis de Tocqueville, suggests that 'the dark side of individualism is a centring on the self, which both flattens and narrows our lives, makes them poorer in meaning, and less concerned with others or society'. See Taylor, 1992, Chapter 1. Other communitarian critics of individualistic autonomy include MacIntyre and Sandel.

[45] See for example the Chinese government's white paper 'The Internet in China' (available online at www.china.org.cn/government/whitepaper/node_7093508.htm). In it, the Chinese government suggests that provisions forbidding amongst other things 'damaging state honor and interests; instigating ethnic hatred or discrimination and jeopardizing ethnic unity; jeopardizing state religious policy, *propagating heretical or superstitious ideas; spreading rumors, disrupting social order and stability*' (emphasis added) must be followed.

The communitarian critique of privacy and autonomy is related to a broader challenge on communitarian grounds to the whole concept of human rights. That challenge was met at least to an extent by the inclusion of economic, social and cultural rights into human rights as a whole, most notably through the International Covenant on Economic, Social and Cultural Rights.[46] In a similar manner, the challenge is met here through the expansion of the concept of autonomy to include what is described above as 'social freedom'.

4.4   Feminist critiques

The essence of feminist critiques is that protection for privacy and autonomy is often a force for patriarchy and conservatism, and that common conceptions of autonomy are generally a reflection of masculine values. Some aspects of the feminist critiques follow somewhat similar lines to those used in the communitarian critique: the idea of autonomy is one that is based on male concepts of independence, rather than the more social and in particular family-based ideals that can sometimes be seen as female.[47] Privacy can be used to protect the dominant position that men have in society, to allow them to maintain their power.

Taking this a step further, privacy can be used as a way of protecting those who abuse their dominant positions, by preventing their abuses from becoming known. The way in which parts of the Catholic Church have at times tried to protect child-abusing priests is an extreme example, more mundane examples might include men using privacy to hide their extramarital affairs from their wives, or finding ways to conceal their assets from their wives to avoid them being taken into account for divorce settlements. In all these cases, it is about privacy being used to protect the power of those who have it, against just claims that are being brought. The furore over the Ryan Giggs 'super-injunction' in 2011 was one of the more graphic examples in recent years.[48]

Feminist critiques are addressed in this book again partly through defining autonomy to include 'social freedom' as noted above and partly by

---

[46] International Covenant on Economic, Social and Cultural Rights, 1966, downloadable from www.ohchr.org/EN/ProfessionalInterest/Pages/CESCR.aspx.

[47] See for example Allen, 2003, and Allen and Mack, 1991. A full examination of feminist perspectives on privacy is beyond the scope of this book, but the strength and importance of their arguments needs to be acknowledged.

[48] The case involved was *CTB* v. *News Group Newspapers* [2011] EWHC 1232 QB. See for example Smartt, 2012.

emphasizing the positive role that privacy rights (particularly on the internet) can play in protecting precisely those aspects of private life that the feminist critique considers important. The kinds of privacy and anonymity that the internet allows can be an enabler and a liberator for women, allowing women and girls the right to roam the net without their gender being revealed, for example, reducing the risks of discrimination of many different kinds. Moreover, similar methods to the suggestions for alleviating security issues could help solve some of the particular problems in this area, catching abusers, producers of child abuse images, stalkers and so forth in the private sphere in the same ways that you can catch terrorists.

The most important and effective answers to both the communitarian and feminist critiques, however, lie in an examination of what the internet would look like, and how it would function, from the perspectives of both women and communities, if the suggested rights were brought into action. That kind of an examination is a central part of the final chapter of this book: a future internet in which these rights were understood and respected would be significantly better from both of those perspectives.

4.5   Transparency critiques and challenges

Transparency critiques revolve around the idea that privacy is an outdated value or is to all intents and purposes unenforceable in today's technological society, and that what is needed is an adjustment to a new way of living.[49] In many ways these are more complex than the critiques and challenges that have been discussed so far – it could be argued that they are more challenges than critiques, a kind of 'technology challenge' or 'information society challenge', something said to have been made inevitable as a result of the developments of technology. Do individuals need to give up privacy in order to function in the new, online world? Whether it is called a critique or a challenge, meeting it is central to the ideas put forward here: ultimately this boils down to the question of whether it is possible to have privacy in this new world. Ultimately, it is posited here that not only is it possible, but it is crucial that a way is found to ensure that it is in place.

One example of just such a challenge is to be found in looking at the future of the web itself. Web 3.0, the semantic web, as it is envisaged by Berners-Lee and others, has the potential to be a great benefit to autonomy, increasing freedom and choice, giving individuals more power

---

[49] See for example Brin, 1998.

to control their own lives,[50] but it is an essentially technological development, and technology is 'value neutral'. What governs the future of the web is not just the technology but *all* aspects of the web, from laws and government actions, business models and commercial practices to community attitudes and social interactions.[51] As the current development of the web symbiosis is beginning to show, the potential of the technology could be turned into precisely the opposite of the laudable and liberating visions of Berners-Lee and others, something that controls us more rather than providing us with more freedom. It is contended here that privacy in general, and internet privacy in particular, is the key to ensuring that this does not happen.

There are three principle variants of the transparency critique:

1. that the struggle for privacy is already lost;
2. that the struggle for privacy is outdated; and
3. that the struggle for privacy is 'wrong', and that we should in fact 'embrace' transparency and make the lack of privacy a virtue to be enjoyed.

Scott McNealy, then CEO of Sun Microsystems, expressed the first of these directly when he told reporters in 1999 'You have zero privacy anyway, get over it.'[52] Mark Zuckerberg, co-founder and CEO of Facebook, is perhaps the best-known proponent of the second version. Essentially his argument has been that, given that more than a billion people use Facebook and put up some of their most personal information there, people are no longer really interested in privacy.[53]

The third variation is more complex – versions of it have been around since David Brin's work *The Transparent Society* (1998). More recently, another angle of it has emerged in Bell and Gemmell's book, *Total Recall: How the E-Memory Revolution Will Change Everything* (2009), though it has also faced its antithesis in Mayer-Schönberger's *Delete: The Virtue of Forgetting in the Digital Age* (2009). This last critique has a close relationship to the old ideas 'If you've done nothing wrong, you've got nothing to fear' or 'If you've got nothing to hide you've got nothing to fear', referred

---

[50] See Berners-Lee and Fischetti, 2000, particularly Chapter 12.
[51] The recognition of this is inherent in the work of cyber-regulation theorists from Lessig to Murray. See for example Lessig, 2006, and Murray, 2006.
[52] Quoted for example in Wired, at www.wired.com/politics/law/news/1999/01/17538.
[53] See for example Chris Matyszczyk's blog on CNET, at http://news.cnet.com/8301-17852_3-10431741-71.html. Zuckerberg has been making related statements to different elements of the media since 2010.

to above, concerning the security challenge. The idea that lack of privacy should be embraced as something positive and transformative to an extent presupposes the truth of the 'nothing to hide/nothing to fear' argument. The converse is also true, at least to an extent. That is, if the 'nothing to hide/nothing to fear' argument is false or flawed, then embracing transparency would need to be done extremely carefully.

Solove, particularly in his 2007 piece, '"I've Got Nothing to Hide" and Other Misunderstandings of Privacy', and his 2011 book, *Nothing to Hide: The False Tradeoff Between Privacy and Security*, challenges that argument convincingly, demonstrating amongst other things how the idea is based on a very limited understanding of what privacy really means. The arguments made by Solove are detailed and compelling, looking at the problem from many different angles. One of particular relevance here is the quote that Solove makes from Judge Richard Posner, that in Posner's view (presented as representative of part of the 'nothing to hide' school) privacy involves a person's 'right to conceal discreditable facts about himself'.[54] In the context of the internet, and particularly when the concepts of profiling, targeting and data aggregation are considered, it is not only the discreditable facts that are at issue. Indeed, as will be shown throughout this book, it is often the least obvious, most apparently mundane or inconsequential of information that makes the difference.

Solove's arguments are powerful, but even so the transparency critique is a strong one in all of its forms, and needs to be carefully addressed. If McNealy is right, this whole discussion is pointless. If Zuckerberg is right, it is an argument that is becoming more and more irrelevant day by day. If Brin, Bell and Gemmell, and others are right, then what is being suggested in this book is retrograde and regressive. These three forms of the transparency critique can all be answered. The case studies here will show that people do still care about privacy and that they are quite capable of winning battles in the area of privacy when the situation is appropriate, when they have the right support and when, using the terms set out in Murray's symbiotic regulation, they find ways to use the regulatory matrix in an appropriate and effective way.

5   Privacy is not the enemy

Perhaps the most important questions of all to ask in this area surround whether privacy matters at all in the final analysis. Is privacy just

---

[54] Solove (2007), originally in Posner (1998).

something that is interesting from a theoretical perspective, a 'right' that matters only on paper or in the minds of philosophers? Is it something that people care about when you ask them, but do not care about enough that they will actually change their habits or actions if it is at all inconvenient?

If the answers to these questions are yes, then that needs to be considered very seriously. They are pragmatic questions, but that does not reduce their importance. Quite the opposite, because in the end this is very much a pragmatic subject. The internet has in many ways been enormously beneficial, whose benefits spring not from philosophical freedoms but from real and practical actions and advantages that people have been able to gain from it. These benefits have emerged as a result of the technological, practical and business developments on the internet, and those developments should not be put at risk for purely hypothetical reasons.

It is contended here, however, that this is not the case with these proposals, for two reasons. Firstly, the risks are real rather than hypothetical, and secondly, the beneficial developments would not be put at risk by taking account of privacy and autonomy. That latter part is crucial and arises because in many ways the debate is often couched in terms of false dichotomies.

The first of these dichotomies is around security. Solove has made the point extensively, most directly in *Nothing to Hide* (2011). As he puts it 'protecting privacy need not be fatal to security measures; it merely demands oversight and regulation'.

Privacy demands a more intelligent, more targeted, more regulated approach to security, but that approach in turn can generate more trust in those responsible for security. Checks and balances over security services are the characteristics of a healthy rather than an unhealthy society, and privacy is one of the key balances against security services.

The second dichotomy surrounds freedom of expression. The debate over the 'right to be forgotten'[55] highlights this, as, in a different context, has the recent debate over press freedom in the United Kingdom, centred around phone hacking and the Leveson Report. Blogger Guido Fawkes put it directly when giving evidence to the Parliamentary Joint Committee on Privacy and Injunctions: 'privacy is a euphemism for censorship'.[56] Indeed, in European Law there is an explicit balance to be kept between

---

[55] See Chapter 7 and Bernal (2014).
[56] Evidence from the Committee can be found at www.publications.parliament.uk/pa/ jt201012/jtselect/jtprivinj/273/27302.htm

Article 8 (the right to respect for private and family life) and Article 10 (freedom of expression) of the European Convention on Human Rights (ECHR). That, however, only tells part of the story and oversimplifies the nature of both privacy and freedom of expression. In other ways, privacy *protects* freedom of expression. Whistle-blowers require anonymity if they are to feel free to express themselves. Vulnerable people need privacy if they are to be brave enough to speak out. Those living under oppressive governments need privacy if they are to express their dissent. Privacy is not just about the powerful protecting their positions of power, and freedom of expression should not be just for the media.

In the age of the internet, this is particularly true: the internet can give the 'little' people an opportunity to express themselves in ways that were previously impossible. It could turn freedom of expression into something much more real than it has ever been before. In that context, privacy is not the enemy of freedom of speech, it is its closest ally.

The third and perhaps the most contentious dichotomy concerns business. In practical terms, privacy is often seen as an enemy of business. Data protection law is seen as a bureaucratic burden. The need for consent is viewed as an unnecessary delay and disturbance of the customer experience. Business lobby groups work hard to try to dilute privacy legislation.[57]

This dichotomy also appears false. Rather than privacy being the enemy of business, privacy should be the ally of business. Privacy helps to foster trust, and in the longer term trust supports business. A customer that trusts a business is more likely to be a loyal and supportive customer. Privacy may well be the enemy of some businesses – the case of Phorm, discussed in Chapter 7, is a prime example – but only those businesses that are excessively privacy-invasive and do not really provide any benefit in exchange for their invasions of privacy.

That last point brings into focus the key point: balance. In the end it is almost all a question of balance. Finding the balances between the needs of governments, businesses and individuals is crucial. Ultimately all three groups will benefit from a safe, secure, 'free' and private internet that provides privacy, security and economic opportunities. That means balancing privacy and security, and privacy and economic development: the essence of the model of the Symbiotic Web, the subject of the next chapter.

---

[57] See for example Chapter 4, Section 2.2, on the proposed reform of the Data Protection regime.

3

The Symbiotic Web

1   The Symbiotic Web

On the surface, the web appears to be a place where there is more freedom to move and act than in real life: international borders can be crossed, often without the surfer even knowing that they are being crossed, censorship appears much more limited and one's identity is seemingly protected. The famous cartoon in the *New Yorker* that proclaimed that 'on the internet nobody knows you're a dog' reflects the common perception of such anonymity.[1] The reality is very different – not only is it possible to know that you're a dog, but to know what breed you are, the names of your doggy friends, which cats you chased yesterday and what kind of dog food you prefer.

Added to this, as Lessig (2006) and subsequently Murray (2006) have shown, the ability of the code writers who create the web pages that people visit to control people's actions and opportunities makes it an environment in which people are potentially subject to much less freedom and less autonomy than in the real world. This means that it is of great importance that what it means to function fully and freely online is understood, as well as what it is that stops this from being possible now, and just as importantly what could stop it from being possible in the future.

This chapter sets out a model – the Symbiotic Web – that helps with the understanding of these developments and their impact. It explains many of the current trends, not least the way in which the gathering of data has accelerated and expanded far beyond the conceptions of most commentators of even just a few years ago. This model forms a backdrop for much of the rest of this book, framing the intellectual context for the substantive case studies in Chapters 5 to 7, helping to explain their significance

[1] The cartoon by Peter Steiner, was published in 1993. In 2000, the New York Times published a piece entitled 'Cartoon Catches the Spirit of the Internet'. See www.nytimes.com/2000/12/14/technology/14DOGG.html?pagewanted=1&ei=5070&en=f0518aafeccf3 6fd&ex=1183089600.

and their implications. Through the understanding that the concept of the Symbiotic Web provides, it becomes possible to see the potential ways forward taking shape in a more logical, connected form. The solutions proposed here – rights-based solutions, balanced with economic and security interests, brought into action through what Murray describes as 'symbiotic regulation' (2006, Chapter 8) – arise through the understanding achieved by use of the Symbiotic Web.

The symbiosis described here is currently essentially benign. Its form might be described as being of the mutualist variety, where both sides of the symbiosis benefit, rather than the commensalist form (where one side benefits and the other neither benefits or suffers) or the parasitic form (where one side benefits to the detriment of the other). It lies behind many of the most positive developments on the internet and has produced a massive expansion in attractive and productive products and services available on the internet. It is a symbiosis that benefits both the individuals who use the internet and the businesses that provide services through the internet.

Nevertheless, there are risks associated with its symbiotic nature, and there is a danger that it could develop into something malign, twisting the mutually beneficial symbiosis into a harmful parasitism, harmful in particular insofar as individual autonomy is concerned. The eventual result, as described here, could be a fractured web, manipulating and controlling those who use it. Berners-Lee and others have set out visions of the future in which the internet becomes more personalised, and users have more and more control (Berners-Lee and Fischetti, 2000). What the malign version of the Symbiotic Web suggests is precisely the opposite: that control could be being taken out of the hands of the users, choices being made for them, rather than by them, and not necessarily for their benefit, but rather for the benefit of those wielding that control.

What is more, the symbiosis that is currently manifesting itself in the web is one that is in some ways duplicated in our 'offline' world. The gathering and use of data in these ways is not limited to online activities, but is happening to a greater or lesser extent throughout our society, from supermarket loyalty cards to transport payment systems such as London's Oyster cards.[2] Moreover, the borders between the online and offline worlds are becoming more and more blurred, as demonstrated forcefully by Google's 'streetview'[3] and 'augmented reality' systems such as Google's Project

---

[2] https://oyster.tfl.gov.uk/oyster/entry.do.
[3] http://maps.google.com/help/maps/streetview/.

Glass.[4] It is not just online businesses that are becoming dependent on the use of personal data, and it is not just people who spend significant time online whose data is being gathered and used. The issue is becoming more pervasive all the time, and the need for solutions is becoming ever more important. The solutions offered here point us in a direction that could help solve – or at least ameliorate – the problems identified, problems that go beyond the virtual into the 'real' world.

1.1   What is the Symbiotic Web?

Symbiosis is where two different kinds of organism exist together in a close and interactive relationship. It can be mutually dependent and mutually beneficial – examples occur in nature such as the birds that live on rhinos, eating the insects that infest the rhinos' skin, feeding the birds and cleaning the rhinos – but it can also be detrimental to one of the parties, like the tapeworms that grow inside people's stomachs, leading to sickness and on occasion death.

A form of symbiosis has developed on the web. Individuals and commercial enterprises are mutually dependent: enterprises have built business models reliant on a currency of personal data, while individuals depend on 'free' access to many services, from search engines to price comparison services, social networking sites and media services such as YouTube, many of the services that now form an intrinsic part of online life. These 'free' services use personal data, obtained through various overt and covert means, as their way of generating revenues through targeted advertising, profile building and the direct sale of personal data, amongst other things. Even many of those services that are not free have moved towards this kind of symbiotic state, gathering personal data as part of their process in exchange for personal information, offering discounts for buying online or 'personalised services' such as, for example, the iTunes Genius system, which selects music for each user based on a profile they have built up, which is in turn rooted in that user's musical taste.[5]

We as individuals are sacrificing one kind of freedom – 'liber' freedom, our privacy and autonomy – for another, 'gratis' freedom, receiving services and convenience without having to pay for them in the pecuniary sense. As the adage goes, there's no such thing as a free lunch. Effectively

---

[4] See for example www.google.com/glass/start/.
[5] Introduced as part of iTunes 8 and now a key part of the system. See www.apple.com/itunes/features/#genius.

we are paying for these services through the surrender of our private information, and ultimately, as will be outlined below, through giving up part of our autonomy. Conversely, the enterprises are sacrificing the opportunity to make money for a less tangible form of reward: information about their potential customers that may or may not be able to be transformed effectively into financial rewards at a later date. So far, for many businesses (most clearly Google and Facebook and similar services) these rewards have been substantial. Whether they continue to be so is another matter, but business models and ways of operating have been built on the assumption that they will be. As more businesses shift into this way of being, this gathering and use of data can only be expected to increase.

The implications of this symbiosis are significant. It helps to explain many of the most important things that are happening in the field. It explains why so much personal data is gathered. Further, it can help us to understand what kinds of data are being gathered, and by whom, and the principal purposes to which such information is being put commercially. Understanding the nature of this symbiosis can also provide good indications as to the ways in which this data may be used in the future, as well as why companies are less than eager to be open about either the data gathering or its purposes. It can also help us to understand the threats to our privacy and autonomy that are arising – and the further threats that might arise in the future – as a result of the ways in which data is being gathered and used, and will be gathered and used in the future.

These threats are complex and manifold, but they centre around the ways in which data can be used to persuade or manipulate people into doing what the data-user rather than the data-subject chooses, whether this means buying products or services, seeing or reading information, visiting particular websites, supplying certain information, or anything else. The implications for autonomy are clear, but it must be remembered that much of this can be and is beneficial: links and information that are well chosen, targeted advertising that is appropriate and useful, and so forth. The economic model that provides free services to users is the one that most appreciate. It is at present, in general at least, a mutually beneficial form of symbiosis. What is important is to understand the risks associated with it, the ways in which it can become something negative and what can be done to prevent this from taking place.

1.2   The evolution of the Symbiotic Web

In the early days of the internet, the worldwide web was to most intents and purposes an 'information bank'. 'Content providers' – for the most

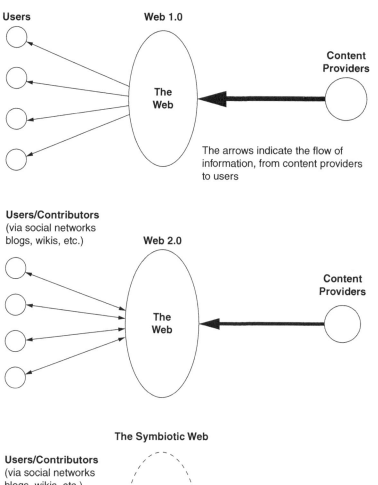

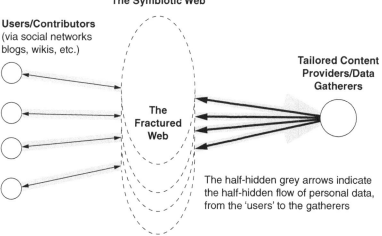

Figure 1 The evolution of the Symbiotic Web

part technical experts or people working at and for institutions or companies – put information on to the web, while most ordinary people were primarily 'users', and accessed and downloaded that information. The flow of information was to a great extent one-way: from the content providers to the users.

The move to a more interactive web was characterised largely by a transformation in the 'users'. Rather than simply accessing information provided for them, users began to supply information themselves: they no longer needed to be technical experts or to be working for large institutions or companies in order to supply that information. To do this, they used a wide range of 'Web 2.0' sites or applications, through web-logs ('blogs'), 'wikis' (collaborative websites such as the web-encyclopaedia wikipedia.com), social networking sites such as Facebook or MySpace, media sites such as YouTube, and expansions in old-fashioned message-boards and equivalents. In the interactive web, information flows into the web not only from the content providers, but also from the users themselves.

In the shift to this more interactive web, information started to flow both ways for the users. The shift to the Symbiotic Web is characterised by a converse transformation for the erstwhile 'content providers'. Not only do they provide information, but they extract it from the users as well, using a wide variety of techniques, from monitoring their activities online to persuading users to volunteer as much personal information as possible. This personal information is in turn used by the content providers to 'tailor' the information they provide to individuals. The supremely successful business models of first Google and then Facebook and the other social networking sites began this process. Google's use of search terms to target advertising demonstrated the potential that access to personal information can provide. As the Google business model developed and other businesses emulated their success, this tailoring has expanded to individualise not just advertising but the content of websites and the suggestions given (and often the options provided) as to where to go next. For search engines, this means that not only the 'sponsored links' and advertisements that appear around search results can be tailored to the searcher, but that the results the searcher finds when they search for a particular term could be different, or in a different order, than those that another person might find if they search for precisely the same term. Given that this is the way that most people navigate the internet, this has a huge impact on what sites people become aware of and as a result actually 'choose' to visit.

This has many implications, but the most direct is that it 'fractures' the web, making it potentially different for each and every individual user, and different in ways that are controlled not by the user but by the content providers. This fracturing is significant, and although it may appear just to be a side effect of the symbiotic collection of data, it has a direct impact on autonomy. Moreover, it makes it clear that the Symbiotic Web is not simply about the gathering of data but about its use.

This shift of control from the user to the content provider is one of the things that distinguishes the Symbiotic Web from many of the ideas presented for the future of the web. Most have anticipated more power being put into the hands of the individual, for example allowing the individual to find what he or she wants or needs using 'intelligent agents' to scour the internet, building on Berners-Lee's concept of the 'semantic web' (Berners-Lee and Fischetti, 2000, pp. 169–70). The future of the web seems less 'liberating' than these concepts suggest. Despite the appearance of the individual taking more control, the reality could be the opposite, with individuals having more of their choices made for them, and control taken out of their hands.

1.3   The emergence of the Symbiotic Web

The Symbiotic Web is already taking shape, using existing technologies such as cookies rather than requiring the development of new, intelligent software that may be years or even decades away from practical existence. Moreover, the moves towards the Symbiotic Web are driven by financial imperatives rather than by the somewhat vague technological speculation that appears to underlie the suggestions being made about the development of the semantic web. That in itself seems likely, in the current climate, to make the future implied by the model of the Symbiotic Web a more probable outcome than the visions of even people as eminent as Berners-Lee, making it all the more important that the situation is better understood, and where necessary appropriate interventions are made.

Even leaving aside the assumptions that many are making about the future development of the web, the emergence of the symbiosis described above was not an expected one. Indeed it has come about directly against many of the predictions that both academics and lawmakers have been making in terms of the development of 'free' services. What many were predicting was the development and use of e-money, particularly for micro-payments. Miller, for example, writing about online payments in Edwards and Waelde, 2000 (pp. 55–6), begins his chapter with a sketch of how he saw a couple's online lives in the near future, and one of the keys was a number of different, small-scale payments for online services.

Indeed, the European Union brought in its 'E-Money Directive'[6] in 2000, anticipating the need for regulation as this kind of system developed and expanded. This has not yet materialised; the EU's evaluation of the E-Money Directive, published in 2006,[7] concluded that there was 'widespread agreement among stakeholders that the e-money market has developed more slowly than expected'.[8] As the Symbiotic Web has come into action, an effective if hidden currency of personal information has meant that there has been little need for the kind of e-money system that is needed for these kinds of small payments.[9] That may change. The 2000 Directive has been superseded by a 2009 Directive,[10] which has already led to renewed micro-payment speculation and the offering of new systems by some of the big players in the internet world.[11] The success or otherwise of these systems has yet to become clear.

2   The make-up of the benign symbiosis

2.1   Search engines

Perhaps the most important element of the symbiosis is the search engine. The Google business model played a central role in the development of the Symbiotic Web, a role that is continuing and even growing, as the business models of Google and the other search engines become

---

[6] E-Money Directive (2000/46/EC), available online at http://eur-lex.europa.eu/LexUriServ/LexUriServ.do?uri=CELEX:32000L0046:EN:HTML.

[7] Available online at http://ec.europa.eu/internal_market/bank/docs/e-money/evaluation_en.pdf.

[8] E-Money Evaluation Report, p. 2.

[9] On the other hand, Rupert Murdoch has suggested that the current 'free delivery' system is a 'malfunctioning model', and there are now charges for access to the Sunday Times online. See www.guardian.co.uk/media/2009/may/07/rupert-murdoch-charging-websites and www.guardian.co.uk/media/2009/jun/03/sunday-times-website. The success or otherwise of the move has yet to be proven, and it has been designed not to replace the data gathering with money, but to supplement it. Moreover, the rapid decline of Friends Reunited, which continued to charge despite the growth of rival social networking sites such as Facebook, suggests that, for mainstream consumers at least, the move away from a 'free delivery' model is unlikely to be easy.

[10] Directive 2009/110/EC, which came into force in April 2011, is available online at http://eur-lex.europa.eu/LexUriServ/LexUriServ.do?uri=OJ:L:2009:267:0007:0017:EN:PDF.

[11] Systems such as Amazon's 'Amazon Coin (www.amazon.com/gp/feature.html?docId=1001166401) and Apple's subscription system (see www.apple.com/pr/library/2011/02/15Apple-Launches-Subscriptions-on-the-App-Store.html).

increasingly sophisticated. At a basic level their part in the symbiosis is clear: they offer an excellent service to internet users, and the service is apparently free. This makes search engines of fundamental importance and a key part of the benign symbiosis. The services provided by search engines – and by Google in particular – are extremely good, and although the Google business model is dependent on targeted advertising, it would not work if Google searches were not sufficiently good to command such a huge user base. In comparison to what had come before it, Google offered (and continues to offer) something that makes the internet far easier to use and far more attractive to the user.

Google provides these services effectively in exchange for gathering vast amounts of search data. In their search logs, search engines record not just the terms that are searched for and the links that are followed as a result of such a search, but the time and location at which the search was made and other details. This data can give a very detailed picture of the searcher's interests and habits, browsing style and so forth, and this can be extremely significant not only in profiling and targeting,[12] but also in working out how best to ensure that the searcher reads and follows particular links. What is more important, because search engines (and again, Google in particular) are used by such huge numbers of people, they are able to analyse patterns and behaviour on an unprecedented scale, and use it to hone their profiling. Google and others use this most directly for their targeted advertising. As much of this advertising is paid for on a 'pay-per-click' basis, it is in the search engine's interest to convince users to click on the advertisements. Google has been extremely adept at this, which is one of the reasons that it has grown to be one of the most successful corporations in the world.

2.2   Communications providers

The second group of key elements of the symbiosis to consider are what can loosely be described as the communications providers: providers of email, messaging, telephony and so forth. Communication was one of the primary initial uses of the internet, and it remains one of the most important. It has become a key part of the benign symbiosis, as most of the communications services are provided to the user free. This includes the large-scale web-based email services such as Gmail, Microsoft's Outlook. com (formerly Hotmail), Yahoo Mail, and most instant messaging systems

[12] See Chapter 5, Section 1.

and many chatroom services such as Microsoft Live Messenger, AIM,[13] Google+Hangouts,[14] Yahoo Messenger,[15] BlackBerry Messenger (BBM),[16] as well as internet telephony services such as Skype.[17] The forms and quality of these services have been improving all the time, incorporating such things as video conferencing, which in the past was an extremely expensive, premium service, and yet they are still in general provided free, a prime example of the essentially benign nature of the symbiosis.

The exchange that is taking place is that when people communicate over the internet, significant amounts of data are gathered and held about that communication. Precisely what is recorded and held can vary significantly. For example, email providers keep records of originators and recipients of messages; internet telephony providers keep records of a user's calls. As well as this 'traffic data' some providers will keep records of the contents of the actual communications themselves. Google and Yahoo Mail are perhaps the best examples of this – the contents of an email can be used to generate targeted advertising in the same way that search engines do with searches. If an email contains particular keywords, the advertisements presented around that email will be tailored accordingly. If a user is writing about planning a holiday, for example, they might find advertisements for online travel agencies.

2.3   Social networking services

Social networking services form the third key part of the symbiosis. Indeed, with Facebook's membership now over one billion it may now be the most significant part of all. They provide a carefully built, user-friendly package of communications tools (including email and instant messaging), networking tools, games and other forms of entertainment. The services they provide would in the past have only been available in highly expensive 'group-ware' that was effectively only accessible to big business. It is now available to anyone, and for free, another example of the benign nature of the Symbiotic Web.

What social networking sites do, effectively, is ask their users to profile themselves. Users put in biographical data, educational data, information about their careers and their tastes in everything from music and food to religion, politics and relationships. In Facebook, some of the

---

[13] www.aim.com.   [14] www.google.com/talk/.   [15] http://messenger.yahoo.com/.
[16] http://us.blackberry.com/apps-software/blackberrymessenger/.
[17] www.skype.com.

more common 'applications' are questionnaires and quizzes, all seemingly for amusement, but in reality allowing Facebook and its advertisers to put together more and more detailed information about the user. Furthermore, Facebook knows who a user's friends are, so can link this data to such friends, giving another dimension to the possibilities. The simplest examples include telling the user what their friends' favourite books and movies are, or informing the user that one of their friends has just started playing a particular game online. The profiles generated from all these forms of 'social data' are currently used primarily for targeted advertising and also to help expand the service, providing more scope for further advertising, more users, and ultimately to make the company itself more valuable, at least in part because of the value of the enormous amount of data that it owns. Though the services they offer are 'free' to the user, their businesses are worth billions of dollars to their owners through their ability to advertise and through the accumulated value of the data that their users supply, [18] which makes them perfect examples of the kind of symbiosis that characterises the Symbiotic Web.

2.4 Internet Service Providers

Internet Service Providers (ISPs) make up the fourth category of key elements of the Symbiotic Web. Though they do not, in the UK at least, generally provide their services for free, prices for internet access have dropped dramatically, and sometimes internet access is 'bundled' with other services in a way that can be presented as free.[19] It may be that they are also being used as 'loss leaders', perhaps in part because providers realise that the potential benefits from the data that may be gathered outweigh the relatively small costs involved in providing the service. They provide this service, with more bandwidth and fewer problems than before, and at a vastly reduced cost, and although the general improvements in technology over the last few years and the increasingly competitive market for internet service provision have been substantially responsible for these

---

[18] The Facebook initial public offering (IPO), in May 2012, initially valued Facebook in excess of $100 billion. That IPO, however, was fraught with problems, and the price fell significantly. Nevertheless, as of May 2013, the company was worth in excess of $60 billion (see for example http://thenextweb.com/facebook/2013/05/17/one-year-post-ipo-facebooks-stock-is-31-under-the-level-at-which-it-went-public).

[19] Examples include Sky TV bundling broadband access with their satellite TV services (see www.sky.com/shop/broadband-talk/).

improvements, the beneficial symbiosis may well have also played a role in this service improvement.

The most significant data type gathered by ISPs is 'clickstream data', the record of the clicks made when browsing the web. Just as for search data, clickstream data is not simply a record of what clicks are made but when, from where and so on. The potential economic benefits derivable from clickstream data have yet to be exploited as fully as Google and others have exploited search data, but the potential is clear: business models such as Phorm, which is discussed below and in depth in Chapter 6, are just the starting point. It should be noted, too, that many other kinds of data can be (and often are) collected while clickstream data is gathered: information such as the type of computer being used, the kind of browsing software being used, the location of the user and so forth.

2.5   Commercial websites

Commercial websites such as Amazon and eBay are some of the most successful and attractive sites on the internet and make up the fifth key element of the Symbiotic Web. Though they do not provide their services for free, they do provide them for less than products acquired in the offline world, and therefore provide a level of convenience that would not previously have been possible.

Direct shopping sites such as Amazon gather data of two distinct kinds: transaction data relating to goods and services that have been bought or bid for, and 'interest' data relating to goods and services that have been looked at or researched on their sites. Both are useful in determining possible future sales, and the latter can include detailed 'clickstream data' (which is discussed in more depth below) including details such as the timing between clicks and so forth, which can be used for profiling and to predict behaviour. Van den Poel and Buckinx (2005), for example, found that detailed clickstream data was the best indicator of future online purchasing behaviour. In particular, they found that it was a significantly better indicator than the actual purchases made, the information that users might reasonably believe was used by online stores.[20]

These two types of data have very different characteristics when considered from the perspective of privacy and autonomy. It appears reasonable to expect the real transactions to be recorded and used for marketing, but

[20]   Amazon, for example, explains its recommendations by saying 'recommended because you purchased ...'

quite possibly unreasonable for the rest of the browsing to be taken into account in the same way. Whether it is reasonable for either of these types of data to be sold on to third parties for aggregation or other commercial use (as in the Beacon system discussed below, and elsewhere) is another question entirely.

2.6   The majority of the web?

To summarise: the five most significant individual elements of the Symbiotic Web have been described above: the search engines, the communications providers, the social networking services, the ISPs and the commercial websites. To a certain extent, however, the symbiosis covers the majority of the web. The pure 'information providers' generally supply their information for free. There are all kinds of other free services available, from 'geographical' services such as Google Maps,[21] Google Earth,[22] Google Street View[23] and the various street finder systems,[24] to the recreational services such as YouTube and its equivalents. New kinds of services are evolving all the time and a large proportion of them are free, built on business models using data gathering and targeted advertising.

The data gathered by these services varies enormously. Controllers of websites can gather the clickstream data that relates to their own sites. When people arrive at their sites, they can gather information such as where they have come from and all the clicks once they arrive, including where they go to next. Then there is the more specific data related to the service provided: for geographical sites, the places people are looking at; for media sites such as YouTube the tastes people have in music and video; for sports sites what sports and teams they follow. All of this data can help in building up profiles, in targeting advertisements and so forth. More types of data and more methods of extraction are being developed all the time.

3   The risks of a malign symbiosis

Though the Symbiotic Web is currently of an essentially positive, mutualist form, providing benefits for individuals, for business and potentially

---

[21] http://maps.google.com/, http://maps.google.co.uk/ etc.

[22] http://earth.google.com/, http://earth.google.co.uk/ etc.

[23] http://maps.google.com/help/maps/streetview/.

[24] There are a number of such services for many locations, including for the UK, see for example www.streetfinder.co.uk/ and www.streetmap.co.uk/.

for society as a whole, there are significant risks associated with the symbiosis, particularly in relation to privacy and autonomy. A new understanding of the potential value of personal information has developed and with it whole new markets, not just different ways to use this information but markets in the buying, selling and aggregation of this data. The competitive drives that accompany these developments will invariably impact on both privacy and autonomy.

The starting point is the understanding that personal information has a commercial value. This has led organisations to gather more and more data, not just for specific current or planned uses, but speculatively, based on an assumption that new uses and new values will be found for this data. And not only is more data gathered, but there is pressure to find new and different ways to gather the data, some of which are detailed elsewhere in this book. As this data is gathered, the organisations are looking for more and more ways to use the information they have. If a business has an asset, it will want to get as much commercial value from it as it can. The more competitive the market, the more attempts there will be to squeeze the maximum value out of the data. New businesses are developing for aggregation of data and profile generation, not only to make money from the existence of the new data, but also to find even more effective ways of using such data for other businesses.[25]

3.1   Who is serving whom? Alliances and favouritism

One of the characteristics of the functioning of social networks is that, in practice, people tend to see them as 'neutral', and even use them as a route to navigate the web. They see them as a 'service' and have been shocked when this 'service' is used to serve the businesses and their allies rather than the users. Facebook's 'Beacon', and behavioural advertisers such as Phorm,[26] acted to the benefit of themselves and their business allies and to the detriment of their competitors, with the users' wishes effectively ignored. The result in both cases was a revolt amongst users and an eventual abandonment of the service.

If similar systems are extended onto search engines it is easy to see how conflicts of interest might result in unfair or misleading search results and consequent manipulation of how people navigate the web. The ongoing

[25] See Ayres, 2007 for details not only of the data aggregators but some of the more imaginative ways in which this data is being used.
[26] See Chapter 6.

EC investigation into the functioning of Google, which originated from cases such as the 'Foundem' case, is exactly on this point, Foundem's complaint suggesting that Google manipulates search results to favour sites that particularly benefit it.[27]

The reality behind Facebook's Beacon was discovered before it came into operation, and the privacy issues surrounding it raised such a furore that Facebook was forced to change it significantly before it started, making it an opt-in rather than opt-out system, amongst other things. This is in itself revealing, in two ways. Firstly, it demonstrates why companies might keep the real reasons for their data policies and practices effectively secret from most of their users, for when users find out what is going on, they often object, and object strongly. Secondly, it suggests some of the possible ways to change things: by raising awareness of practices so there are more objections; by making it harder for companies to keep such practices secret; and by making it harder for companies to use practices that do not require real express, informed consent, of an 'opt-in' rather than 'opt-out' form.[28] Beacon was eventually abandoned in September 2009, in part at least as a result of the exposure of its privacy-intrusive nature.

Phorm's 'Webwise' was another example of how these kinds of alliance can form and the impact they can have.[29] Phorm's Webwise system would have allowed some of the UK's biggest ISPs to analyse individuals' browsing behaviour. This would allow potential advertisers to target users, by 'intercepting' the clicks made as a user surfs the web, analysing them and building up a database of users' entire internet activity. Effectively, Phorm intended to harness the value of clickstream data. Phorm raised a plethora of legal, ethical and commercial issues, as it monitors a user's entire online activities, and as such was challenged as a possible breach of wiretapping regulations, as a breach of data protection legislation and as another step towards a surveillance society. It was also being seen by some as an interference with other websites' commercial interests. It could, for example, gather all the search data entered into the Google search page

[27] Google is being investigated under competition law after a complaint by UK price comparison site Foundem, French legal search engine ejustice.fr and Microsoft's Ciao. See for example www.telegraph.co.uk/technology/google/7301299/Google-under-investigation-for-alleged-breach-of-EU-competition-rules.html. As of May 2013, the situation had not been fully resolved. See for example www.v3.co.uk/v3-uk/news/2268051/foundem-advises-eu-to-reject-googles-proposed-antitrust-settlement.

[28] The Facebook Beacon story is discussed in Chapter 6, Section 5.3. For a summary from Facebook's own perspective, see http://blog.facebook.com/blog.php?post=7584397130.

[29] See www.phorm.com/, and for a look at the negative side of Phorm, see www.badphorm.co.uk/page.php?2. Phorm is examined in detail in Chapter 6.

before Google themselves had gathered it. The issues raised by Phorm
are complex and concerning in many ways, and are examined in depth
in Chapter 6. Phorm's importance lay not just in its proposed functions but in what it implied about where the symbiotic nature of the web
might cause it to go, and how, as noted above, the competitive drives that
underpin the Symbiotic Web will manifest themselves in more and more
imaginative and potentially risky ways of using – and exploiting – the
data that is being gathered.

3.2   Tailoring and Balkanisation

Another key set of risks arises through the process of 'tailoring' web pages
for individuals, which as discussed above is one of the fundamental features of the Symbiotic Web. As businesses learn more about their customers – and are able to derive more information through new profiling and
data aggregation businesses – they are able to 'tailor' services even more.
This tailoring can include such potentially pernicious practices as price or
service discrimination. If a business can learn enough about a customer
to know how much they might be willing to pay for something, which
becomes more and more possible as they gather more data about that
customer, then they can set prices (and display those prices on their web
pages) individually for that customer, prices that might be either higher or
lower than those offered to others.

With the development of the Symbiotic Web, companies can potentially
learn much more about their customers than ever before, and not just the
kind of information that the customer wants them to know. Information
such as social class, salaries earned, home ownership, purchasing history
from other businesses and so forth can be available through data aggregation,[30] or via commercial alliances such as those already forming through
Beacon and Phorm. Profiling techniques, together with the increase in
available information, can allow companies to predict with more and
more accuracy not just what their customers might be persuaded to buy,
but how much they might be willing to pay for it. This in itself has its problems. The idea of 'price discrimination' might just seem like good business practice, offering better prices to regular customers, for example, but
it has a downside as well. While lowering prices for regular customers to

---

[30] See Ayres, 2007, particularly pp. 33–4 for an examination of the predictive use of data.
    As Ayres puts it, 'data mining can let business emulate a kind of aggregate omniscience.
    Indeed, because of Super Crunching, firms sometimes may be able to make more accur-
    ate predictions about how you'll behave than you could ever make yourself.'

reward their loyalty is both common and appropriate, it is also possible that tailoring might result in higher prices for others who are viewed as more likely to be willing to pay more, and that would not be a good thing, at least not from the customer's perspective. All of this becomes possible in the Symbiotic Web and as the competition between businesses grows, and as the availability of data and the technical and technological capabilities for processing it become better and more available, the drives to use it become stronger.

As noted above, tailoring can apply not only to content, but to links provided – most pertinently in search results[31] – which ultimately results in the personalisation of the web experience and could be seen as a 'fracturing' of the web.[32] This brings with it a further set of risks. The internet that a user is 'exposed' to is becoming one that is controlled for them in ways that ensure that a user only sees things that people think that they will like. They know the users' tastes, who their friends are, what kind of work they do, the kind of music they like and movies they watch, and present to them only those things that they think these individual users will be interested in. Personalised news pages will cover the topics the news providers 'know' the user cares about, possibly only from the news sources that they 'know' the user trusts. The products and services offered for the user to buy will be only those that match the profile of the user that sellers have built up. From the point of view of the seller this makes perfect sense, since these are the products the user is most likely to buy. The events, TV shows and movies that the user is told about are similarly chosen to suit what is known about them, which, again, makes perfect sense to the providers. When the user searches for something, the search results, too, are chosen taking into account what the search engine knows about the user, what the user likes and what the user is interested in.

The result may be something instantly attractive, comfortable and unthreatening to the user. One somewhat extreme way to look at it would be to consider a social networking site such as Facebook, where a member really does only see their friends (and only their friends see them), and all the applications suggested to the member and advertisements presented to them are tailored to what Facebook knows about them. The Symbiotic

---

[31] From December 2009, Google has 'personalised' all search results, unless the searcher actively opts out (see http://googleblog.blogspot.com/2009/12/personalized-search-for-everyone.html). See the discussion by search engine blogger Danny Sullivan at http://searchengineland.com/google-now-personalizes-everyones-search-results-31195.

[32] Some aspects of this tailoring, and how it is starting to emerge in reality on the internet, are discussed in Pariser, 2011.

Web could end up producing an internet that functions like one big social networking site, where people only see things that the providers think they will like, and never see things that providers don't think they will like and indeed are specifically excluded from places where controllers do not like their profile. While this might be attractive in one way – we'll like almost everything we see, and never know what else we are missing – it is vastly less positive and stimulating than the current version of the internet. It is a kind of 'sanitised' internet, where the chances of coming across something surprising and really new are limited.

One particularly pernicious version of tailoring is a phenomenon that can be described as 'back door Balkanisation', to extend Sunstein's metaphor from Republic.com. Sunstein (2007) discussed how the internet could have a tendency to polarise opinion and create niches with narrow and potentially extreme political views or interests. While Sunstein writes largely about a phenomenon that takes place through the choices made by individuals, what could potentially happen through the Symbiotic Web would be without the knowledge or understanding of the user, let alone through any kind of conscious or even subconscious choice: Balkanisation through the back door. Effectively, if through their profile a user is deemed to hold a particular political, religious or ideological stance, this kind of system could drive that user into a more extreme version of that stance, with dangers not only for the individual but also for society as a whole. The fact that it happens automatically would make it even more pernicious, and potentially even more dangerous than the phenomenon described by Sunstein. Sunstein's theories have been much criticised,[33] but, as a significant part of that criticism rests on the rights of the individual to make his or her own choices, the backdoor Balkanisation that accompanies the Symbiotic Web is something quite different: at the very least it needs to be considered seriously.

Taking this a step further, there is the potential for individual service providers and web providers to make conscious and possibly damaging choices, checking profiles of users before deciding what kind of information to provide. Nightmare visions such as 'whites-only websites', which check visitors' profiles to determine whether they should be allowed to see certain content, will be both a technical and practical possibility in the near future. It should be remembered that this kind of profiling can

---

[33] Perhaps Sunstein's strongest critic is Eugene Volokh, of the Volokh Conspiracy (www. volokh.com/), but there has also been active criticism in print, such as that by Dan Hunter in Hunter, 2001.

be 'inclusive', only allowing access to particular content for an 'approved' kind of person, or 'exclusive', allowing access for everyone except a 'banned' type. The potential for misuse is significant.

3.3   Risks associated with particular data types

There are also risks associated with the gathering of particular data types. With communications data, for example, where data such as the content of communications is held, even if the primary use is simply for targeting advertising and commercial profile building, there is the potential for misuse. Wherever and however data are held such material can be vulnerable, so it is not just what the communications provider might do with the data that is of concern, but what more malign use others might make of it. Security and privacy of communications are key human rights, particularly in times and places of political oppression. The well-publicised examples of dissidents being imprisoned in China as a result of information provided by Yahoo! about their communications are just one of the ways in which this can cause problems.[34] There are similar possibilities with other kinds of data, most notably the data gathered and stored by social networking sites, with their in-built self-profiling, and with geographical and in particular geo-location data, with its potential for finding the person in the 'real' world as well as the online world.

It should also be remembered that while there are particular issues concerning each of the data types discussed above, the overall effect is greater than the sum of the individual parts. Google, for example, combines the information gathered by search with that gathered on Gmail, through Google Maps, Google Street View, Google Earth and so forth.[35] The opportunities for profiling, for aggregation and for other forms of research multiply as more data becomes available (Ayres, 2007).

Much of the concern expressed so far has related to the risk of the symbiosis becoming unbalanced, as commercial forces drive organisations to find more ways to gather data, and use that data to control the individuals about whom the data has been gathered. The range of ways in which this control can be exercised has not yet been explored beyond a surface level. All that has been seen to date has been regular advertising techniques and

---

[34] See e.g. http://en.rsf.org/china-yahoo-settles-lawsuit-by-families-14–11–2007,24240.html.

[35] This combining of data became explicit with the change in Google's privacy policies in March 2012. See http://googleblog.blogspot.co.uk/2012/02/googles-new-privacy-policy.html.

persuasion through the presentation of links and so forth. Powerful as these methods are, there are deeper possibilities. As Lessig (2006) has suggested, code writers wield enormous power on the internet, and through the design of the architecture, new ways to monitor and control individuals can and will be developed.

3.4   The burgeoning market in data

Perhaps the most significant potentially malign result of the Symbiotic Web, however, is simply the burgeoning market in data,[36] about which users have been, at least until recently, largely ignorant. Businesses are becoming acutely aware of the value of gathering data, but at the same time evidence suggests that when customers are aware that their data is being gathered for such purposes, they do not like it. The reactions to the Facebook Beacon affair and the controversy over the emergence of Phorm are two pieces of evidence to support this. Though in some cases it is made clear that data is being gathered, it is often far from clear, and even when it is clear, the true uses to which the data is being put are rarely revealed. Individuals are generally kept in the dark, and this in itself leads to a loss of autonomy.

The very existence of this massive quantity of data represents a risk. Digital information, wherever it is and however it is stored, is vulnerable, whether from hacking, inadvertent or inappropriate selling or giving away of data, hardware and software failure, hardware theft or loss, or administrative or security failures. Once the data has been 'lost', the potential for criminal misuse is huge. Identity theft and other forms of financial fraud are already a significant problem.[37] As new kinds of information become available – particularly profiling and equivalent information – the potential for better-targeted and more pernicious identity-related crimes increases dramatically. Data vulnerability and the potential consequences of such vulnerability are examined in Chapter 7. Furthermore, as noted earlier, the existence of the data makes it tempting for those who have access to it to find new uses for it that are not necessarily in character or proportional to the reasons for which

---

[36] See Ayres, 2007, particularly pp. 134–8, for an examination of the growing market in data.

[37] In the UK, for example, police estimated identity theft in 2012 to cost £3.3 billion. See NFA Annual Fraud Indicator 2013, online at www.gov.uk/government/uploads/system/uploads/attachment_data/file/206552/nfa-annual-fraud-indicator-2013.pdf, p. 29.

the data was gathered in the first place. This 'function creep' has been particularly evident in recent years in relation to data gathered for anti-terrorism purposes. Notable examples include the use of the Regulation of Investigatory Powers Act (RIPA) 2000,[38] which was presented as a means to tackle terrorism and other serious crimes, to deal with dog fouling[39] and to spy on a couple to determine whether they were using a false address to get their child into a local school.[40] Function creep may come into play for commercial reasons and in commercial contexts even more often that it does for security or law-enforcement purposes, and is a risk whenever data is held, so the more data is being held, the greater the risk.

4 Governments and the Symbiotic Web

The development of the Symbiotic Web has been essentially driven by commercial forces, and primarily for commercial interests, but governments have already had an important role in shaping it, and that role could become more significant in the future. The symbiosis, in its benign form, can be seen to be very much in the interests of government. It can help provide happy and satisfied citizens, thriving businesses, technological innovation and, almost as a side product, substantial amounts of data that can potentially be extremely useful for governments. In broad-brush terms a government likes to have more information, not for sinister reasons, but because information can help it to do its job better. The more information it has about its citizens, the more accurately and appropriately government can design and implement policies to support them and to satisfy their needs. This general need covers almost every aspect of government, from housing and employment policies to taxation and health, and not just the more contentious areas such as crime prevention and security. As a consequence, it is in the general interest of *most* governments to firstly support the symbiosis and secondly do whatever is necessary to ensure that it remains benign, for many, though not all, of the malign possibilities for the symbiosis, as outlined below, are not at all in the interests of government.

---

[38] Available online at www.legislation.gov.uk/ukpga/2000/23/contents.
[39] See for example www.telegraph.co.uk/news/uknews/1584808/Council-spy-cases-hit-1000-a-month.html.
[40] See for example http://news.bbc.co.uk/1/hi/england/dorset/7341179.stm.

4.1   Tensions and balance

The tensions of the symbiosis apply also to governments: there are pushes towards privacy and pushes against it, and those pushes, as shall be shown in the next chapter, are played out in the way that governments attempt to use law to regulate the internet. 'Privacy-protective' legal regimes such as data protection are in tension with 'privacy-invasive' laws such as those surrounding surveillance and data retention. Data protection is of particular importance. It has strong principles and could potentially form the basis of what would be an excellent protection of individual privacy. Indeed, it has already played a significant part in moderating the actions of corporations and governments in terms of the gathering and processing of personal data, and hence in shaping the development of the Symbiotic Web. Data protection law, however, suffers from many problems, including its inconsistent implementation through national law and its often inadequate enforcement. Although reform is currently on the agenda, many of these problems are likely to remain.[41]

Data retention, in some ways the converse to data protection, is also playing its part in shaping the Symbiotic Web, though in a very different way. Data retention essentially requires ISPs and other communications providers to hold data and make it available to the authorities when requested.[42] There is a direct tension between data protection and data retention: one effectively asks for less data to be held, and for less time, while the other asks for more data to be held, and for longer.

This reflects the common tension between privacy and security, and points to one of the primary difficulties facing governments when dealing with the internet. In essence, governments have a balancing act to perform in relation to personal data. They must protect the privacy and autonomy of individuals, promote and support their businesses in achieving economic success, and at the same time ensure security for their citizens. Maintaining that balance is difficult, and unless the issues involved are appreciated and understood it is easy for privacy and autonomy to be squeezed by the competing economic and security interests. Indeed, the EU Data Protection Directive declares in its preamble that 'the establishment and functioning of an internal market' requires 'that personal data should be able to flow freely from one Member State to another', in other

---

[41] Data protection is discussed in detail in Chapter 4, Section 2.
[42] Data retention is discussed in detail in Chapter 4, Section 3.

words, that our economic success relies on the ability of personal data to flow freely.[43]

4.2 Harnessing the Symbiotic Web

Many of the risks associated with the Symbiotic Web that apply to commercial operators also apply to governments. Governments have similar temptations to simply gather data 'just in case', and to assume that the more data they have the better they will be able to perform their various tasks. The dangers associated with this potentially excessive data gathering tend to be underplayed, particularly in the security context, where the 'nothing to hide' argument is commonly used.[44]

The result of this has been an approach that attempts (and seemingly sometimes succeeds) to provide extreme levels of surveillance. This approach can be primarily legal, such as the attempt to bring in the Communications Data Bill in the UK,[45] or it can be more secretive and more directly technological. The most dramatic and potentially important example of the latter has been the revelation, through the leaks of Edward Snowden, of the previously hidden internet surveillance programmes of the US National Security Agency (NSA) and the UK's Government Communications Headquarters (GCHQ).[46] Precise details of these programmes are not clear – and may well never become clear – but the idea of perhaps the most significant of them, the PRISM programme, seems fairly direct in the way that it uses existing services and their data. According to the information given in *The Guardian*, PRISM is intended to provide the NSA with access to information gathered and held by nine major internet providers: AOL, Apple, Facebook, Google, Microsoft, PalTalk, Skype, Yahoo! and YouTube.[47] This list includes many of the biggest names on the internet and in particular what might loosely be described as the 'social' internet. Whether these revelations are entirely true remained unclear at the time of writing, but the intent appears evident: to monitor and analyse the way in which the 'new' internet is being used. Security agencies seem to be attempting to tap into the way that the search engines, social

---

[43] From paragraph (3) of the Preamble to The Data Protection Directive, Directive 95/46/EC. Available at http://eur-lex.europa.eu/LexUriServ/LexUriServ.do?uri=CELEX:31995L0046:EN:HTML.

[44] See Chapter 2, Section 4.1.   [45] See Chapter 4, Section 3.2.

[46] The stories about these programmes were published in *The Guardian*, starting in June 2013. See www.guardian.co.uk/world/prism.

[47] See www.guardian.co.uk/world/2013/jun/06/us-tech-giants-nsa-data.

networks and other services are already profiling, analysing and targeting people on the internet, letting Facebook, Google and Apple do much of their work for them.

Some of this is out in the open. In July 2013, for example, the UK government announced that it was monitoring Twitter and other social media in order to be able to get early warnings about protests regarding the proposed cull of badgers,[48] a controversial policy that had already caused public unrest. The appropriateness of this kind of approach is complex and potentially contentious. Headlines such as the BBC's 'Whitehall chiefs scan Twitter to head off badger protests',[49] for example, do not sit happily with rights to free association and free assembly enshrined in the major human rights conventions. What is clear, however, is that this kind of monitoring is happening, and to an increasing extent.

Harnessing the Symbiotic Web is not an approach restricted to security. In other areas such as combating illegal online activities such as the illegal downloading of music and child abuse images, one of the most common approaches appears to be to get commercial enterprises to do much of the work on behalf of the authorities, at its simplest to gather and hold the relevant data, but sometimes to go beyond that and detect and report suspicious activities, or even to actually police them, though many of these plans end up coming to nothing.[50] In all these examples, the authorities are trying to take advantage of the new kinds and volumes of data being gathered for commercial use, and using it for their own, very different purposes. As further new kinds of data appear, the authorities are continually assessing whether they can use that data. With the expansion of social networking sites, for example, the UK government first considered expanding the terms of data retention to include social networking data as well as the more conventional communications data that it originally covered,[51] and then, ultimately, through the Communications Data Bill, tried to expand those terms to include substantially all internet traffic.[52]

---

[48] See the Government Communications Plan 2013/14, downloadable from https://gcn.civilservice.gov.uk/about/201314-government-communications-plan/.

[49] See www.bbc.co.uk/news/uk-politics-22984367.

[50] Examples include the UK government's plan to get ISPs to detect and ban users who illegally download music and video files. This plan, like many other schemes, had to be abandoned as getting the ISPs to do all the work turned out to be fraught with legal and technical complications. See for example http://entertainment.timesonline.co.uk/tol/arts_and_entertainment/music/article5586761.ece, from January 2009.

[51] See for example http://news.zdnet.co.uk/security/0,1000000189,39629479,00.htm.

[52] See Chapter 4, Section 3.2.

Governments work with the data gatherers in many other ways. Examples include the UK government considering turning to Tesco for data on the UK's migrant population.[53] The commercial data gatherers have encouraged this, presenting good examples of how their data can be used in positive ways, to assist both governments and the people. A dramatic example of this is Google Flu Trends, which uses search data to analyse outbreaks of flu state by state in the United States, and claims to be able to do so up to two weeks earlier than 'traditional systems'.[54]

In these cases, the authorities are effectively piggybacking onto the Symbiotic Web, using not only the data that is gathered but the ways that data is processed and used, for their own purposes. This emphasises the reasons that governments are supportive of the symbiosis. When one considers how the profiling and targeting performed by commercial enterprises is likely to be extremely similar to the profiling and targeting government agencies might wish to do in their struggles against crime and terrorism, or indeed against disease, the reasons become even clearer. That, of itself, is something that suggests a need to be wary. When the interests of governments and businesses coincide so closely, it is crucial that the needs of individuals do not suffer.

5   Managing the symbiosis

If the beneficial nature of the symbiosis is not maintained, many of the best features of the existing internet may risk being lost. The idea of a common knowledge base, a place where people can speak and act freely, a system that can support dissidents and the oppressed, and encourage community and global interaction in a positive way: all these things are under threat, as well as the privacy and autonomy of individuals. The internet can – and to a large extent currently does – represent a great opportunity for users to grow as people, expanding their horizons, their knowledge and their breadth of experience. Any throttling of that opportunity is in itself a restriction of autonomy. For all these reasons, it is important that everything is done to ensure that the benefits and the essentially benign nature of the web symbiosis are maintained, and that the risks are addressed appropriately.

---

[53] See for example http://blogs.ft.com/westminster/2008/04/can-tesco-help-the-government-count-how-many-migrants-are-in-the-uk/.
[54] See www.google.org/flutrends/, and for an academic analysis Ginsberg *et al.* (2009).

So what, if anything, can be done? How can regulators manage this symbiosis and make sure that it evolves in positive rather than negative ways? What role would be appropriate for governments and other regulators to play, and how should they play it? What place is there for other forms of regulation or control, in Lessig's terms, for markets, for norms and for code? And what, crucially, could the role of rights be in this context?

One of the functions of human rights is to provide protection for individuals against more powerful forces, most directly those of governments, but increasingly also those of business. That is particularly important here. The forces behind the Symbiotic Web are powerful and potentially dangerous, and individuals need to be protected. The current methods, not in a real sense based on rights, do not seem to be providing an adequate solution; a rights-based solution could be far more effective. There are a number of possible ways forward, each of which suggests a different kind and level of involvement for governments and other regulators.

The first option would be to try to break the dependence, to make the use of personal information in this way impossible through stronger, better-enforced laws. Current data protection laws should theoretically be a good start. In particular, the principles of data minimisation, of using data only for a set, lawful process and not allowing further processing, and the need for express, informed consent before data is gathered or processed, could potentially provide a great deal of protection. In reality they appear to fail to live up to their promise, whether because of weak implementation or because of poorly resourced enforcement. If sufficiently strengthened and properly enforced, they could make a significant impact. This, however, could effectively mean the end of the Symbiotic Web, as many of the business methods that have driven its development would become effectively illegal. Not only might this mean giving up all the positive aspects of what is a benign symbiosis, but it would mean having to come into conflict with very powerful business interests, which would be difficult, to say the least.

The second, and converse, approach would be to try to change the paradigm and 'give up' on privacy to a great extent. It may be an option to accept the trade in personal data, encourage personalisation, and deal with the consequences by penalising excessive or inappropriate use and encouraging understanding in the general public. Though it might appear a purely pragmatic solution, it might end up with something beneficial, as suggested by writers such as David Brin.[55] There are, however, far too many negative consequences for this to be a practical possibility. The various case studies throughout this book should make this abundantly clear.

The third approach would be to do very little, and allow markets and norms to redress the balance. There are some signs so far that this kind of approach might work: the increased newsworthiness of privacy breaches and excessive government surveillance, for example, suggests that things might be changing. The intervention of lawmakers might be producing even better results. As will be detailed in Chapter 5, Google has reduced the time that it holds onto individualised server logs of search data from an initial unlimited period to eighteen months, then to nine months, to a great extent because of the pressure exerted by the Article 29 Data Protection Working Party, the EC body responsible for oversight, advice and expert opinion concerning data protection.[56]

The fourth approach, and the one advocated here, is to weaken the dependence, to loosen the symbiosis and strengthen the rights of the individual. This would alter the balance, but still allow and support the mutually beneficial symbiosis. It could be brought about through a combination of legal, technological and other measures. The case studies throughout this book, most notably those concerning Google and Phorm, strongly support this suggestion. Achieving positive results has required a mix of measures, including strong and active community pressure and some kind of legal support.

5.1 Symbiotic regulation for the Symbiotic Web

The starting point is to have adequate, well-expressed, coherent, consistent and up-to-date rights: the rights set out in Chapter 1. These rights have been expressed in terms designed with the Symbiotic Web in mind, using Murray's regulatory model, 'symbiotic regulation'.[57] It is not simply a coincidence of labels that both ideas use the concept of symbiosis, though their origins are different.[58] Symbiotic regulation starts with a recognition

---

[55] Most notably in Brin, 1998.
[56] See http://ec.europa.eu/justice/data-protection/article-29/. The Article 29 Working Party is one of the key bodies in the regulation of data privacy.
[57] See Murray, 2006.
[58] The term Symbiotic Web was coined by the author, and the concept introduced in Bernal, 2010b.

that the relationships in the web are complex, and that the best way to achieve regulatory results is to work with those existing relationships rather than seek to impose something authoritarian upon them.

The first step to achieving a regulatory result, as outlined by Murray, is to map out the relationships involved. This is precisely the purpose of the Symbiotic Web: to be a model of the relationships between individuals, businesses and others in the web as it currently exists.

The next steps are to establish the appropriate response, from a regulatory perspective. There are already some clues as to how this might work. A key part of the symbiotic regulation approach is to work with existing relationships, 'tweaking' them to produce results. It is clear that existing relationships are, in some cases, already producing these results. The Article 29 Working Party's relationship with Google, for example, has existed for some time; it was the Working Party's 'tweaking' that seemed to make Google change policy. Similarly, the existing relationship between Facebook and its users was the key to halting the Beacon system in its tracks[59] and has had a number of other effects on Facebook, more recently in convincing it to reverse a change in policy about the deletion of data when users delete their profiles.[60] These examples also highlight another feature of symbiotic regulation: the development and support of an active, positive community of users, able to participate in the regulatory process rather than to be merely passive subjects of it.

5.2   New business models

Just as the movement towards the Symbiotic Web was driven by a new business model – the Google/Facebook personal data/targeted advertising model – the movement to moderate it and keep it benign will in all likelihood require the same. If new business models, not dependent on the gathering and use of personal data (or using it in a less intrusive, less manipulative way) could be developed, that would surely lead us in a more positive direction. The Google v. EC case study provides some evidence that this may already be happening. Google's relatively bloodless acceptance of a reduction of data retention periods might be because they are developing a different model for their business, but pressure

---

[59] See Chapter 6, Section 5.3.
[60] The policy change covered new terms and conditions, but the key terms seemed to be about the deletion (or rather non-deletion) of some data even when profiles were deleted. See for example http://news.bbc.co.uk/1/hi/technology/7896309.stm.

from lawmakers, from the computer and hacker communities, and most importantly from users, could make this happen faster. What is more, as Google and others become more aware of their place in the symbiosis, and of the way in which maintaining the benign nature of the symbiosis benefits them as well as individuals, they can become drivers towards positive solutions, rather than seeking to delay or block them.

One way in which this might already be happening is that, as revealed in their actions over search log retention periods, Google believes in setting global standards for their global business. For example, Google sets global deletion periods for their search logs, though outside Europe there appears no legal need for data deletion at all as data protection rules do not apply. Global solutions make much more sense for the internet, and perhaps global businesses like Google can help drive governments into developing those global solutions. This is another example of symbiotic regulation in action.

This is where a rights-based approach can be particularly effective. Rights can work not only as practical ways to bring about change – the Google story is just one example – but as global standards to aspire to, and principles that can guide future actions. The existence of a right can help to establish in people's minds that the subject of the right is of importance: here, to establish the idea that our privacy and autonomy on the internet are important. If commercial actors, in particular, wish to be seen to do 'the right thing' (Google famously states that 'You can make money without doing evil'),[61] then we need to ensure that they know what 'the right thing' is. Rights-based approaches fit perfectly with the symbiotic regulation model suggested above, working directly with existing relationships principally by changing the perspective from which those relationships are viewed. These rights are not seen as 'absolute', as 'trumps' that overrule other laws or interests, but as part of the balancing act, as part of what Murray (2006, Chapter 8) calls the 'regulatory matrix'. Moreover, the existence and expression of these rights can support, inform and empower the key communities that are at risk of being 'squeezed': the communities of individuals whose autonomy and privacy are under threat. The rights set out in this book are conceived specifically with this role in mind.

---

[61] Item 6 on Google's statement of corporate 'philosophy', accessible at www.google.com/corporate/tenthings.html.

4

Law, privacy and the internet – the landscape

1 The role of law in the internet

Making laws for the internet is very difficult. There are many reasons for this, including the speed of technological development, the lack of speed of lawmakers, the seemingly borderless nature of the internet, the limited technological understanding of lawmakers, and the power of various lobby groups.

The question of how to react to that difficulty, and how and whether it might be possible to make better laws for the internet, is a complex one. Since the inception of the internet, a number of different approaches has emerged. Three in particular need careful consideration: that of the cyber-libertarians, the cyberpaternalists and the network communitarians.

1.1 Cyberlibertarians and cyberpaternalists

The essence of the cyberlibertarian argument, in broad terms, is that not only is 'real-world' law likely to be ineffective in 'cyberspace' but it is also inappropriate and unsuitable. Barlow's famous 'Declaration of the Independence of Cyberspace'[1] in 1996 put it directly:

> You have no moral right to rule us nor do you possess any methods of enforcement we have true reason to fear.

Experience since 1996, and in particular the growth of laws both designed for and applied to the internet, makes cyberlibertarian arguments somewhat harder to sustain than they might once have been. However, there is still something to be said for some of their key arguments. Certainly many of the laws discussed here have significant problems with enforcement and with practicalities, many of which appear to arise from the lawmakers' lack of understanding either of the technical issues around

---

[1] Online at https://projects.eff.org/~barlow/Declaration-Final.html.

the internet or the nature and behaviour of the people who spend time online.[2]

What can loosely be described as the cyberpaternalists, from Reidenberg and Lessig onwards, emerged at least in part in direct response to the cyberlibertarians. They suggest a very different approach: effectively that not only can real-world lawmakers apply their laws to the internet, but that they must. From the cyberpaternalist standpoint, lawmakers need to engage with the issues much better, and most importantly, from Lessig's perspective, to engage with the code writers in order to utilise the potential of code to provide much more effective regulation. That, from the cyberpaternalist point of view, could allow the development of the kind of internet that 'we' want. As Lessig puts it:

> We can build, or architect, or *code* cyberspace to protect values that we believe are fundamental. Or we can build, or architect, or code cyberspace to allow these values to disappear. There is no middle ground. (2006, p. 6)

1.2 Network communitarians: the active community

The different perspectives of the cyberlibertarians and cyberpaternalists appear on the surface to have little common ground, but on one thing they do seem to coincide: lawmakers have been, and to a great extent still are, ineffective at putting together laws that work well for the internet. Why this is the case has been the subject of much investigation and analysis, and new schools of thought have emerged. The idea of 'network communitarianism' put forward by theorists such as Murray takes a more subtle approach than either the cyberlibertarians or the cyberpaternalists, building on some of the strengths of both sides of the argument. It takes the importance and strength of the online community from the cyberlibertarian school and uses it to modify the models put forward by Lessig and others. Rather than the 'pathetic dot' that Lessig used to symbolise an individual worked upon by law, norms, markets and code, Murray suggests an 'active matrix' of users, not just worked upon by these regulatory modalities but acting upon them in turn.[3]

That kind of a regulatory model seems to be closer to the reality of the internet as it currently exists, as the case studies set out in the chapters that follow this demonstrate. The online community can be – and in practice

---

[2] See for example Reed, 2012, Chapter 7.
[3] Murray's model is set out in detail in Murray, 2006, particularly Chapter 8.

is – an active community, and does manage to have an impact on all the other factors. It has an impact upon markets, bringing down some business ideas. Phorm, which is discussed in Chapter 6, is just one example. It can even bring down laws: the effective defeats of the Stop Online Piracy Act (SOPA),[4] PROTECT IP Act (PIPA),[5] the Anti-Counterfeiting Trade Agreement (ACTA)[6] and the UK's Communications Data Bill[7] have come about to a significant extent because of the actions of the online community. It sets, establishes and eventually overturns norms. It is also directly involved in both the writing and the use of code. The way in which privacy-protective software and systems have been developed by the 'community' is one of the notable trends emerging from the stories discussed here.

What that means in terms of the law is complex but important. Although law is not necessarily the most important factor in relation to people's experiences and their autonomy online, it does have a significant impact. The better that laws can be made for the internet, the more autonomy and the better experiences people can have in their online lives.

As Reed suggests, one of the key problems with making laws for cyberspace is the mismatch between laws and 'cyber reality': understanding what the citizens of cyberspace expect and believe to be their rights can help deal with this mismatch. If lawmakers do not understand this, their laws will be ignored or bypassed. As Reed puts it:

> cyberspace actors are likely to obey laws which they think ought to be obeyed, and ignore those whose authority they do not accept, or whose obligations they find meaningless. This is irrespective of whether those laws are actually applicable or enforceable against them. (2012, p. 211)

This once again brings to the fore the function of the kind of privacy rights suggested here. If lawmakers are aware of what people expect and believe to be their rights, they could find it easier to make laws that work better for the internet community, and hence are more likely to be accepted and obeyed, and more likely to be effective and enforceable.

1.3   Law, privacy and autonomy – and the role of rights

The laws that affect privacy and autonomy online to a great extent exemplify the delicate balancing of rights and needs that is inherent in the

---

[4] See Section 3.3 below.   [5] See Section 3.3 below.
[6] See Section 3.3 below.   [7] See Section 3.2 below.

internet, and are central to the model of the Symbiotic Web set out in the previous chapter. That balance is evident in a number of ways:

1. It is evident within laws and directives. Article 8 of the European Convention on Human Rights, for example, following the familiar pattern for European directives, first sets out the right to privacy, then sets out when and how it can be overridden. Similar caveats and exceptions are naturally included in many equivalent laws.
2. It is evident between laws. Laws that protect privacy (data protection laws, for example) are balanced by laws that enable invasions of privacy (data retention and interception and surveillance laws, for example).

In European Law, the balancing of rights is explicit, and in general there is no presumption that one right overrides another. Privacy and freedom of expression, for example, are given equal theoretical protection under European Law. The question is how to find an appropriate balance between the two.

Privacy and freedom of expression are just two of the rights that need to be kept in balance. As discussed in earlier chapters, the rights and interests of governments in security and of businesses in economic success all need to be kept in balance. There are tensions between all the different rights and interests, and there are laws that try to clarify the ways in which the interplay between them can best be managed and how the appropriate balances can be found.

In practice, this means that laws can impact upon privacy in a number of key ways:

1. Laws can work to protect individual privacy. Perhaps the most important of these laws in the internet context are data protection laws.
2. Laws can work to enable and support infringements and invasions of privacy, setting out terms under which those invasions of privacy are deemed legitimate and appropriate. Examples of these kinds of law are data retention laws, surveillance laws such as the Regulation of Investigatory Powers Act (RIPA), copyright enforcement laws and agreements such as the Anti-Counterfeiting Trade Agreement (ACTA), SOPA and PIPA, mooted anti-pornography laws and others.
3. Laws can outlaw or block ways in which people can protect their own privacy, for example laws requiring people to give up encryption keys (including RIPA) and laws demanding that people use 'real names' such as those introduced in China and mooted elsewhere.

None of this is quite as straightforward as it might seem. For example, laws that ostensibly protect privacy can also to an extent deceive and allow overconfidence in the degree of privacy protection provided, and end up in reducing real privacy. Some might suggest that this could apply to most of data protection and related law.

It should be noted that another key consequence of the difficulties that are encountered in making appropriate laws for the internet is that those laws themselves are subject to regular and significant change. Indeed, at times it seems as though they are almost constantly in flux. At the time of writing, for example, the entire European Data Protection regime was under review, with a substantial reform under discussion,[8] while the most important development in UK internet surveillance law in recent years, the Communications Data Bill, was lying dormant, awaiting possible redrafting and reintroduction after what might fairly be described as a mauling at the hands of a parliamentary committee.[9] There are similar stories elsewhere in the world: in the United States, for example, the Cyber Intelligence Sharing and Protection Act (CISPA) is currently being considered, while in Australia a full review of national security laws, including measures for extensive surveillance of the internet, is under way. Precisely where any of these laws will stand at this book's publication date is unclear – but that is part of the point with the legal landscape of the internet. Laws are regularly changing – perhaps not as fast as the technology, and not necessarily as dynamically or effectively as they should be, but they are changing.

This state of flux has implications for a discussion of the legal landscape of internet privacy. Firstly, and most importantly, it means that the focus should be on the principles, not on the details, not only for the discussions here but also in the minds of the lawmakers. Indeed, that is one of the principal points of the rights-based approach. It is easy for lawmakers to pay attention only to the technical details of law rather than the bigger picture, and in this field the bigger picture matters a great deal. The effect of law is as much in shaping norms and in encouraging appropriate business models as it is in specific enforcement, and that requires principles as well as detail. Secondly, it is important to be aware of the possibility of changes

---

[8] In July 2013, the status of the Data Protection reform package was still very unclear, with many potential amendments still on the table and votes in the European Parliament having been delayed several times.

[9] The full report of the committee is available online at www.parliament.uk/business/committees/committees-a-z/joint-select/draft-communications-bill/news/full-publication-of-report/.

in the future. That, too, is one of the points of the rights-based approach. Setting out appropriate rights can improve the chances of effective and appropriate changes in law in the future and just as importantly reduce the chances of ineffective, inappropriate and even counterproductive laws being brought in.

2   Privacy-protective law

Some kind of right to a private life is explicitly set out in most international human rights conventions. Article 8 of the European Convention on Human Rights (ECHR)[10] says that '[E]veryone has the right to respect for his private and family life, his home and his correspondence', while Article 12 of the Universal Declaration of Human Rights says that '[N]o one shall be subjected to arbitrary interference with his privacy, family, home or correspondence … [E]veryone has the right to the protection of the law against such interference.'

The implications of this are direct: protection for privacy in some form is built into almost every legal system, whether explicitly in statute or via some kind of common-law principle. These laws are, as noted above, often subject to significant caveats and exceptions. The caveats brought into Article 8 of the ECHR, for example, are broad. Article 8.2 says:

> There shall be no interference by a public authority with the exercise of this right except such as is in accordance with the law and is necessary in a democratic society in the interests of national security, public safety or the economic well-being of the country, for the prevention of disorder or crime, for the protection of health or morals, or for the protection of the rights and freedoms of others.

The interpretation of these kinds of exception is one of the biggest challenges to privacy in law; in practice, it could be possible to find a way to include almost any invasion of privacy into one or other of these categories. Certainly the competing interests of governments in security and businesses in economic success could fit well within them.

Nevertheless, the right to privacy does receive significant legal protection. This is increasingly true in the digital environment: by June 2013 there were data privacy laws in ninety-nine countries, and the trajectory was upwards.[11] The most important of these laws and, indeed, in many

[10] Downloadable from www.echr.coe.int/Documents/Convention_ENG.pdf.
[11] See Greenleaf, 2013.

ways the driver of the spread of data privacy laws, has been European data protection law.

2.1   Data protection and the Data Protection Directive

The Data Protection Directive (DPD)[12] is a key pillar in European privacy regulation. The principal idea is for citizens and residents of the EU to have some degree of control over what information is stored about them, and what is done to that information, and that they should be assured that the data is processed, stored and used only for appropriate and legitimate purposes.[13] At the same time, it is intended to allow personal data to flow freely across European borders, allowing businesses and governments to take advantage of the opportunities that such free flow of data should allow.

It is a powerful piece of legislation and sometimes a point of pride for European privacy advocates, particularly in comparison with the situation in the United States.[14] Nevertheless, there are problems with it, not least the inconsistent and sometimes weak implementation across the states of the European Union as well as weaknesses in its enforcement, as the case studies in Chapters 5, 6 and 7 will reveal.

The DPD arose directly from the felt need to provide some of the protection required under Article 8 of the ECHR. Article 1, setting out the objectives of the DPD, states: 'In accordance with this Directive, Member States shall protect the fundamental rights and freedoms of natural persons, and in particular their right to privacy with respect to the processing of personal data.'[15]

The scope of the DPD is set out in Article 3, which states that it applies to 'the processing of personal data wholly or partly by automatic means, and to the processing otherwise than by automatic means of personal data which form part of a filing system or are intended to form part of a filing system'.[16] Effectively, this means that it covers all computer systems

---

[12] Directive 95/46/EC, downloadable from http://ec.europa.eu/justice_home/fsj/privacy/docs/95–46-ce/dir1995–46_part1_en.pdf.

[13] See 'Data Protection in the European Union', http://ec.europa.eu/justice_home/fsj/privacy/guide/index_en.htm.

[14] As Cate (1997, p. 98) puts it: 'protection for information privacy in the United States is disjointed, inconsistent, and limited by conflicting interests'. Little has changed in the intervening period.

[15] DPD, Article 1.   [16] DPD, Article 3.

and prevents any possible avoidance techniques involving transferring computer systems onto paper records or their equivalents.

Article 3 allows exceptions for operations concerning public security, defence, state security and the criminal law (following the principles in Article 8.2 of the ECHR, as noted above) and for processing 'by a natural person in the course of a purely personal or household activity'. The scope is broad, potentially covering, for example, all commercial, financial, medical and recreational systems as well as the vast majority of government records, and most of the data on the internet.

The definitions used in the DPD, set out in Article 2, are where the legislation's strengths and weaknesses start to appear. 'Personal Data' is defined as 'any information relating to an identified or identifiable natural person ("data subject"); an identifiable person is one who can be identified, directly or indirectly, in particular by reference to an identification number or to one or more factors specific to his physical, physiological, mental, economic, cultural or social identity'.[17] This is a broad, strong definition. The definition of what constitutes an 'identifiable' person is similarly strong, and the process of identification could cover many kinds of profiling as well as the more obvious direct definitions, but it is (perhaps inevitably) somewhat vague and subject to argument.[18]

'The data subject's consent' is defined as 'any freely given specific and informed indication of his wishes by which the data subject signifies his agreement to personal data relating to him being processed'.[19] Again, it can be argued that this is a strong definition, but terms such as 'freely given' and 'informed' are hard to pin down. This makes the role of the Article 29 Data Protection Working Party,[20] the EC body responsible for interpreting and advising on the implementation of the Directive, of critical importance.

Article 7 of the Directive details the criteria for making data processing legitimate, fulfilling the 'in accordance with the law' part of Article 8.2 of

---

[17] DPD, Article 2(a).

[18] The Information Commissioner's Office in the UK produces a 'specialist guide' as to what constitutes personal data, downloadable from http://ico.org.uk/~/media/documents/library/data_protection/detailed_specialist_guides/personal_data_flowchart_v1_with_preface001.ashx. The guide was produced in response to a narrower than expected interpretation of the term in a Court of Appeals case (*Durant* v. *FSA* [2003] EWCA Civ 1746; [2004] FSR 28; *The Times*, 2 January 2004). The fact that it was needed reflects the problems in the language of the UK's implementation of the DPD, the Data Protection Act 1998 (available online at www.opsi.gov.uk/Acts/Acts1998/ukpga_19980029_en_1), which to this extent at least follows the DPD closely.

[19] DPD, Article 2(h).   [20] See http://ec.europa.eu/justice/data-protection/article-29/.

the ECHR. The first and perhaps most important is when 'the data subject has unambiguously given his consent', an issue that is fundamental if the impact on autonomy is to be considered. Other basic categories, again following the principles of Article 8.2 of the ECHR, include compliance with a legal obligation, protecting the vital interests of the data subject and performance of a task carried out in the public interest.[21]

There are two specific categories relevant to business use:

> for the performance of a contract to which the data subject is party or in order to take steps at the request of the data subject prior to entering into a contract;[22]

or:

> for the purposes of the legitimate interests pursued by the controller or by the third party or parties to whom the data are disclosed, except where such interests are overridden by the interests for fundamental rights and freedoms of the data subject which require protection under Article 1 (1).[23]

Essentially, this means that either a contract must be entered into with consent to the processing expressly given, or the data processing must not be of sufficient importance to the individual concerned to warrant protection.

Article 6 of the DPD sets out data quality requirements:

- Data must be accurate and kept up to date, and 'every reasonable step' must be taken to ensure it stays that way.
- Data must be collected only for 'specified, explicit and legitimate purposes', and not 'further processed in a way incompatible with these purposes'. This protects against 'function creep', a significant risk for personal data.[24]
- Data must be 'adequate, relevant and not excessive in relation to the purposes for which they are collected and/or further processed'. The 'not excessive' part is crucial – this is part of the critical concept of 'data minimisation'.
- Data must be 'kept in a form which permits identification of data subjects for no longer than is necessary for the purposes for which the data were collected or for which they are further processed'. Effectively, this calls for anonymisation of data as soon as possible.

---

[21] DPD, Article 7(a), (c), (d) and (e).   [22] DPD, Article 7(b).
[23] DPD, Article 7(f).   [24] See Chapter 7, Section 2.

These latter three protections (against function creep, for data minimisation and for minimum retention periods) are particularly important in the context of the internet, but are also especially difficult to monitor and enforce.

There are other important elements to data protection set out in the DPD. Most important amongst them are the right of users to access data held about them, special protection for 'sensitive' personal data, an obligation on organisations to keep data secure and an obligation not to send data out of the jurisdiction of the DPD unless the place to which it is being sent can ensure an 'adequate level of protection for the rights and freedoms of data subjects in relation to the processing of personal data'.

Each of these elements hits upon an important issue in relation to privacy, though the degree to which they provide meaningful protection is another matter. A right to access is only relevant if it is made user-friendly: it would need to be easy to exercise the right, and the data provided would need to be in an easily understood form. 'Sensitive' personal data is important, but as will be discussed,[25] differentiating between sensitive and non-sensitive data is far less simple than it might appear. The most sensitive of information, from sexuality to health and financial details may be derivable from the most mundane of data such as shopping records or eating habits, so protecting the sensitive while providing no protection for the mundane may be effectively meaningless, and even counterproductive.

Similarly, asking organisations to keep data secure is very important, but the fundamentally vulnerable nature of data must also be acknowledged. As will be shown in Chapter 7, data in any form, held by any organisation and in any way can be vulnerable. Some of the organisations with the most technological expertise, the best resources and the biggest incentives to keep data secure have in practice been unable to do so. Finally, the idea of controlling where data may or may not be transferred is both laudable and important, but the nature of the internet, particularly in the era of 'cloud computing', means that enforcing it is far harder than it might appear. In practice, when operating on the internet, it is neither obvious nor necessarily important (from a user's perspective) where a website – or indeed data – physically exists. The implications of this are profound but deeply challenging: the ultimate solution would be to have similar standards of protection everywhere. If that could be reached, it would not matter where data was held. That is another of the purposes of the rights set

---

[25] This subject is discussed in Chapter 6, Section 3.3.

out here: to try to move towards global principles, rather than local and conflicting legal rules. Though complete uniformity is ultimately impossible, a greater degree of convergence should be attainable. Coherent and understood rights should help to bring this about.

In summary then, in terms of privacy, data protection is intended to do the following:

- define personal data very broadly as any data that can be linked to an individual;
- only allow processing of that data for legitimate, specified reasons, made clear to the data subject at the time the data is gathered;
- ensure that only the minimum data is held and only for the minimum period; and
- require that those holding data keep it securely and not allow it to be transferred to a place where there is less protection.

2.2   Implementation and reform

There are problems in the ways that the DPD has been implemented across EU member states. There are not just variations between states, but significant problems that appear to apply throughout the EU, most notably under-resourced enforcement,[26] patchy compliance by data controllers and a low level of knowledge of their rights among data subjects.[27] Nonetheless, the First Implementation Report concluded that:

> Despite the delays and gaps in implementation, the Directive has fulfilled its principal objective of removing barriers to the free movement of personal data between the Member States. The Commission also believes that the objective of ensuring a high level of protection in the Community has been achieved since the Directive has set out some of the highest standards of data protection in the world.[28]

For these and many other reasons the data protection regime – and the DPD in particular – is currently the subject of reform. At the time of writing, that reform was very much in flux, with the draft up before the European Parliament and literally thousands of potential amendments on the table. Precisely how it will turn out is as yet unclear: the European

---

[26] See Burghardt, Böhm, Buchmann, Kühling and Sivridis (2010).
[27] See the First Implementation Report: http://eur-lex.europa.eu/LexUriServ/LexUriServ.d o?uri=COM:2003:0265:FIN:EN:PDF.
[28] Summary of the First Implementation Report: http://ec.europa.eu/justice/data-protection/document/transposition/index_en.htm.

Commission has put forward what looks on paper to be a bold and strong directive, but there is intense lobbying on behalf of the internet 'industry' and certain governments to either water down or even reverse some of the terms of the proposed reform,[29] while the impact of the PRISM and related revelations[30] has led some to suggest a strengthening of that reform. It remains in flux, as with other key areas of the law in this area.

The key reforms to the regime under consideration are the following:

1. replacement of the DPD with two new instruments:
   a. a Data Protection Regulation, covering most situations; and
   b. a separate Data Protection Directive, covering the 'processing of personal data by competent authorities for the purposes of prevention, investigation, detection or prosecution of criminal offences or the execution of criminal penalties, and the free movement of such data';
2. a specifically defined 'right to be forgotten and to erasure';
3. a 'right of data portability', allowing people to transfer their data from one system to another (e.g. for social networking);
4. clarifying the scope of the data protection regime to effectively cover all services and systems worldwide that are aimed at European citizens; and
5. providing extensive and powerful financial penalties: up to two per cent of the global turnover of the companies concerned.

These developments could address some of the key weaknesses of the current regime. Using a 'regulation' rather than a directive would mean that rather than having separate implementation in each member state, the regulation would apply directly, cutting down on inconsistent or incomplete implementation, as demonstrated in the UK, for example, over Phorm.[31] The separate directive would be to allow greater leeway for governments over their approaches to deal with crime, though how this would work out in practice is somewhat unclear. The right to be forgotten and erasure is a big and complex area of debate,[32] as is the right of data portability. Broadening the scope of the regime and adding much more powerful financial penalties would enable the European authorities to have some kind of real power to deal with the big, global companies such

---

[29] See for example the analysis by Jan Albrecht MdEP of the lobbying over Data Protection Reform, online at www.janalbrecht.eu/themen/datenschutz-und-netzpolitik/lobbyism-and-the-eu-data-protection-reform.html.
[30] See Chapter 3, Section 5.2, and Section 3.2 below.
[31] See Chapter 6.   [32] See the discussion in Chapter 7.

as Google and Facebook. As a consequence they are some of the potential reforms most subject to criticism, particularly from the powerful lobby groups.

It remains to be seen how much of the reform actually comes into operation and when. The debate and discussion is likely to continue for some time, even beyond the finalisation of the instruments themselves. What are perhaps more interesting than the details of what is actually enacted are the principles that are established, and where the balance is found between the different lobbying groups. When any new regime is in place, this balance is unlikely to be stable.

2.3   The E-Privacy Directive and the 'Cookies Directive'

The E-Privacy Directive[33] was created as a supplement to the DPD, intended to address developments in communications technology. It was an adaptation of and replacement for Directive 97/66/EC,[34] 'concerning the processing of personal data and the protection of privacy in the telecommunications sector', which itself 'translated the principles' set out in the DPD into 'specific rules for the telecommunications sector'.[35] This somewhat complex evolution of directives demonstrates a number of things: firstly, that the EU takes the issue of data privacy seriously and is constantly looking at what needs to be done to protect it; secondly, that its efforts have not been entirely successful, as directives have needed to be superseded and amended and have become increasingly specialised; thirdly, that this is probably in itself inevitable as the technology and its application have been proceeding apace, and that regulation is almost always 'playing catch-up'.

The aim of the E-Privacy Directive is:

> to ensure an equivalent level of protection of fundamental rights and freedoms, and in particular the right to privacy, with respect to the processing of personal data in the electronic communication sector and to ensure the free movement of such data and of electronic communication equipment and services in the Community.[36]

---

[33] Directive 2002/58, available online at http://eur-lex.europa.eu/LexUriServ/LexUriServ.do?uri=CELEX:32002L0058:EN:HTML.

[34] Downloadable from http://eur-lex.europa.eu/LexUriServ/LexUriServ.do?uri=CELEX:31995L0046:en:HTML.

[35] Directive 2002/58/EC, paragraph 4 of the Preamble.

[36] E-Privacy Directive, Article 1.1.

The E-Privacy Directive places obligations on providers of electronic communications to provide security and confidentiality and to erase or anonymise traffic data when it is no longer needed, putting the general principles of data protection into place for the electronic communications sector. The confidentiality requirements should specifically prevent interception of communications or retention of communications data, but it should be noted that the E-Privacy Directive does not apply to the interception of communications by the authorities for the purposes of national security, crime prevention and related areas.[37]

The E-Privacy Directive also covers the issue of unsolicited emails – specifically those used for marketing purposes – establishing an 'opt-in' regime, allowing such emails only to be sent where there is 'prior consent'.[38] Although this appears a very specialised term, it points to one of the most important issues in relation to internet privacy and autonomy: where and how consent can be gained and when it can be assumed.[39] The receipt of unsolicited emails may sometimes be considered little more than an annoyance, and the improvements in spam-filtering systems have reduced that still further, but there are broader implications when other kinds of 'communications' are considered.

Those implications have been played out in the saga of the so-called 'Cookies Directive'. The name is somewhat misleading; the relevant parts of Directive 2009/136 actually implement an amendment to the E-Privacy Directive rather than introducing a new and separate directive.[40] The new terms require prior, informed consent to be gained for any cookie to be installed on a computer except where that cookie is 'strictly necessary for the delivery of a service requested by the user'.

The 'Cookies Directive' emerged in part as a response to the Phorm saga,[41] and has itself been the subject of immense controversy. It has been described as 'breathtakingly stupid',[42] and its implementation and enforcement has been highly inconsistent and incomplete, and is in some ways a prime example of the problems that arise in putting together laws for the internet. The intentions are good: to regulate privacy-invasive practices by the online behavioural advertising industry. In practice, however, it appears to do little or nothing to control this, and instead places a burden on people operating a wide range of non-invasive businesses, as well

---

[37] See E-Privacy Directive, Article 15.1.   [38] E-Privacy Directive, Article 13.

[39] As discussed in Chapter 2, Section 3.

[40] The Directive, labelled PE-CONS 3674/09, is available at http://register.consilium.europa.eu/pdf/en/09/st03/st03674.en09.pdf.

[41] See Chapter 6, Section 5.   [42] See www.out-law.com/page-10510.

as annoying a great many people: the main response by website operators has been to place a banner on the top of their websites asking people to click to accept cookies. That kind of consent is effectively close to meaningless and just creates frustration and reduces trust.

The 'Cookies Directive' is in some ways a prime example of how not to put together privacy-protective law. It was put together in haste and without proper discussion with the key stakeholders – the operators of ordinary websites – or with experts in either the technology or the law. The process through which it came about should be seen as a cautionary tale.[43]

2.4   The Cybercrime Convention and the Computer Misuse Act

A final category of laws that can be considered, at least in part, protective of privacy, are those that protect against what can loosely be described as 'criminal' invasions of privacy. In the United Kingdom, that means the Computer Misuse Act 1990 (as amended) (CMA)[44]; internationally, the most important document is the Council of Europe Convention on Cybercrime.[45] The two are closely aligned: the CMA was amended to ensure that the UK satisfied its obligations under the Convention on Cybercrime. The Convention itself has been signed by fifty countries, and not just in Europe: the United States, Canada and Japan are amongst the signatories.

There are two particular ways in which privacy comes into play here: hacking to access private data, and the use of 'spyware' to monitor private computer activity. Section 1 of the CMA says:

1.   a person is guilty of an offence if –
      a.   he causes a computer to perform any function with intent to secure access to any program or data held in any computer, or to enable any such access to be secured;
      b.   the access he intends to secure, or to enable to be secured, is unauthorised; and
      c.   he knows at the time when he causes the computer to perform the function that that is the case.

---

[43]   This process is outlined in detail in Chapter 6, Sections 3–5.
[44]   Available online at www.legislation.gov.uk/ukpga/1990/18/contents.
[45]   Available online at http://conventions.coe.int/Treaty/en/Treaties/Html/185.htm.

Effectively, then, the CMA makes it illegal to access private data without appropriate permission: amongst other things, this covers hacking and unauthorised access.

The extent to which the CMA and Convention on Cybercrime cover spyware is another matter. As Murray puts it:

> There is doubt over whether spyware and adware is outlawed by the Computer Misuse Act 1990, the UK's criminal law on unauthorised access to computers and data and unauthorised modification of data, due to the fact that the customer 'consents' to its installation when they agree to the licence terms for the piece of software they do want. (Murray, 2013, pp. 187–8)

This highlights one of the perennial problems with 'criminal' aspects of invasions of privacy: the thorny issue of consent.[46] Where access is clearly and overtly without permission, criminality is clear, and where consent is clearly and unequivocally given legality is clear, but there is a huge grey area, an area in which the criminal law struggles both conceptually and practically.

3   Privacy-invasive law

The converse to the privacy-protective laws are those designed to enable privacy invasions to happen, to make those invasions legitimate, thus satisfying the overriding requirement of Article 8.2 of the ECHR. These kinds of law prioritise another right or need, whether it is national security, crime prevention, administrative or economic necessity, property or other rights, tipping the balance so that the privacy invasion is considered proportionate and appropriate. The most direct and clear of these is national security, from which emerged the concept of data retention.

3.1   Data retention

The Data Retention Directive (DRD)[47] arose directly from counterterrorism. One trigger for the passing of the directive was the terrorist attacks in London on 07 July 2005, which were referred to directly in paragraph 10 of the Preamble to the Directive. The idea was essentially that governments and other agencies engaged in counterterrorism might

---

[46] See Chapter 2, Section 3.
[47] Directive 2006/24/EC, available online at http://eur-lex.europa.eu/LexUriServ/ LexUriServ.do?uri=CELEX:32006L0024:EN:HTML.

be able to find terrorists or potential terrorists through their actions (and data trails) on the internet. Data retention, therefore, requires those who provide 'publicly available electronic communications services' or 'public communications networks'[48] to keep records sufficient to identify individuals involved, for periods of up to twenty-four months, so that when necessary a government agency can examine those records to try to catch the people concerned. While data protection is essentially a European concept, data retention is something taken seriously all over the world and in particular in the United States.

The DRD is technically an amendment to the E-Privacy Directive, which itself demonstrates the sometimes conflicting needs and motives at play within the EU: there are those at the EU who want to counter some of the most important principles of data protection in the name of either security or law enforcement.

Article 1 sets out the subject matter and scope of the Directive and has a number of key elements:

- It applies to 'providers of publicly available electronic communications services' and 'public communications networks'.
- It requires the retention of 'certain data' 'in order to ensure that the data are available for the purpose of the investigation, detection and prosecution of serious crime, as defined by each Member State in its national law'.
- It applies to 'traffic and location data on both legal entities and natural purposes and to the related data necessary to identify the subscriber or registered user'.
- It does not apply to the 'content of electronic communications, including information consulted using an electronic communications network'.

The DRD is intended to ensure that email services, digital telephony services (including mobile telephony services) and their equivalents, and where appropriate internet access providers, keep sufficient information to enable law enforcement agencies to determine who has been communicating with whom,[49] and when and how, but not what they have actually been communicating. Precisely what that data should consist of is set out in the Directive for each of the main services covered by the DRD: fixed network telephony and mobile telephony, internet access, internet

---

[48] DRD, initial description.
[49] Including records of unsuccessful call attempts – see DRD, Article 3.2.

email and internet telephony.[50] On the face of it, it does not apply to search engines, but as the conflict between Google and the EU over search log retention revealed, that did not deter Google from using it for its own purposes.[51]

The data must be made available to 'the competent national authorities in specific cases and in accordance with national law' – and it is left up to the national law to determine 'necessity and proportionality requirements', subject to the 'relevant provisions of European Union law or public international law, and in particular the ECHR as interpreted by the European Court of Human Rights'.[52]

It is in appearance a very simple directive, befitting its political rather than technical or practical motivations. One of the intentions of the DRD is to harmonise the data retention legislation that currently exists in a number of member states.[53] International organisations (of which Google is a prime example) can use a lack of harmonisation to attempt to avoid legislation entirely. This laudable aim is unfortunately far from successful as the terms of the Directive still allow member states significant leeway in key areas, not least in terms of the periods of obligatory data retention: the Directive allows retention periods from six months to two years.

The implementation of the DRD has been neither straightforward nor consistent. As well as the various legal challenges noted below, sixteen of the member states (including the UK) took advantage of provisions allowing for a postponement in implementation of the Directive.[54] The UK's implementation, the Data Retention (EC Directive) Regulations 2009,[55] was drafted to attempt to overcome the technical and financial objections of UK ISPs and phone operators who complained about being expected to provide and pay for technical solutions to store data, but in the process of drafting ran up against concerns from both a legal and political perspective, drawing criticism from the Information Commissioner's Office[56] and other experts and political opponents.[57]

The DRD has been subject to significant criticism. In principle it is in direct tension with data protection: data protection is intended to reduce

---

[50] DRD, Article 5(1).   [51] See Chapter 5, Section 2.   [52] DRD, Article 4.
[53] DRD, Article 1, and Preamble paragraphs (5) and (6).
[54] Declarations made by these sixteen member states are included in the Directive.
[55] Available online at www.legislation.gov.uk/uksi/2009/859/contents/made.
[56] The ICO said that 'We have real doubts that such a measure can be justified, or is proportionate or desirable.' See www.ico.gov.uk/upload/documents/pressreleases/2008/proposed_government_database.pdf.
[57] See for example http://news.bbc.co.uk/1/hi/technology/7410885.stm and http://news.bbc.co.uk/1/hi/uk/7409593.stm.

the amount of data held and the length of time it is held, while data retention effectively increases the amount of data held and the length of time for which it is held. Peter Hustinx, the European Data Protection Supervisor, has said that 'The Data Retention Directive – turned the rules upside down'. In its official response, the Article 29 Working Party said 'Traffic data retention interferes with the inviolable, fundamental right to confidential communications' and went on to question 'whether the justification for an obligatory and general data retention ... is grounded in crystal-clear evidence'.[58]

The Working Party's criticism has been extensive.[59] In an opinion issued in 2005,[60] prior to the enactment of the DRD, it made suggestions that it hoped would lead to changes. These included the observation that the aims of the DRD, although ostensibly to fight terrorism, in practice allowed data retention for 'the purpose of the investigation, detection and prosecution of serious crime, as defined by each Member State in its national law',[61] function creep within a single directive, and precisely the kind of function creep that has characterised the worst kind of antiterrorism legislation.[62]

The Working Party also noted that no evidence had been presented to clearly justify compulsory and general data retention. This is characteristic of antiterrorism legislation but is particularly relevant in this area, with the unprovable justification that to provide such evidence would require revealing methods of detection and prevention that would compromise security. The Working Party also suggested that there are other methods of investigation or detection that infringe on privacy much less, notably the 'quick-freeze procedure', which involves surveillance and data retention only in well-founded cases, where law enforcement agencies specifically request the storage of certain data.

The Working Party also proposed that the DRD should suggest maximum rather than minimum periods of data retention, providing protection for citizens against over-zealous member states, and a raft of specific safeguards intended to ensure proper scrutiny and control of the process, even if the major criticisms of the DRD outlined above were rejected. These

---

[58] Opinion 113 of the Working Party, page 2, downloadable from http://ec.europa.eu/justice/policies/privacy/workinggroup/wpdocs/index_en.htm.

[59] The Working Party had also issued strong opinions against previous, failed, attempts to institute data retention, in 2002 (Opinion 64) and 2004 (Opinion 99).

[60] Opinion 113, footnote 38.

[61] DRD, Article 1.

[62] See for example Gearty (2006), Chapter 4, for an exploration of the problems of anti-terrorism legislation.

included provisions against data mining and further processing,[63] and against the use of retained data solely for public order purposes, clear definitions of data categories to be held, and a 'no-contents' provision ensuring that only traffic data and not content would be held. These last two (clear categorisation and 'no-contents') were included in the final Directive.

Other than these few specific safeguards, none of these criticisms resulted in changes to the draft Directive. All remain relevant and have been the basis for continuing criticism since the DRD came into force on 3 May 2006. The Working Party issued a further opinion, subsequent to the adoption of the DRD, again voicing its reservations, urging 'uniform, European-wide implementation of the Directive'[64] and stressing the need for stringent and specific safeguards. The Working Party's concerns about consistency have proved well grounded at least in one way: Google used the inconsistencies and vagueness of the DRD as one of its tools in its attempt to rebuff the challenges of the Working Party over retention periods for search logs.

Further criticism has been directed at other countries' proposals for individual implementation of the DRD currently envisaged.[65] In the Netherlands, the Dutch Data Protection Agency issued an opinion suggesting that the bill proposed to implement the DRD breached Article 8 of the ECHR,[66] while Digital Rights Ireland wrote to the Irish government threatening legal action to scupper the Irish government's attempts to implement the DRD.[67] Further, the Irish government itself took action to attempt to have the DRD repealed, effectively on the grounds that it was passed as though it were a trade directive, not a security directive,[68] the latter directives being much harder to pass, with more stringent requirements including a unanimous rather than simple majority vote.[69] In April

---

[63] Both discussed in Chapter 5.

[64] Opinion 119 of the Working Party, downloadable from: http://ec.europa.eu/justice/policies/privacy/workinggroup/wpdocs/index_en.htm.

[65] For an analysis of the implementation issues in Bulgaria, Romania, Germany, Cyprus, the Czech Republic, Hungary, Poland, Slovakia and Slovenia see Kosta (2013).

[66] The Dutch Data Protection Authority's opinion is downloadable from www.dutchdpa.nl/downloads_adv/z2006–01542.pdf?refer=true&theme=purple.

[67] See www.digitalrights.ie/category/data-retention/.

[68] Under Article 95 of the Treaty Establishing the European Community, downloadable from http://eur-lex.europa.eu/en/treaties/dat/12002E/pdf/12002E_EN.pdf. Measures based upon Article 95 must have as their 'centre of gravity' the approximation of national laws to benefit the functioning of the internal market.

[69] See http://curia.europa.eu/jurisp/cgi-bin/gettext.pl?lang=en&num=79939084C19060301&doc=T&ouvert=T&seance=REQ_COMM, and for an analysis www.out-law.com/page-7310.

2008 an *amicus* brief was submitted to the European Court of Justice by forty-three non-governmental organisations (NGOs) from eleven countries in support of this case, suggesting that data retention 'violates the right to respect for private life and correspondence, freedom of expression and the right of providers to the protection of their property'.[70] The conclusion drawn by the European Court of Human Rights in *S. and Marper v. the United Kingdom*, that 'the mere retention and storing of personal data by public authorities, however obtained, are to be regarded as having direct impact on the private-life interest of an individual concerned, irrespective of whether subsequent use is made of the data'[71] added weight to this argument.

In the light of the decision over passenger record numbers,[72] where a similar argument prevailed, this case appeared to have a reasonable chance of success, but in the event failed on 10 February 2009. The Court suggested that the act of retention, as specified by the DRD, was simply an obligation on service providers and that the DRD essentially harmonised that obligation, and hence could be viewed as a trade directive. The security aspects – the investigation, detection and prosecution of crime – were held to be a separate issue, independent of the DRD.[73]

In December 2007, more than 30,000 German citizens took up a case against the implementation of the DRD in Germany.[74] In March 2010, responding to the challenge, the German Federal Constitutional Court struck down their implementation of the DRD, describing the law as a 'particularly serious infringement of privacy in telecommunications'.[75] The DRD is not currently implemented in Germany as a result.

In Bulgaria certain terms of their government's implementation of the DRD were repealed in 2008 for their vagueness,[76] while in Romania

---

[70] See www.vorratsdatenspeicherung.de/images/data_retention_brief_08–04–2008.pdf.

[71] *S. and Marper v. the United Kingdom*, Applications nos. 30562/04 and 30566/04, European Court of Human Rights, Judgment, 4 December 2008, para. 121.

[72] *European Parliament v. Council and Commission*, Joined cases C-317/04 and C-318/04. In May 2006, arrangements to transfer the 'passenger name records' of air passengers from the EC to the US Bureau of Customs and Border Protection, which had been set up on the basis of Article 95 of the Treaty Establishing the European Community, were held to be illegal and annulled.

[73] The case is Case C-301/06, *Ireland v. European Parliament and Council of the European Union*, and the judgment may be viewed at http://eur-lex.europa.eu/LexUriServ/LexUriServ.do?uri=CELEX:62006J0301:EN:HTML.

[74] See for example www.dw-world.de/dw/article/0,2144,3025009,00.html.

[75] See for example http://news.bbc.co.uk/1/hi/world/europe/8545772.stm.

[76] See for example http://edri.org/edri-gramnumber6-24bulgarian-administrative-case-data-retention/.

in 2009 the Constitutional Court declared data retention itself to be in breach of the fundamental right to secrecy of correspondence.[77] The exact impact of this declaration has yet to be determined. A new draft law was presented in June 2011, but reports suggest that it is substantially the same as the law that was previously rejected by the Constitutional Court, and that its fate may be the same.[78]

Criticism of the DRD has continued. In December 2010, Peter Hustinx called for a European Commission review of the DRD to prove that it had achieved results – by demonstrating the number of cases where it had actually been needed – or repeal it. As Hustinx put it:

> The Directive is without doubt the most privacy invasive instrument ever adopted by the EU in terms of scale and the number of people it affects.[79]

In July 2013 a hearing of the Grand Chamber of the European Court of Justice took this a step further, asking for proof of the necessity and efficiency of the DRD: this has been seen by some as the first stage towards the eventual repeal of the Directive.[80] The authorities, however, show few signs of dampening their enthusiasm for the concept. Indeed, there are signs that the idea could be spreading: in the United States, the Department of Justice has been renewing calls to introduce mandatory data retention for ISPs, something that has not appeared possible to date and goes counter to the US principles of free trade.[81] To academics such as Claire Walker, data retention seems to have become part of the landscape. As she put it: '[C]ommunications data retention and interception have become a non-negotiable fact of modern life' (Walker, 2009, p. 333).

3.2   Interception and surveillance

Data retention law works in principle by requiring those who already gather data to hold it and make it available. Interception and surveillance

---

[77] See for example www.openrightsgroup.org/blog/2009/data-retention-rejected-by-romanias-courts.

[78] See for example http://edri.org/edrigramnumber9-13new-draft-data-retention-romania/.

[79] Hustinx's speech can be found at https://secure.edps.europa.eu/EDPSWEB/webdav/site/mySite/shared/Documents/EDPS/Publications/Speeches/2010/10-12-03_Data_retention_speech_PH_EN.pdf.

[80] See for example http://policyreview.info/articles/news/data-retention-might-not-be-proportional-risks/170. The Advocate General was due to report on this hearing in November 2013.

[81] See for example http://news.cnet.com/8301-31921_3-20029423-281.html.

law works more directly: by enabling authorities to gather data themselves or to tap into feeds of data being gathered by others. This distinction is not quite as clear as it might appear, however. Firstly, because data retention law can require more data to be gathered than might otherwise have been gathered, and secondly, because some of the laws used for interception and surveillance are also used to access data retained under data retention law: the Regulation of Investigatory Powers Act 2000 (RIPA)[82] is an example.

RIPA is a broad and extensive Act, covering many different aspects of police and intelligence gathering, including the use of covert human intelligence, but it is particularly focussed on the field of communications and dealing with technological developments. Amongst other things, RIPA makes provision for:

> the interception of communications, the acquisition and disclosure of data relating to communications, the carrying out of surveillance ... and the acquisition of the means by which electronic data protected by encryption or passwords may be decrypted or accessed.

What RIPA does, in practice, is to allow a wide range of public bodies to intercept communications,[83] to acquire existing communications data (data held as a result of data retention, for example)[84] to perform surveillance,[85] and to demand encryption keys.[86] RIPA includes terms to govern the warranting of interception, to restrict the use of intercepted material and so forth. In practice it has proven controversial. Cases coming to the fore suggest that the uses of the law have been stretched on a fairly regular basis, including such matters as dog fouling, fly-tipping and checking the addresses of children for determining catchment areas for schools.[87] Keith Vaz MP, Chair of the Commons Home Affairs Committee, was reported to have said:

> I am astonished that this very serious legislation is being misused in this way in cases which seem to be petty and vindictive. We have just completed an inquiry into the surveillance society and we have noted that there has been a huge growth in the use of these laws.[88]

---

[82]   Online at www.legislation.gov.uk/ukpga/2000/23/contents.
[83]   Governed by RIPA, Part I, Chapter 1.   [84]   Governed by RIPA, Part I, Chapter 2.
[85]   Governed by RIPA, Part II.   [86]   Governed by RIPA, Part II.
[87]   See Big Brother Watch, 2012.
[88]   See www.telegraph.co.uk/news/uknews/1584808/Council-spy-cases-hit-1000-a-month. html.

As well as enabling invasions of privacy to take place, the way in which RIPA deals with encryption is an example of another key role of law in relation to privacy: dealing with the ways that individuals attempt to protect themselves. This is a trend that is likely to become a more significant part of the legal landscape for privacy in the future, particularly as the drive towards 'real-names' policies heats up.[89] There is little law in this area so far in most parts of the world, though China appears to have begun the process, with indications that they will now require real names to register for internet access.[90]

RIPA is a controversial law, particularly as its apparent misuses have been well documented and well publicised. It is, however, already considered to be significantly out of date, and newer forms of surveillance and interception law have been on the agenda for some time. In the UK, in 2008, the then Labour government introduced an initiative known as the 'Interception Modernisation Programme', but after public pressure and political opposition this programme was dropped. It was revived in 2012 by the Conservative/Liberal Democrat Coalition government in the form of the Communications Data Bill. This bill has also faced significant opposition, and after a fierce debate and a highly critical report from a specially convened Parliamentary Committee[91] was temporarily withdrawn and at the time of writing had been effectively abandoned.[92]

That, however, may be a short-term result: the drives behind this form of surveillance are strong and persistent, and events that are even in appearance 'terrorism related' can trigger more calls for it. The brutal murder of a soldier on the streets of Woolwich in May 2013, for example, led to calls for the revival of the Communications Data Bill only a short time after its abandonment.[93] Similar events will produce similar calls. The PRISM, Tempora and related revelations seem to have done the reverse, pushing back the possibilities of the bill being revived once more. The situation is highly volatile.

---

[89] This drive is examined in Chapter 9, Section 3.2.

[90] See for example www.infowars.com/china-may-require-real-name-registration-for-internet-access/.

[91] The report is available here: www.publications.parliament.uk/pa/jt201213/jtselect/jtdraftcomuni/79/7902.htm.

[92] See for example www.guardian.co.uk/world/2013/apr/25/snoopers-charter-nick-clegg-agreement. The Communications Data Bill was not included in the Queen's Speech of 9 May 2013, available online at www.gov.uk/government/uploads/system/uploads/attachment_data/file/197434/Queens-Speech-2013.pdf.

[93] See for example www.telegraph.co.uk/news/uknews/terrorism-in-the-uk/10076002/Woolwich-attack-Snoopers-charter-could-have-prevented-machete-tragedy.html.

The essence of surveillance of this kind is simple and direct: monitor and gather *all* 'communications' data with the exception of the 'content' of communications (which is effectively protected by the E-Privacy Directive) and hold it for subsequent use. Precisely what counts as 'communications' data and what counts as 'content' is a subject of some contention and is unlikely to be easily resolved. Indeed, the separation into the two categories is based to a great degree on an old-fashioned view of communications. How this kind of programme would be implemented is also a subject of some contention: proponents of the Communications Data Bill were at pains to point out that there would be no 'central database' of communications data. Instead it would be distributed in a number of places, with a search and filtration system to allow users to access all the data. How this might work out in practice has yet to be seen, but in qualitative terms the idea is clear. All communications should be monitored and that includes all activity on the internet.

It is logical that all activity would need to be covered, because in practice almost any part of the internet can be used to communicate. Conversations do not just happen by email or instant messages, or on social networks such as Facebook. They might happen in online role-playing games, or via comments on blogs, or even through product reviews on Amazon. One of the characteristics of the online 'community' is that methods of communication change all the time and that whenever some new service or system appears, new and unexpected uses of that service or system develop. As a consequence, if surveillance of all kinds of *communications* is required, then surveillance of all *internet activity* is required.

This kind of surveillance, however, raises a lot of questions and presents a lot of risks, considered throughout this book. The overriding question is whether universal rather than targeted is appropriate. This is perhaps the most important, touching directly on the paradigm shift suggested in this book. With universal surveillance, privacy becomes very much the exception rather than the norm. If the norm is to be privacy, surveillance, even for national security purposes, needs to be the exception and hence needs to be targeted rather than universal. Further, universal rather than targeted surveillance is directly incompatible with the right to roam the internet with privacy as set out in Chapter 1.

The big struggles that have taken place over the attempts to introduce universal surveillance systems hint at the underlying struggles. To a great extent, it appears as though people do not want to be watched all the time, regardless of the 'need' for security. The battle over the Communications Data Bill in late 2012 was 'won' by the opponents of the bill, to an extent by managing to characterise it as a 'Snoopers' Charter', and getting that characterisation to stick. In the short term at least, the opponents of the bill appeared to 'win' the battle for hearts and minds.

Laws following similar principles are either already in place or being contemplated in many countries around the world. In Sweden, the 'FRA Law' (*FRA-lagen*), passed in 2008, allows the warrantless tapping of all internet traffic that crosses Swedish borders. It too has faced significant opposition,[94] not just within Sweden, but from Finland, Denmark and Norway, with whom Sweden shares its borders.[95] In Australia, similar measures are being considered under the National Security Review, though they are also facing strong opposition, and at the time of writing it had been postponed until after the election in 2013.[96] In India, the 'Central Monitoring System', which performs similar surveillance, has come into effect, but without, it seems, any specific legal basis.[97] In France, in the aftermath of the PRISM revelations, a similar system is strongly rumoured to exist.[98] The various conflicts over this form of surveillance reflect the underlying tension between privacy and security; that tension is inherent and unavoidable.

It is in the United States, however, that the issue of internet surveillance is being played out most forcefully and dramatically. At the time of writing, the Cyber Intelligence Sharing and Protection Act (CISPA) had been passed by both Houses, though it has had a similar mix of proponents and opponents as the Communications Data Bill has in the UK, and faced a possible veto from the White House. It follows similar lines to the Communications Data Bill, and may even be broader in scope. The opposition to CISPA has also been broad-based. Tim Berners-Lee, for example, has been quoted as saying that it 'is threatening the rights of people in America, and effectively rights everywhere, because what happens in America tends to affect people all over the world.'[99]

---

[94] See for example Klamberg (2010).

[95] See for example http://edri.org/edrigramnumber6-21fra-surveillance-society/ and http://edri.org/edrigramnumber6-16wiretapping-swedish-way/.

[96] See for example www.wsws.org/en/articles/2012/07/asio-j14.html.

[97] See for example http://cis-india.org/internet-governance/blog/indias-big-brother-the-central-monitoring-system.

[98] See for example www.lemonde.fr/societe/article/2013/07/04/revelations-sur-le-big-brother-francais_3441973_3224.html and www.guardian.co.uk/world/2013/jul/04/france-electronic-spying-operation-nsa.

[99] Quoted in *The Guardian*, online at www.guardian.co.uk/technology/2012/apr/18/tim-berners-lee-google-facebook.

What CISPA would legitimise, however, may well already have been taking place, albeit without an entirely clear legal basis. The PRISM programme appears to suggest that large-scale surveillance of internet activity is already taking place under the auspices of the National Security Agency (NSA). The primary legal basis for PRISM appeared to be the FISA Amendments Act of 2008 (FISAA):

> Notwithstanding any other provision of law, upon the issuance of an order in accordance with subsection (i)(3) or a determination under subsection (c)(2), the Attorney General and the Director of National Intelligence may authorize jointly, for a period of up to 1 year from the effective date of the authorization, the targeting of persons reasonably believed to be located outside the United States to acquire foreign intelligence information.[100]

The intelligence services of other countries have been given access to some of the data gathered through PRISM: in the UK, this was said to be authorised by the Intelligence Services Act 1994.[101] Similar programmes around the world came to light in the immediate aftermath. Tempora in the UK, through which, according to *The Guardian*, 'GHCQ taps fibre-optic cables for secret access to world's communications',[102] is perhaps the most pervasive, but far from alone.[103] It is a seemingly necessary characteristic of the activities of the intelligence services that they remain 'secret' and to a degree obscure, though the level and degree of that secrecy and obscurity can clearly vary. What is clear, however, is that intelligence services do seek to perform surveillance on the internet, but if the principles of liberal, democratic societies are to be taken seriously that surveillance should require an appropriate, proportionate and balanced legal basis. In Europe this is set out under Article 8.2 of the ECHR, as discussed above, and confirmed by a series of judgments in the European Court of Human

---

[100] The Foreign Intelligence Surveillance Act of 1978 Amendments Act of 2008, online at www.gpo.gov/fdsys/pkg/PLAW-110publ261/content-detail.html. The paragraph quoted is FISAA, s. 1881(a). Precisely how the complex and detailed legislation in the United States, including the USA PATRIOT Act, online at www.gpo.gov/fdsys/pkg/PLAW-107publ56/pdf/PLAW-107publ56.pdf, The Foreign Intelligence Surveillance Act of 1978 (FISA) and FISAA have been used to enable this kind of surveillance of the internet remains somewhat unclear. It appears likely to remain so, even after the events surrounding the PRISM leak have been absorbed.

[101] Online at www.legislation.gov.uk/ukpga/1994/13/contents. See also www.guardian.co.uk/world/2013/jul/17/prism-nsa-gchq-review-framework-surveillance.

[102] www.guardian.co.uk/uk/2013/jun/21/gchq-cables-secret-world-communications-nsa.

[103] The equivalent French surveillance programme, for example, was disclosed in *Le Monde* at www.lemonde.fr/societe/article/2013/07/04/revelations-sur-le-big-brother-francais_3441973_3224.html.

Rights.[104] Its application, however, is, and needs to be, worldwide. As Frank La Rue, UN Special Rapporteur on the Promotion and Protection of the Right to Freedom of Opinion and Expression put it in his report to the Human Rights Council in April 2013:

> Legal frameworks must ensure that communications surveillance measures:
>
> (a) Are prescribed by law, meeting a standard of clarity and precision that is sufficient to ensure that individuals have advance notice of and can foresee their application;
> (b) Are strictly and demonstrably necessary to achieve a legitimate aim; and
> (c) Adhere to the principle of proportionality, and are not employed when less invasive techniques are available or have not yet been exhausted. (La Rue, 2013, para. 83)

At present, these frameworks, insofar as they exist, are neither consistent nor transparent, but the fallout from the PRISM revelations may be that this transparency and consistency are demanded.

3.3   IP surveillance laws

One of the prime motivators for surveillance on the internet is concern over the distribution of 'illegal' content. There are concerns about a wide range of content: child sexual abuse images; obscene content; content inciting racial or religious hatred; terrorist-related material such as 'bomb-making kits'; defamatory content; and, perhaps most significantly, content infringing copyright and other intellectual property (IP) rights. The wish to reduce or remove such content from the internet and to catch those producing, distributing or consuming such material is a strong incentive to perform surveillance on the internet. That incentive lies behind a number of laws and agreements, some of which have come into force, others of which are still being fought over.

In the UK, the Digital Economy Act 2010, while it does not explicitly enable surveillance for the purposes of enforcement of copyright, does have terms that seem to implicitly allow it. It makes reference to 'copyright infringement reports' that state that there 'appears' to have been an infringement of copyright, including a description and evidence of that

---

[104] For an analysis of the law and the relevant cases, see Fura and Klamburg, 2012, Section 3.1.

apparent infringement.[105] Gathering such evidence would require surveillance and effectively an invasion of privacy.[106]

Similar laws are in existence – and often under challenge – in many
parts of the world. The HADOPI Law in France has provision for forcing
an ISP to monitor an IP address if a copyright holder alerts them to a
potential infringement, though how the copyright holder identifies that
potential infringement is another matter. For this and other reasons, principally connected to the proportionality of the measures, the HADOPI
Law was deeply contentious, and in July 2013 was abandoned, having only
achieved one successful prosecution since its introduction in 2009.[107]

In the United States, attempts have been made to bring in broad-based
copyright enforcement laws that include wide-ranging surveillance
powers. SOPA in particular included terms that indicated that a high level
of surveillance would be required. Indeed, some suggested that it would
effectively have mandated the use of Deep Packet Inspection,[108] looking
into every detail of a user's communication with the internet.[109] Both
SOPA and its companion bill, PIPA, were ultimately withdrawn, primarily
as a result of a concerted campaign by both advocacy groups and internet
industry representatives. Although privacy was just one of the reasons for
the defeat of those bills, it did appear to play a significant part.

Surveillance for the enforcement of copyright is not limited to national
efforts. Indeed, the push for the enforcement of copyright is very much
an international one, with ACTA as the most direct manifestation of that
push. ACTA was a multinational treaty intended to address many different aspects of intellectual property enforcement, including dealing with
what can loosely be described as 'piracy' and other forms of online copyright infringement. This could potentially have included significant levels
of surveillance. As the Open Rights Group (ORG) puts it, ACTA would:

- encourage Internet Service Providers to police the activities of internet users by holding internet providers responsible for the actions of

[105] Digital Economy Act 2010, s. 124A (3). Online at www.legislation.gov.uk/ukpga/2010/24/
contents.

[106] Though parts of the Digital Economy Act 2010 have still not come into force, in
September 2013 content providers were seeking to use surveillance through voluntary
agreements with ISPs. See for example www.theguardian.com/technology/2013/sep/01/
record-labels-broadband-database-illegal-downloads.

[107] See http://m.guardian.co.uk/technology/2013/jul/09/france-hadopi-law-anti-piracy.

[108] A more detailed look at Deep Packet Inspection is in Chapter 6, Section 2, where Phorm
is examined.

[109] See for example http://news.cnet.com/8301-31921_3-57328045-281/sopas-latest-
threat-ip-blocking-privacy-busting-packet-inspection/.

subscribers, conditioning safe harbours on adopting policing policies, and by requiring parties to encourage cooperation between service providers and rights holders; and

- encourage this surveillance, and the potential for punitive disconnections by private actors, without adequate court oversight or due process.[110]

ACTA, however, suffered the same fate as SOPA and PIPA. Strong resistance organised by advocacy groups such as the Electronic Frontier Foundation (EFF), European Digital Rights (EDRi) and ORG resulted in the rejection of the Treaty by the European Parliament in June 2012, effectively neutralising the Treaty worldwide, at least for the time being. Whether a way is found by the supporters of ACTA to revive the agreement has yet to be seen. As for SOPA and PIPA, it is unlikely to be the end of the story. In one form or other, it is highly likely that laws to enforce intellectual property rights will continue to be pushed, and those laws will almost certainly include some kind of provision for surveillance.

Content held or distributed in breach of intellectual property rights is only one of an array of illegal or 'inappropriate' content or communications for which surveillance might be considered appropriate. Child abuse images, obscene material, hate speech, 'cyber-bullying', 'terrorist materials' such as bomb-making kits and so forth might suggest similar approaches, and while there is no evidence yet of specific privacy-invasive laws to cover these areas, they would be logical extensions of current policies. New ideas to combat each of these areas are being regularly mooted, from making people 'opt in' to pornographic content (thus building databases of those who choose to opt in) to real-names policies on all social networks to enable easy location of those engaged in cyber-bullying. Though there are good reasons to bring forward many of these ideas, they generally have an impact upon privacy in one way or another. Maintaining the balance between the various rights and interests is the challenge and, just as for the other related areas already examined, the situation seems to be constantly in flux.

4   Privacy-related law: the overall landscape

What has been described in this chapter so far paints only part of the picture of how the law impacts upon privacy, not just in the UK and Europe,

---

[110] See Open Rights Group press release June 2010, available online at www.openrights-group.org/blog/2010/acta-international-three-strikes-surveillance-and-worse.

but around the world. The complex nature of privacy, as discussed in the first two chapters, is reflected in the law. What might loosely be described as 'old-fashioned' privacy invasions – paparazzi with telephoto lenses, private detectives hacking mobile phones– are subject to the common-law torts of breach of confidence and, more recently, 'misuse of private information'.[111] This kind of privacy law is also in some degree of flux in the UK, partly as a result of the Leveson Inquiry and its aftermath.[112] It is not directly relevant to internet privacy, but the principles established and used in those cases are similar, again based on the balancing of rights. The way that the debate around this law – and around the role of the press itself – has become so heated is similarly a reflection of the difficulty with which an appropriate balancing of these rights can be found. There are also laws that allow overrides to privacy in very specific fields: money laundering legislation, for example, which places obligations on banks, accountants, solicitors and others to file reports when they suspect clients of laundering the proceeds of crime or terrorism-related property.[113]

4.1   Privacy law in the United States

The focus of this chapter has been for the most part on the situation in the UK and in Europe, but it has also touched upon the legal situations elsewhere in the world. The United States is particularly important in this context, in part because of its historical background and economic dominance over the internet as a whole. More specifically, however, because it is the base of the key internet companies, such as Google and Facebook, whose business models have been (and continue to be) crucial in shaping the internet environment, particularly insofar as privacy is concerned.

A number of US laws have already been referred to in this chapter – SOPA, PIPA and CISPA, for example – but that only touches the surface of the state of privacy law in the United States. The principles are similar in many ways to those in the UK. The idea of 'right to privacy' emerged from the seminal article by Warren and Brandeis (1890) of the same title

---

[111]   Developed from *Campbell* v. *MGN* [2004] UKHL 22.
[112]   See www.levesoninquiry.org.uk. The Leveson Inquiry arose as a result of the phone hacking scandal, where members of the press invaded the privacy of large numbers of people. The implementation of the Leveson Report that followed the Inquiry has caused a great deal of contention, and at the date of writing the recommendations had not been implemented.
[113]   Under s. 330 of the Proceeds of Crime Act 2002 and the Terrorism Act 2000, as amended respectively. See Brown, 2012 for an analysis of this and other sector-specific laws allowing overrides to privacy.

in the Harvard Law Review, with the right broadly defined as a 'right to be let alone'. Related to that is the idea of a 'reasonable expectation of privacy', a concept that applies in the UK as much as in the United States.

It is particularly relevant in relation to surveillance. There is direct constitutional protection against *unreasonable* 'search and seizure', via the Fourth Amendment, which says:

> The right of the people to be secure in their persons, houses, papers, and effects, against unreasonable searches and seizures, shall not be violated, and no Warrants shall issue, but upon probable cause, supported by Oath or affirmation, and particularly describing the place to be searched, and the persons or things to be seized.

How the Fourth Amendment is interpreted in relation to the internet is complex and developing: each new situation seems to call upon a new interpretation.[114] That, as before, is characteristic of the tensions and complications of applying law to the internet and can only be expected to continue. The PRISM revelations brought this tension to the fore dramatically. On 4 July 2013 demonstrations were held across the United States under the banner 'Restore the Fourth', suggesting that the NSA's surveillance plans were contrary to the Fourth Amendment, at least in spirit.[115]

When data is looked at in the United States, the situation is very different from that in the EU. There is no general data protection, but there are specific protections for certain kinds of data via a series of laws, including the Health Insurance Portability and Accountability Act (HIPAA), the Video Privacy Protection Act (VPPA) and the Fair Credit Reporting Act (FCRA) amongst others. The situation is made even more complicated by the existence of specific data protection laws in different states. The overall picture that emerges is complex and multifaceted.

In practice, it may well be the Federal Trade Commission (FTC)[116] that does the most to regulate privacy on the internet in the United States. In its role as a protector of consumer rights, and in particular in protecting consumers from unfair or deceptive practices, it has forced agreements out of many of the major players on the internet. Google and Facebook have agreed to regular 'privacy audits' by the FTC, each for a period of

---

[114] In 2012, for example, it was ruled in Rhode Island that the seizure of text messages from mobile phones was a breach of the Fourth Amendment. See http://arstechnica.com/tech-policy/2012/09/police-seizure-of-text-messages-violated-4th-amendment-judge-rules/.

[115] See for example www.guardian.co.uk/world/2013/jul/04/restore-the-fourth-protesters-nsa-surveillance.

[116] www.ftc.gov.

twenty years.[117] In addition, Google has been fined $22.5 million for misrepresenting privacy assurances to users of Apple's Safari.[118] The extent to which this enforcement is effective is another matter. How the audits will work in practice and whether they will result in any change in how either company operates have yet to be seen. In both examples, the questions to be decided were whether the companies were being *deceptive*, that is, were they actually doing what they said they were doing in their privacy policies, and whether those privacy policies themselves were *unfair*. Both *deceptive* and *unfair* are somewhat nebulous terms and, moreover, treat people just as consumers deserving of protection rather than as citizens with rights.

That may seem to be a merely semantic difference, but it has significant implications for the relationship between people on the internet and the authorities. The relationship between citizens and their governments is very different from that between consumers and businesses.

4.2   Privacy law around the world

Elsewhere in the world similar stories are played out, with differences based on specific issues in particular places. One particular piece of legislatioin worthy of note was passed in Mexico in 2012: their 'Geolocalization Law'.[119] This allows the police and other authorities warrantless access to geo-location data from mobile phones, specifically to combat kidnapping problems. The privacy implications are significant, not least when the relationship between the police and the drugs cartels are considered.[120]

The levels of protection given to data privacy worldwide vary a good deal, but the drive by the European Union to bring about more uniformity – and better protection – has had an impact in at least two ways. Firstly, the data protection rules that prohibit transfers to countries not providing sufficient protection mean that those countries

---

[117]   The settlement agreements can be found online at www.ftc.gov/os/caselist/1023136/1103 30googlebuzzagreeorder.pdf and www.ftc.gov/os/caselist/0923184/111129facebookagre e.pdf respectively.

[118]   See http://ftc.gov/opa/2012/08/google.shtm.

[119]   'La Ley de Geolocalización', 2012. See http://dof.gob.mx/nota_detalle.php?codigo=5243 973&fecha=17/04/2012 (in Spanish).

[120]   See for example http://arstechnica.com/tech-policy/2012/04/mexican-geolocalization-law-draws-ire-of-privacy-activists/.

wishing to get internet-related business from the EU will have to raise their standards. Secondly, the EU rules are seen at least by some as a kind of 'gold standard' of data protections, and countries wishing to establish themselves as being on the vanguard of privacy would like to follow those standards. Accordingly, data protection laws are spreading round the globe: Hong Kong[121] and Malaysia[122] are just two recent examples.[123]

Similarly, the level of laws enabling surveillance and invasions of privacy worldwide varies a great deal. The situations in the UK, the United States, Australia and Sweden have been discussed above; elsewhere, for the most part, the law is either less clear or has been less discussed. In many places it appears as though internet surveillance happens as a matter of course, with the authorities having a free rein. In India, for example, the Information Technology Act of 2008 grants the government the power to 'issue directions for interception or monitoring or decryption of any information through any computer resource', so long as it 'is satisfied that it is necessary or expedient to do in the interest of the sovereignty or integrity of India, defense of India, security of the State, friendly relations with foreign States or public order or for preventing incitement to the commission of any cognizable offence relating to above or for investigation of any offence'.[124]

The internet surveillance laws in more oppressive regimes are another question, and the extent to which they are directly authorised by law or the authorities have sufficiently sweeping powers to assume that it is possible is a somewhat moot point. Either way, it appears clear that internet surveillance is happening in many such countries.[125]

---

[121] The Personal Data (Privacy) (Amendment) Bill 2011, available online at http://legco.gov. hk/yr10–11/english/bills/b201107081.pdf.

[122] Malaysia's Personal Data Protection Act 2010 (PDPA), available online at www.kkmm. gov.my/pdf/Personal%20Data%20Protection%20Act%202010.pdf, passed in 2010 and came into force in August 2013.

[123] See for example DLA Piper's 'Data Protection Laws of the World', available online at www.dlapiper.com/data-protection-laws-of-the-world-handbook-2013/.

[124] Information Technology Act of 2008, s. 69. Available online at http://cybercrime.plan-etindia.net/it-act-2008.htm.

[125] See for example the Privacy International report on the worldwide use of internet surveillance technology at www.privacyinternational.org/media-articles/researchers-find-25-countries-using-surveillance-software and their analysis of the situation in Russia at www.privacyinternational.org/blog/lawful-interception-the-russian-approach#footnote2_yxim4h8.

4.3   Privacy law in tension

The examples discussed above are just that: examples. The full picture is too complex and rapidly changing for a detailed analysis here. Indeed, taking a snapshot of the situation at one particular time would be misleading; the constant and continuous change is one of the defining features of privacy law in the current climate. The legal landscape for privacy on the internet is complex and in constant flux, but one thing that is clear from this is that the same essential issues, the same balances and the same tensions are being played out in most countries around the world.

Perhaps even more than complexity and flux, the primary characteristic of privacy law is one of tension: tension within laws and tension between laws, as well as underlying tensions between the different groups involved and their respective rights and needs. Some laws are struggling to get passed, others are facing challenges after they have been passed. There are struggles over implementation and enforcement – in the case of the 'Cookies Directive' it appears clear that even some of the authorities themselves don't really want to have to enforce the law.[126] These struggles work in both directions: both privacy-protective laws (e.g. the 'Cookies Directive' and the reform of the Data Protection regime) and privacy-invasive laws (e.g. the Communications Data Bill, CISPA, SOPA, PIPA and ACTA) have had – and are still having – significant difficulties.

It is important to understand why this is the case. It is one of the reasons that internet privacy rights, as clearly expressed and understood as they can be, could be particularly useful. The confusion, the contention and the enfolding practice are key to the case studies that are central to the three chapters that follow this, most specifically in Chapter 5, where the conflict between the Article 29 Working Party and Google over search data takes centre stage.

---

[126] See Chapter 6, Section 5.2 for more details.

5

Navigating the internet

1 Search engines and their role

One of the most significant developments in relation to the internet over the last two decades has been the emergence of the search engine and in particular the rise of Google. In fifteen years, Google grew from a research project to being one of the largest companies in the world.[1] Many different factors lie behind that growth, but the fundamental role that search engines play in navigating the internet is key.

The amount of information available on the internet is staggering, and finding the information that you want or need is vital if the internet is to be genuinely useful. The nature of the information –generally in a relatively open, digital form – means, however, that there are ways to sort through that immense amount of information. Alternatives are emerging, but the search engine, and Google's in particular, is the simplest, clearest and most popular way to sort through that information and to navigate the internet.

The result of this is that search engines to a great extent govern what people find on the internet and the choices that are made available to people about where and what to visit. The way in which they do this is critical, particularly from the perspective of autonomy.

1.1 How does Google make its billions?

The search market is competitive, and though Google is dominant (with close to 90 per cent of the UK market according to some estimates,[2] and

---

[1] Measuring the 'size' of companies is complex, but by most measures Google is in the top few companies in the world. According to *The Wall Street Journal*, for example, in January 2013 Google ranked third in the world in terms of market capitalisation, at \$248 billion. See http://online.wsj.com/article/SB10001424127887323539804578264024260588396. html.

[2] This figure comes from March 2013, from http://theeword.co.uk/info/search_engine_market.html.

approximately 67 per cent of the US market[3]), there are other big players in the market, particularly in the United States, where Microsoft's Bing (with approximately 15 per cent market share) and Yahoo! (with approximately 10 per cent) provide strong competition. Since Yahoo! is now 'powered by' Bing, Microsoft has an effective 25 per cent market share in the United States. There are also important regional players, most importantly China's Baidu, which although specifically Chinese accounts for some 8 per cent of searches worldwide, and the Russian Yandex, which offers searches in a number of languages including English and French as well as Russian.[4] Smaller players such as AOL and Ask also compete, even if their market shares remain very small, as do 'privacy-friendly' alternatives such as DuckDuckGo.[5]

Google's business model is supremely effective: its revenue for the first quarter of 2013 was almost $14 billion.[6] How is Google so successful? At first sight searching doesn't appear to be an obvious profit-maker. It's free to use, and looks as though it is just a service, provided out of some sense of public goodwill. Google's website, for example, is a paragon of clarity: a clear white page, devoid of advertising or distraction, with a blank box in which to enter your search data.[7]

That simplicity belies the complex nature and consequences of the data that is entered in the box. 'Googling', a term now in many dictionaries,[8] is one of the first things that many people do if they are interested in something or in someone. As a consequence, search data is potentially some of the most revealing data of all, including the most intimate and private of information (looking for new jobs or romance, problems with health, sexuality, etc.) but also the most mundane of information that reveals a great deal about our ordinary lives, such as which movies we enjoy and which film stars we admire, or what products we buy. Google and their competitors understand this, knowing first of all that if they know what we want to find they can do their best to provide it, not just to help guide us to the places we would like to find but to the places that their advertisers would like us to find.

---

[3] Figure from January 2013, see http://searchenginewatch.com/article/2244472/Google-Once-Again-Claims-67-Search-Market-Share.

[4] Yandex is the fourth largest search engine worldwide, after Google, Baidu and Yahoo! See for example http://searchenginewatch.com/article/2242374/Yandex-Just-Passed-Bing-to-Become-4th-Largest-Global-Search-Engine.

[5] See Section 3.2 below.

[6] See http://investor.google.com/earnings/2013/Q1_google_earnings.html

[7] www.google.com

[8] For an online example, see www.merriam-webster.com/dictionary/google.

The intimate information can be important and potentially highly damaging. From teenagers exploring homosexuality or researching abortion to almost anything connected with religion, there is great potential for harm. The mundane information, however, may have even more significant implications for autonomy, but to understand why, we need to look more closely at how a search engine functions.

There are many possible models for running a search engine, from the basic 'telephone directory' style search engine to the sophisticated data-gathering model used by Google and most of its competitors. The way that Google works begins to become clear when you complete your search: the advertising appears with the results, not with the initial search. The most significant part of Google's business model is its ability to provide *targeted* advertising, appropriate to the user concerned, and thus more likely to be successful. Because Google understands the nature of search data and knows how to use it, the targeted advertising works. Google can prove it, because its records show not only who looked at the advertising but also who clicked on it: who actually visited the sites of the advertisers. Moreover, when someone visits that advertiser's site, they can tell that they have come from Google. Advertisers have been convinced that Google's advertising revenue is the key to its success. As the case study below will show, however, this ability to target advertising is not mentioned by Google's Privacy Counsel Peter Fleischer anywhere in his explanation to the Working Party as to why Google retains identifiable search logs.

Different degrees of targeting are possible, including the most recent idea, behavioural targeting, the subject of the next chapter. The degree of targeting depends on the kind of information available and used. The most direct uses only immediately available information: first and foremost the term searched for, but also information such as the general location of the searcher, the time of day the search is made, the ISP that the searcher uses and so forth. The more sophisticated models of Google and others use much more information: profiles built up from the logs of all the terms that the user has ever searched for before, together with other data from Google services such as places looked for on Google Maps or Google Earth, that aspect of clickstream data that shows which links from our Google searches we actually follow, and for how long, even the texts of emails sent through Gmail. Other data purchased from third parties can be aggregated with this, building even more detailed profiles and allowing for even more accurately targeted advertising.[9] This advertising may appear not just on the search results pages, but on any pages provided by any of the many other Google services, including your Gmail webmail pages. The integration of all these services, primarily through Google's social network Google+, is proceeding apace, making the integration of all the data gathered via these services easier and in general automatic.

It is crucial to remember that the first and most important reason that Google succeeds is because its search engine is very effective. When it first appeared it was streets ahead of the competition, which is why it gained so many users, and hence was so good for advertising. Google wishes to maintain that advantage in order to maintain its pre-eminent position in the market. Its collection and mastery of its database of personal information, personal searches and so forth is one of the keys to maintaining that advantage. Google knows this, which is why it is not going to give it up without a fight.

1.2   The role of search engines in the Symbiotic Web

Some of the problems arising from the involuntary personalisation of the internet have been discussed in Chapter 3. They are relevant here for two reasons: firstly, because the nature and quantity of search data make it ideal for exactly the kind of profiling that forms the starting point for personalisation, and secondly because of the role that search engines play.

The Symbiotic Web is to a great extent about the way that choices are offered to people, chosen for them, by others, on the basis of the information that others have about them. In particular, it is about the web pages people are guided to and that are suggested to them. Search engines play a crucial role in this. If the principal way people navigate the web is by using a search engine, then the places that the search engines suggest to them are where they are likely to go. This has two direct implications. Firstly, when people 'google' something, they almost always only go to sites on the first page of search results,[10] and how a site gets to that first page is essentially up to the search engine. Secondly, as noted above, when search engine results are presented, the page is surrounded by advertisements and 'sponsored links'. Since 2010, Google has been blurring the

---

[9] An introduction to the effectiveness of profiling can be found in Ayres, 2007.

[10] It has been estimated that ninety per cent of users never look beyond the first page of search results on Google. See for example www.creativelipi.com/search-engine-optimization.html.

boundaries between search results and such sponsored links, mixing the results where something might appear in both categories.[11] Moreover, as noted earlier, the issue of potential bias for commercial reasons in Google's search results has been subject to EU investigation.[12]

These two factors already make the role of search engines in 'shaping' the experience of web users, controlling them and reducing their autonomy, of considerable importance. That is just the first stage. The next is that not only advertisements but actual content is chosen for people. Where Google is concerned, this means that the search results presented are not simply the results of searching for the terms that have been put in, but have been altered ('tailored') based on the individual's prior searching records, and not just the records of what they've previously searched for, but of which of the links that have been presented have actually been followed. Since the end of 2009, Google has personalised search results unless the user specifically opts out.[13]

Most of this is not harmful in itself. Indeed, much of it is helpful and makes a user's experience of the internet more rewarding. The problem is that it takes control out of the hands of the user, in a way that is often in effect dishonest, and puts it in the hands of the search engine's creators, in this case Google. For the most part, the motives of these creators are at worst pecuniary, but that may not always be the case, and even so it compromises the web user's autonomy, controlling the options made available to them.

There is a potentially more sinister side to this tailoring. Most people use Google as their prime method for navigating the internet, so the honesty and transparency of Google searching is critical to ensuring that the internet is something that can be used with the kind of openness, equality and neutrality that give it its strengths, and its possibilities as a tool to improve openness and freedom, rather than as one of limitation and control. If the links presented as the result of a Google search can change depending on the profile of the visitor, there is then scope for discrimination. This discrimination could arise through differential pricing and differentiated access to services based on anything from locale to ethnic origin, education or health. Websites might not even be visible to visitors who are not deemed 'suitable'.

---

[11] See Danny Sullivan's comments on the subject at http://searchengineland.com/google-blurs-the-line-between-paid-unpaid-results-again-36268.

[12] See Chapter 3, footnote 27.

[13] See http://googleblog.blogspot.com/2009/12/personalized-search-for-everyone.html.

As Ayres (2007, Chapter 1) has suggested, profilers believe (and they may often be right) that they know people's tastes better than they know them themselves, so the opportunity for people to have their online lives 'shaped' for them by others can be extreme. With the massive growth in social networking sites, they not only know the internet user, they know their friends, and they use that information for their own purposes.

All of this combines to make the role of search engines, and of the data that they collect, particularly important. Google, the biggest of the search engines by a considerable margin, is in an unparalleled position in terms of gathering personal data and in using that data in ways that can potentially impact upon people's autonomy. That brings a level of potential power that naturally draws the attention of regulators, especially the kind of interventionist regulators prevalent in the EU.

2   Google and the Article 29 Working Party

Relations between Google and various elements of the European authorities have been edgy for many years, an edginess that sometimes seems to reach a level of real conflict. This exemplifies some of the bigger tensions surrounding the regulation of the internet, and in particular over privacy: the tension between individual privacy and business models, the tension between the United States and the EU, and between the generally *cyberpaternalist* views of regulators and the near *cyberlibertarian* views of some US companies.[14] Companies in general often prefer not to be regulated, and Google is no exception.

The events looked at here, surrounding a conflict over the retention of search data, also highlight the pressures inherent in the way that law deals with privacy on the internet, as discussed in detail in the previous chapter. As will be seen, Google attempted to use those tensions – in particular, the tension between data protection and data retention – in order to try to avoid being subject to the kind of privacy regulation that might interfere with its business model. That it ultimately failed to do so has potentially significant implications.

2.1   A dispute over search data

Search data became the first real battleground in the conflict between data protection and data retention. Two aspects of searching lie behind this:

---

[14] See Chapter 4, Section 1 for a discussion of cyberpaternalism and cyberlibertarianism.

the nature of the data gathered, and the crucial role that search engines play in our navigation of the internet, as has been discussed above. This combination of factors not only gives search engines the massive business opportunities that have made them billions, but also raises significant concerns.

Search data is a particularly significant form of data when examined from the perspective of autonomy and privacy for a number of reasons. The first of these relates to its nature: as well as including some of the most private and even intimate things, the most mundane and ordinary things we search for can be perfect information for profiling.

Secondly, this importance lies in the role searching plays in the internet. As noted above, it is the primary method not only of finding things but also of navigating the web. This has direct implications when looking at our ability to find our 'own' way around the web, rather than having ways chosen for us: search engines have a direct role to play in the Symbiotic Web, in particular in terms of the personalisation aspect.

The third factor is that of choice, a crucial factor from the perspective of autonomy. Searching and search data are important because there is little choice involved as to whether to use a search engine at all. Almost all search engines work similarly, gathering data and using it for their own purposes. As searching is a fundamental tool of the internet, this makes it almost impossible to use the internet at all without data being gathered. Alternatives to searching – and privacy-friendly versions of searching – are now beginning to emerge,[15] but at the moment they are very much the exception rather than the rule, and some of them have even more significant implications for privacy than the ordinary, current forms of search.

Fourthly, and perhaps even more importantly from the perspective of autonomy, there is the issue of consent. As discussed in the previous chapter, consent is one of the keys to data protection: if you can obtain express, informed consent from someone to use their data, some of the key aspects of data protection law are effectively bypassed.[16] The argument that search engines obtain any kind of consent at all, let alone express, informed consent, is highly contentious given that it is not made clear when you make a search that any data whatsoever is being gathered. Other kinds of data such as the 'social' data gathered by social networking sites do at least have a log-in procedure and terms and conditions to be agreed to, providing a surface level of consent. How Google's particular

---

[15] See Section 3 below.   [16] See Chapter 4, Section 2.

methods of obtaining what it considers to be consent for the use of search data fit with the terms of data protection will be looked at below.

These are just some of the reasons that search data became the first real battlefield when the conflict between data protection and data retention was fought, in the dispute between Google and the EU Article 29 Working Party. It was a conflict of deep significance not least because it could have been the first of many such confrontations, as the struggle over data retention spread into different areas and different kinds of data. The latest forms of internet surveillance (such as that envisaged in the Communications Data Bill and apparently practised through PRISM and related programmes) suggest gathering and retaining *all* internet data.

2.2   The Article 29 Working Party

Interpretation and advice on the implementation of the Data Protection Directive (DPD) has been placed in the hands of the Working Party on the Protection of Individuals, otherwise known as the Article 29 Working Party,[17] or simply the Working Party, which is composed of representatives of the supervisory authorities on data protection of each of the EU member states, including the UK's Information Commissioner. In many ways it is a strong, expert and authoritative body unafraid of taking on the biggest players in the market. It was the Working Party that was at the centre of the EU dispute with Google.

Google's dominant position in the crucial search market – and in the internet world as a whole – made it an ideal target for the Article 29 Working Party. What is more, it exemplifies some of the most important problems arising from the tension between data protection and data retention, showing how in practice businesses can use these tensions to their own advantage, one of the reasons why more needs to be done to protect the individual. The Article 29 Working Party appeared to know that, and to understand that its role required it to take this bull by the horns.

There was a huge amount at stake, not just the tension between data protection and data retention. This included the long-term power relationships between big business and the European regulators and the question of how an American corporation would react not just to a European regulator but to a European principle, data protection being still an essentially European concept. European competition regulators had been locking

---

[17] Established by Articles 29 and 30 of the DPD.

horns with Microsoft for years, and in 2007 appeared finally to have won, with Microsoft accepting their fine of nearly half a billion Euros.[18] Now, it seemed, the regulators were going after the second of the American monoliths of the internet industry, Google.

The Working Party did not choose Google as its target because Google is the 'worst' of the search engines providers. If anything, it appeared to be one of the more ethical providers. Certainly the records of Yahoo! and Microsoft in China did not inspire much confidence in terms of ethical practice,[19] while Google could at that stage justifiably claim that it was the only one of the major providers to resist the US government's attempts to subpoena vast amounts of consumer data in the name of counterterrorism.[20] Google's dominance of the market may, however, have been of concern to the regulators. Searching is the primary method of navigating the internet, and Google dominates the search market, so how Google works is of crucial importance in how the internet functions for the vast majority of users.

As services become more personalised and tailored, to a significant degree precisely because of the way Google uses people's search data, that 'neutrality' and independence is compromised. So too is Google's role as a 'disinterested' navigator of the internet. The question for regulators is whether there is any kind of obligation on Google to prevent this from happening, or, if not, whether more effort was needed to ensure that users of Google and other search engines understand the processes, so that they can make appropriately informed decisions.

The Working Party may also have been attempting to cement its place as the world's primary setter of data protection and privacy standards and policies. As the analysis in the previous chapter set out, privacy-related law and standards around the world are far from consistent: harmonisation would be highly desirable. The Working Party would like to be at the heart of that harmonisation process, guiding and shaping it. As the drive towards reform of data protection in Europe has proceeded, this has seemed to become more likely: the reforms currently on the table[21]

---

[18] See for example http://news.bbc.co.uk/1/hi/business/7056288.stm.

[19] See the Amnesty International Report, 'Undermining Freedom of Expression in China: The Role of Yahoo!, Microsoft and Google' at www.amnesty.org/en/library/info/ POL30/026/2006.

[20] See for example http://news.bbc.co.uk/1/hi/technology/4630694.stm. The extent to which Google could claim this kind of 'moral high ground' was challenged in 2013, when it was implicated in the PRISM revelations along with the majority of the other big players in the internet world.

[21] See Chapter 4, Section 2.2

envisage a strengthened version of the Working Party, to be called the Data Protection Board, with more responsibilities and powers.

It may also be true that this whole process may be seen as just a part of the internal conflict within the EU, between those who support the idea of data protection in the name of human rights and those who are striving for stronger data retention laws, in the name of the fight against terrorism. The vehemence of the opposition shown by the Working Party to the data retention laws from their initial conception, as described in Chapter 4, lends some credence to this.[22]

It may be, however, that the most direct and obvious reason was the real key: the Working Party considered that Google's methods of gathering, holding and using data fail to comply with at least the spirit and intent of data protection legislation. On the face of it this can certainly be argued. The DPD requires that data be 'kept in a form which permits identification of data subjects for no longer than is necessary',[23] and it cannot really be said to be 'necessary' that Google makes as much money as possible from us as individuals.

2.3   Should identifiable search data be retained?

What the Working Party and Google were arguing about is the retention of search data in a form that can be linked – identified[24] – with the person who made the search. At the start of the dispute Google kept a permanent record of everything that you searched for, building up a detailed profile of all your searches and thus of your interests, tastes and tactics in using the internet. The Working Party questioned whether such records should be maintained, and whether they were in compliance with EU data protection legislation.

The first salvoes were fired at the 28th International Data Protection and Privacy Commissioners' Conference, held in London in November 2006,[25] where a strongly worded resolution on privacy protection and search engines was passed, making three key points: that search engines should inform their customers up front about the data being gathered;

---

[22] The significance of the issue is reflected throughout the 'human rights world' – indeed, the title of Conor Gearty's 2006 book *Can Human Rights Survive?* shows how seriously the challenges to human rights are taken – and the challenges from antiterror legislation form a key part of that book.

[23] See Chapter 4, Section 2.1.

[24] The issue of identity is a contentious one and is discussed further in Section 3.

[25] See www.privacyconference2006.co.uk/.

that search engines should offer services in a 'privacy-friendly manner'; and that data minimisation should be regarded as crucial.[26]

It was a general resolution, more a statement of principles than a specific call for action. It did signify intent and was a sign of things to come in another way, in that the dispute took place in public, with both sides allowing their 'private' correspondence to enter the public domain as they appeared to try to win hearts and minds (of the other key regulators, the rest of the industry, the public, and legal and other commentators) as well as making their legal points.

The next move came in the form of a letter from the Working Party to Peter Fleischer, Google's 'Privacy Counsel' for their European operations, on 16 May 2007, and made public almost immediately online.[27] In it, the Working Party questioned Google's need to keep identifiable search records, suggesting that Google's current practice 'does not seem to meet the requirements of the European legal data protection framework'.[28]

The areas of possible non-compliance arise essentially from principles rather than precise legal rules. The key relevant principles of data protection, as described in Chapter 4, are:

1. the purposes for which data is kept must be specified;
2. data should only be held when it is 'strictly necessary' for the provision of the service;
3. services should be offered in a 'privacy-friendly manner';[29]
4. data linked to an individual user should only be kept when that user has given their 'explicit, informed consent'; and
5. data minimisation: the minimum amount of data should be held for the minimum amount of time.

The Working Party asked Google to explain why the data was kept, and why for so long. At the time that the dispute began, it was being kept indefinitely, and by the time the letter was sent their policy was to hold search log data for eighteen to twenty-four months. The Working Party was asking Google to justify itself, and asking it publicly.

---

[26] The resolution is downloadable from http://ec.europa.eu/justice_home/fsj/privacy/news/docs/pr_google_annex_16_05_07_en.pdf.

[27] Letter from Peter Schaar to Peter Fleischer, 16 May 2007, made available online at http://ec.europa.eu/justice_home/fsj/privacy/news/docs/pr_google_16_05_07_en.pdf (accessed 30 June 2010).

[28] *Ibid.* p. 1.

[29] This principle was set out in the Resolution on Privacy Protection and Search Engines of the 28th International Data Protection and Privacy Commissioners' Conference, November 2006.

Peter Fleischer responded on 10 June 2007 with a six-page letter that was also made public immediately through Google's own blogs.[30] It was a long and detailed letter, but essentially boiled down to the following:

1. Google needs to keep its search data in order to keep improving the quality of its searches, and to fight fraud and abuse.
2. Google believes it is in compliance with all legislation by keeping logs for eighteen to twenty-four months.
3. The principles of data retention mean that Google is obliged to keep its data for twenty-four months.

The first point appears to be a red herring: there is no need for data used to improve the quality of service to be kept in an identified form, and in general fighting fraud and abuse has to be faster than eighteen to twenty-four months to be of significant use.[31]

The second and third points are more complex. One key part of Fleischer's argument is very hard to refute: that the laws and directives concerning data protection and data retention are vague and often contradictory, as discussed in the previous chapter. He quoted back to the Working Party some of its own criticisms of the DRD, in particular, that it lacks clarity in many ways, that its implementation across EU states is inconsistent, and hence that the rules that govern a provider such as Google are far from clear. When you add to the equation regulations from other jurisdictions and Google's stated policy to provide 'one level of privacy protection for our users worldwide',[32] his argument does appear consistent and logical.

Fleischer claimed that there are few hard and fast rules, and that Google's eighteen to twenty-four month policy is as close to compliance as it can get and is proportionate to the risks involved. However, as a concession, Fleischer announced that Google would reduce their data retention to a flat eighteen months, a concession made out of goodwill, for Fleischer reminded the Working Party that it might have to raise the limit again, as a result of 'future data retention laws'.[33] This small phrase may have been

---

[30] Letter from Peter Fleischer to Peter Schaar, 10 June 2007, made available at http://64.233.179.110/blog_resources/Google_response_Working_Party_06_2007.pdf (accessed 30 June 2007).

[31] The existence of the AskEraser (see Section 3 below) also shows that one of Google's competitors believes it can fight fraud and abuse without holding identified data for more than 'a few hours'.

[32] Letter from Peter Fleischer to Peter Schaar, 10 June 2007, p. 1.

[33] Letter from Peter Fleischer to Peter Schaar, 10 June 2007, p. 5.

the most important part of the whole letter, as will be explained below. Essentially, however, Fleischer's argument hinged on the supposition that data retention 'trumps' data protection.

The Working Party responded almost immediately to Fleischer's letter, first of all by saying directly that the DRD did not apply to search data and hence that Fleischer's attempt to use data retention as a reason to hold the data did not apply.[34] It did not publish any further correspondence, but instead let it be known that the terms of its enquiry into search engines would be broadened to cover more than just Google, and that it would respond in detail in the early part of 2008.[35]

This response appeared on 4 April 2008,[36] in the form of a comprehensive, published opinion covering searching and search engines generally rather than Google in particular. In it, the Working Party affirmed its view that the DPD *does* apply to search data while the DRD *does not*.[37] The Working Party also concluded that '[s]earch engine providers must delete or irreversibly anonymise personal data once they no longer serve the specified and legitimate purpose they were collected for'.

The opinion contradicts all the substantial arguments put forward by Google, going through each of the 'purposes and grounds' suggested by Google and others as reasons for their retention of data (improvement of services, securing the system, prevention of fraud, accounting requirements, personalising advertising, collection of statistics and law enforcement)[38] and rejecting them as grounds for long-term data retention. Most are 'too broadly defined to offer an appropriate framework to judge the legitimacy of the purpose', while the question of 'reprocessing' data collected for one purpose for another that might be incompatible with it is also considered a problem.[39]

That left two possible grounds for data retention: consent and contractual agreements. On these, the opinion is unequivocal: ordinary, anonymous users cannot be considered to have given consent and the 'de facto contractual relationship' when using a search engine in its usual form 'does not meet the strict limitation of necessity as required in the

---

[34] They responded within one week, by 27 June 2007. See www.out-law.com/page-8179.

[35] See e.g. www.news.com/EU-privacy-body-to-take-months-on-Google-probe/2100-1029_3-6212794.html?tag=html.alert.hed.

[36] Working Party 'Opinion on data protection issues related to search engines', 00737/ EN WP 148, at http://ec.europa.eu/justice_home/fsj/privacy/docs/wpdocs/2008/ wp148_en.pdf.

[37] Working Party Opinion 148, Executive Summary, p. 3, and in detail on pp.12–13.

[38] Working Party Opinion 148, pp. 15–18.   [39] Working Party Opinion 148, p. 16.

Directive'.[40] The Working Party specifically reminded search engines of the Directive's requirements in this area, and noted that 'search engines should make clear to users what information is collected about them and what it is used for', something that search engines (and Google in particular) conspicuously fail to do.

In conclusion, the Working Party did 'not see a basis for a retention period beyond 6 months', and suggested that if search engine providers wished to retain data beyond that six-month period, they would have to 'demonstrate comprehensively that it is strictly necessary for the service'.[41] The opinion is a strong, broad and authoritative response, meeting Google's letter head-on and flatly contradicting it on almost every point.

2.4   Google's reaction: a regulatory result?

In the face of such an unequivocal response, Google eventually reacted, six months after the opinion was issued. In a blog post on 8 September 2008, Google said:

> Today, we're announcing a new logs retention policy: we'll anonymize IP addresses on our server logs after 9 months. We're significantly shortening our previous 18-month retention policy to address regulatory concerns and to take another step to improve privacy for our users.[42]

This step could be seen as a victory of a kind for the Article 29 Working Party. In effect, the pressure it exerted made Google change its policies concerning data, from initially holding it indefinitely, to holding it for eighteen months and, then, here, to nine months. There are limitations to this change: the data is being anonymised, rather than deleted, and the extent to which that anonymisation is effective is somewhat debatable.[43] Nonetheless, it does show that companies such as Google do respond to pressure when that pressure is appropriately applied and is backed up by public opinion. That last point is, perhaps, the biggest key here. Google understands the importance of the community and of the community's views. If enough people care sufficiently about privacy, Google will do something about it. In the case of data retention periods, it did.

In its response, Google explicitly states the challenge:

---

[40] Working Party Opinion 148, p. 17.   [41] Working Party Opinion 148, p. 19.
[42] http://googleblog.blogspot.com/2008/09/another-step-to-protect-user-privacy.html.
[43] See Chapter 7, Section 4.4.

> it's difficult to find the perfect equilibrium between privacy on the one
> hand, and other factors, such as innovation and security, on the other.
> Technology will certainly evolve, and we will always be working on ways
> to improve privacy for our users, seeking new innovations, and also find-
> ing the right balance between the benefits of data and advancement of
> privacy.

This is not a challenge just for Google but for everyone involved in the
internet. Ultimately, it is the challenge of the Symbiotic Web: how to make
sure that the symbiosis remains positive. What this case study suggests
is that the process through which the balance is maintained is one that
involves effort, thought and discussion between all the related parties.
Google's reaction came through, as they put it:

> literally hundreds of discussions with data protection officials, govern-
> ment leaders and privacy advocates around the world.[44]

This is symbiotic regulation in action. All the various relationships came
into play and ultimately, at least to an extent, the community produced a
reaction. As shall be shown in the case studies in Chapters 6 and 7, this
pattern has been repeated in other key areas.

3   Implications and ways forward

Should we, as private individuals, be concerned about these practices?
First of all, it must be noted that whether they *really* threaten our privacy and hence our autonomy is much more significant than whether they
comply with the precise terms of the DPD.

Search engines play a vital role in the navigation and use of the internet
for the vast majority of users. This means that there is a strong argument
for people possessing a significant interest in changing search engines'
current and possible future practices. Two questions arise: what is the
outlook for the future? And what are the implications for attempts to find
solutions? There are three connected issues to resolve: firstly, the resolution of the specific dispute between the EU and Google; secondly, the
possibilities of finding a privacy-friendly future for internet navigation
in general; and thirdly, resolving the overall tension between data protection and data retention. The three issues are intrinsically linked, and
by finding solutions to one it may be possible to find ways forward in the
others.

---

[44] http://googleblog.blogspot.com/2008/09/another-step-to-protect-user-privacy.html.

3.1   The continuing dispute between Google and the EU

The protracted negotiation that has taken place between Google and the Article 29 Working Party may have been part of Google's intention, to stretch out negotiations as long as possible while it investigated different options and business models. What appears to have been the final outcome has been a kind of workable compromise. Google might still be vaguely hoping that other parts of governments come to their 'rescue'. The mention of 'future data retention laws' in Fleischer's letter suggested this. In fact, he mentioned it twice, also suggesting that individual countries might implement stronger data retention laws.[45] The principles behind data retention – to be able to find and catch terrorists, organised criminals, paedophiles or pornographers through their internet use – apply as much to search data as they do to emails or telephone calls, no matter what the letter of the law currently says. Google may have been trying to remind governments of that, to ensure that new, stronger data retention legislation is brought in, applying as much to search as to email, so that Google can use that to trump privacy rights. This has not happened as such, though the developments over internet surveillance laws and indeed practice discussed in Chapter 4 do suggest something similar. To an extent, however, it appears that Google may have moved on and realised that privacy is such an important issue that it needs to be embraced rather than resisted. If so, it would be a very interesting and important development, a move towards the 'privacy-friendly future' that is envisaged in Chapter 10. Drawing such a conclusion, however, would be highly premature. Although there are signs that this might be the direction in which Google and others are moving, there are also significant signs of movement in precisely the opposite direction.

Indeed, it must be remembered that for Google, as for any business, what matters is the bottom line, and that it will use whatever it can to protect and enhance that bottom line. In this case, it attempted to use data retention law – and indirectly the fight against terrorism – in order to support its business. More recently, it has enlisted the emotive protection of 'free speech' in its wish to oppose the 'right to be forgotten', when it looks again more as though it is its business model that it really wishes to protect, and its costs that it wants to keep down.[46]

---

[45] Letter from Peter Fleischer to Peter Schaar, 10 June 2007, p. 3.
[46] See Chapter 7, and Bernal, 2014.

In the short term, though, not much could be expected from the legal process and both sides appeared to know it, which is one of the reasons they did almost everything in public. Hearts and minds were as important as the legal process. Ultimately, much depends on what the public wants and politicians believe is possible. If the interests of individuals' privacy are to be protected, the arguments need to be won at this level. The conflict between Google and the EU regulators has continued since the search data retention story was resolved. Google's consolidation of its various privacy policies (over sixty of them) into a single agreement in 2012 raised the hackles of the regulators, and at the date of writing regulatory action by a number of them was on the cards.[47] It has remained an emotional conflict as data protection reform has progressed, with Fleischer comparing regulators to Don Quixote in February 2013.[48] Though in his blog Fleischer reminded the regulators that 'things don't end well for the noble knight', this does not seem likely to be a story that comes to a conclusion in the immediate future.

3.2 Privacy-friendly internet navigation?

What options exist if there is to be a more privacy-friendly way to navigate the web? There are other search engines, but, as noted above, if anything most of them have worse privacy policies and practices than Google. In addition, the whole industry knows that gathering private data is one of the keys to Google's success, a key that they appear to be more likely to try to copy than to reject.

There are, however, privacy-friendly versions of search evolving. One of the smaller search providers, Ask.com, offered a service called the 'AskEraser',[49] which effectively allowed you to access Ask's search engine without having your data recorded and also allowed you to delete any search records that Ask already held on you. It seemed to satisfy most of the privacy requirements suggested here. In any event, Ask.com discontinued the AskEraser in January 2014.[50]

There are caveats to the privacy provided by the service in that Ask does agree to cooperate with law enforcement agencies:

---

[47] In April 2013, Google faced action in six countries including the UK. See for example www.out-law.com/en/articles/2013/april/google-facing-regulatory-action-in-six-eu-countries-over-privacy-policy-issues/.

[48] See http://peterfleischer.blogspot.co.uk/2013/02/dox-quixote.html.

[49] http://about.ask.com/en/docs/about/askeraser.shtml.

[50] See the Electronic Frontier Foundation analysis: www.eff.org/deeplinks/2008/03/search-privacy.

> Ask.com must abide by federal, state, and local laws and regulations. Even
> when AskEraser is enabled, we may store your search activity data if duly
> required or requested to do so by law enforcement or other governmental
> authority. In such cases, we may retain your search data even if AskEraser
> appears to be turned on.

This weakens the privacy, but does mean that privacy is overridden only
when requested: the default remains privacy, as the paradigm shift underlying the ideas here would suggest.

Ask.com's market share is very small – less than one per cent[51] – and
this may lie behind its willingness to buck the industry trend and offer a
real alternative to the mainstream. In addition, the AskEraser button is
small and gray so unless a user knows what they want in terms of privacy they are very unlikely to find it or use it. What is more, the AskEraser
is an opt-in service; you have to choose privacy, it is not the default. It
may even be that Ask.com offers it precisely for that reason: it satisfies the
privacy lobby but makes little difference to the amount of data they can
gather, the depth of their profiling and the effectiveness of their targeted
advertising.

There are also other, more specifically and practically 'privacy-friendly'
search engines emerging. DuckDuckGo states on its access page[52] that
'We believe in better search and not tracking', and provides a detailed
explanation of how it differs from Google and others.[53] Startpage[54] bills
itself as 'the world's most private search engine' and makes privacy its
central point:

> Startpage, and its sister search engine Ixquick, are the only third-party
> certified search engines in the world that do not record your IP address or
> track your searches.[55]

The existence of the AskEraser and of services such as DuckDuckGo and
Startpage does show that if the search engines wanted to, they could offer
the kind of services that might be approved of by privacy advocates. The
question is whether the more mainstream search engines want to provide
these services. The evidence so far seems to suggest that they do not.

---

[51] See e.g. www.karmasnack.com/about/search-engine-market-share/.
[52] https://duckduckgo.com.
[53] 'Google tracks you. We don't. An illustrated guide.' Online at http://donttrack.us.
[54] www.startpage.com.
[55] www.startpage.com/eng/protect-privacy.html. See also an analysis of the effectiveness
      of these services in protecting privacy by advocate Alexander Hanff at www.alexander-
      hanff.com/startpage-and-ixquick-search-in-privacy.

3.3   Technological alternatives and new pressures

There have been attempts to find ways to use Google's existing service in a manner that protects our privacy better. There are 'anonymisers' such as proxify[56] and TOR,[57] which theoretically enable you to surf the internet and use Google without leaving your identity by routing the search through independent servers. There are services such as hidemyass.com that use Virtual Private Networks (VPNs) and web proxies to 'surf anonymously online, hide your IP address, secure your internet connection, hide your internet history, and protect your online identity'. [58] Most of these, however, need to be specially sought out and carefully checked before use – and tend to only provide limited protection, can slow down browsing and even make some parts of the internet inaccessible.

Moreover, to help internet users in general, relatively obscure independent solutions are not enough. They have always existed, but only protect those people 'in the know', who are not likely to need protection in any event as they know good practice.[59] What are needed are more mainstream solutions where privacy becomes the default option, and data gathering and data retention have to be 'opted into' or, as the Working Party suggested, operate only where users have given 'explicit, informed consent'.

Are mainstream technological solutions possible? One solution would be for a browser provider to build anonymous search into its standard product. There are many technical problems to providing such a solution, not least the bandwidth and processing power needed to route the searches. There are cost implications, and there would be huge political and market pressures *not* to provide this kind of service, not least from Google whose business plan it would undermine. It is easy to imagine how governments would portray them – 'tools for terrorists' – and how strongly they would oppose them in the current political climate.[60] Nonetheless, it might not be impossible: Microsoft and Mozilla, the makers of Internet Explorer and Firefox respectively, have recently taken 'privacy-friendly' steps with their browsers in relation to behavioural advertising, evidently believing that this is something their customers want.[61]

---

[56] http://proxify.com/.   [57] See www.torproject.org/.   [58] www.hidemyass.com.
[59] There are strategies to cut down the risks (e.g. www.eff.org/wp/six-tips-protect-your-search-privacy).
[60] This may have already happened at some US universities, where nodes for anonymising services were provided, but rumour suggests that there was pressure to remove them by law enforcement agencies. These rumours remain unsubstantiated – but the nodes have been removed.
[61] See Chapter 6, Section 5.1.

Search engines, moreover, are facing more pressures. Though they are currently the principal method through which people navigate the internet, alternatives are emerging. Social networks act to an extent as gateways, with people following links that they find or that are suggested to them by their friends or by the system itself. Facebook has taken this a step further with the launch of 'Graph Search', which to an extent automates the process, amongst other things allowing you to search through the 'social' information provided by your 'friends'.[62] Twitter can be used to 'crowdsource' information: if a Twitter user has a significant number of followers, they can tweet a question and simply wait for the answers. The move to the use of mobile platforms such as Apple's iOS and Google's Android has brought in the use of 'apps' – small programmes that operate on your smartphone or tablet – that can bypass browsers. Apps are 'found' using app stores rather than by using search. Further technological advances such as the voice-based systems like Apple's Siri partially bypass search: a user literally 'asks' Siri for information, and Siri answers, using a variety of different sources which may or may not include a particular search engine.

Many of these alternatives have privacy implications of their own – and often even more potential problems than those presented by search – but they could also have a significant impact on search itself, putting further pressure on search providers' revenues. That, as the model of the Symbiotic Web suggests, puts further pressure on search providers to squeeze more income from their search data, and hence puts more pressure on privacy. Even if Google has an inclination to become more privacy friendly the growing pressures on its business model may be too strong for that inclination to take hold.

3.4   Change from the community?

So, on the face of it, all that leaves is the possibility of change from the community, norms, in Lessig's terms,[63] or more directly the kind of community action suggested by network communitarians such as Murray. This is where symbiotic regulation can come into play. Google has shown itself to be responsive to customers' needs and wishes, and if it believes that its users really desire privacy or even anonymity it will find a way to provide it, building a business model that incorporates it. Google now

---

[62] See https://en-gb.facebook.com/about/graphsearch.
[63] See Lessig, 2006.

earns more revenue outside the United States than in the United States,[64] so pressure from international markets such as the EU will be likely to have more impact than in the past.

If sufficient community pressure is put on Google, the company might offer solutions itself, perhaps in the form of a 'premium' service for those willing to pay, offering varying degrees of anonymity, or by showing the options directly on its own website. This latter method could allow Google to make the case directly for non-anonymised search, by allowing them to explain to users (in a form of words agreed with the regulators, for example) why Google would like to retain their search data, and how it can offer each user a better, more personalised search service as well as better, more appropriate advertising, a feature that people might appreciate. It might even find that by being more open, direct and honest about the way its search works, the public responds positively and keeps using Google in its current form – or even in a more 'intrusive' form, giving away more personal details, as in Google+ – but this time with full, explicit and informed consent.

Following this kind of logic, there may be other ways for the Working Party and other regulators to proceed even if they accept that it may not be possible to win the argument directly or through the legal process. One way could be to say to Google 'you can have your data retention if and only if you provide good access – highlighted on your search pages themselves – to all the data you hold on the user, in a form they can read and understand, giving them a chance to correct or delete if appropriate'.

That could satisfy most of the Working Party's requirements, and if combined with up-front information (perhaps as part of a short, blunt, log-in process) most of the rest of the problems could be resolved. The precise form of this information could be agreed between Google and the Working Party. This could benefit both:

- From the Working Party's perspective, the user's rights under data protection are satisfied much more. The right to know, see and understand what data is being stored is a fundamental data protection principle.
- From Google's perspective, it could actually allow their profiles to be improved, and thus allow advertising to be targeted even more accurately.

---

[64] Google's sales figures for the first quarter of 2008 showed 51 per cent of sales outside the United States for the first time, and this trend has continued. See for example http://news.bbc.co.uk/1/hi/business/7353677.stm.

There are many objections to such a solution, and it could involve large costs to implement, though they would be likely to pale into insignificance compared to the near half-billion Euros the EU fined Microsoft. Nonetheless, it gives an idea of how some degree of horse-trading might be possible. Indeed, Google has gone some way towards implementing this through its 'Google dashboard',[65] providing access to some of the data that is held about individuals and moving closer to implementing something at least partly akin to the idea of collaborative consent.[66]

3.5   The future of data retention

The struggle over data retention is far from over. As discussed in the previous chapter there are still strong forces working in both directions, as the emphasis on counterterrorism shows few signs of dissipating and the security challenges to privacy remain both present and powerful, as the drive towards full internet surveillance demonstrates. The privacy lobby, however, seems to have some momentum of its own, illustrated by the strength of the Working Party's opinion. That momentum has continued in many ways, not least in the strength of the proposed reforms to the data protection regime.[67] Public interest and concern over privacy appear to be growing all the time, and it seems likely that there will be a growing level of opposition at least to mandatory, generalised data retention. As noted in the previous chapter, introductions of broad-based internet surveillance have met with significant resistance whenever they have occurred.

Some aspects of the problems relating to search data have not even been addressed. One of these is the issue of profiles themselves. Even when search data etc. is deleted, it is possible that profiles derived from that data could be retained and considered 'current' rather than past data, and thus not covered by any requirement to delete data older than a certain age. These could include categorisations or more sophisticated descriptions of individuals, and other kinds of profiling data. How does data protection legislation cover this? How would it in the envisaged reforms? At the moment this seems far from clear, but it should, and pressure should be put on regulators to ensure that it is.

At the moment the fight is over data protection and data retention, but perhaps it should go further, and move on to the right to have data about

---

[65] See www.google.com/dashboard.   [66] See Chapter 2, Section 3.
[67] See Chapter 4, Section 2.

you deleted, and not just if the data is not true. As noted above, there are many reasons to care about the amount of data being gathered and processed. The combination of these and the risks of data vulnerability that will be discussed in Chapter 7 make a strong case for a right to delete personal data, the third of the rights suggested in this book.

4 Conclusions and rights-based solutions

The first and clearest conclusion from the case study is that the tension between data protection and data retention exists, not just theoretically but in practice, and that it is an issue that has not yet been resolved. What is more, it is an issue that is of serious concern not only to the Working Party but also potentially to everyone. Currently, data retention applies only to traffic data arising from telephony, email and their equivalents – which in itself is a significant concern, as the Working Party has signalled – but if it is extended to cover search data, as Google has suggested that it might and as the movement towards more universal internet surveillance[68] indicates, that concern would be much magnified. Further extensions to cover other forms of data could make this even worse. Such extensions would offer threats to privacy and autonomy, and should be opposed.

The question then is whether the compensating 'goods' that arise from data retention are sufficient to override these concerns over autonomy. The 'goods' arise in three areas; economic benefits to business, security benefits to governments and 'service' benefits to consumers – the positive aspects of better targeted advertising and providing more appropriate links. The first of these is difficult to argue. There are effective business models that do not rely on this kind of data retention, though they might not have the potential for quite such astronomical profits. The second, the security question, is hard to answer fully but the Working Party questioned 'whether the justification for an obligatory and general data retention ... is grounded in crystal-clear evidence',[69] and offered suggestions of alternative ways to solve these security problems.

The third of these goods, 'service' benefits to consumers, is beneficial, but would be as beneficial if it was done with consultation and consent. On the surface, therefore it seems that the 'goods' are not sufficient to justify this kind of constriction on our autonomy. At the very least, further

---

[68] See Chapter 4, Section 3.
[69] Opinion 113 of the Working Party, page 2, http://ec.europa.eu/justice_home/fsj/privacy/docs/wpdocs/2005/wp113_en.pdf.

investigation is needed and further evidence provided as to the benefits of allowing this to take place.

4.1   A right to roam with privacy

As has been shown, the way that search engine providers currently gather, hold and use search data represents a risk to both privacy and autonomy. If the balance between the interests of businesses, governments and individuals is to be found this needs to change. Following the kind of balanced, rights-based approach suggested in this book is one way that this change could be brought about. Here that would mean *the right to roam the internet with privacy.*

This right could solve many of the problems surrounding search engines. In essence, it would be a right to roam the internet without data being gathered about you.

This 'right to roam with privacy' would cover all the principal methods of navigating the web. It would, for example, not only cover search data but also clickstream data, whether it is gathered by ISPs or directly from websites monitoring where their visitors have come from and are going to, as well as all the emergent new methods of navigating the internet discussed above. The right would not be an absolute right, but would be the default position. If a website, ISP, search engine or other navigation provider wishes to gather data, they would need to get genuine, informed consent or have some other competing right that can outweigh the obligation to the person roaming the internet: a targeted investigation into criminal activity, for example.

This could effectively require the search engine providers to offer two levels of service: a basic, effectively anonymised one as a default, and a personalised, data-gathering one as an option. The basic one could operate similarly to the AskEraser, with data kept only for hours unless there is a specific reason to hold it for longer, allowing targeted rather than general data retention. The premium service could work as Google does now, but require a registration and log-in process that would be set up clearly enough to satisfy informed consent requirements. This could be designed to allow the search engine to actually gather more information than before, and potentially allow a business to benefit from it, but without compromising privacy and our autonomy. Indeed, it could be argued that Google has set up an infrastructure to allow this to happen already: its normal search could be without gathering, and search through Google+ could (and does) allow all the data gathering and more.

When applied to ISPs, there could be a similar two-level approach: a basic service without data gathering, and a 'super' service with data gathering, to which a user needs to opt in. That 'super' service could be cheaper, but it should be made clear to subscribers why it is cheaper, and what the subscribers are giving up in order to get their discount. It may well be that the vast majority of subscribers would choose cheapness over privacy, but they should be given that choice.

The right to roam with privacy would work in balance with the interests of security and of economics. An apposite analogy is that of CCTV, something that should not be used universally but can be useful where it is really needed. For security purposes, where information leads the authorities to be concerned about a particular individual, that individual's activities (including search and clickstream data) can be followed. Similarly, if certain websites are of interest, those sites can be monitored, and visitors to them 'tagged' and tracked. For economic purposes, commercial sites can track people so long as appropriate, standardised warnings are placed on those sites to alert visitors, the equivalents to the signs saying 'CCTV is used in this area'. Where sites want to gather more than the basic data, they would require registration and log-in procedures, again with appropriate warnings beforehand.

The right to roam with privacy would have implications not only for the actions of the likes of search engines and ISPs, but for behavioural advertisers (which are looked at in depth in the next chapter) and for surveillance and data retention by governments. As noted in the previous chapter, there is an increasing movement towards a 'universal' form of internet surveillance where everyone operating on the internet is subject to surveillance at all times, with their actions both monitored in real time and the data gathered and held for later use. A right to roam with privacy would make such surveillance inappropriate: it would require privacy to be the default, and surveillance the exception. In particular, it would demand a targeted rather than universal approach: 'surveillance minimisation'.[70] There would need to be a reason before surveillance takes place: this reflects the need to balance rights, as suggested throughout this book. The strong resistance shown in so many places – not least the UK – whenever universal surveillance has been suggested is indicative of the feeling that many people have that they have a right *not* to be under surveillance. That in turn implies a right to roam the internet with privacy.

---

[70] See Chapter 10, Section 2.4.

Having an established and coherent right of this kind has a number of benefits. First of all, it could help in the process of harmonising legislation. As the case study showed, where there are conflicts or inconsistencies, businesses will take full advantage. Fleischer managed to bring into his argument not only the conflict between EU data protection and data retention regulations but conflict between European and US regulation, and even with specific rules in Germany.[71] Clear and consistent rights have a better chance of producing clear and harmonised legislation.

Secondly, it could help to ensure that individual pieces of legislation are clearer, unambiguous and more precise. Particularly in such a technical area, legislation needs to be carefully and clearly drafted. The Data Retention Directive was not; it has holes big enough to drive a juggernaut through, and Google did just that.[72] Such lack of clarity again allows businesses to take advantage, to the potential detriment of individual privacy and autonomy. As will be seen in Chapter 7, a similar story has developed over the 'right to be forgotten', and the lack of clarity has been one of the weapons that opponents of the right have been using to attack it.

Thirdly, it could help regulators to work better together. The fact that Google was able to use the EU's own data retention regulations as what was, in effect, an excuse not to comply with data protection regulations highlights the problem here. Those drafting the data retention regulations should have responded better to the Working Party's opinion on the matter. Again, clear and strong rights can reduce the chances of internal disputes between regulators.

4.2   Solutions in practice

The kinds of right being considered here would operate in balance with the interests of businesses and government, recognising that businesses and governments can play a positive role. Privacy advocates can sometimes have a tendency not to recognise this; there has been something of a movement to demonise Google,[73] to present it as the 'bad guy' in every way. Not only is that missing the point (for Google has made using the

---

[71] See letter from Peter Fleischer to Peter Schaar, 10 June 2007, page 4.

[72] See letter from Peter Fleischer to Peter Schaar, p. 3, for a comprehensive attack on the clarity of the Data Retention Directive.

[73] Books such as Vaidhyanathan's The Googlization of Everything' paint Google almost entirely in black. See for example HYPERLINK "http://techliberation.com/2011/03/09/book-review-siva-vaidhyanathan's-"googlization-of-everything"/" http://techliberation.com/2011/03/09/book-review-siva-vaidhyanathan's-"googlization-of-everything"/.

internet far easier and more productive) but it appears highly unlikely to produce results. Google has created an image of itself as publicly responsible and responsive to consumer wishes. The most likely way to get Google to change is to work with it, following the logic of symbiotic regulation, not to fight against it.

Similarly, a lesson to learn from the case study is that regulators do sometimes work for the benefit of their constituents. The Working Party has been bold enough to take on not only one of the biggest players in the internet world, but to stand up to another part of its own system, the data retention lobby, who are backed by much stronger, more powerful and better organised supporters. Privacy advocates should recognise this, applaud the Working Party for its efforts so far and encourage it to continue to fight for their corner.

The dispute between Google and the Working Party has been a crucial test, but it is one that is still unfinished. Will Google ultimately react positively and imaginatively and come up with radical solutions that both protect privacy and enable it to build its business? Will it take what might be called 'the Microsoft approach' and essentially ignore almost everything that the regulator says, and accept the fines when they finally come along? Will those who wish to extend data retention to cover more and more areas rescue it from its dilemma? Alternatively, will the lobbying efforts against a stronger data protection regime, in which Google has played a part, reap returns in the form of a more 'business-friendly' form of regulation, one that interferes less with its business model?

Ultimately, the most important question is whether the suggested solutions have any real chance of success. In particular, in this case, is a right to roam with privacy conceivable from a business perspective? That issue will be examined in depth in the last three chapters of this book. It will be suggested that though it would require adjustments to their business models, these could and should be far from insurmountable. If there is sufficient public interest and political support, it could be possible.

6

Behavioural tracking

1 Behavioural tracking and targeting

Behavioural tracking and targeting epitomise some of the key aspects of the Symbiotic Web. In simple terms, behavioural trackers gather data from people browsing the web and use that data to tailor the information that those people receive, usually in order to make a profit. The data gathered may be extensive and detailed: not just the websites visited but when, how, what links are followed, every click made and the timing between them, the device used to browse, the precise software used and much more. All this information can be analysed, and profiles can be built based on people's behaviour.

There are two stages to the process: the *tracking* – that is, the monitoring of what a user is doing on the web – and the *targeting*, which is using that tracking in order to send the tailored information, whether it be advertising or other content. The distinction between the tracking and the targeting is an important one, and one that, as will be seen, behavioural trackers and targeters sometimes seem to want to gloss over. The 'Do Not Track' initiative, for example, may well turn out in practice to allow people to block off targeted advertisements, but not stop the tracking itself. Data will still be gathered, profiles will still be constructed, and may well be used for purposes other than direct targeting of advertising.

Both the tracking and the targeting parts of the process have important implications. These, together with the fact that behavioural targeting has been one of the fastest growing features of the internet in recent years, make their examination particularly useful in the study of the implications and problems associated with the symbiosis.

1.1   Who does behavioural tracking and targeting?

Behavioural targeting in one form or other is already common on the net. Amongst others it is already used by Google,[1] Yahoo!,[2] AOL[3] and Microsoft,[4] as well as by a number of specialist advertising and marketing companies such as AudienceScience,[5] Omniture[6] and Netmining.[7]

The marketing industry is highly enthusiastic about behavioural targeting, suggesting that not only does it work well for advertisers,[8] but that it gives customers what they want, 'improving user experiences' and suggesting that audiences actually welcome this kind of activity. Mark Wilmot, writing in *Marketing Daily* in 2009, said:

> Something amazing happens when marketing efforts are actually relevant to people. We see this step as initiating that crucial dialogue. And shoppers, for their part, are replying; essentially giving permission to marketers to learn their habits and respond accordingly.[9]

What he meant by 'essentially giving permission' reveals a great deal about the way that the advertising industry views the issue of consent: as something that customers do automatically, implicitly, just by participating in their programmes or accepting their services, without any kind of real debate or discussion.

Privacy advocates take a diametrically opposite view, seeing behavioural targeting as a pernicious and potentially dangerous practice.[10]

---

[1] Most directly through Google AdSense. See www.google.com/adsense/static/en_US/ AfcOverview.html?sourceid=aso&subid=ww-ww-et-pubsol&medium=link.

[2] See http://advertising.yahoo.com/adsolution#product=Behavioral.

[3] See http://advertising.aol.com/.

[4] See http://advertising.microsoft.com/en-uk/behavioral-targeting.

[5] See www.audiencescience.com/.

[6] See www.omniture.com.

[7] See www.netmining.com/.

[8] A US study commissioned by the Network Advertising Initiative (NAI), a coalition of online marketing companies, suggested that in 2009 behaviourally targeted advertising was more than twice as effective as ordinary 'Run of Network' advertising (measured by average conversion rate) (6.8 per cent v. 2.8 per cent). See Beales, 2009.

[9] In *Marketing Daily*, 28 July 2009, www.mediapost.com/publications/article/110489/put-out-the-welcome-mat.html.

[10] See for example Privacy International's view at www.privacyinternational.org/article. shtml?cmd%5B347%5D=x-347–559082, or the Center for Democracy & Technology's guidelines at www.cdt.org/privacy/pet/Privacy_Controls_IPWG.pdf.

A 2009 study by a group from the University of Pennsylvania and the Berkeley Center for Law & Technology suggested that the American public is closer to the views of the privacy advocates than those of the marketing industry: 66 per cent of adults did not want marketers to tailor advertisements to their interests, rising to between 73 per cent and 86 per cent when they were informed about the methods involved in gathering and using data.[11]

1.2   Phorm, behavioural tracking and symbiotic regulation

The story of the most controversial of the behavioural tracking and targeting systems, Phorm's 'Webwise', illustrates many of the problems associated with behavioural tracking. The failure of Phorm's Webwise and the reasons behind that failure are salutary lessons for businesses, governments and others, particularly for those wishing to use behavioural targeting and tracking. Seen through the lens of symbiotic regulation, it was an inability to appreciate the complexity and nature of the regulatory matrix in which Phorm operated that lay behind many of its mistakes, and in the end led to the failure of its business idea. Ultimately, Phorm failed because it did not understand the nature of the Symbiotic Web. Symbiosis succeeds when both sides of the symbiosis benefit from the relationship, as happens to a substantial degree with business models such as those of Google, Facebook and others. With Webwise, only Phorm stood to benefit. In effect, it was offering a parasitic rather than a symbiotic model.

Painfully, almost tortuously, that parasitic model collapsed: the parasite was rejected and effectively purged from the system. That purging has had some serious implications, not all of which are positive. A technologically innovative and potentially beneficial stream of business ideas may be lost, delayed or hamstrung as a result. This might have been avoided if the situation had been better understood.

Part of the misunderstanding relates to the kind of rights that people think they should have and the rights that Phorm and other behavioural trackers believe that they have. People appeared to believe that they had the kind of privacy rights that would prevent monitoring and tracking of the sort performed by Phorm's Webwise, while Phorm stuck by a legal interpretation of rights, as set out in the Data Protection Act, which it interpreted in its own particular way. This highlights one of the principal

---

[11] See Turow, King, Hoofnagle, Bleakley and Hennessy, 2009, particularly p. 3.

problems in the field and one of the most important reasons to establish clearly understood rights: the gap between detailed law and principled rights. The new proposed right, the right to monitor the monitors, would help to bridge that gap.

1.3   Tracking, targeting and consent

One of the most important points to come out of this case study is the need for the web symbiosis to be a consensual one: not only must both sides of the relationship benefit, but they must understand that benefit, and consent to the process. Behavioural trackers have so far ridden somewhat roughshod over the idea of consent, dealing with it on at best a superficial level and often effectively avoiding it entirely. If a way can be found for this to be changed it could not only protect the rights of the individuals and in particular their autonomy, but also provide an environment in which business ideas have a better chance of success.

The concept introduced in Chapter 2, 'collaborative consent', is particularly applicable here. The internet provides a medium for immediate and interactive communication that allows a continuous, two-way process to be possible and the symbiosis of the Symbiotic Web to remain both benign and consensual. This kind of consent is not only apt but the only kind of consent that is appropriate.

2   Does any of this matter? Isn't it just about advertising?

Behavioural tracking and targeting are primarily used for advertising, and it is possible therefore to consider this issue not to be of great significance. The regulatory suggestions to date have largely only concerned the advertising industry. That, however, does not take into account the full nature of current uses or the future potential of the techniques and systems that have been developed.

Firstly, while targeting is currently about advertising, the techniques developed and systems used will be equally useable for other kinds of targeting. The same systems used to target people to sell to can be used to target people for scams or other identity-related crimes, and the more accurately scammers can target their scams, the more likely those scams are to be successful. Governments and others can use targeting techniques for their own purposes, both appropriate and contentious. Here, as in other areas, both criminals and governments are likely to 'piggyback' on commercial efforts, both copying techniques and actually accessing and using commercial data and systems for their own purposes, something that will be looked at in more depth in Chapter 7, when data vulnerability is examined, and which came very much to the fore in 2013 as a result of the PRISM revelations. So though targeting is currently largely concerned with advertising, it is not always so, nor is it necessarily going to remain the case.

Secondly, advertising on the internet has one significant difference from most forms of advertising: its success or failure can be proven. Advertisers can and do know whether people have followed their advertisements, and can then keep monitoring to see whether they have made a sale. Much of the advertising on the internet is on a 'pay-per-click' basis, so that advertisers only pay when potential customers actually click on their advertisements and visit their sites. This in turn means that advertising providers such as Google will only place advertisements that people will follow, and because of the enormous scale of Google and others, it means that they have accurate and analysable records of which kind of advertisements work, why, when and on whom. Ultimately, that is likely to mean that advertising will be more successful and more persuasive.

2.1   Profiling

The profiling used by behavioural trackers has very little to do with psychological or sociological profiling, but instead is a mathematical, analytical system, and as a consequence significantly more accurate. It starts from the kind of thing that an Apple iTunes user might see: a recommendation for something by Crosby, Stills and Nash because there is a song by Joni Mitchell in their library. iTunes does not recommend Crosby, Stills and Nash because Apple employs specialists in folk rock to tell them what people who listen to Joni Mitchell might like, but because they have built up a database of millions of users' musical tastes, and it shows that many people who have Joni Mitchell on their system also have Crosby, Stills and Nash on their system. It is a mathematical exercise, not an aesthetic one.

This has a number of implications. It means that for accurate profiling of this kind you need extensive databases; this is one of the reasons for the gathering of vast quantities of data. The data thus gathered is used not only for information about the individual concerned, but to help target others more accurately too. It also means that profilers need powerful computer systems capable of working with the immense databases thus compiled. These two factors together mean that the best and most successful profilers (and targeters) tend to be the largest companies, with the largest number of users and the deepest pockets, such as Google, Apple and Amazon. This in turn has regulatory implications: it puts particular emphasis on the need and ability to regulate these biggest of companies, and it means that if ways can be found to ensure that the biggest of companies behave ethically, appropriately and in ways that are positive for individuals, then significant strides will have been made to solve the overall problems.

The next key implication of this method of profiling and targeting is that it has the potential to be much more accurate than 'traditional' psychological, sociological or 'human expert' profiling. Ian Ayres (2007, pp. 1–10) gives a series of examples of how this kind of statistical analysis outperforms human experts in even the most surprising and often counterintuitive fields, from success in sports to assessing the potential quality of a particular year of Bordeaux wine. As the amounts of data and the power of computers have increased dramatically in recent years, and as the analytical techniques have been developed and refined, these profiling and predictive systems have become more and more accurate. This trend seems certain to continue: future systems are likely to be more refined and potentially far more accurate.

Further to all of this, another level of analysis becomes possible when data is aggregated, not just similar and apparently closely related data, but seemingly unconnected and dissimilar data, to create even greater data sets and allow much more complex and detailed profiling. For example, if you start with data about musical taste, then add age and location data, and then add to that data about income, occupation, education and marital status, the number of further possible inferences that can be made increases exponentially. The sample sizes are sufficiently large that statistical analysis is very powerful, and applying the kind of predictive techniques discussed by Ayres makes targeting even more effective (2007, pp. 135–8). The 2013 study by Kosinski and others has confirmed the power and accuracy of this profiling, and its ability to make inferences from the most apparently trivial of data.

2.2   Imperfect profiling

This kind of profiling and targeting is by its nature imperfect, but from a commercial perspective this does not really matter. An advertiser does not need all its targets to follow its advertisements, or to make a sale to all those who follow its advertisements, it just needs enough of both to find sufficient real customers. For other purposes, however, imperfect targeting can have significant implications: those engaged in counter-criminal activities, for example, need to ensure that they do not round up the innocent with the guilty, while serving an inappropriate advertisement may have implications wider than just failing to make a sale, particularly where products might have sensitivities, such as books about religion or sexuality.

The problem of imperfect identification needs particular attention. When data is gathered from one particular device, how can it be possible to tell the identity of the person using that device? Is it the same person who generally uses that device? Where devices are shared, for example in a family household, how can the website visited tell which member of the family is using the device at a particular time? If there are casual or visiting users, will the data gathered from their use of the device be merged in with that by the regular user? There are systems on most computers, tablets and so forth to allow individuals to set up secure, personalised profiles, but are they always used? Can it be appropriate for a website visited or other profiling system to assume that they are being used?

Phorm, the subject of the central case study here, seemed to be doing exactly that. In an online interview with the BBC, Phorm's spokesperson replied to a question about 'surprise' advertising appearing – e.g. a man researching wedding venues whose partner is then bombarded by advertisements for dresses and rings – that 'most people have a separate login if they are sharing a computer'.[12] This is a bold assumption to make, and the consequences of it being wrong could be significant.

2.3   Predictive profiling

A particular area of concern in relation to autonomy is the use of profiles to predict people's behaviour, and the use of those predictions to control that behaviour. A prime example of this is also detailed in Ayres, 2007, (pp. 30–1): the use by Harrah's casinos of profiling information to effectively manipulate its customers into spending more money. Harrah's tries to assess an individual's 'pain point': the amount of money a particular gambler can lose in one session and still enjoy the experience. This pain point is calculated based upon a combination of personal and demographic details and Harrah's own data gathered about all its customers' gambling habits. Harrah's regular customers use a swipe card system to gamble, so Harrah's knows exactly how much money a customer has lost at any time.

---

[12] In http://news.bbc.co.uk/1/hi/technology/7283333.stm.

When that customer is nearing their pain point, Harrah's sends a representative called a 'luck ambassador' to interrupt them and offer them a free drink or a meal, and Harrah's also knows what kind of food or drink that customer usually buys when they visit Harrah's casinos. This break cuts off the pain, and leaves the customer refreshed and ready to spend more money in Harrah's after they have had their food or drink.

The Harrah's example is an 'offline' example, but the techniques used give some idea both as to what can become possible with this kind of system and the dangers of businesses having too much information about their customers. Do Harrah's customers know what is happening to them? Did they consent to be monitored and manipulated in this way when they signed up for the swipe card system that has gathered all their data? From a legal perspective, almost certainly: the small print on the agreement that they signed will have covered all such eventualities. Whether they really understood that agreement, let alone how Harrah's would be using the data that they had agreed that Harrah's would be able to gather, is another question.

For all these reasons behavioural tracking and targeting are not 'just' about advertising; they are much more significant than that. The advertising industry has barely scratched the surface of the possibilities that could be developed from behavioural tracking, targeting and profiling.

3   Phorm

The story of Phorm demonstrates many of the issues that are of concern here. Phorm attempted to implement a system that would monitor and analyse people's entire web-browsing behaviour, using that analysis to profile those people and target them for advertising. The way that it intended to do that monitoring, the extent to which it was done surreptitiously, and without the meaningful consent of those being monitored, made it highly controversial. This controversy eventually brought about the failure of Phorm's business plan in the UK. The manner of that failure and the roles played by the online community, by other businesses, by privacy advocate groups, and by politicians and lawmakers both in the UK and Europe are revealing. The role of the online community and privacy advocates in the process was crucial: they highlighted what Phorm was doing and why it was of concern, they lobbied and brought other groups onto their side, alerted politicians and lawmakers, including those in Europe, eventually leading to the abandonment of Phorm by its erstwhile business allies, and the collapse of Phorm's business model.

The story provides a graphic demonstration of how regulation on the internet can function in practice, and how and why Murray's theory of symbiotic regulation can be applied, as suggested throughout this book. It also helps to outline the role that rights can play in the process.

3.1   The origins of Phorm

Phorm was controversial from the beginning. The company that became Phorm began as 121Media, in what the BBC describes as 'the murky world of adware and spyware'.[13] Phorm is at pains to point out that its origins lay in adware rather than spyware,[14] though its principal product, PeopleOnPage, was classified as spyware by F-Secure, one of the main anti-spyware software providers.[15] As Kent Ertugrul, Phorm's founder, puts it:

> what happened was it became very clear to us that there was no distinction in people's minds between adware – which is legitimate – and spyware. So we did something unprecedented which was we turned around to our shareholders and we shut down all our revenues. We weren't sued, we weren't pressed by anyone, we just said 'this is not consistent with the company's core objectives.'[16]

121Media withdrew all its products and reformed as 'Phorm'[17] and began to develop its 'Webwise' system, in the then emerging field of behavioural targeting. With Webwise, Phorm took behavioural tracking to a new level. It did not just track particular aspects of surfers' web activities, activities on particular websites or uses of particular web services, but attempted to track their entire web activity. With a few specific exceptions, every website visited, every click made, every service used would be logged. Moreover, though its initial service was based on targeted

---

[13] See the BBC technology pages 'Phorm: Your Questions Answered', on http://news.bbc. co.uk/1/hi/technology/7283333.stm.

[14] Adware is effectively a way to acquire software: a user can download a product 'for free', but must accept advertising as a consequence. Spyware is a more intrusive version, which, generally unbeknownst to the user, installs software onto their system to monitor their activities and serve 'appropriate' advertisements to them, while at the same time often slowing or corrupting their computer systems. For an analysis of the differences between them, see www.webopedia.com/DidYouKnow/Internet/2004/spyware.asp.

[15] See www.f-secure.com/sw-desc/apropos.shtml.

[16] From an interview with Kent Ertugrul in *The Register*.

[17] www.phorm.com/.

advertising, from the start its ambition was greater: it wanted to provide 'a personalised internet', including both advertising and content.

> Webwise will automatically start working for you by understanding your interests from the pages you visit, matching them to the content of millions of websites, and providing you with personalised content and relevant advertising.[18]

In this way Webwise can be seen as epitomising the Symbiotic Web, gathering personal data, monitoring individuals' behaviour, and attempting to tailor their whole web experience on the basis of that behaviour.

Achieving this depth of monitoring involved two key things: some inventive technology and an alliance with cooperative ISPs. Richard Clayton of the Computer Laboratory at the University of Cambridge analysed the technology in depth.[19] As he puts it:

> The basic concept behind the Phorm architecture is that they wish to take a copy of the traffic that passes between an end-user and a website. This enables their systems to inspect what requests were made to the website and to determine what content came back from that website. An understanding of the types of websites visited is used to target adverts at particular users. (Clayton, 2008, p. 2)

The way Webwise does this can be broken down into three key phases: monitoring, analysing and targeting.

Phase 1: Monitoring – the tracking phase

A user's web activity is monitored by intercepting the instructions given by the user at the ISP level and attempting to filter out what it believes is useful from that activity, building up a profile of the individual user. Webwise does not monitor all internet traffic produced by a user: it monitors only web traffic, rather than email, file transfer or other non-web traffic. It also makes an attempt to ensure some degree of privacy by ignoring 'known' webmail sites (based on a list maintained by Phorm) and sites that are private enough not to permit search engines to examine them.

This monitoring mechanism involves putting a 'false' cookie onto the user's computer by masquerading as the website that the user wishes to visit. For example, if the user sends out a command to visit www.bbc.co.uk, a computer run by the ISP will pretend to be www.bbc.co.uk and

---

[18] From www.phorm.com/consumers/index.html.
[19] First of all in Clayton, 2008. The Phorm 'Webwise' System, at www.cl.cam.ac.uk/~rnc1/080518-phorm.pdf, and then continuing analyses in Clayton's blog at www.lightbluetouchpaper.org/.

send back a cookie to the user's PC as though it was www.bbc.co.uk. That cookie will contain an individual 'identifier' that is then used by Phorm to monitor the activities of that user on the www.bbc.co.uk domain. That identifier (known as a UID) is used as the principal way of identifying a user throughout the Webwise process, and is one of the ways in which Phorm claims to maintain privacy. It is a randomly generated number, with no connection to the individual. The efficacy of this anonymity is a complex issue – and a crucial one. Phorm uses it not only as what it believes is a way to ensure that it is not covered by data protection law (since the data it holds is not linked to an individual, just to a UID) but as a way of portraying itself not just as a 'privacy-friendly' company but as a company in the vanguard of the fight *in favour* of privacy.

At first glance this UID system would appear to offer the kind of anonymity that Phorm suggests, but this was hotly disputed. As Nicholas Bohm of the Foundation for Information Policy Research puts it:

> If parts of the visited site use the HTTPS protocol for secure browsing, the cookie containing the Phorm UID will be sent to the site, where the UID can be read; and if a webmaster wishes to do so, he can read the UID in any case using Javascript. The result is that any site which holds any personally identifying information about a user, and many do, can associate that information with the Phorm UID and indeed also with the user's IP address visible to the site. In view of this, Phorm's claims for the anonymity of its processes are, to put it no higher, a considerable exaggeration. (Bohm, 2008, p. 2)

Moreover, what may be technically possible now is not necessarily an indicator of what may be possible in the future. As Ross Anderson, Professor of Security Engineering at the Cambridge University Computer Lab has said, historically, anonymising technology has never worked.[20]

There is another side to the question of anonymity for Phorm and for all behavioural trackers. Interaction with the real world can effectively bypass all these attempts at anonymity. Suppose, for example, a web surfer has browsed for something they would wish to keep private. A relatively harmless example could be one partner secretly researching wedding venues, not wishing their partner to know about it. The Phorm system may not know who that person is but anyone *in the real world*, someone watching them over their shoulder, for example,[21] who sees that person

---

[20] Quoted in the *Evening Standard*, in March 2008. See www.thisislondon.co.uk/standard-home/article-23449601-web-users-angry-at-isps-spyware-tie-up.do;jsessionid=D5AA1541C91446314EAD7013363AB159.

[21] Known as 'shoulder surfing'.

served with a personalised advert while they browse, will be able to identify them. The link can be made in the world of atoms, even if it is not made in the world of bits. Moreover, several people might share the same computer and not always log in using different accounts; a system such as Webwise would mean that they might be served by advertisements targeted at each other, and hence learn things about each other that might compromise their privacy. Phorm may provide technical and legal anonymity, but that anonymity could be fatally flawed in the real world.

Phase 2: Analysis

The analysis phase works by examining the individual web pages visited by a particular user. It operates in a similar way to the way in which search engines inspect web pages, extracting and examining the words on the page, comparing them with other pages to determine what kind of a page it is. For search engines, this is then used to determine which search terms should lead to the listing of a page, while for Webwise it is used effectively to determine the profile of a person. The processes are similar, the results converse. There is also one very big difference: when a page is analysed by a search engine, the owner of that page should at least in some senses benefit from that analysis, as their pages will be more easily found by the right kind of people. When a page is analysed by Phorm, the owners of websites whose pages are scanned do not benefit. The prime beneficiaries are Phorm and their clients, who will be better able to find potential targets.[22]

Once the analysis of a page visited has been performed, the Webwise system distils it into a short record: the URL of the page, the top ten words with which it can characterise the page, the search terms the user might have used to find the page at first, and the UID of the user.

Phase 3: Targeting

These short records are matched against 'channels' that have been set up by Phorm on instructions from Phorm's advertisers. If this profile matches with the specification of the channel, then that UID becomes eligible for an advertisement from that channel, and a further 'date-

[22] Phorm assumed that if a website permitted search engines to examine it, then it would also consent to Phorm's analysis. As Phorm's representatives told Richard Clayton 'we work on the basis that if a site allows spidering of its contents by search engines, then its material is being openly published. Conversely, if the site has disallowed spidering and indexing by search engines, we respect those restrictions'. See Richard Clayton's analysis (2008). There are also parallels with the arguments made in the much discussed case of *eBay* v. *Bidder's Edge*, 100 F.Supp.2d 1058 (N.D. Cal. 2000).

stamped' record is made, recording the name of the channel and the UID. The earlier record, containing the visited URL, the search terms and the frequent words, is immediately discarded. Then, if the user visits a participating website (one that takes advertisements from Phorm), the system will look up which channels a UID is matched to, and an 'appropriate' advertisement from one of those channels will appear on that website. Which advertisement appears depends on the rules set up by the website and by the relevant channels. If more than one advertisement is eligible the advertisement that makes Phorm the most money is placed.

Phorm's channels are in effect profiles: categories into which individuals are being put, which are used to determine what kind of content will be delivered to them. These categories are defined and set by Phorm and its clients, for the benefit of Phorm and its clients, not for the individual. Where there is an option, the option chosen is the one that financially benefits Phorm the most. That is the essence of this kind of profiling and precisely the kind of risk associated with the Symbiotic Web.[23]

There is one significant difference between Phorm and other behavioural advertisers. Webwise monitors and analyses *all* an individual's activities, not just those on a particular site or system. Google's behavioural targeting, by comparison, generally works only on data gathered through searches made using Google's search engine and other Google services, so if a user searches with Yahoo! or Bing instead, that data will be neither available nor used by Google for their analysis. Amazon analyses a customer's activity on the Amazon site, and Facebook the activities on the Facebook site, though Facebook's recent 'Beacon' service extended this through the formation of an alliance of online retailers, allowing each of them to share the data gathered during visits to the others' sites.[24] Webwise took it to a new level, gathering data not just from a selection of sites and services, but from all sites and services except those that specifically and actively opt out of the system.

The way that Webwise did this is by working at the ISP level. From a practical perspective it was a system that needed to be deployed by an ISP, so that it could be in a position to intercept all the web surfer's activities. The key to

---

[23] This method of analysis and targeting is very simple, boiling down a web page into a ten-word record, then matching it against an existing set of pre-created channels, rather than designing and creating channels based on an analysis of users' behavioural patterns. It would be false to assume, however, that the simplicity of the analysis is something that would be true either for Phorm as it develops or for future behavioural targeting systems.

[24] See Section 5.3 below.

the Phorm business model was that Phorm aimed to work very closely with three of the UK's largest ISPs: BT, TalkTalk and Virgin Media.

3.2   Phorm and the law

Nicholas Bohm, of the Foundation for Information Policy Research, in his legal analysis of Phorm (2008), suggested that the deployment by an ISP of the Phorm architecture would involve four different forms of illegality, for which the ISP would be primarily liable, and for which Phorm would be liable as an inciter:

1. Interception of communications, an offence contrary to Section 1 of the Regulation of Investigatory Powers Act 2000 (RIPA). This relates to the monitoring phase, where the Phorm architecture, as managed and operated by the ISP, intercepts the instructions sent by the surfer to a website (in the example above, to www.bbc.co.uk) in order to copy them (2008, pp. 3–11).
2. Fraud, an offence contrary to Section 1 of the Fraud Act 2006. This relates to the way in which the Phorm server masquerades as the target server, in order to make the surfer's web browser accept the Phorm cookie (in the example above, the Phorm server would falsely represent itself to be the BBC server) (pp. 11–12).
3. The risk of committing civil wrongs actionable at the suit of website owners. Bohm suggests the example of the Bank of England, which like many other websites states categorically in its published privacy policy that it does not 'use cookies to collect information about you'. When Phorm is in action, it would look to most users as if the Bank of England is doing precisely that. Although the monitoring cookie would actually have been placed by Phorm, it would look to a user as though it were a Bank of England cookie. The owner of the site might therefore have civil remedies for false implication or even defamation, or potentially passing off or trademark infringement, where the name in the cookie includes a trademark (p. 16).
4. Unlawful processing of sensitive personal data, contrary to the Data Protection Act 1998 (DPA) (pp. 12-14).

These four issues hint at the deeper issues that lie behind not just Phorm but other behavioural targeting systems. The RIPA issue concerns the privacy of an individual's actions on the net to start with: whether people want or expect their web browsing to be private or not. The second and third issues are issues of good faith: when a surfer visits a website, can they expect that their interactions with that website just to be with that website, and not with another, unconnected third party?

The last of these legal issues, the data protection issue, is the most complex. Browsing activities can be some of the most personal, most intimate and most sensitive of activities, concerning everything from personal tastes to relationships, jobs and finance, plans for the future, even personal peccadilloes. Is there an expectation that this kind of thing is considered private?

Phorm sought advice from the Home Office on the RIPA issue. They asked two questions: firstly, do Phorm's actions constitute 'interception of communications' or not, and secondly if they do, is it lawful interception? There were delicate legal issues such as whether a 'person' has intercepted the communications, as required for RIPA to apply according to Section 2(2) of RIPA, or whether the contents of the communications have been 'made available' to that person, as required by Section 2(8) of RIPA. On the second question, if interception is deemed to have taken place, then it can only be lawful if both the sender and the intended recipient of the communication have consented to that interception. Phorm relied on the idea that surfers have consented to their service in some form (either through the terms and conditions of their ISP, or through some kind of direct consent whose precise form would be determined when their service comes into action) and on the assumption that if a website consents to be spidered for search engine purposes, then it has consented to have communications to it intercepted for Phorm's purposes. This latter assumption is highly debatable.

The memo received in response became available on the internet, and was far from conclusive on either question, but ultimately suggested that Webwise would be legal if the users gave explicit consent.[25] The nature of the correspondence between Phorm and the Home Office, however, as well as the advice that was eventually issued, gave rise to significant controversy and played a part in the eventual fall of Phorm.[26]

3.3   Phorm, sensitive personal data and consent

If all web browsing is intercepted, that web browsing will be likely to include information about the user that would be classified as 'sensitive personal

---

[25] See for example http://cryptome.org/ho-phorm.htm. The memo itself was 'leaked' to the web. See for example www.theguardian.com/technology/blog/2008/mar/12/homeofficeonphormitslegal.

[26] See Section 4 below.

data' according to the DPA. This is defined as information as to racial or ethnic origins, political opinions, religious beliefs, trade union membership, health, sexual life, any court proceedings existing and so forth.[27]

Schedule 3 of the DPA, which governs sensitive personal data, demands specifically *explicit* consent to its processing, and the processing may only be lawful if it is 'necessary' in the sense that it is needed to protect 'the vital interests of the data subject or another person' or for particular purposes related to the particular type of data.[28] There are a few exceptions, where the information has already become public, for example.[29] Some of the exceptions relate to particular data types, but overall these conditions are strong. They require that 'sensitive personal data' should only be processed where clearly necessary, rather than when a processor can benefit for business purposes.

The idea that sensitive personal data should require more stringent conditions is one that makes a good deal of sense, particularly from the perspective of advocates of autonomy and of human rights. The developing techniques of data aggregation and profiling, however, mean that it needs to be considered much more carefully. For example, though data concerning whether a person suffers from diabetes would be classified as 'sensitive personal data', data about whether the subject is a regular purchaser of sugar-free chocolate would not. Similarly, data about whether a man was homosexual would be considered to be 'sensitive personal data', but data suggesting that their preferred holiday destinations were San Francisco or Sydney or that they were members of the Barbra Streisand fan club would not. None of these facts specifically indicate that the individuals are respectively diabetic or homosexual, but if profiling is applied, even automatically, the chances of the individuals being classified within categories that consist mainly of diabetic or homosexual people would be high. What is more, these examples show only the more obvious and intuitive kinds of connections that could be made, and any kind of 'sensitive' data can be inferred from what appears to be non-sensitive data. With detailed processing and large-scale data aggregation, even the most seemingly innocuous data, from sports followed or the kinds of news items read to choice of snacks or time of surfing on the internet, can become highly significant. The data itself is not sensitive personal data but is capable of revealing sensitive personal data.[30]

---

[27] DPA, Schedule 2.   [28] See DPA, Schedule 3, for data-type-by-data-type details.
[29] DPA, Schedule 3, paragraph 5.
[30] See for example Kosinski, Stillwell and Graepel, 2013.

The chances that web-browsing behavioural data would neither contain sensitive data nor sufficient data from which sensitive data could be derived would be very small. That, therefore, could imply that the conditions set out in the DPA should apply. More importantly, it shows one of the weaknesses of the category system set out in data protection legislation. The categories of personal and sensitive personal data are becoming blurred and confused. On top of this the separation between personal and non-personal data is being further confused, as the idea of anonymisation,[31] with Phorm's UID system a prime example, comes under contestation. Data can shift between categories depending on time, processing and context.

If sensitive personal data rules apply to Phorm, specific, explicit consent must be obtained. Indeed, this issue of consent is the crux of the whole story.[32] Many aspects come into play here – issues of identity, for example, as discussed above. The person who is browsing the internet and having their details processed may well not be the person who entered into the contract with their ISP or the person who clicked 'OK' at any point where asked by Phorm, if indeed that has happened at all.

That raises another key issue: the question of whether to make a system 'opt-in' or 'opt-out'. How consent for the system would be gained was initially left to the ISPs to decide as and when they implemented it, though the initial impression gained from Phorm was that opt-out might be the norm.[33] After the privacy furore that arose when Phorm's nature began to go public, as detailed below, and after an opinion by the Information Commissioner's Office (ICO),[34] Phorm eventually decided to insist on an opt-in system. As the continuing controversy over 'Do Not Track' demonstrates clearly, the opt-in/opt-out issue remains a critical one.

4   The rise and fall of Phorm

Phorm raised a wide range of issues, from the technological nature of its interception and inspection systems and the various technical legal points highlighted by Bohm's legal analysis, to the deeper and less concrete concerns over people's every activity being monitored and exploited for financial gain. What is equally interesting is how these various issues

---

[31] See Chapter 7, Section 4.4.   [32] See Chapter 2, Section 3.
[33] See for example an interview on the BBC at http://news.bbc.co.uk/1/hi/technology/7283333.stm.
[34] See www.theregister.co.uk/2008/04/09/ico_phorm_tougher/.

played out as Phorm attempted to bring its Webwise service into operation. Whether the legal points put forward by Bohm and others had
technical merit (or would succeed in court) did not appear, in practice, to
have been as important as the part that their existence *as challenges* has
played in what appears to be the ultimate demise of Phorm.

The story reveals a great deal about the reality of regulation in this
field and the relative strengths and importance of the various interest
groups involved, from Phorm and its business allies to the privacy advocacy groups, the hackers and computer-users' community, the various
governmental groups at different levels and from different locations and,
just as importantly, the many other businesses who have their own interests in the field. All these different interest groups played key parts in the
process. In order to understand how and why Phorm failed, we need to
understand these parts.

4.1   A public dispute

The controversy over Phorm was largely played out in public and more
particularly and appropriately over the internet itself. Hackers and digital
rights and privacy groups reacted strongly from the moment the proposed
service became known. The Open Rights Group started a 'Stop Phorm'
campaign,[35] while Ross Anderson, referring to the three ISPs who were at
that stage proposing to implement Phorm's Webwise, said 'The message
has to be this: if you care about your privacy, do not use BT, Virgin or
Talk-Talk as your internet provider'.[36] Tim Berners-Lee told the BBC that
he would change his ISP if it introduced a system such as Webwise.[37] The
technical and legal analyses provided by Clayton and Bohm respectively
underpinned this campaigning, which was followed in detail by online
technical news providers such as *The Register*[38] and *Wired*.[39]

One of the most contentious issues, through which much of the initial drama was played out, was the discovery that in 2006 and 2007, prior
to the existence of Phorm's Webwise becoming public, BT had carried

---

[35] www.openrightsgroup.org/campaigns/stop-phorm.
[36] Quoted in the *Evening Standard*, 6 March 2008, www.thisislondon.co.uk/standard-
home/article-23449601-web-users-angry-at-isps-spyware-tie-up.do;jsessionid=D5AA1
541C91446314EAD7013363AB159.
[37] See 'Web Creator Rejects Net Tracking' at http://news.bbc.co.uk/1/hi/
technology/7299875.stm.
[38] See www.theregister.co.uk/2008/02/29/phorm_roundup/ for a summary of all the various Phorm stories covered by *The Register*.
[39] See for example www.wired.com/epicenter/2009/04/uk-web-spying-f/.

out 'secret' trials of the system, involving tens of thousands of end-users, without those users' consent. When the trials' existence became public, through a report leaked onto the internet, there was an outcry from privacy groups, and the City of London Police met with BT representatives to informally question them about the trials. The City of London Police decided not to pursue a formal investigation, suggesting that there was no criminal intent on behalf of BT, and, crucially, that there was 'implied consent' by the end-users.[40] This latter claim was highly contentious, and Bohm suggested that the police claim on the former was a misunderstanding of the legal requirements for criminal consent.[41] Nonetheless, though nothing specific materialised from the controversy of the secret trials, the outcry about them caused BT significant embarrassment, provided a powerful weapon for anti-Phorm campaigners and added to the impression that Phorm itself was somehow 'underhand', secretive and potentially illegal.

4.2   Phorm's defence and government involvement

Phorm's defence to these attacks included a PR campaign involving founder Kent Ertugrul talking directly to the media, including being interviewed by the BBC,[42] *The Guardian*[43] and *The Register,*[44] as well as attempting to engage directly with the UK government, specifically to ask the ICO to confirm that Phorm's UID anonymity system meant that it was compliant with the DPA. Phorm believed that data protection did not apply to its system, as the data it gathered, processed and used did not constitute 'personal data'. The ICO did, effectively, confirm that this was the case, though it also expressed the view that 'opt-in' consent would be required for any further trials and for the eventual rollout of the service.[45]

When faced with the legal analysis produced and distributed by Bohm, Phorm sought advice from the Home Office concerning RIPA. The issuing of this advice became the centre of another controversy, as emails between

[40]   See for example www.theregister.co.uk/2008/09/22/bt_phorm_police_drop/.
[41]   Also see www.theregister.co.uk/2008/09/22/bt_phorm_police_drop/.
[42]   www.bbc.co.uk/blogs/ipm/2008/03/phorm_an_interview_with_kent_e.shtml.
[43]   www.guardian.co.uk/technology/blog/2008/mar/06/yourquestionspleaseforkent.
[44]   www.theregister.co.uk/2008/03/07/phorm_interview_burgess_Ertugrul/.
[45]   See ICO press release at www.ico.gov.uk/upload/documents/pressreleases/2008/new_phorm_statement_040408.pdf and reporting at www.theregister.co.uk/2008/04/09/ico_phorm_tougher/.

the Home Office and Phorm were released that appeared to show that the company had helped to edit this draft legal interpretation of Phorm by the Home Office, in an attempt to ensure that the service would be seen as appropriately 'legal'. Baroness Sue Miller, the Liberal Democrat spokeswoman on Home Affairs, accused the Home Office of 'collusion', calling the exchange of emails 'jaw-dropping', and said that 'The fact the Home Office asks the very company they are worried is actually falling outside the laws whether the draft interpretation of the law is correct is completely bizarre.'[46] Both the Home Office and Kent Ertugrul vigorously denied this interpretation of the exchange of emails.

Further complications followed. In response to 'several questions from UK citizens and UK Members of the European Parliament', the European Commission inquired into how the UK government had responded to the complaints about Phorm from users.[47] EU Telecoms Commissioner Viviane Reding sent a letter to the UK government – this time to the Department for Business, Enterprise and Regulatory Reform (BERR) – asking for an explanation as to how Phorm's technology conformed with EU data protection and privacy laws. BERR replied, after a delay, providing an explanation, the key points of which depended on Phorm's UID-based anonymity, together with a confirmation of the requirement in the Home Office memo that explicit consent would be required.[48] Phorm, in BERR's opinion, complied with EU privacy law.

This view was immediately challenged by the Open Rights Group and others, in part based upon Bohm's legal analysis. They noted specifically the requirement for both sides of a communication to need to consent to an interception of a communication, so not only did web surfers need to consent, but website owners, and stressed once more the inadequacy of Phorm's UID-based anonymity. The EC inquiry concluded that if the UK believed that Phorm complied with UK privacy law, then that law must not be a correct implementation of the relevant EU directives. After much communication with the UK government, in April 2009 the Commission launched an action against the UK government, calling for changes in UK law. In the words of Viviane Reding:

---

[46] See http://news.bbc.co.uk/1/hi/technology/8021661.stm.

[47] http://europa.eu/rapid/pressReleasesAction.do?reference=IP/09/570&format=HTML&aged=0&language=EN&guiLanguage=en.

[48] BERR's reply to Commissioner Reding was not made public, but BERR did disclose to *The Register* the key points, which were then published on the internet at www.theregister.co.uk/2008/09/16/phorm_eu_berr/.

We have been following the Phorm case for some time and have concluded that there are problems in the way the UK has implemented parts
of EU rules on the confidentiality of communications.[49]

Both Phorm and the ISBA ('the voice of British advertising') tried to dis-
suade the EC from continuing their action,[50] while the Open Rights Group
and others actively supported it, and publicised the existence of the action
through the media. In October 2010 the Commission confirmed that as
the UK government have not changed the law as the Commission suggested, they would be taking the UK to the European Court of Justice to
force it to do so.[51] Ultimately the UK government acquiesced, making the
appropriate changes as requested by the EC.[52]

4.3   The fallout from a rancorous dispute

The disputes between privacy advocates and Phorm became increasingly
rancorous as the affair wore on. A number of 'anti-Phorm' websites appeared
such as Badphorm,[53] Dephormation[54] and the Anti-Phorm League.[55]
In response to some of the more vociferous of anti-Phorm campaigners
Phorm set up its own campaigning site, Stopphoulplay.com. Phorm was
forced to admit to 'overzealous' editing of its Wikipedia entry, after having
deleted sections critical of Phorm and links to some further stories.[56] In the
words of BBC correspondent Darren Waters, 'This is a battle with no sign
of a ceasefire, with both sides settling down to a war of attrition, and with
governments, both in the UK and the EU, drawn into the crossfire.'[57]

This, then, was the far from simple background. Legal challenges,
technical disputes, serial campaigning, possible police action, EU action
against the UK government, smear campaigns and propaganda, and all
the while Phorm attempting to start its business operation. The result of it
all began to become clear in 2009. Before that stage it had looked as though

---

[49] See again http://europa.eu/rapid/pressReleasesAction.do?reference=IP/09/570&format
=HTML&aged=0&language=EN&guiLanguage=en.
[50] See for example www.marketingweek.co.uk/isba-urges-ec-to-quit-legal-action-over-
phorm/2065075.article.
[51] See http://europa.eu/rapid/pressReleasesAction.do?reference=IP/10/1215&format=HT
ML&aged=0&language=EN&guiLanguage=en.
[52] The case was closed in January 2012. See http://europa.eu/rapid/press-release_IP-12-
60_en.htm?locale=en.
[53] www.badphorm.co.uk.   [54] www.dephormation.org.uk/index.php.
[55] www.antiphormleague.com/index.php.
[56] See www.theregister.co.uk/2008/04/08/phorm_censors_wikipedia/.
[57] www.bbc.co.uk/blogs/technology/2009/04/phorm_hoping_to_stop_phoul_pla.html.

Phorm was likely to succeed, with the UK government apparently firmly behind it, three of the biggest ISP's planning to use its service, an apparent endorsement from noted privacy advocates and a guarded approval from the ICO. Then business reality began to kick in, as other businesses and other government departments began to respond seriously to the furore generated by the whole affair.

In April 2009, Amazon.com announced that it would not allow Phorm to scan any of its domains.[58] Others followed, including the Nationwide Building Society.[59] The hammer blow fell when BT announced that it would not be implementing Phorm, followed immediately by TalkTalk and then Virgin Media. Phorm's shares fell forty per cent on the announcement, and it looked as though Phorm's business model was in danger of total collapse. Phorm responded by bringing out new products, notably its content-tailoring service, 'Webwise discover', which 'will allow visitors to any website to automatically find content within that site based on their interests from across the web'. Then, in August 2009, the Office of Fair Trading (OFT) announced that it was investigating the use of personal information in internet advertising, questioning the use of tailored advertising and the possibility of tailored prices based on personal information.[60] Phorm's share price fell once more, this time more than twenty per cent, as a result of the announcement.[61] The All Party Parliamentary Communications Group (apComms) had also undertaken its own enquiry into internet traffic, covering amongst other things, behavioural advertising, and issued its report in October 2009.[62] This report recommended that:

> the Government review the existing legislation applying to behavioural advertising, and bring forward new rules as needed, to ensure that these systems are only operated on an explicit, informed, opt-in basis.[63]

In September 2009 potentially the final blow fell with the resignation of Phorm's Chief Technology Officer, Stratis Scelparis.[64] Phorm abandoned its efforts to operate in the UK. Since then, Phorm has made efforts to

---

[58] See http://news.bbc.co.uk/1/hi/technology/7999635.stm.
[59] See www.guardian.co.uk/business/marketforceslive/2009/jul/21/phorm.
[60] See www.guardian.co.uk/media/2009/aug/20/internet-targeted-advertising-oft-investigation.
[61] See www.guardian.co.uk/media/2009/aug/20/advertising-digital-media.
[62] See www.apcomms.org.uk/uploads/apComms_Final_Report.pdf.
[63] *Ibid.*, p. 21.
[64] See www.telegraph.co.uk/finance/newsbysector/mediatechnologyandtelecoms/media/6209787/Phorm-loses-technology-chief.html.

re-emerge in different places around the world, in South Korea, Brazil, Romania, Turkey and most recently China[65] – without significant apparent success.

5   Regulation of behavioural tracking

The aforementioned investigations by the OFT and apComms are just part of the fallout. Phorm was the focus, but it drew attention to the whole of behavioural advertising, adding controversy to a developing practice, leading to serious contemplation of regulation on both sides of the Atlantic. The European regulatory fallout detailed below arose directly from Phorm, as outlined in Section 4.2 above.

The route to the contemplation of regulation in the United States was less direct; it was a reaction to the whole practice of behavioural targeting rather than just to Phorm. Nonetheless, Phorm played an important part, at least from the perspective of the lobbyists who have supported the idea. As Jeff Chester, of the US-based Center for Democratic Technology (the CDT), put it in May 2008: 'This is such an important story ... In the UK, there's been a huge firestorm over Phorm. But there's been close to nothing here.'[66] That 'firestorm' catalysed the pressure groups into action, and eventually the US authorities began to consider action.

5.1   Regulation in the United States: Do Not Track

In September 2009 a coalition of privacy and consumer rights groups (including the CDT) wrote an open letter to the House Committee on Energy and Commerce calling for the regulation of behavioural advertising.[67] A number of bills relating to the idea have been introduced,[68] but

---

[65] See for example www.telecompaper.com/news/phorm-signs-two-isp-agreements-in-china–920900 from January 2013.

[66] Quoted in *The Register* at www.theregister.co.uk/2008/05/16/congress_questions_nebuad/.

[67] See http://arstechnica.com/tech-policy/news/2009/09/privacy-advocates-want-regulation-of-behavioral-advertising.ars for a discussion of the issues, and www.uspirg.org/reports/usp/online-behavorial-tracking-and-targeting-legislative-primer for the letter itself.

[68] See for example the Building Effective Strategies To Promote Responsibility Accountability Choice Transparency Innovation Consumer Expectations and Safeguards Act or BEST PRACTICES ACT, available online at www.govtrack.us/congress/bills/111/hr5777 or the Do-Not-Track Online Act of 2011, available at http://commerce.senate.gov/public/?a=Files.Serve&File_id=85b45cce-63b3–4241–99f1–0bc57c5c1cfff.

they have been strenuously opposed by the advertising industry[69] and have shown no signs, to date, of being passed by either House. Instead, what is being actively pursued is the 'Do Not Track' (DNT) initiative: a mixed, largely self-regulatory approach, involving not just lawmakers but more importantly the internet industry.[70] The idea is to allow users to control whether they allow behavioural targeting through their browser settings. Behavioural advertisers would be expected to design their advertising systems to look for these settings and then follow them.

The makers of the most used browser software are working in collaboration with this plan: Microsoft, Mozilla, Apple and Google have implemented it in various ways for their Internet Explorer (IE), Firefox, Safari and Chrome browsers respectively. From the perspective of privacy and autonomy, however, there are flaws in DNT that work in the opposite direction. The first is that they are in general 'opt-out' rather than 'opt-in' – a critical issue – with the notable exception of IE. That exception shows one of the key problems with DNT. When Microsoft announced that it was going to set the new version of IE with DNT on by default, the reaction by the internet advertising industry was dramatic and direct. Industry spokespeople suggested that if Microsoft did this, they would simply ignore the settings.[71] In effect, unless Microsoft left DNT off by default, DNT would not work at all.

This reveals the second and most important flaw: DNT relies on the goodwill of the trackers in order to function.[72] Mozilla took another approach, one that appeared a bit harder for the advertisers to avoid. In its most recent version of Firefox, it changed the defaults so that third-party cookies were disabled by default,[73] and as most current forms of tracking rely on the use of third-party cookies, that would bypass the need for trackers' compliance with DNT terms. It may be, however, a short-term 'fix' as other methods of tracking are available and will be developed. Further to that, there is still an issue as to whether DNT will really mean 'do not track'. Some within the industry want DNT to signify simply that targeted advertisements will not be placed: effectively, that 'do not track'

---

[69] See for example 'Tech Firms Warn Privacy Bill Will Harm Economy' on CNET, at http://news.cnet.com/8301-31921_3-20011435-281.html.

[70] See http://donottrack.us/.

[71] See for example www.zdnet.com/microsoft-sticks-to-default-do-not-track-settings-in-ie-10-7000002289/.

[72] See for example www.pcworld.com/article/217556/donottrack_in_chrome_and_firefox_different_approaches_same_fatal_flaw.html#tk.mod_rel.

[73] See for example www.pcmag.com/article2/0,2817,2415810,00.asp.

would really mean 'do not target'.[74] Even so, the moves by both Microsoft and Mozilla show both a willingness of browser makers to engage with the issue and to take on the trackers, and an understanding that the users, their customers, do not want to be tracked without their consent. And, perhaps, that they have a *right* not to be tracked.

5.2   Regulation in Europe: the 'Cookies Directive'

In Europe in September 2009 Meglena Kuneva, the consumer affairs Commissioner, told a gathering of ISPs, major websites and advertising firms that they were violating 'basic consumer rights in terms of transparency, control and risk', through data collection and behavioural targeting.[75] Following this, in October 2009, came the adoption of an EU Directive that has become known as the 'Cookies Directive'.[76]

This piece of legislation has such far-reaching implications that Struan Robertson, the editor of Out-Law.com and a respected blogger in the field, has called it 'breathtakingly stupid'.[77] It modifies existing European legislation to effectively require that any cookie can only be stored on a user's computer, or accessed from that computer, with that user's explicit, informed consent. This would cover not just such things as advertising but any kind of web analytics and indeed the functioning of most modern websites, as cookies are used by most websites in one form or another to store, for example, user preferences.

The UK government enacted the Directive as the Privacy and Electronic Communications (EC Directive) (Amendment) Regulations 2011,[78] but the implementation has not had as dramatic an effect as might have been feared, if the media coverage of the issue had been believed. Most websites seem to have complied with it by putting a banner at the top of the website to inform the user that cookies are being used, a banner that needs to be clicked on to be removed, thus producing opt-in 'consent' meeting the requirements of the Article 29 Working Party,[79] though consent that in real terms appears close to meaningless.

---

[74] See for example www.eff.org/deeplinks/2012/04/some-companies-choose-do-not-target-over-do-not-track-what-are-user-attitudes and www.nytimes.com/2013/07/21/opinion/sunday/dont-track-us.html?_r=2&. At the date of writing, this tension remained unresolved.

[75] Reported in www.theregister.co.uk/2009/03/31/kuneva_behavioural/.

[76] See Chapter 4, Section 2.3.   [77] www.out-law.com/page-10510.

[78] Available at www.legislation.gov.uk/uksi/2011/1208/contents/made.

[79] Based on their Opinion 2/2010 from June 2010, WP171, and in particular Section 4.1.1. See http://ec.europa.eu/justice/policies/privacy/docs/wpdocs/2010/wp171_en.pdf.

The story in the EU appears in some ways similar to that in the United States. There are real gaps between what the industry wants, what the law-makers are proposing and what might actually be useful to users. There are two key differences between the approaches. Firstly, in the United States, the law has not yet been enacted and may well not come into force for a long time, if at all. Secondly, in the United States there has at least been an attempt (and a partially successful one) to get the industry on board. In both cases, however, the principal result is uncertainty.

This uncertainty arises in part at least from a problem of trust: as a result of the practices of Phorm and others, many people have lost trust in the advertising industry over such things as behavioural advertising. The advertisers, too, have lost trust in the European regulators. That gap in trust, and the uncertainty that follows it, cannot be good for the beneficial aspects of the web symbiosis.

5.3   Symbiotic regulation as best practice?

Whether the effective failure of Phorm is an individual incident or representative of an overall movement has yet to be seen, but the regulatory crackdown does suggest the latter. Looked at through the lens of symbiotic regulation, it can be argued that Phorm's demise resulted from Phorm's failure to appreciate the complexity of the regulatory matrix. Phorm is a good example of how symbiotic regulation works, and why, if a good regulatory result is to be achieved, it needs to be harnessed.

The regulatory matrix in which Phorm operates is complex. Many of the different relationships within it have had their impact: Phorm's relationship with its customers; Phorm's relationship with its business allies and its competitors; all the various parts of the UK government's relationships both with Phorm and with the people; the hackers and the advocacy groups' relationships with people, with other businesses, with the UK government and with the EU; the EU's relationship with the UK; and finally, as the culmination of all these things, other businesses' relationships with their customers – for that, in the end, must have been what caused BT and the other ISPs to withdraw, and hence Phorm to fall.

It appears that Phorm took too simplistic a view of the regulatory environment, relying on its ability to lobby and negotiate with government, to form alliances with businesses and to provide an inventive technological solution. It looked to find solutions that could be argued to meet with the letter of the law: the arguments that Phorm put forward about compliance with data protection law had enough substance to convince the ICO, the

Home Office and BERR to give Phorm their support and approval. It is a similar misunderstanding to that made by Kent Ertugrul when he tried to distinguish between legal adware and illegal spyware: he did not appreciate that what people believed and felt could be more important than the letter of the law. The public does not like adware, even if it is legal, and sees very little difference between it and spyware. Effectively, Kent Ertugrul was saying that the public was 'wrong' not to distinguish between the two, but that he would have to bow to their 'wrong view' in abandoning his system. He did not appear to accept that the public might be right in not liking adware because it interfered with what they considered to be their rights. The letter of the law was not what the public cared about, rather what they thought to be *right*.

Compliance with the letter of the law is not enough when norms and markets come into play. Phorm drastically underestimated firstly the feelings of the community with regard to privacy – as the 2009 study of American attitudes to behavioural advertising suggested and the 2013 Ovum report confirmed[80] – and secondly the power of the community to influence other parts of the regulatory matrix. Ultimately, through the various advocacy groups, through public campaigning and through the EU, the community managed to get its view across. Phorm was seen as 'anti-privacy': this image gathered momentum.

Whether these perceptions actually lay behind the key events in Phorm's ultimate downfall – BT's withdrawal, the refusal of websites such as Amazon.com to be scanned – is questionable, for in both cases there were other factors involved. In Amazon's case, letting Phorm scan its website could potentially have robbed it of some of its crucial competitive advantages, as its ability to monitor its own enormous customer base is a key part of its business model, while for BT, it might simply have been a matter of not wanting to throw good money after bad. In Amazon's case, however, the fact that it chose to talk about the privacy issues as a part of its reasoning was very revealing. BT did not mention privacy; it said very little except that it was no longer pursuing Phorm as an option. For BT, admitting that privacy issues played a part in its decision would have been very difficult, suggesting that it had at best initially misjudged the situation, and at worst broken the law in its earlier trials of

---

[80] See Turow, King, Hoofnagle, Bleakley and Hennessy, 2009, and www.out-law.com/en/ articles/2013/february/most-consumers-would-activate-do-not-track-privacy-settings-if-they-were-easily-available-according-to-ovum-survey/.

the service, but the adverse publicity and overall image of Phorm cannot have helped the cause of BT's continued participation.

This analysis of Phorm's failure is made with the benefit of hindsight, but the story of Facebook's Beacon, which has a number of similarities to the Phorm saga, adds weight to the suggestion. Through Beacon, Facebook shared data with an alliance of online retailers, allowing each to use the other's information about individuals in order to better target advertising and services.[81] Beacon was contentious to say the least; the public outcry was vociferous. Facebook's initial response was to change the way Beacon operated – primarily to change it from 'opt-out' to 'opt-in' – but ultimately Facebook was forced to abandon the system completely, after settling a class action lawsuit that had been brought in California accusing not only Facebook but a number of its allied retailers of breaching various US wire-tapping and privacy laws.[82] Just as in the case of Phorm, community reaction was strong enough to bring about the end of a service that went beyond what people thought was right. Furthermore, it was through the manipulation of all the various relationships in the regulatory matrix – relationships between individuals and Facebook, between individuals and governments, through the use of the law, through working with businesses – that this result was brought about. Just as in the case of Phorm, a lot of the trouble could have been avoided if Facebook had been more aware of both public opinion and of the ability of the public to bring that opinion to bear.

Some other services – Google Street View being perhaps the best example – have produced somewhat similar reactions from privacy advocates, and in some ways appear even more intrusive and yet have not suffered the same fate as Phorm and Beacon.[83] The reasons for this are not simple, but in symbiotic regulation terms, the regulatory matrices in

---

[81] For an analysis of Beacon see www.facebook.com/notes/facebook/thoughts-on-beacon/7584397130.

[82] Facebook abandoned Beacon on 21 September 2009. For an examination of the class action suit, see www.wired.com/threatlevel/2008/08/facebook-beacon/, and for the suit itself see www.wired.com/images_blogs/threatlevel/files/facebook_beacon_complaint0812081.pdf. The settlement included Facebook's allocating US$9.5 million 'to create a foundation to fund products that promote online privacy, safety and security'. See www.concurringopinions.com/archives/2009/09/facebook-settles-beacon-lawsuit.html. The result of the suit was finally confirmed in February 2013; see http://arstechnica.com/tech-policy/2013/02/appeals-judges-will-allow-9–5m-facebook-privacy-settlement/.

[83] Action has been taken against Google Street View in some countries. Switzerland is one example, see www.techradar.com/news/internet/swiss-take-legal-action-over-google-street-view-650241, while in Japan there are other concerns about the misuse of images – see www.searchenginejournal.com/google-street-view-in-japan-faces-various-complaints/13048/.

which they operate are different. Google has both a stronger base position and a better reputation with the public, and, it appears, a better grasp of how to get the community on its side. Moreover, Street View offers a service that is both useful and attractive to users: a benefit, in exchange for the intrusion, and an example of how the symbiosis of the Symbiotic Web can function. Even though Street View has had considerable adverse publicity (particularly in relation to the revelation that cars taking photos for use by Street View had been 'scraping' data from private Wi-Fi networks) that adverse publicity has not dampened public enthusiasm for the use of the service.

6　Ways forward and rights-based solutions

The Phorm affair caused the UK government considerable problems. It faced a legal challenge from the EU and was forced to change its law. It was accused of collusion with what was perceived to be a 'dodgy' business, and was portrayed as riding roughshod over people's privacy and rights, and all of this to back a business idea that ultimately ended in failure. If it had had a better idea of the likely outcome, and a better understanding of what it was that mattered to people – why, in the end, people were sufficiently distressed by Phorm to bring about its downfall – then the government could have avoided the whole farrago.

Further, it is not just Phorm and the UK government who have found themselves in difficulties, but the whole of the online advertising industry. It faces a regulatory crackdown not only in Europe but potentially in the United States as well – a crackdown that could potentially damage its entire business model – and even opposition from the browser makers. It now has a continuing need for serious lobbying, which, at a time when finances are being stretched to breaking point for many, is a distraction and a drain on resources it can little afford. That, too, could potentially have been avoided if the situation had been better understood and the rights that people believed themselves to have had been properly appreciated.

6.1　A right to monitor the monitors

Behavioural advertising highlights the need for rights governing surveillance, monitoring and tracking. The reaction to Phorm, and the successful resistance to its implementation of Webwise, suggests that people feel very strongly about this and indeed that they have a right not to be monitored.

Phorm made much of its system of anonymisation, and of the fact that it did not hold data, that the vast bulk of the data gathered was immediately deleted and that its system was therefore compliant with data protection legislation. One key question is whether even if their system of anonymisation had worked perfectly, even if the data had been immediately deleted, would monitoring of an individual's internet activities then have been acceptable?

This crystallises one of the problems with data protection legislation: it focusses on data rather than on privacy. Privacy concerns whether we have the right not to be watched, not just whether those who watch us should be able to record and store the images of what they see. Having our internet activities monitored amounts to having our private actions watched. As Berners-Lee puts it:

> To allow someone to snoop on your internet traffic is to allow them to put a television camera in your room, except it will tell them a whole lot more about you than the television camera.[84]

It is not just privacy advocates and internet experts such as Berners-Lee who are concerned about this kind of monitoring. In the 2009 survey of American attitudes to behavioural advertising, sixty-eight per cent of adults stated that they would definitely not allow tailored advertising that results from 'following the websites you visit and the content you look at', even in a manner that keeps them anonymous, with a further nineteen per cent saying that they probably would not allow it.[85]

Taking this into account, along with the strength of the reaction to Phorm, there is a strong case for a right not to be monitored. This would extend the 'right to roam the internet with privacy'. It would have similar limitations: allowing, for example, security services to monitor when they have demonstrated that they have sufficient reason to monitor particular people or particular websites, and have obtained appropriate authorisation.

This right, however, should be taken a step further. Not only do people have a right not to be monitored, but when they *are* monitored and accept that monitoring – in a commercial rather than security or criminal investigatory context – they have a right to monitor those who are doing the monitoring, and to control how and when that monitoring

---

[84] To a meeting in Parliament organised by Baroness Miller, as reported in *The Register* at www.theregister.co.uk/2009/03/11/phorm_berners_lee_westminster/.

[85] See Turow, King, Hoofnagle, Bleakley and Hennessy, 2009, p. 16.

takes place. In this context, 'monitoring' includes such things as intercepting, inspecting, viewing, analysing, comparing, categorising, or otherwise examining or processing information that may be linked to an individual or their activities, even where records of or data arising from that monitoring are not gathered or held, or where the data are immediately anonymised.

6.2   Collaborative consent to behavioural tracking

What behavioural targeters and trackers do is technologically innovative and potentially useful both for the businesses involved and the individuals who use it, but there are clear problems concerning the impact it has on individuals' privacy and autonomy. In the same way that the overall challenge for regulators and technologists is to find a way to keep the beneficial symbiosis of the Symbiotic Web in balance, the most important question arising from the Phorm saga is whether a way can be found to harness and support these kinds of technological innovation and these kinds of potential benefit in a way that does not impact upon privacy and autonomy in too detrimental a fashion. The key to the solution is consent: if a way can be found for the individuals concerned to have a real, autonomous and consensual choice as to whether and how to participate in programmes like these, all sides could benefit.

A route towards this has already been suggested in Chapter 2: collaborative consent. Making consent a two-way, continuous and interactive process fits the nature of behavioural tracking, and there are already signs that such an application might be possible. The technological aspects of implementing both the right to monitor the monitors and collaborative consent in a tracking context have already started to be developed. Systems such as Ghostery[86] and Abine's DoNotTrackMe[87] both monitor tracking cookies and allow users to control which ones are and are not allowed to keep tracking, and these solutions are becoming more user-friendly and effective all the time. They still remain largely the province of privacy advocates and what might loosely be described as 'geeks'. The moves by Microsoft and Mozilla over their browser settings, however, offer an indication that interest in this kind of thing may become more widespread.

---

[86] www.ghostery.com.   [87] www.abine.com/dntdetail.php.

6.3   A future for behavioural tracking?

Are there ways that behavioural tracking can be used without sacrificing autonomy, ways that can put the benefits into the hands of the users rather than just into the hands of the advertisers?

One way could be to recast behavioural tracking as a profiling *service*: you would volunteer to be profiled, to allow your web browsing to be monitored and allow the profiler to provide a content tailoring service. That profile could be placed under your own control, used for tailoring content not just for the advertiser's benefit, but for your own. This might be what Phorm was suggesting (albeit unwillingly) with its subsequent 'Discover' service, which was intended to allow users to decide when to use the service to scour websites to find relevant content.

What is more, it could be part of a reshaping of the internet, helping to bring about the kind of positive model of Web 3.0 suggested by Berners-Lee. Berners-Lee's 'intelligent agents', the key to the semantic web, could be programmed using behavioural tracking. A user could switch on their behavioural tracking system, surf the net, then turn the tracking off and examine the profile that the tracking system has produced, before handing that profile to the intelligent agent and sending it on its way. Ayres suggests that computerised, automatic profiling, based on mass statistics and well-developed algorithms, tends to be far more accurate than those produced by individuals themselves. As Ayres (2007, Chapter 5) has shown, people are often remarkably bad at making estimates and at knowing their own preferences. This way, the advantages of the technology could be brought to bear without threatening privacy or autonomy, and the more positive future that the beneficial aspects of the Symbiotic Web could bring might become possible.

7

Data vulnerability and the right to delete

1   Vulnerability and autonomy

When people feel that their personal data is vulnerable, they seem to care a great deal. If people's most personal information can be easily lost, and potentially put into the hands of criminals or others who could or would wish to use it against them, people feel in danger. If their data is vulnerable, the people themselves are vulnerable. If their data is threatened, people themselves feel threatened. The use (and misuse) of data can result in direct threats to autonomy, but there is a *feeling* of a threat to autonomy that is of great importance too. If the problems are to be addressed, they must be addressed at both levels. People must *have* more control over their data and they must *feel* that they have this control.

The nature of the threat to autonomy presented through the vulnerability of data is qualitatively different from the majority of the threats discussed in this book so far. In most of those cases, there was at least some degree of intentionality behind the gathering and use of the data, certainly from the perspective of the data gatherer. Search engines intend to gather data from those who search; those who search put their search terms into the relevant box intentionally and intend the search engine to use that data to present them with appropriate possibilities. When someone browses a website, they do in general intend to look at the site and could be expected to understand that the owners of that site may know that someone has visited, even if they do not know what else might be told by and what might be done with that information. When data vulnerability is examined, that intent is missing: what happens to the data was not, at least in general, envisaged either by the person who initially gathered the information or by those who are the subjects of the data. This represents a new level of lack of control and a new set of potential risks.

1.1   Data minimisation and the right to delete

Ultimately, wherever and however data exists, it is vulnerable, in many different ways. Conversely, and crucially from the perspective of privacy and autonomy: if data does not exist, it cannot be vulnerable. If a way can be found to take more control over what data actually exists – to make the data protection principle of 'data minimisation' become something that has real impact – that could make a significant difference.

The key to this is a change in the paradigm that governs the retention of data: those who hold data should have to justify their holding, rather than the data subjects needing to find a reason for the data not to be held. In effect, this would mean a 'right to delete' personal data, unless there is a strong reason for the data to be held. Through this change in paradigm and the establishment of this right, businesses could be encouraged to develop new business models: models that do not depend on the holding of vast quantities of personal data.

This idea of a right to delete is subtly but importantly different from the idea of a 'right to be forgotten', as currently under discussion by European regulators for inclusion in the forthcoming revision of the data protection regime.[1] Quite how such a right might work in practice is still not entirely clear, but the connotations of the name of the right as well as the implications of its implementation are of concern and have been subject to criticism. A right to be forgotten looks like the rewriting or erasing of history, or a kind of censorship. The right to delete is about the control of data, not about censorship, and if properly understood and implemented is not in conflict with freedom of expression. It should not be seen as a way to rewrite or conceal history or as a tool for celebrities or politicians; it is rather a basic and pragmatic right available to all.

Equally importantly, a right to delete imposes different duties on different people than what might be understood as a right to be forgotten. It changes the rights being balanced and the duties that are imposed on others: it is balanced against businesses' 'right' to hold data rather than against individuals' rights to remember. Of course we have the right to remember things; it is much more questionable whether businesses have a right to hold our personal data. We can impose duties (both moral and legal) on businesses to delete, but we cannot impose duties on people to forget.

---

[1] See Chapter 4, Section 2.2.

1.2   A theoretical and pragmatic right

At a broad-brush level, the interests theory of rights[2] supports the assertion of such a right: the issue of data vulnerability indicates that we have a strong interest in keeping our data secure, and hence a strong interest in deleting data that concerns us. That interest implies the existence of a right of some sort.

The second reason is a more basic one: that we have a claim to such a right because we *believe* that we *should* have it. That is a bold assertion, and more work would need to be done to fully endorse it, but it does have support from empirical studies, and in particular the 2009 University of Pennsylvania's study of attitudes to behavioural advertising.[3] In that study, ninety-two per cent of those surveyed believed that there should be a law that requires 'websites and advertising companies to delete all stored information about an individual, if requested to do so' (Turow, King, Hoofnagle, Bleakley and Hennessy, 2009, p. 20), the single strongest finding of the entire study. Drawing firm conclusions from surveys such as this is a perilous business, but a finding like this does at least indicate that it is something that needs to be considered seriously. Support for the idea – at a pragmatic level – seems to be gaining ground: even Google's chairman Eric Schmidt has endorsed it. In May 2013 he was quoted as saying 'The lack of a delete button on the Internet is a significant issue. There is a time when erasure is a right thing.'[4]

There are good reasons to believe that it is an appropriate right to assert. One of the most important of these comes down to the deeper question of to whom the data really belongs. If it is in any real sense 'ours', then when we allow others to gather and hold that data, we trust the people to whom we hand it over to deal with it responsibly, but we still retain some rights over it. One approach that has been suggested, most notably in the United States, is to consider a 'property rights' approach to personal data: to grant individuals some kind of property right in their personal data that would 'enable individuals to bargain over which personal data to reveal to which firms for what purposes'.[5] That approach, offered in part in an attempt to

---

[2] See Chapter 2, Section 1.2.   [3] See Chapter 6, Section 6.1.

[4] In *Business Insider*, 6 May 2013, online at www.businessinsider.com/schmidt-internet-needs-a-delete-button-2013–5.

[5] Discussed in Samuelson, 2000. Samuelson goes through the arguments made elsewhere by people such as Kenneth C. Laudon, Patricia Mell, and Richard S. Murphy and others, advocating a property right in personal data, before outlining her own 'licensing' approach.

use a market-based solution rather than the strict legal control approach of European data protection, has been analysed in some depth in academic literature. A particularly pertinent analysis comes in Samuelson's article (2000), which suggests a form of 'licensing approach' rather than a direct property right.

The idea that individuals should be able to bargain with those who gather and use their data is attractive, but making this workable appears very difficult. It could very quickly become highly complex and, as when considering consent, all that is likely to happen in practice is that people will scroll through whatever rights they are being offered and click 'OK' to whatever is being suggested. One of the most important aspects of any system to give individuals control or more autonomy is that it should be simple to understand and simple to use. Complex legal licensing systems or property rights, however legally precise or superficially attractive they might appear, are unlikely to be simple in practice.

That is one of the strengths of a 'right to delete' approach. It is simple and direct, and makes it clear what is important, and it shifts the balance of power in any subsequent 'bargaining' process over rights over data and its use. Property rights fail to capture the distinctive nature of the relationship between a person and their personal data. Personal data is not like other property, something owned, something separate from the individual, something that can be bought and sold in the marketplace.[6] Instead, personal data can be looked at as part of what might be described as an 'extended self'.

1.3   Personal data as part of an extended self

Personal data is different from property both in qualitative terms and in terms of its impact and potential use. Firstly, data may have little or no intrinsic value without its connection to its owner – indeed, much of its value is in its connection to its owner. A car, for example, is of value in itself. The information that a particular person owns a particular kind of car, on the other hand, has very limited value unless something is known about the person who owns it, and it is of most value of all if exactly who

---

[6] For an examination of the way that attitudes to personal data have been moving towards an overly 'material' form, see Simon G. Davies, 1997. The changes that Davies highlighted in 1997 have become even more pronounced in the years since then.

that person is becomes known, for then it can reveal further information used in selling that kind of car, or in selling further things to the person who owns the car. The distributors of that car can more accurately focus their marketing, and other companies can attempt to advertise or sell more accurately to the person. Add to this the ability to reach that person (and their friends, relations, colleagues and classmates) directly and automatically by knowing their email address, Facebook ID or Twitter tag, and the data becomes even more of a gold mine.

Secondly, the loss of control over data can have much more impact than the value of the property itself. Indeed, the value of the data to the person might often only exist in any real terms in connection with loss of control over it. The information that someone owns a particular car may not seem of great value, but if its leaking could subject that person to an avalanche of unwanted junk mail, cold calls or spam email, then keeping control of it and preventing that avalanche matters. When combined or aggregated with other data, the value of keeping control could be much more important. If, for example, some kind of statistical inference can be made from the kind of car owned to a risky form of lifestyle, it could impact upon credit ratings, insurance costs and so forth. For more sensitive kinds of data – or data from which more sensitive information can be derived – the implications could be even more significant.

This combination of factors makes the connection between the person and the personal data much stronger and more 'entwined' than is the case with a conventional property relationship. Psychologists such as Clark and Chalmers (1998) have investigated the concept of an 'Extended Mind', attempting to answer the question 'Where does the mind stop and the rest of the world begin?' They have looked at the interaction between the mind and the perceived environment, particularly in the context of computer (and other technology) use, and suggest that the barrier is not as clear-cut as it might at first seem. The connection between a person and their personal data, particularly insofar as it is used in the online environment, is stronger than a connection between a person and conventional property, or indeed than past connections between a person and the information held about them.

Further, it is through that data that the person interacts with and has an impact on the online environment, and the accumulation of that data makes up how the person is perceived and experienced by the online environment and by other people operating in that online environment. It is in that sense, too, that a person's personal data can be seen as part of what might be considered their 'extended person'. If autonomy is to be taken seriously it needs to be exercisable over this extended person.

2   The reality of data vulnerability

Arguments over data vulnerability are not merely theoretical. Indeed, it is the reality of data vulnerability that matters the most, and over recent years examples of data loss and data vulnerability have proliferated.

2.1   Commercial data risks

There are significant risks associated with the way that businesses deal with data, some of which have already been discussed in Chapter 3 when the model of the Symbiotic Web was set out. Commercial pressures often mean that data security is not top of the agenda for a business, which can lead to a wide range of potential vulnerabilities. Organisational matters, senior management responsibility problems, low levels of staff competence and a lack of staff training, pressures on time and on costs, the use of untrustworthy third-party contractors – issues that, as shown below, have been highlighted by reports into government data losses[7] – are all likely to arise in a commercial setting, driven in part by commercial pressures.

There are also more direct risks that have been highlighted in practice. On 17 November 2009, the Information Commissioner's Office (ICO) issued a press release[8] to highlight a particularly pernicious problem. Employees of a mobile phone company appeared to have sold details relating to customers' mobile phone contracts, including their contract expiry dates, to competitors who had then used the material to cold call those customers in an attempt to induce them to switch suppliers. The ICO investigation revealed that 'substantial amounts of money' had changed hands. The identity of the company involved was revealed very swiftly in the press as T-Mobile, and that thousands of their customers were involved.[9]

---

[7] See Section 2.5 below.
[8] ICO press release, 17 November 2009, www.ico.gov.uk/upload/documents/press-releases/2009/mobile_phone_records_s55_171109.pdf.
[9] See www.telegraph.co.uk/technology/mobile-phones/6591726/T-Mobile-customers-hit-by-data-sale-scandal.html.

It was not the ICO who uncovered the issue, but T-Mobile, after an internal investigation following customer complaints.[10] The immediate question that arises is how many other similar breaches have gone undiscovered or unreported? For T-Mobile the whole story was an embarrassment. To have to admit to having had such a lapse in security is something that could not do anything but damage to the company. Would other companies in similar circumstances be so quick to come forward?

Another key kind of commercial vulnerability of data was demonstrated when the US owner of XY Magazine and its associated website, whose target readership and subscriber database consisted of young homosexual boys, filed for bankruptcy in 2010. XY's creditors applied for possession of the company's user database, quite logically from their perspective: it was probably the company's most valuable asset. The database included around a million users and by its very nature revealed some of the most personal and sensitive information about people in an enormously vulnerable situation. The potential for harm was huge, and the legal situation was far from clear. The Federal Trade Commission in the United States expressed concerns, and suggested that the sale of the database could be in violation of the legal prohibition of 'unfair or deceptive acts or practices', and ultimately the publisher and former partners agreed to destroy the database rather than sell it.[11]

The XY Magazine case received a great deal of media attention, drew in privacy advocates such as Simon Davies of Privacy International[12] and was another example of how community pressure was able to produce a positive result for privacy. It is almost certain, however, that it is just one of many examples of data being sold or transferred as a result of bankruptcy or similar procedures. Where data is so obviously 'dangerous' the kind of attention shown to XY Magazine was able to prevent the transfer of data, but less clearly sensitive data is far more likely just to be sold as part of the normal sale of the assets of a company, particularly in the US legal environment where no data protection law exists.

2.2   Hacking and technological vulnerability

Hacking and other forms of technological attacks can and do occur, and there is a constant 'battle' between hackers and those employed to make

---

[10]   As reported in *The Register* at www.theregister.co.uk/2009/12/09/tmobile_ico/.
[11]   See www.eff.org/deeplinks/2010/08/publisher-former-partners-agree.
[12]   Quoted in the BBC report on www.bbc.co.uk/news/10612800 and the *New Statesman* at www.newstatesman.com/magazines/2010/07/gay-magazine-creditors-legal.

systems secure. Data in almost any situation can potentially be vulnerable to some kind of technological attack or intrusion.

A particularly striking example of this kind of vulnerability happened in April 2011, when hackers went into the Sony Playstation Network and stole the personal details of more than 100 million users.[13] These details included names, home addresses, email addresses, dates of birth, phone numbers, gender information and 'hashed password', and in some cases direct debit details, credit card numbers and expiry dates. The direct debit and credit card details came from what Sony described as an 'outdated database',[14] which in itself raised a lot of questions, most importantly, why that database even existed, let alone was accessible online for hackers. In terms of data minimisation – a common thread for many of the cases here – it is hard to see any justification for its existence. In January 2013, the ICO fined Sony £250,000 for the data breach.[15]

When the nature of Sony is considered, the hack is very revealing. Sony should be amongst the most technologically advanced and sophisticated organisations, with access to the best experts in security and in particular network security, yet they were hacked, and hacked with great success. If Sony can be hacked, is anyone secure? Almost all of the big technology companies have found themselves victims of hacks in recent years: Twitter,[16] Facebook[17] and Apple[18] were all hacked in a span of a few weeks in February 2013, for example.

It does not always take particularly great technical expertise to access data on the internet in ways that are neither illegal nor constitute any kind of 'attack'. In May 2011, Matthijs R. Koot, a PhD student in the Netherlands, used simple techniques to mine Google's databases and put together a database of 35 million Google users including names, email addresses and biographical details. As Koot puts it, it was 'completely trivial for a single individual to do this',[19] and the process was entirely within Google's rules, as they allow indexing of their public user information.

---

[13] Sony acknowledged that 77 million users of Playstations and 25 million users who access the Playstation Network through PCs or Facebook may have had their data stolen. See www.soe.com/securityupdate/pressrelease.vm and www.soe.com/securityupdate/index.vm.
[14] www.soe.com/securityupdate/pressrelease.vm.
[15] http://ico.org.uk/news/latest_news/2013/ico-news-release-2013.
[16] See www.bbc.co.uk/news/technology-21304049.
[17] See www.bbc.co.uk/news/world-us-canada-21481101.
[18] See www.bbc.co.uk/news/technology-21510791.
[19] See for example www.theregister.co.uk/2011/05/25/google_profiles_database_dump/.

There is another angle to consider when looking at hacking: hacking that may be linked to the actions of governments. One particular example, the Chinese 'Google hack', is discussed in depth below.[20] Though there has been considerable debate about who was responsible, no one has attempted to deny that the hacking attack took place. Indeed, the whole concept of 'cyberwarfare' is predicated by the understanding that systematic attempts to hack into systems not only *can* happen but *are* happening.

2.3   Vulnerability to governments

Governments often have a wish to acquire data from other sources, whether they be commercial, academic or other organisations. They use a wide variety of means to acquire this data, some of which are on a grand scale and in an insidious form, as the emergence of the PRISM revelations has demonstrated graphically.

Most directly, governments can attempt to acquire data using legal action. In August 2005 for example, the US Department of Justice (DoJ) filed a request for data to Google, requesting not only search data but related web addresses. The Department of Justice wanted the data as a part of its attempts to combat child abuse images.[21] Initially, the DoJ requested a substantial amount of information: all the websites that could be located using particular search terms and details of all the specific searches that were made on those terms over the two-month period covering June and July 2005, but this was eventually narrowed down to only 5,000 sample searches from Google's search log. Google resisted the initial government requests, and actively defended the subpoena, resulting in a decision at a California District Court[22] that was somewhat inconclusive: Google was ordered to supply some of the URL data, but not the search data. Expert opinion as to who exactly 'won' the case is divided, but Daniel Solove concludes that 'Overall, I view this opinion as a victory for information privacy'.[23]

The case was interesting from many different perspectives. Firstly, it demonstrated that the DoJ saw the potential for the use of search data,

---

[20] See Section 2.4(a) below.
[21] Specifically for its defence in the case *ACLU* v. *Gonzales*, No. 98-CV-5591, pending in the Eastern District of Pennsylvania. The case involved a challenge by the ACLU to the Child Online Protection Act (COPA), 47 U.S.C. § 231.
[22] *Gonzales* v. *Google, Inc.*, No. CV 06–8006MISC JW (17 March 2006).
[23] As part of his analysis of the case at www.concurringopinions.com/archives/2006/03/the_google_subp.html.

both Google's database of URLs and its record of searches made. Secondly, its initial approach to Google was simply to 'ask' for the data rather than go through a legal procedure. It emerged during the case that other search engine providers, notably Yahoo!, Microsoft and AOL, were not subject to similar subpoenas because they probably did provide the information asked of them or at least came to some sort of accommodation with the DoJ behind closed doors.[24]

One reaction to this has been the introduction of 'transparency reports' by the major players in the field. Google, for example, now provides a six-monthly 'User Data Requests' report. As Google puts it:

> Like other technology and communications companies, Google regu-
> larly receives requests from governments and courts around the world to
> hand over user data. In this report, we disclose the number of requests we
> receive from each government in six-month periods with certain limita-
> tions. Usage of our services have increased every year, and so have the
> user data request numbers.[25]

These numbers are large: in the fourth quarter of 2012, Google received 21,389 requests, and fully or partially complied with sixty-six per cent of them. Other companies provide similar reports: Facebook, Twitter and LinkedIn, for example, produce partial reports.[26] After pressure from privacy advocates,[27] Microsoft began producing their own, including data from Skype, in March 2013. These reports indicate the scale of the issue: governments can and do request access to people's personal data, and those requests are often complied with.

The PRISM revelations and their aftermath have put all this into per-spective, suggesting that the level of government access to commercially held data and commercial systems is on an even greater scale than pre-viously considered, and that the transparency reports to date had not been entirely 'transparent'. The intent of PRISM and related programmes appears clear: to gain access to the data and systems of communications companies and others whenever and however needed.[28] What also appears clear is that governments of different nations cooperate with each other

---

[24] See for example Phillip Lenssen's blog at http://blogoscoped.com/archive/2006–03–18-n45.html.

[25] See www.google.com/transparencyreport/userdatarequests/.

[26] See the EFF's 'When the Government Comes Knocking, Who Has Your Back?', online at www.eff.org/pages/when-government-comes-knocking-who-has-your-back.

[27] See www.eff.org/deeplinks/2013/03/victory-transparency-microsoft-releases-report-law-enforcement-requests-user-data.

[28] See Chapter 3, Section 5.2 and Chapter 4, Section 3.2

in sharing this information and intelligence. The degree of cooperation between the US National Security Agency (NSA) and GCHQ in the UK, for example, is a matter of speculation, but it is likely to be significant.[29]

Data held in one country can also be vulnerable to laws passed in other countries. Perhaps the most relevant of these in the UK and EU relates to the powers set out in the United States through the USA PATRIOT Act of 2001. Section 215 of the Act, which revises the Foreign Intelligence Surveillance Act of 1978 (FISA), provides that designated FBI personnel may apply to the FISA court for an order requiring the production of business records relevant to an investigation concerning international terrorism or clandestine intelligence activities. Applications to the FISA court do not require 'probable cause', but simply a claim by the FBI that the records are needed for an ongoing investigation into something that can loosely be classified as related to international terrorism or intelligence activities. What is more, the terms of the law demand that individuals served with a warrant under FISA rules may not disclose, under penalty of law, either the existence of the warrant or the fact that records were provided to the government.[30]

This makes data gathered and held in the United States particularly vulnerable – with huge implications for cloud computing, for example – but there is another possibility that is relevant here. The USA PATRIOT Act's requirements cover US companies and allow the US authorities to access data held by those US companies, and this may be so even when that data relates to and was gathered from a non-US company. When in 2008 the US defence company Lockheed Martin bid for the contract to run the 2011 UK census it was speculated that the USA PATRIOT Act might have allowed US authorities access to all the data gathered by Lockheed Martin as a part of that UK census. Questions on the subject were raised in the Commons Treasury Subcommittee, and while Angela Eagle, the then Treasury Minister, told the Subcommittee that she had received legal assurances that this would not happen, the doubt and the question remain. Angela Eagle's exact words were that she was 'pretty confident' that there would be robust safeguards on the security of data.[31]

---

[29] See for example www.guardian.co.uk/uk/2013/jun/21/gchq-cables-secret-world-communications-nsa.

[30] For analyses of the reality of Section 215 of the USA PATRIOT Act see the Friends Committee on National Legislation analysis at www.fcnl.org/issues/item.php?item_id=344&issue_id=68 or the EPIC analysis of the USA PATRIOT Act at http://epic.org/privacy/terrorism/usapatriot/.

[31] As reported to the BBC. http://news.bbc.co.uk/1/hi/uk_politics/7231186.stm.

Lockheed Martin did eventually win the contract, after assurances were made that the data would remain in the UK and under the ownership of the Office for National Statistics, but the larger issue remains: for a company owned under one jurisdiction and operating under another, the laws of both jurisdictions might apply.

There is another scenario to consider: where data is gathered by one company and then that company is taken over by another company. In particular, if a UK company gathers data and then that UK company is bought by a US company, could the USA PATRIOT Act allow US authorities to access all the personal data owned by that UK company? At the very least, there is a conflict of law: data protection law in Europe against the USA PATRIOT Act, FISA and so forth. Moreover, it could provide another potential area for uncertainty, and hence vulnerability. An individual data controller, faced by a request from the US authorities, might not be clear enough to know that they do not need to comply – indeed that they must not comply – and hence may allow access even when they should not.

2.4   Government use of illegally acquired data

A practice that has emerged in recent years is the use by governments of illegally acquired data. Two particular examples are notable from the last few years: the Chinese 'Google hack' and the use by governments of stolen bank data from Liechtenstein and Switzerland. Though these two cases might seem at first to have little in common, when looked at more closely they have significant similarities.

(a)   Google and China – the 'Google hack'

In January 2010, Google reported that it had been the subject of a 'highly sophisticated and targeted attack on [its] corporate infrastructure'.[32] Google had 'evidence to suggest that a primary goal of the attackers was accessing the Gmail accounts of Chinese human rights activists' and that:

> as part of their investigation, but independent of the attack on Google [they] have discovered that the accounts of dozens of U.S.-, China- and Europe-based Gmail users who are advocates of human rights in China appear to have been routinely accessed by third parties. These accounts

[32] Revealed in the Official Google Blog at http://googleblog.blogspot.com/2010/01/new-approach-to-china.html.

have not been accessed through any security breach at Google, but most likely via phishing scams or malware placed on the users' computers.[33]

The revelation of this hacking attack started a row that brought the US and Chinese governments into direct conflict. Hillary Clinton, the US Secretary of State, called on Beijing to investigate the Google hack,[34] while the Chinese state-run news agency Xinhua attacked Google for having 'intricate ties' with the US government and of 'providing US intelligence agencies with a record of its search engine results'.[35] Google used the event to trigger a withdrawal of cooperation with China's requirement for a strictly censored search engine, providing instead a simplified, uncensored search facility based in Hong Kong.[36]

It may never become clear whether the Chinese government was directly involved in the hacking of the data. What is clear is that someone had been trying to access this kind of data, presumably because they believe they can find a use for this data, and the most obvious potential user of this kind of data is the Chinese government. There are a number of possibilities, the most obvious of which are that the hackers were working directly for the Chinese government that they were independent but commissioned by the government, or that they were independent but believed that they could sell the data they hacked to the Chinese government.

(b)   Liechtenstein and Swiss banking data

A seemingly very different example is the use of hacked or otherwise illegally obtained data to find and convict tax evaders. The practice emerged in Germany in 2008, when the German government purchased information taken from the Liechtenstein bank LGT[37] in a complex story that eventually effectively forced Liechtenstein to drop most of its banking secrecy laws.[38] *The Sunday Times* reported that the German foreign intelligence service had paid 5 million Euros for the data[39] and that HM

---

[33] Again, see the Official Google Blog at http://googleblog.blogspot.com/2010/01/new-approach-to-china.html.

[34] See http://news.bbc.co.uk/1/hi/8472683.stm.

[35] See http://news.bbc.co.uk/1/hi/8578968.stm.

[36] See http://googleblog.blogspot.com/2010/03/new-approach-to-china-update.html.

[37] See for example www.reuters.com/article/idUSLDE6160KO20100207.

[38] See for example http://online.wsj.com/article/SB124727784329626615.html.

[39] See http://business.timesonline.co.uk/tol/business/industry_sectors/banking_and_finance/article3399526.ece.

Revenue & Customs (HMRC) in the UK had acquired similar information for £100,000.[40]

Then in February 2010, the German state of North Rhine-Westphalia announced that it had bought Swiss bank data as part of its drive to deal with tax evaders, after having been given the go-ahead by the German federal government to buy the information, even if it had been obtained illegally.[41] The German authorities did not use the information they had acquired just to catch tax evaders, but by publicising the fact that they had acquired this data – and would do their best to acquire similar data in the future – to try to convince other tax evaders to come forward voluntarily. This kind of 'persuasion' was successful: Reuters reported that 5,900 German citizens owing around 500 million Euros came forward in the months following the initial revelation of the data acquisition.[42]

In March 2010 *The Sunday Times* revealed that the authorities in Germany had been joined by their equivalents in France in the acquisition of this kind of data, and that those in the UK were also considering following the same path. According to *The Sunday Times*, Hervé Falciani, a French software engineer, had illegally obtained the details of 24,000 customers with accounts at HSBC's private bank in Switzerland while working for the company in Geneva.[43] Falciani had already sold some of the information to the French government, and HMRC in the UK was apparently about to receive some of that information from their French equivalents as a part of an information exchange. A 'senior tax official' was quoted as saying:

> It's fair to say that the prospect of getting hold of this information has generated some excitement here.[44]

The Swiss authorities asked the French to return the data, but though the French authorities agreed, they kept copies of the files and used them to try to root out tax evaders. France's tax office is thought to have subsequently recovered around half a billion Euros.

(c) An emerging practice?

The media responses to the two examples were very different. The suggestion that the Chinese government might have been behind the Google

---

[40] See www.timesonline.co.uk/tol/money/tax/article3423428.ece.
[41] See www.reuters.com/article/idUSLDE61P1FN20100226.
[42] Also reported in www.reuters.com/article/idUSLDE61P1FN20100226.
[43] See www.timesonline.co.uk/tol/news/politics/article7061114.ece.
[44] See again www.timesonline.co.uk/tol/news/politics/article7061114.ece.

hack provoked a mixture of anger and fear, links to the ideas of cyber-warfare and a general sense of paranoia about the way that the Chinese government seeks to suppress any kind of dissent, and the hackers were presented as stooges in the hands of a totalitarian state, while the banking data hackers/whistle-blowers have been portrayed as heroes, helping to bring tax evaders to justice.

From the perspective of the governments concerned, however, the two scenarios are actually very similar. In both cases the governments feel they have an overwhelming need (and duty) to locate and catch people perpetrating serious crimes – for the German, French and UK governments, people evading taxes, for the Chinese, people putting the stability and security of their state in jeopardy. In both cases the governments are using whatever means they can find to perform that duty. Further, governments believe that this kind of move will be popular. As German Finance Minister Wolfgang Schäuble puts it:

> In view of growing social tensions caused by globalization, the financial market crisis and the ludicrous bonus payments on the one hand, along with growing unemployment on the other, it would be completely unbearable if the state didn't do everything possible to ensure taxes were collected fairly.[45]

The Chinese government has not claimed responsibility for the Google hack but it would be easy to frame a similar argument in support of such actions: that to respond to growing social tensions caused by globalisation (of communications) it would be completely unbearable if the state didn't do everything possible to prevent subversives from destroying the Chinese state and way of life. To take it a step further, consider the case of terrorism. A significant part of the so-called 'war on terror' has been based on the premise that almost everything should be allowed that can help to stop the terrorists from destroying the West's way of life. Indeed, as the PRISM affair has revealed, the US government has used this kind of logic to justify its own large-scale internet surveillance.

For the Chinese Government, subversion and dissent would certainly be defined as serious crime under its national law. There are strong parallels, therefore, between the use of data for the 'war on terror', for the catching of tax evaders and for the suppression of dissent and subversion. In all

---

45 www.reuters.com/article/idUSLDE6160KO20100207.

these cases the importance of the objective seems to have overridden the need for an 'appropriate' method of obtaining the data.

The precise legal status of data acquired in this way is not entirely clear. There are conflicting and competing imperatives. In the case of the stolen bank data the German government has a duty to do what it can to collect tax fairly, but also has obligations under the Convention on Cybercrime, which it has both signed and ratified.[46] Those obligations include a requirement for international cooperation and the extradition of those who commit computer crimes including the theft of data,[47] so the Swiss authorities would have expected the German government to arrest and hand over to them the hackers/whistle-blowers who stole the data from the Swiss banks, together with the data that had been stolen. No such actions have taken place. The German government has effectively deemed its duties under domestic tax law to override its obligations under the Convention on Cybercrime. Indeed, it has gone further, for it can also be argued that by buying the data and by signalling that it would buy similarly acquired data in the future, the German government has effectively encouraged the commission of further data thefts, or the sale of the data to other countries. The further sale of data to the French and UK governments adds weight to this suggestion and demonstrates the way in which the existing international data security framework, of which the Convention on Cybercrime is a key pillar, is being denied effectiveness by signatory states.

Acquiring the data through this kind of a process might also give governments more freedom in terms of how it is used than they would have if they acquired them in a more conventional way. Data protection law requires specification of purpose – but if data is gathered in this 'indirect' way, how is that purpose specified? Governments might use the same definition as set out above from the Data Retention Directive: that the purpose is the 'investigation, detection and prosecution of serious crime', which would then give them freedom to use the data exactly as they want in accordance with this goal. All that might even be sidestepped depending on the particular implementation of data protection law. The Federal Data Protection Act in Germany, for example, says that data may be collected without the participation of the data subject if:

---

[46] See also Chapter 4, Section 2.4. The Convention on Cybercrime is downloadable from http://conventions.coe.int/Treaty/EN/Treaties/html/185.htm. Germany ratified the Convention on 9 March 2009. See https://wcd.coe.int/ViewDoc.jsp?id=1416299&Site=DC

[47] Convention on Cybercrime, Chapter III.

a legal provision prescribes or peremptorily presupposes such collection.[48]

German tax evasion laws would provide precisely that kind of legal provision. Either way, the purpose specification and consent requirements of data protection law can potentially be avoided.

(d)   Easy targets or slippery slopes?

In most of the examples above, the 'targets' chosen by the governments are what might be described as 'easy targets', in the sense that they are exactly the kind of 'offenders' that the public would want to get 'caught'. The people concerned, whether they are tax evaders or terrorists (and sometimes the creators or consumers of child abuse images) might even be described as 'enemies of society' – though that emphasises again the parallels with the Chinese government's drive to root out subversives and dissidents.

It is not unusual for these kinds of offences to be used to bring in laws that have far wider implications and cover far more people than their significance would suggest, and for the rights of ordinary individuals to be restricted as a consequence of the desire to apprehend them. The struggle to maintain civil liberties in the face of the demands of security is echoed strongly in this field. The practices and policies that have emerged to catch tax evaders, terrorists and murderers could equally be used to catch more minor 'offenders' in the same way that antiterrorism laws have been used in the UK to prevent protests against the arms trade,[49] and the powers of RIPA used to catch the owners of fouling dogs.

This pattern can be viewed in a number of ways. Some privacy advocates see it as a kind of 'Trojan horse' phenomenon; the 'easy targets' are used as an excuse to bring in powers or systems that governments would have liked to bring in anyway. Looked at another way, it is simply a matter of efficiency. If the systems, laws or powers exist, why not use them for other things? The local councils who have used their CCTV cameras to deal with dog fouling might well have seen it that way, and if a vast system of cameras like those used to enforce the London Congestion Charge

---

[48] German Federal Data Protection Act, Section 4(1). Downloadable including English translation from www.bdd.de/Download/bdsg_eng.pdf.

[49] In the case of R. (on the application of Gillan) v. Commissioner of Police of the Metropolis [2003] EWHC 2545 (Admin), Gillan and Quinton challenged the use of antiterrorism laws to stop and search them at an arms trade protest. They lost, lost again on appeal and again in the House of Lords, but the European Court of Human Rights overturned that decision, in Gillan v. United Kingdom (4158/05) (2010) 50 E.H.R.R. 45; 28 B.H.R.C. 420.

exists, why not use those cameras for other important purposes such as the prevention of terrorism?[50] Either way, the phenomenon does appear to exist,[51] and the implications in relation to data could be even greater than those in the material world, if the possibilities for aggregation, analysis and data mining are considered.

2.5   The HMRC and other government data losses

Governments hold an ever-increasing huge amount of data and have demonstrated significant levels of data vulnerability. The HMRC child benefit CD loss in 2007 was particularly spectacular, both in its scale and its consequences. As the then Chancellor of the Exchequer put it:

> The missing information contains details of all child benefit recipients: records of 25 million individuals and 7.25 million families. Those records include the recipient and their children's names, addresses and dates of birth, child benefit numbers, national insurance numbers and, where relevant, bank or building society account details.[52]

The discs were lost in transit between HMRC and the National Audit Office (NAO), and rather than containing just a sample of records, for audit purposes, they contained the entire child benefit database, primarily because it was easier and cheaper to copy over the whole database than to do proper sampling. In the aftermath of this loss, the government commissioned a full investigation into the affair, performed by Keiran Poynter, Chairman of PricewaterhouseCoopers LLP. The report ('The Poynter Report') revealed a complex combination of individual errors, communications failures and institutional deficiencies at HMRC.

In all, according to Poynter 'more than thirty HMRC staff from four different departments, and a number of NAO staff, played some part in the story'. Poynter (2008, pp. 8–11) points to such factors as placing operational concerns above security risks, failures to keep to official procedures, failures to either seek or consider appropriate authorisation for removal of data off-site, the routine use of insecure methods of data

---

[50] As reported in *The Register*: see www.theregister.co.uk/2007/07/18/smith_n_mcnulty_surrender_to_jihadi_bunglers/.

[51] Function creep has been recognised and studied in various forms relating to this and associated fields such as ID cards, DNA databases and sex offenders registers. Examples of academic work in this field include Greenleaf, 2008, Dahl and Sætnan, 2009, and Thomas, 2008, respectively.

[52] See *Hansard*, 20 November 2007, online at www.publications.parliament.uk/pa/cm200708/cmhansrd/cm071120/debtext/71120-0004.htm#07112058000527.

storage and transfer, and also institutional HMRC factors such as an insufficiently strong and poorly communicated information security policy and a lack of awareness and training on information security amongst HMRC staff.

Another highly public loss of data occurred shortly after the HMRC data loss: the theft, in January 2008, of a Royal Navy recruiter's laptop, which contained the unencrypted personal records for more than 600,000 recruits and potential recruits. This too was the subject of a detailed government review, this time undertaken by Sir Edmund Burton for the Permanent Under Secretary, Ministry of Defence ('The Burton Review', 2008).

The events were much simpler than those of the HMRC data loss: the Royal Navy recruiter left his laptop overnight locked in the boot of his car, from which it was stolen. The recruiter concerned was 'in clear breach of physical security rules' (Burton, 2008, Part 1, p. 8). Further investigation revealed that this was not a unique occurrence. Since 2003 nine other recruiters' laptops had been stolen, and in at least three of those cases the thefts had been under similar circumstances, taken from parked cars. Security policies were simply not being applied.

Why the laptop had contained the entire database, and why the data was unencrypted was another mixture of practical and systemic problems. Complex administrative changes, technical problems with implementation, failure to comply with stated policy, all combined to produce a disaster.

The fact that the laptop contained the entire database has uncomfortable parallels with the events of the HMRC data loss. In essence, it appeared that the laptops all contained all the data largely because that was easiest, which meant that the details of about a million people (recruits, potential recruits, 'next-of-kin' and so forth) were being held on *all* the MOD recruitment laptops. As a matter of design, the laptops synchronised their databases with the full database on the MOD main server (Burton, 2008, Part 1, p. 9). This is an almost exact reversal of the principle of data minimisation.

The Burton Review's main conclusions in terms of data were strong: that '[t]he Department is not treating information, knowledge and data as key operational and business assets', that '[i]nformation risk is not being formally managed at executive boards across the Department, with a small number of exceptions' (Preliminaries, p. 3) and that 'there can be little assurance that information is being effectively protected'. Ultimately, as Burton puts it, '[a] serious security event of this nature was inevitable' (Preliminaries, p. 4).

The parallels with the Poynter Report into the HMRC data loss are clear. The problems start with management and management systems, and work all the way down. Most importantly of all, in both cases, the data minimisation issue is fundamental to the severity of the problems. The HMRC discs should have held only a small sample of the child benefit data, but in fact held information for all 25 million people, while the MOD laptops could have held only relevant data but actually held the entire database.

Many other examples of government data loss have come to light since the HMRC data loss, revealing the same kinds of failing as those identified by both the Poynter Report and the Burton Review: failures of policy and of implementation of policy, individual errors, failures of subcontractors to fulfil their duties and so on. The cumulative impact of these various data losses and related problems was recognised as significant by the authorities. As well as the Poynter Report and Burton Review into the HMRC and MOD data losses respectively, in June and July 2008 there were a number of other official investigations and reports. The Independent Police Complaints Commission investigated the HMRC data loss and reported on that investigation.[53] At the direct request of the Prime Minister, Sir Gus O'Donnell produced a report into 'Data Handling Procedures in Government'.[54] July 2008 saw the production of the *Data Sharing Review* by Richard Thomas and Mark Walport.

In November 2008, the ICO produced its own report 'Taking Stock, Taking Action'(2008b), which examined all of the above investigations and reports and attempted to draw appropriate conclusions from them all. There are common themes from all the reports, such as problems arising from the use of third-party contractors, and the need for better management systems, more responsibility, and, at more senior levels, better information risk management and better training for staff. The ICO report (2008b, p. 7) concluded:

> While we recognise that much work has been done in improving information governance over the last year and are realistic in recognising that one can never completely eliminate the risk of data loss, the fact that the ICO continues to receive significant numbers of notifications of information losses indicates that both the public and private sector have to continue to improve in this area.

[53] Downloadable from www.ipcc.gov.uk/sites/default/files/Documents/investigation_commissioner_reports/final_hmrc_report_25062008.pdf.

[54] Downloadable from www.gov.uk/government/publications/data-handling-procedures-in-government.

The most important point arising from the ICO report is the recognition that 'one can never completely eliminate the risk of data loss'. Even when procedures are in place they are not always followed, and communication between individuals and departments is rarely completely clear.

2.6   *The reality of data vulnerability: the big picture*

The organisations studied in this analysis include those that 'ought' to have the strongest security: high-tech companies such as Sony, and the most privacy and security-conscious organisations such as the banks of Switzerland and Liechtenstein. The government departments examined in the previous section, HMRC and the MOD, are respectively the department with some of the most sensitive personal data (specifically financial data) and the department that should have had the best understanding of security. Both showed a vast range of weaknesses at almost every level: strategic, managerial, individual and technological. These kinds of weakness are not limited to governmental departments: something very similar happened to the HSBC Bank in 2009, two of whose departments lost CDs with 180,000 and 2,000 customers' data respectively, putting those customers at significant risk.[55]

The Swiss bank scenario demonstrates a number of important things: not just the fact that governments seem willing to condone or even promote the illegal acquisition of data so long as it is in a 'good cause'. The simple fact that the thieves were able to steal the data in the first place may be even more important. Further, the interaction between the vulnerability *of* governments with the vulnerability of information *to* governments needs to be considered. As has been shown, government bodies have a wide range of ways to acquire data, with various levels of legality. Once they have acquired this data, that data becomes potentially even *more* vulnerable. Moreover, the more information is copied and transferred, the more opportunities for vulnerability appear.

When the activities of leakers and whistle-blowers, from WikiLeaks to the likes of Edward Snowden, are added to the picture, the conclusion is clear. Data, wherever it is, however it is held and whoever it is held by, is vulnerable.

---

[55] HSBC was fined £3.2 million by the Financial Services Authority for these data losses. See for example www.telegraph.co.uk/finance/newsbysector/banksandfinance/5886419/HSBC-fined-3.2m-for-losing-customers-details.html.

3 Data vulnerability – solutions?

There are a wide range of tools that can be used to help improve the data vulnerability situation, many of which have been identified by the reviews into the various incidents outlined above.

3.1 Changes in existing law and practice

The most direct way to deal with data vulnerability is through changes in existing law and practice. In the UK, this could begin with the ICO's suggestion of increased fines and harsher sentences to deal with data losses and failures of data security, and in particular, the possibility of custodial sentences (something that arose from the T-Mobile data selling scandal discussed above). The possible penalties have been increased – from April 2010, fines could be as great as £500,000[56] – but to date custodial sentences have not been introduced. The Information Commissioner also suggested enabling extradition in some cases. Given the nature of the internet, that would seem logical.

While there may be benefits to these ideas in terms of deterrence, there are also significant weaknesses. Deterrence can only have a chance of functioning if the potential offenders believe that there is a significant likelihood of their being caught, which is only likely if the enforcement arms of data protection authorities are substantially strengthened. That too is something that could potentially make a difference, improving data security and reducing data vulnerability. Even so, the nature of current law and practice, and the principle of proportionality, mean that this kind of law – and in particular the idea of penalties harsh enough to act as a deterrent – could only apply to significant breaches and clearly 'sensitive' data. Problems relating to data vulnerability do not just apply to large-scale events or to directly sensitive data: the vulnerability of seemingly innocuous data is also important, and the accumulation and aggregation of individually insignificant pieces of data can have a significant impact. These kinds of breach are less likely to be detected and, even if they are detected, are highly unlikely to incur substantial penalties. More to the point, it would not be appropriate for them to do so.

---

[56] Details of the penalties are available at http://ico.org.uk/enforcement/~/media/documents/library/Data_Protection/Detailed_specialist_guides/ico_guidance_on_monetary_penalties.pdf.

3.2   Better use of technology

There are technological tools that can help with data security, the most obvious being the use of encryption. However, experts do not believe that encryption is anything more than a tool in the overall scheme of things. Ross Anderson, Professor of Computer Security Engineering at Cambridge University, and one of the leading experts in cryptography in particular and computer security in general, when asked 'How well-encrypted must data be, in order to be safe?' replied:

> You are in a state of sin. This is a wrong question to ask, for many reasons. 'Whoever thinks his problem is solved by encryption, doesn't understand his problem and doesn't understand encryption' (Needham and Lampson).[57]

Quite how true this is can be seen by the examples of both HMRC and the MOD in this chapter. In the HMRC case, the policy was in place for encryption, the technology for encryption existed, but it was not applied. In the MOD case, though the encryption technology had been specified, its application had been delayed a number of times, inconsistently and in some cases incorrectly installed, and it was rarely actually used by the personnel involved.

What is more, even encrypted data is potentially vulnerable in two different ways. Firstly, the encryption itself can potentially be hacked or broken. There is an ongoing battle between the developers of encryption technology and the hackers trying to break it. Any code can and will eventually be broken. The question is whether those who are attempting to keep the data secure stay ahead of those who are attempting to break it. This then requires those who use encryption to keep that encryption up to date, which leaves further scope for human error. That leads to the second weakness: the use of encryption requires human interaction, and even if the encryption cannot be 'broken', sometimes the human can. As Ross Anderson puts it:

> As designers learn how to forestall the easier techie attacks, psychological manipulation of system users or operators becomes ever more attractive.[58]

Most directly, people might be persuaded or forced either to release the keys to their encryption or even not to use the encryption properly at all. This is Ross Anderson again:

---

[57] In an interview for simple-talk.com, at www.simple-talk.com/opinion/geek-of-the-week/ross-anderson-geek-of-the-week/.

[58] *Ibid.*

> Deception, of various kinds, is now the greatest threat to online security. It can be used to get passwords, or to compromise confidential information or manipulate financial transactions directly.[59]

So what does all of this imply? Simply that though technological tools are a crucial part of the process of improving data security and reducing data vulnerability they are far from being the whole solution.

3.3   Changes in the community and culture

An overriding requirement, emphasised in all the reports that have been made into the data losses, is that all the issues concerning information vulnerability and security need to be taken more seriously at every level. That must start from the very top. The ICO's position paper, 'Taking Stock, Taking Action', for example, suggested that a 'role should be created at board level in larger organisations to deal specifically with information risk', and that '[a] post at senior executive level should oversee information security' (2008b, p. 6). The changes must be reflected throughout the organisation, and include proper and professional information risk management policies, periodic reporting of information risk at board level and clear lines of accountability, together with proper staff training and support.

The Poynter Report and Burton Review (and the ICO position paper following all the reviews) focus on that awareness simply in terms of individuals' roles as employees of their organisations, but the real problem and indeed the potential solution run deeper. If people were more aware of the issues of data security and vulnerability – and indeed of data privacy – in their ordinary personal and social lives, then it would be far easier for them to understand the importance of data security in their professional lives. They would find it easier to understand and implement information security policies, they would care more if the data encryption systems on their computers were not functioning properly and they would be less likely to fall for the kind of deceptive practices used by sophisticated cyber criminals.

3.4   Taking data minimisation seriously

Even if the law is both improved and better enforced, if the culture of organisations is more 'data conscious', and if security technology is used

---

[59] *Ibid.*

appropriately and effectively, there will still be problems and risks that cannot be completely eliminated. Human error, human nature, human malice, technological error and technological developments, commercial demands and community pressures, such as the need to fight terrorism or catch child abusers or murderers, are just some of the challenges. Ultimately, wherever data exists, it is vulnerable, so the only way not be vulnerable is not to exist. The ultimate weapon in the fight against data vulnerability is to eliminate the very existence of data wherever possible.

The starting point for this is stronger, better-understood and better-implemented data minimisation. The concept of data minimisation is built into data protection law. It combines the third and fifth principles: that data should be 'adequate, relevant and not excessive' and 'not kept for longer than is necessary'. It is, however, a concept that seems to be paid far less attention than it should, partly, perhaps, because the terms are very difficult to define. What is 'excessive' and how long is 'necessary'? In specific cases European regulators have argued the point at length,[60] but in general the answers to the questions have been left to the discretion of the businesses concerned. Unless specifically challenged, those businesses can choose how much data to hold and how long to hold it for. As things stand, it appears that most businesses choose to hold more data than they need, for longer than they need to.

The best way – perhaps the only way – for things to change positively in this field is for new business models to develop: models that take data minimisation seriously. If a way can be found to put data subjects more in control of the data minimisation process, then not only will people be more in control of their own data but businesses would be put in a position where they *have* to develop business models that do not depend on their ability to gather whatever data they choose and hold it as long as they like.

4   A change in assumptions and the right to delete

What is needed is a paradigm shift. The assumption should be that unless you have a strong reason to hold it, data should not be held.[61] The holders should need to justify their data holding. The shift of assumptions in

---

[60] Notably the search engine case discussed in Chapter 5.
[61] This assumption does theoretically exist in data protection law, but as the case studies in this chapter demonstrate, the reality is very different, and data minimisation is neither effectively followed nor enforced.

favour of deletion rather than retention implies a general right to delete data. In general, a data subject should have the right to have any data held relating to them deleted, and those holding that data must put into place systems that allow that right to be enforced at any time.

4.1   Forgetting and deletion

This right to delete should not be seen as akin to the 'right to be forgotten'. As suggested at the start of this chapter, what is being suggested is not about rewriting history or about censorship: it is about placing more effective, better controlled and realisable limitations on the government or commercial holding of more data than is needed. To describe it as a 'right to be forgotten' could even be seen as misleading or disingenuous; it is not about forgetting, but about control and autonomy. Talking about a right to be forgotten is attractive in some ways but it can also distract from the more important point. There are reasons why people might not have a right to be forgotten – rewriting history is something that is rightfully considered contentious or even dangerous – but they are not reasons not to have a right to delete. A right to be forgotten can be seen as a rejection of society and something ultimately undemocratic,[62] whereas a right to delete, properly set out and balanced with other rights, can be something precisely the opposite and act as a support and protection for individuals in their interactions with society.

Much of the opposition to the idea of a 'right to be forgotten' has been based on the idea of it being an infringement on free speech. Jeffrey Rosen in the *Stanford Law Review Online* (2012) wrote that 'it represents the biggest threat to free speech on the Internet in the coming decade'. Rosen quotes the notorious case of the murderers of German actor Walter Sedlmayr attempting to remove the mention of their criminal history from Sedlmayr's Wikipedia page, which does indeed reveal a real attempt to 'rewrite history'.[63] In the light of such stories, it is easy to see how the right to be forgotten can be characterised as a threat to free speech, but a limited and qualified right to delete would not have the same impact. Moreover most of what would generally be described as 'free expression'

---

[62] Suggested for example by Tessa Mayes at the Westminster Media Forum, 22 March 2011, and in her article in *The Guardian* at www.guardian.co.uk/commentisfree/libertycentral/2011/mar/18/forgotten-online-european-union-law-internet.

[63] See for example www.nytimes.com/2009/11/13/us/13wiki.html.

would be specifically exempt as set out below: the right to delete is intended to be primarily about data held rather than stories told.

It is hard to escape the conclusion, however, that behind the 'free speech' rhetoric, there is another agenda operating: that of free enterprise.[64] The right to be forgotten does interfere with free enterprise, placing restrictions and limitations on certain business models, and potentially placing expensive burdens on others. The same could be said about the right to delete: it *does* interfere with free enterprise, but appropriately so, placing appropriate restrictions on the way that businesses can use people's data. It is a step towards putting data minimisation in the hands of the individual. It is a shift in defaults: rather than asking when people should have the right to delete personal data, the opposite should be asked: in what circumstances and what kind of data should people *not* have the right to delete. The default should be that an individual *can* delete data.

4.2   When would the data subject not have the right to delete?

There are six principal categories of reasons for which data might need to be preserved regardless of an individual's wishes to delete it – where the presumption in favour of deletion can be rebutted.

1. **Paternalistic reasons:** where it is in the individual's interest that the data be kept, and society can override the individual's desire. A clear example of this is medical data.
2. **Communitarian reasons:** where it is in the community's interest that the data be kept. This might include criminal records, for example.
3. **Administrative or economic reasons:** where the economic or administrative needs of society require records to be kept. This could include tax records and electoral rolls.
4. **Archival reasons:** for keeping a good, accurate and useful historical record. This might include newspaper archives and blogs. This category is very important, and could be governed through a system by which a particular database is agreed to be 'archival' in nature – and thus not covered by the right to delete – but also restricted in the uses to which it can be put and so forth. This is in itself another contentious issue. The British Library and others use a recently granted 'right to archive', effectively archiving web pages without needing to get permission

---

[64]   A more detailed examination of the conflict over the right to be forgotten, and the role of free speech and free enterprise, can be found in Bernal, 2014.

from the website owners.[65] At first sight this might appear to be precisely the opposite of the shift of assumptions being suggested in this chapter, but in reality the two rights are compatible: both require close scrutiny and regulation of an archive.

5. **Free expression reasons:** the right to delete is not intended to chill free expression and should concern data rather than stories. There is a difference between published expression and held data – indeed, some of the most important data, such as profiling data, which is discussed specifically below, is never published, but held and used rather than *expressed* in any meaningful way. It should be noted, however, that free expression is never absolute, even in the United States, but subject to restrictions, as set out for example in Article 10(2) of the ECHR. One of those restrictions is 'the rights of others' – the right to delete should be one of those rights. Where there is a free expression claim, there is a balancing exercise to be performed.

6. **Security reasons:** where the data is needed for security purposes. This might include records of criminal investigations or such communications records as are set out in data retention laws. This category is by its nature highly contentious, and should be subject to close scrutiny – including political scrutiny – and regularly reassessed, applying a principle of proportionality to assess whether the impact on privacy is so severe that it is *not* overridden by the interests of security.

Effectively, these are limitations on autonomy, but limitations that are understood and reasonable in society. They can be compared with the data protection principle of 'fair and lawful processing' concepts (consent, vital interests, administration of justice, functions of crown and public interest), 'processing exemptions' (research, history and statistics, and the special purposes exemptions: journalism, artistic use and literary use) and the exemptions to access rights set out in Schedule 7 of the Data Protection Act 1998.[66] All of these cover similar ground, so the concept of such limitations should be familiar and acceptable. Indeed, setting out these terms from a rights perspective could be part of a harmonisation process, making all these areas consistent and coherent.

---

[65] The British Library, the National Library of Scotland, the National Library of Wales, the Bodleian Libraries, Cambridge University Library and Trinity College Library Dublin have all been granted this right, as of April 2013. See British Library Press Release at http://pressandpolicy.bl.uk/Press-Releases/Click-to-save-the-nation-s-digital-memory-61b.aspx.

[66] Data Protection Act 1998, ss. 28, 29, 33, Sch. 7(9), Sch. 7(1), Sch. 7(8) respectively.

It should be specifically stated that 'supporting your business model' should not be a sufficient reason to deny data deletion. This could be viewed simply as taking data minimisation seriously, but needs to be explicit. One of the purposes of rights is to spell things out so that people understand the principles and begin to understand the reasons behind those principles.

4.3   Highlighting profiling and other derived data

The exemptions set out above cover the kinds of data for which deletion should not be possible, but there is another end of the spectrum: a category of data that would need to be specially highlighted as 'available for deletion'. That is, not just data that the data subject has the right to delete, but data to which attention must be drawn and for which there is a simple, direct and clear method of deletion. The most obvious example of this would be 'profiling' or 'channelling' data so that an individual would be able to delete information derived about them from their behaviour in one form or another. The reasons for highlighting this kind of data are twofold: firstly, because this kind of data can represent the most direct threat to autonomy, and secondly because profiling or derived data could be a way that data gatherers attempt to avoid or circumvent data minimisation rules in relation to the time that data is held. For example, if someone searched for and looked at a particular website in January 2009, the fact that they performed that search could theoretically only be retained for six months, until July 2009.[67] If at that point, however, while deleting that search log data in accordance with agreed deletion periods, the search engine provider creates some new 'profiling' data, categorising the person as a 'visitor of websites of that kind in early 2009', that profiling data could be classified as 'new' data in July 2009, and then kept for a further six months, before being incorporated into some new form of profiling data, and kept for another six months. Intelligent use of profiles can effectively extend data retention for unlimited periods, and hence special provision needs to be made to cover it.

4.4   Deletion and anonymisation

There is a close relationship between deletion and anonymisation. As and where it is technically possible the right of data deletion could be

---

[67] If the periods of data retention suggested by the Article 29 Working Party in their recommendations to Google as discussed in Chapter 5, Section 2 were followed.

augmented with a form of subsidiary right: the right to have data ano-nymised. The primary right would be to delete data, but in certain cir-cumstances a data controller could offer the option to anonymise the data instead, with the data subject's consent.

The relationship between deletion and anonymisation is not, however, a simple one. If a right to delete is enacted, a data controller could poten-tially avoid the possibility of that data being deleted by prior anonymisa-tion. As the data would no longer be linked to an individual, no individual would have the right to delete it. Moreover, data is not always related to just one person: a group photograph in which a number of the people pictured are 'tagged' would be an example. That could bring a conflict of rights: if one person wants the data deleted but the others do not, whose rights have priority? Anonymity could apply here as well. In the photo example, it would be the tag that could be deleted rather than the photo-graph itself, effectively using the subsidiary right of anonymisation.

Further, anonymisation is far from a reliable process. There is evi-dence to suggest that much supposedly 'anonymised' data can be 'de-anonymised', by combining it with other, often public, data sources. In 1997 Latanya Sweeney demonstrated that by combining an anonymised hospital discharge database with public voting records a range of identi-fiable health data could be produced. Computer scientists have contin-ued to work on de-anonymisation; their models are getting substantially stronger and more applicable to the kind of data now being generated on the internet. In a 2008 paper, Narayanan and Shmatikov of the University of Texas demonstrated that, by combining the databases of Netflix and the online movie database IMDB, if you knew the county someone lived in and one movie that they had rented in the last three years, they could be uniquely identified eighty-four per cent of the time. Moreover, they sug-gested that their results could be generalised and applied to most other similar databases.[68] Work in this field has continued, and its implications are significant. At worst, it can be argued that anonymisation is simply an illusion, and even at best it means that it needs to be considered very care-fully and its weaknesses taken seriously.[69]

[68] Narayanan and Shmatikov, 2008. Available online at www.cs.utexas.edu/~shmat/shmat_oak08netflix.pdf.
[69] See for example the work of Paul Ohm (2010). Ohm analyses the work of computer scien-tists from Sweeney onwards and suggests that a full understanding of the weaknesses of the anonymisation process is required if methods to protect privacy are to be effective.

4.5   The virtue of forgetting

As noted above, the idea of a 'right to delete' should not be seen as a 'right to be forgotten' – there are technical, practical and emotional reasons to differentiate between the two. Nonetheless, there are still aspects of forgetting that are closely related and both important and beneficial. Viktor Mayer-Schönberger has written compellingly about the virtues of forgetting in *Delete* (2009). Mayer-Schönberger analyses how the developing 'default' of perfect digital memory takes control out of the hands of the individual, as their information and history becomes an indelible part of a mass of information usable and controllable by others. Moreover, it removes some of the positive effects of the passing of time. Digital memory can bring back information that has been forgotten for a reason, as part of the brain's method of navigating through life. As Mayer-Schönberger (2009, p. 118) puts it:

> forgetting is not an annoying flaw but a life-saving advantage. As we forget, we regain the freedom to generalize, conceptualize, and most importantly to act.

Forgetting, in these terms, is crucial for autonomy. Mayer-Schönberger's analysis is deep and detailed, providing strong arguments in favour of forgetting, and against the ideas presented by Bell and others[70] that digital memory is an essentially beneficial development. Furthermore, Mayer-Schönberger has suggested a solution to the problem of 'excessive remembering' by digital systems: the idea of expiration dates on information – as he puts it, 'reviving forgetting'. His suggestion is an ingenious and interesting way to find solutions to the problem, and in practice could have many benefits.

Establishing and implementing a right to delete could take it a step further, particularly from the perspective of autonomy, as it would put more control in the hands of the individual. The two could and should work together: the implementation of expiry dates on certain forms of data would provide a kind of overarching control over data, while the specific right to delete would provide further autonomy and put further pressure on businesses to develop better, faster-acting and more flexible business models.

This last point is the most important. The ultimate weapon against data vulnerability is the elimination of that data. Where data does not exist, it is not vulnerable. If businesses no longer create so much data, or no longer hold so much data, there is less data to be vulnerable and hence less vulnerability for individuals.

---

[70] In Bell and Gemmell, 2009, for example.

8

A rights-based approach

1 Putting the rights together

Three rights have been proposed in the course of this book so far: a right to roam the internet with privacy in Chapter 5; a right to monitor the monitors in Chapter 6; and a right to delete personal data in Chapter 7. Though these rights are important individually, they become significantly more effective when considered together. To understand why this is, and how the relationships between the three rights operate and are important, it is useful to divide the personal data process into three phases: the gathering, utilisation and holding of data. These three phases are related and intertwined, as are the related rights: for data gathering, the right to roam with privacy; for data utilisation, the right to monitor the monitors; and for data holding, the right to delete. The three combine to provide a coherent rights-based approach to people's engagement with the internet.

1.1 Data gathering and the right to roam the internet with privacy

The first and potentially most important of the phases is the data gathering phase. If the data gathering does not take place, there is no data to be utilised and no data to be held. For that reason, the *right to roam the internet with privacy* is not only the first of the rights to consider but the most important, particularly from the perspective of autonomy.

The right, as set out previously, would be a right to roam the internet and use its fundamental tools, without being monitored and without personal data being gathered. The key point of this right is that following the change of paradigm suggested in Chapter 1, the default position is that data is *not* gathered for storage and use unless an express choice has been made, for example by logging in to a premium, specified service. That then leaves the questions of what 'roaming' the internet means and what can be considered the internet's fundamental tools.

As for what constitutes a 'fundamental tool of the internet', the starting point is to look at current habits and market shares – at present, for example, search engines are amongst the fundamental tools of the internet, and ISPs are required in order to roam the internet. Search engines, for example, would effectively be required to offer their basic services in an alternative, 'privacy-friendly' form. For Google that might mean that rather than just the one search box there could be two search options: Google could call them 'basic search' and 'super search', the latter allowing Google to gather data but also provide tailored results and to offer 'better' services.[1]

With other tools, there are more questions to ask: to start with, how many people are using the services (both in absolute and market-share terms) and for what purpose. Where use of a particular service becomes the norm rather than the exception, that service could be said to be fundamental, and when there is doubt, the benefit of that doubt should lie with the individual. For some websites it would depend on whether the user was 'signed in' or not, and the kind of data that could be acceptably gathered without explicit consent would vary. Online retailers such as Amazon, for example, could (and would) gather actual transaction data, which they need for financial records, but would not be permitted to gather clickstream or 'browsing data' linked to the user from those visiting their websites unless the user had signed in. With other, not so directly commercial websites – news sites such as the BBC's, for example – unless some kind of sign-in process happens, gathering clickstream or browsing data could only happen in a strongly anonymised form. When the users sign in, the consent process begins and the second of the rights discussed in this book kicks in: the right to monitor the monitors.

The paradigm shift argued for here would mean that unless there is a good reason for tracking – that is, unless tracking is a fundamental part of how the service functions (as opposed to how the *business model* for the service functions) – then it should be possible to use the service without tracking. A news or information website, for example, has no 'need' to track or to gather information, while a social networking service works on the basis of membership and linking between members, so would require that information to be gathered and used.

That does not mean, however, that news and information websites would not be able to track, but that they would need to find a way to track that was consensual. Some potential business models are discussed below,

---

[1] See Chapter 5, Section 4.1.

but there are many ways in which this could work. The key is that if it is to the customer's benefit that tracking happens, the service needs to find a way of demonstrating that benefit to the customer and of limiting any associated risks. Membership schemes that do this are already developing and are placing the relationship between the customer and the business on a much more even footing.

As systems for profiling develop, tracking has the potential to become more pernicious. Such extreme examples as 'whites-only websites'[2] give some idea of why the idea of a right to roam with privacy should have general rather than specific application, and why tracking should be the exception rather than the rule, particularly if the internet is viewed as a 'public' resource. The idea of a 'no blacks' sign in a shop window is universally condemned in modern societies; a right to roam with privacy would provide protection against similar, hidden, but equally pernicious, practices online. Perhaps of more direct relevance, policies such as surreptitious price setting based on profiles could be curtailed.

The right to roam with privacy is intended as a principle and a guide; how it would apply in practice is something that will develop over time as habits and expectations develop. As will be shown later in this chapter, there are a number of possible business models that could function effectively while still satisfying the new rights. It could be possible, for example, to have 'membership' or 'paid-for' services (such as the subscription version of the websites of *The Times* newspapers)[3] that generate income without tracking or gathering information about the user. Once entry to the 'private' section of the website has been made, there would be no need for the website owner to track the user and so the right to roam with privacy would still function.

A right to roam the internet with privacy is a radical suggestion. It would require a significant change in the approaches of search engines, ISPs and other web providers, and in governments' approaches to security, as it would be directly contradictory to the current policy of near-universal surveillance and data retention[4] and all that surrounds it. It is, however, something that could ultimately be of benefit to all. It is also part of the process of changing the paradigm of internet use so that privacy is the default, and surveillance and data gathering is the exception, either

---

[2] See Chapter 3, Section 3.2.

[3] www.timesplus.co.uk/welcome/index.htm. *The Times* websites, however, currently require payment *and* still track and gather data.

[4] See Chapter 4, Sections 3.1 and 3.2.

opted into or brought into play when needed for security or other similarly important reasons. Those exceptions could include security exceptions. Security services could, for example, monitor particular users (even particular ISPs) or particular websites or services, when they have reason to believe that monitoring those users, sites or services would be useful and proportionate. Similarly, commercial web services would need to record certain transactions for legal purposes, and record certain data for reasonable economic purposes, but again, those purposes would need to be justified and specified.

1.2   Data utilisation: collaborative consent and the right to monitor the monitors

As and when data gathering is to happen – when it is consented to – more control and understanding of the process needs to be provided to those who are being monitored, those about whom data is being gathered. This control needs to cover not simply the data gathering process but the data utilisation process: people have rights not only over when, how and where data is gathered about them but when, how and where it is used.

The *right to monitor the monitors* – and the concept that could support it, *collaborative consent* – is the start of a process through which that control can be made possible. The key to the right and its underpinning concept is another aspect of the privacy paradigm shift. In this case, it translates to an understanding that the consent that is given to a data gatherer is a privilege. It should be taken seriously, both in terms of ensuring that the initial consent is one that is informed and understood, but also in that it is consent that can be modified or withdrawn at the will of the individual concerned, as their understanding develops, as their knowledge increases, and as their views and opinions change.

As set out in Chapter 2, collaborative consent has two key aspects. Firstly, it treats consent not as a discrete, one-off decision but as a process. Secondly, it looks at consent as a two-way agreement. The 'consenter' is allowed and enabled to see to what they have consented and to monitor, modify or withdraw that consent in real time; and the enterprise seeking the consent must communicate and collaborate with the 'consenter' not just at the start of the process but throughout. That means not just when the data is gathered, for example while browsing the web, but also when it is used. That might mean when a targeted advertisement based on gathered data appears, or when tailored content or recommended links appear, or when the price offered for goods or services is similarly tailored for an individual. Collaborative consent requires a two-way process, a form of dialogue between the enterprise and the individual. The internet provides the kind of medium for immediate and interactive communication that allows such a process to be possible.

From the perspective of the Symbiotic Web, collaborative consent has a crucial advantage: if those who are monitoring and targeting people require continued consent from those being monitored and targeted, they will need to communicate the benefits that those being monitored and targeted are getting. That in turn means that they first need to ensure that a benefit really exists, not just in the minds of the providers, but a real benefit that the user can understand and appreciate.

Once the data has been gathered, the third of the rights set out in this book comes into play. Rights are needed not only over what happens to personal data as it is gathered and processed, but also over what happens to that data after it is gathered. For that, one further right is required, *the right to delete.*

1.3   Holding data and the right to delete

Wherever and however data is held, it can be vulnerable, whether to technological failure, human error, human malice, business pressures, political pressures, hacking, leaking, theft, legal loopholes or a wide variety of other risks. Ultimately, the only way to ensure that data is not vulnerable is for it not to exist at all. That is the starting point when considering the holding of data and the first part of the reasoning behind the suggestion of a *right to delete.*

The second part is one of the key questions asked throughout this book: is 'personal' data in any sense 'ours'? If the answer to this question is essentially positive, then what needs to be considered is the kind of rights individuals have over data relating to them. As for the issues of data gathering and processing, what is needed is a paradigm shift. The assumption should be that unless there is a strong reason for data to be held, data should not be held. Data holders should need to justify their holding, rather than the other way around. This can be looked at as an extension to the logic behind the concept of collaborative consent. Consent needs to be continually renewed, but this time the consent is not just for the gathering of data but also for the holding of data.

This shift of assumptions is a shift in defaults: rather than asking when people should have the right to delete personal data, the opposite should be asked: in what circumstances and what kind of data should people not have the right to delete? This follows a similar logic to the exceptions to the right to roam the internet with privacy. The six principal categories of reasons for not deleting data are: paternalistic, communitarian, administrative, archival, free expression and security-based. As noted in Chapter 7, it should be specifically stated that 'supporting your business model' should not be a sufficient reason to deny data deletion. The exceptions that are suggested should ensure that the right remains in balance and indeed supports the positive balance that underlies the concept of the Symbiotic Web.

In the end, this idea boils down to ensuring that those holding data understand that holding data connected to an individual is a privilege, and one that can in most circumstances be revoked at any time. The organisations holding data should be asking the individual: 'Can we keep your data please?' as a real question, asked in a meaningful way, and with the answer being properly respected.

1.4   Three rights together: protecting autonomy, balanced with the needs and rights of others

In summary, then, for the three phases – the gathering, utilising and holding of data – three respective rights are proposed: the right to roam with privacy, the right to monitor the monitors and the right to delete. The right to roam with privacy is the overriding right. The right to monitor the monitors kicks in when that initial right is waived. The right to delete applies to the data once it has been gathered. The three are intended to work as a coordinated set, with the intention of moving to a situation where the gathering, using and holding of data is seen as a privilege rather than the default.

The crucial point here is that the rights are intended to protect autonomy. They are intended to preserve such autonomy as already exists in the internet, protecting it from the emerging threats discussed here, both the theoretical threats suggested by the model of the Symbiotic Web in Chapter 3 and the practical threats discussed in the case studies in Chapters 5, 6 and 7.

These rights are not what might be called 'fundamental' rights, but rather are 'mechanistic', designed for the world as it now is, and for the relationship between the online and 'real' worlds as they are currently developing. They can be seen as both positive and negative rights: freedom *to* roam and use the internet and at the same time freedom *from* surveillance and from manipulation. They are alienable rights; the alienability of the right to roam with privacy is critical to the way that it works and to the way that the internet works in its symbiotic form.

They are rights held in balance with the rights and needs of other individuals, of governments and of businesses. It is not the intention for the rights to stop the gathering, using or holding of data: that gathering, using and holding of data is what fuels the current beneficent symbiosis and provides individuals with so many useful, entertaining and enlightening tools and services. Governments have the right to do what is required to preserve security, to encourage and support business, and so forth. Businesses need the freedom to do what they find necessary in order to function. The needs and rights of all must be balanced. The rights suggested here are not intended to override the rights of others. Rather, they are intended to shift the balance of control more in favour of individuals – to give them more autonomy within the process – and thus give the symbiosis the best chance of continuing to grow and develop positively.

That it is the function of rights regimes to maintain a balance has been played out in recent cases. In first *Scarlet* v. *SABAM*,[5] and then *SABAM* v. *Netlog*,[6] the European Court of Justice ruled against the imposition of general filtering mechanisms to screen for copyright infringing materials, first on an ISP and then on a social media provider. The balance between individual rights to privacy and freedom of expression on the one hand and intellectual property rights on the other must be maintained. As the press release from the European Court of Justice on *SABAM* v. *Netlog* puts it:

> Such an obligation would not be respecting … the requirement that a fair balance be struck between the protection of copyright, on the one hand, and the freedom to conduct business, the right to protection of personal data and the freedom to receive or impart information, on the other.

1.5   How the rights might apply

How might these rights change current services on the internet? Looking first at a search engine, the right to roam with privacy would mean that search engines' 'basic' services should be available in a form that does not track or record search terms linked or linkable to the searcher. As noted above, a search engine provider could offer an alternative service – a 'super

---

[5] See http://curia.europa.eu/jcms/upload/docs/application/pdf/2011–11/cp110126en.pdf.
[6] See http://curia.europa.eu/jcms/upload/docs/application/pdf/2012–02/cp120011en.pdf.

search' – and explain that data would be gathered but that the service would be 'better' in the sense of being more tailored. An explicit exchange is being made: 'better' search results in exchange for more data being gathered. At that point, the right to monitor the monitors would kick in, and they would have to provide regular notifications as to when data was gathered, label any advertisements that were targeted or any content that was tailored and so forth, and also provide real-time access to all data held, including, following the right to delete, an easy and simple way to delete that data.

For a shopping website, the right to roam with privacy would mean that it should always be possible to 'browse' a shopping website without data about that browsing being gathered. Individuals should know that their browsing is private unless they have signed in and committed themselves to having that browsing monitored. Real transaction data would still be gathered, and the services would be free to make recommendations and so forth based on those real transactions, which is effectively what Amazon.com does when it makes personal recommendations. The right to monitor the monitors would only apply when and if a customer signs in and agrees to have their browsing monitored. It would have no effect on the transaction data, which is required to be held for administrative reasons. Similarly, the right to delete would only apply to browsing or related data, not to transaction data. If the shopping site also uses advertisements, where those advertisements are targeted based on monitoring, just as with search engines, those advertisements would need to be clearly labelled.

For a news or information website, the right to roam with privacy would apply in that it should be possible to surf without data being gathered. That should mean that even for 'paid' services such as *The Times* + subscription service, it should be possible to surf with privacy. Once again, it might be possible to have 'super' services that allow browsing data to be gathered, perhaps with fewer ads on the page, taking a leaf out of the book of the apps market on smartphones. Here, apps are often available in two forms, one free but where there are advertisements cluttering the small screen of the smartphone, the other costing money but 'ad-free'. The right to monitor the monitors would apply throughout, and again, the right to delete simply and easily should be available.

The area where the rights would be at the same time the simplest and the most controversial is when applied to ISPs. In its essential form, the right to roam with privacy should apply to ISPs across the board, preventing the kind of universal data gathering and use applied by Phorm's

Webwise.[7] It would also directly contradict the essence of the kind of general data retention regime or universal surveillance systems currently popular with governments. Though that would be a big political challenge, from the perspective of privacy and autonomy it would be a crucial step forward.

2   Autonomy by design

The idea of 'Privacy by Design' was conceived and developed by Dr. Ann Cavoukian, Ontario's Information and Privacy Commissioner, in the 1990s,[8] but has since become widespread, though generally as an aspirational tool rather than an idea with any legal force. In the UK, the Information Commissioner's Office (ICO) has been pushing it as an approach to data protection since November 2008. As the ICO puts it:

> Privacy by Design is an approach whereby privacy and data protection compliance is designed into systems holding information right from the start, rather than being bolted on afterwards or ignored, as has too often been the case.[9]

The Privacy by Design programme is intended to 'encourage public authorities and private organisations to ensure that as information systems that hold personal information and accompanying procedures are developed, privacy concerns are identified and addressed from first principles' (ICO, 2008a, p. 2). As set out in the report, the concept of Privacy by Design is a good one, though its strengths and weaknesses reflect those of the ICO in general, and indeed those of the data protection regime as a whole. The principles are essentially good, but it suffers from working largely through 'recommendation' rather than having much real force, it places more emphasis on encouraging the flow of data than it does on individual rights and it appears not yet to have had as much effect in reality as it does in theory.[10] The concept, however, is a good one: that privacy should be planned for from the very first, and that it should be taken into account through all phases of the data cycle.

---

[7] See Chapter 6.   [8] See www.privacybydesign.ca/index.php/about-pbd/.
[9] In www.scl.org/site.aspx?i=ne19845.
[10] The title of a March 2011 event organised by the Society for Computers and Law, 'Privacy by Design: "Grand Design" or "Pipe Dream"?' gives some indication as to the doubts that exist about the effectiveness of Privacy by Design in reality. See www.scl.org/site.aspx?i=ev18730.

2.1   Autonomy by design: the change of paradigm

Looking at the three rights set out so far, and taking the idea of Privacy by Design as a starting point, a new concept can be suggested: *'autonomy by design'*. Privacy by Design was all about data management under the old paradigm: autonomy by design is about data management under the new paradigm. The focus should be on the individual and on managing the data from the point of view of that individual and that individual's rights. As data is gathered it should be put into a format that helps the individual at the same time as it is put into a format that suits the business. What suits the individual? Knowledge, understanding and control, which means that the individual has to be able to *know* what data is held, *understand* why it is held and how it is used, and then be able to *control*: controlling what is gathered (via the right to roam with privacy), controlling how it is used (via the right to monitor the monitors and collaborative consent) and controlling what is held (via the right to delete).

If data is put into such a format from the moment it is gathered, and mechanisms are put into place to allow both access and control over that data in real time, then all three rights can be promulgated and brought into play together. The same systems can allow the user to turn the data gathering off, to look at and modify what data is being gathered, and what data has already been gathered, and to delete the data that is being held. This is taking the concept of Privacy by Design to a new level, to autonomy by design.

Phorm's Webwise – and to an extent other behavioural targeting systems – show that it is possible to make instantaneous use of data, if the software that does the work is designed accordingly. Why not use that kind of approach to analyse and prepare the data for presentation and use by the individual at the same time? If it can be done for the benefit of the business, it can be done for the benefit of the individual. Using the logic of the Symbiotic Web, doing so for both is more likely to produce a positive outcome for both.

In the ICO's 'Privacy by Design Report' (2008a) it was suggested that organisations should 'incorporate subject access request (SAR) functionality at the design stage ... [it is] in the interests of both organisations and individuals to ensure that systems are designed to automatically service SARs' (2008a, p. 24). Autonomy by design would take that a stage further. Both the business and the individual would benefit in the medium to long term if systems are designed from the outset not only to service the relatively bureaucratic and essentially legalistic process of a SAR, but to give the individual real and practical access to their data, in real time, together with the ability to correct, control and delete that data, and indeed to manage the data gathering process (including, crucially, the possibility of turning it off). Google's developing 'dashboard' system shows that this would be possible and hints at how it might work in practice.[11]

2.2   Autonomy by design: user-friendly rights

A crucial requirement of all these rights is that they would need to be both practical and user-friendly. That is one of the key features of autonomy by design. At present, it is generally far from the case, whether it is access to data (as in the use of the Google dashboard or Google ads settings[12]) or the deletion of data, as those who try to delete their accounts from Facebook, for example, will have experienced. There is no reason for this not to be possible. Organisations such as Google and Facebook have the highest levels of expertise in making all kinds of services accessible, user-friendly and attractive. If the will was there, they could do the same with the deletion of data. Combining the systems required for monitoring the monitors with an ability to immediately delete data would be a simple way to make this possible.

Further, with these rights in place, there would be pressure on enterprises to apply their considerable skills to find ways to present the data that they gather in user-friendly ways. If the user has the option to prevent data gathering (as the right to roam with privacy would require) and to delete any data that has been gathered, then if they are presented with something confusing or over-complex they are likely to exercise those negative options. It would be in the interests of the business to make the process as user-friendly and easily understood as possible, indeed, as quick and slick as possible, so that the user moves quickly through the processes and on to the real uses of the systems and services, the uses that make money for the enterprises. Autonomy by design, in a user-friendly form, would satisfy the requirements of both businesses and individuals, and could begin to provide the kind of systematic underpinning of a future, autonomy- and privacy-friendly internet.

For the rights to have this kind of pressurising effect, they would have to be backed by appropriate legal tools, enforcement mechanisms and penalties, such as the substantial fines that are now exercisable by the ICO in the UK, or have been applied by the European Commission

---

[11] www.google.com/dashboard.   [12] See www.google.com/settings/ads.

against Microsoft for anti-competitive practices. It is likely, for example, that the substantial fines applied against Microsoft played at least some part in persuading Google to give way (insofar as it did) to the Article 29 Working Party over data retention periods.[13] A general understanding and acceptance of these rights, however, makes the establishment of those legal mechanisms more possible.

Just as with collaborative consent, autonomy by design is ultimately about harnessing the strengths of the internet: its immediacy, its inter-activity, its powers of analysis and so forth. Businesses are continually striving to harness these strengths for their own benefit; autonomy by design would harness them for everyone's benefit. Though that may not immediately appear to be as attractive to businesses as something more focussed on their short-term bottom line, in the end they should benefit. Once more, this is the logic of the Symbiotic Web coming into play: when businesses and individuals both benefit, that benefit is more sustainable.

Autonomy by design is a form of multifaceted regulation. In Lessig's terms, it works by using code, law, norms and markets at the same time. More accurately, if it should come to pass it would be best achieved through symbiotic regulation. In the end, it will work as and when the different pressures in all those fields make it desirable. Here there are lessons to be learned from the field of online banking. In the early days of the internet, the idea of making payments online was considered highly risky and was discouraged. Now it is mainstream. This transformation has taken place as a result of a combination of the needs and desires of people to do business online, of banks to take advantage of these desires, and of the abilities of the legal and technical communities to find functional solutions to the problems. Making secure payments online works because of the technology, the legal infrastructure and the way in which people have been persuaded that it is safe: the code is there, the law is there, the market is there and the norm has been established.

The banking example is just one example of 'security by design'. The ICO Privacy by Design Report analyses how security by design was effectively introduced and how the lessons from it could be applied to Privacy by Design. It suggests five key factors: understanding the threat, management standards, executive awareness, language and frameworks, and organisation and responsibilities.[14] The report is good as far as it goes, indicating the technical and organisational challenges, some of which, the organisational ones in particular, would apply in an even more significant way to the

---

[13] See Chapter 5. [14] ICO, 2008a, p. 23.

introduction of autonomy by design. These key challenges could be better met with the introduction and acceptance of rights such as those suggested here. Well-communicated rights would help the management of businesses to understand something of the threat and to improve executive awareness. Well-written rights could help provide the language and framework, and help frame the management standards, as well as providing motivation and direction towards setting up appropriate organisational structures and setting appropriate responsibilities. Autonomy by design and the rights work hand in hand: autonomy by design would be a way to enable organisations to meet the challenges of the rights, while the rights would also help support the establishment and acceptance of autonomy by design.

2.3   Business in the new internet

Establishing and instituting rights such as these would place burdens on businesses. They would be required to create systems to allow individuals knowledge of the monitoring and access to their data, in an understandable and user-friendly form. They would have to allow individuals to control and even delete data that they, the businesses, could in the past have held and used as they wished, and benefited from both financially and strategically. Are these unnecessary or disproportionate burdens? On the surface, and from the businesses' point of view, they might seem so, but if the gathering, processing and holding of data about individuals is seen as a privilege rather than a right, and a privilege that must be earned, it is neither disproportionate nor inappropriate. Putting these kinds of systems in place is part of the price that must be paid to earn that privilege, and any business model that relies on deceiving or taking advantage of individuals is not a model that a good society and good legal system should support. It should be possible to develop business models that respect these rights and respect both customers and others from whom data might be gathered. There are many potential approaches, some of which are set out below.

Model 1: the anonymous, non-data gathering model

In this model, no data is gathered about either the person browsing or their activities. At first glance this could be viewed as representing the 'old-style' internet, as it existed before the Google/Facebook business models transformed the internet, but it is still a model that could function effectively. Moreover, not all of the advances made in the development of business models for the internet rely on tracking or gathering of data. Advertisements, for example, can be 'tailored' or targeted in some way without collecting data or monitoring the individual. Tailoring based on the route from which the individual arrived, for example, would not breach privacy and still maintain all the suggested rights.

There is a significant amount of additional information available for tailoring without having to infringe on the browser's privacy or record any data. For much of the internet (news and information sites, blogs and wikis for reading rather than contributing, for example) this is the model that should be prevalent.

Model 2: the instant tailoring model

In this model, data would be gathered 'on the fly', results tailored and displayed, and all data deleted as it is used, learning from the positive features of Phorm's Webwise. Systems using instant tailoring would have to be clearly signalled, and would have to find positive ways to deal with the consent issue by, for example, using collaborative consent in a simple form, notifying the user and allowing opting out of targeting. This should be possible; the failure of Phorm should not be seen to be the death knell for instant tailoring. Phorm's demise was brought about by many factors, the technological elements being far from decisive.

This kind of model would be suitable for more commercially focussed websites than those using the anonymous, non-data gathering model. In this model there are other tools available: anonymisation and aggregation. Once again learning from some of the positive elements of the Phorm model, it is possible to gather data and use it for analysis without identifying the individual involved, either as part of a quantitative analysis of behaviour of visitors to a website or users of an internet service (via a form of aggregation), or as part of a profiling system that identifies a type of user without linking that type to a specific individual (a form of anonymisation). It must be remembered, anonymisation is a tool to be used with caution, as it can be possible to 'de-anonymise' records.[15]

Model 3: the 'instant collaboration' model

Instant collaboration would mean a kind of 'mini-membership' system, whereby a user could enter into a short and most importantly very temporary relationship with a service, via something like a simple online form. Once again this would be learning from the positive aspects of Phorm, but this time suggesting the establishment of an immediate relationship with the surfer, a relationship based on collaboration and understanding.

---

[15] See Chapter 7, Section 4.4.

The collaboration would be immediately terminated if such a service was just browsed away from or ignored, and in those cases data would need to be immediately and automatically deleted.

A key point here is that the idea of instant collaboration should be one that grows as people begin to understand the way that the web symbiosis works. If people become more aware of the way that data is gathered and used on the internet, they should become more aware of the reasons for this kind of collaboration and the benefits that it can provide. They will also become more accustomed to the practice and more willing to participate, and the providers should become better at implementing the systems, making them more user-friendly and attractive. If the web symbiosis is to continue to grow and develop positively, that overall level of awareness and understanding must increase – that is part of the key to a more autonomous internet. An example of a website that might use this model would be a 'casual' shopping site, one that relies principally on one-off or irregular customers. As noted for the instant tailoring model above, the tools of aggregation and anonymisation would be possible with this model, with similar caveats.

Model 4: the long-term collaboration model

Here, a user would establish some kind of permanent membership with a service or site. This is essentially another 'traditional' model, but in a much more collaborative and controllable form. Access to data would have to be provided, as well as choices about how it is used, simplification and so forth, and the immediate ability to delete all data, really and effectively. Social networking services are perhaps the best current examples of the systems that would use this sort of model, though the simplicity and clarity of how they work in relation to surveillance and personal data would have to be significantly changed. This is an area where autonomy by design should come into its own.

Different businesses would use different models, and variants and hybrids of them. Each of the models has advantages and disadvantages in particular situations. A news and information site, for example, would be most likely to use an instant tailoring or instant collaboration model, while a social network needs long-term collaboration.

2.4   Would privacy 'break' the internet?

Even the business models that are most obviously privacy-invasive may not be as successful as they appear: privacy invasion, and in particular always-on, effectively non-consensual tracking may not be fundamental to the economic functioning of the internet. The stock market seems far less convinced by Facebook's business model than it might have been: the price of Facebook's shares fell to less than half its price within three months of its initial public offering (IPO).[16] Moreover, Microsoft's drive to setting 'Do Not Track' as the default in Internet Explorer 10[17] suggests that industry belief that tracking is 'necessary' is far from universal. There was significant pressure from many in the advertising industry for Microsoft to shift its stance, but that pressure did not prevail, at least in the first instance.

What does this mean? As it stands, the evidence that privacy intrusion produces business success is not as certain as it might seem. It means that business models have to constantly evolve, as indeed they are. The Google v. EU case study shows one of the ways in which this is happening: Google found a way to do business in a more 'privacy-friendly' form, under pressure from the Article 29 Working Party. This gives some clues as to the way in which others might follow. With appropriate pressure, businesses can and do find better and more privacy-friendly ways forward, though beforehand they may have claimed it to be impossible.

The rights suggested here, and the methods through which they can come into effect – symbiotic regulation, generally a gradual and piecemeal approach, evolution rather than revolution – should mean that it is possible for most businesses to find a way to meet the needs, the rights, of their customers. Some will fail, of course, in ways similar to the ways in which Phorm failed, but this is nothing unusual in business. The businesses that find a way to evolve as their environments change are those that are successful.

2.5   Leaner and more efficient businesses

Embracing these rights would encourage efficiency and 'leaner' business models. That leanness and efficiency would cover not only the data – the idea of taking data minimisation seriously should be fundamental to the future internet – but the systems and interfaces around data. The volume of data would need to be controlled, the forms in which they are stored would have to be more systematic and efficient, and access, manipulation

---

[16] See for example www.guardian.co.uk/technology/2012/aug/20/facebook-shares-drop-half-stock?CMP=twt_fd.

[17] See Chapter 6, Section 5.1.

and control over the data would need to be faster, cleaner and clearer. It should encourage greater efficiency, which in turn should help and support businesses that do it well. If done without the negative aspects demonstrated by examples such as Phorm, and with more transparency, consultation and coherence, it could provide something new and different. The innovative skills of those who have developed businesses such as Google and Facebook should be able to create similarly innovative and imaginative ideas that could function in this new environment. Indeed, ideas and businesses could thrive and take the internet onto a new, far more autonomous level.

3   A rights-based approach?

One question underlying all this work is whether, in the first place, a rights-based approach is appropriate or likely to be effective. Further, is it not true to say that the current European data protection regime is 'rights-based' anyway? In principle it is 'rights-based', at least in the sense that its origins include Article 8 of the European Convention on Human Rights, the right to respect for privacy (embracing a right to a private life).[18] In practice, however, data protection is more about the regulation of data flow than the protection of individuals' privacy, and it is treated to a great extent as a piece of technical legislation to be complied with rather than as a statement of rights and principles, and though the proposed new data protection regulation has more of a focus on individual rights, it remains more focussed on the data than the individual.[19]

In the UK, the ICO produced a comprehensive report to the Ministry of Justice about the current state of the data protection regime, and how it sees the future of that regime, particularly in terms of the current review of the Directive.[20] While it highlights the successes and failures of the regime and provides positive recommendations throughout, it still places the emphasis on the data flow, with the protection of individual rights simply something to take into account when encouraging data flow. In the online world as it exists now, it does not seem that data flow needs much encouragement – quite the opposite, as the various case studies here have demonstrated and as the imperatives of the drives within the Symbiotic

---

[18]   See paragraph 10 of the Preamble to the Data Protection Directive – Directive 95/46/EC, available at http://eur-lex.europa.eu/LexUriServ/LexUriServ.do?uri=CELEX:31995L00 46:en:HTML.

[19]   See Chapter 4, particularly Section 2.2.   [20]   ICO, 2010.

Web would suggest. Though the data protection regime has some of its roots in rights, its realities are more focussed on economic drives. Rights are treated more as a qualifier, an influence, than as the backbone of the regime.

So long as the primary focus remains on economic success, privacy and autonomy are likely to be squeezed, as so much of this book has shown, from the Google data retention story and the saga of Phorm to the numerous examples of data vulnerability. A more direct and genuinely rights-based approach would put that focus back on the rights of the individual. It would look at the issues from the perspective of the individual, and how the individual experiences things, how the individual is affected by events, and how that individual can understand those events, rather than the precise and technical details of what may or may not be happening to particular pieces of data.

What is more, one of the implications of the current approaches to data, privacy and related areas is that the law (and in particular data protection law) tends to be very technical and opaque. This is another reason for a rights-based approach. Where there is confusion, conflict or lack of clarity in law (central to many of the case studies set out in this book) then what is needed is something to fall back on, to guide and to set principles.

3.1   Technological neutrality

There are further reasons why a rights-based approach is particularly appropriate in this field. The first is that of technological neutrality. A rights-based approach can get closer to being 'technologically neutral' than a more legalistic approach. Looking from the perspective of the individual and their experiences rather than in detail at a particular form of technology gives more of a chance to set principles that can be applied when technologies develop. When working solely with law, approaching technological neutrality is possible, but has pitfalls: if the law is too specific, it can be sidestepped, while if it is too general, it is hard to apply. As new technologies emerge, or new ways of using data are developed, well-expressed rights are not as easily sidestepped, neutered or avoided as are more specific laws. The combination of rights setting the principles and specific laws used for enforcement has a better chance of success.

The problems surrounding technological neutrality can be further examined by looking at some particular examples:

(a) Phorm's Webwise

Phorm's Webwise was at least arguably compliant with data protection legislation in the UK because of the way that it used its UID system to avoid storing what could technically be described as 'personal data', though in the eyes of the public it seemed to infringe on privacy, and 'should' have been illegal in terms of the effect of what it did rather than the technological specific. It could be said that Phorm's Webwise breached peoples' rights, even if it might not have broken the law, and the EU pursued the UK government over its implementation of the Data Protection and e-Privacy Directives in relation to Phorm, and forced a legislative change.[21]

(b) Flash cookies

'Flash cookies' provide another example of the importance of technological neutrality and the advantages of a rights-based approach. Effectively, flash cookies could be used to sidestep legislation that targets 'traditional' HTML cookies, though flash cookies can end up even more intrusive, having no set expiry date and being able to regenerate previously deleted HTML cookies, for example. As security expert Bruce Schneier put it:

> Unlike traditional browser cookies, Flash cookies are relatively unknown to web users, and they are not controlled through the cookie privacy controls in a browser. That means even if a user thinks they have cleared their computer of tracking objects, they most likely have not.
>
> What's even sneakier?
>
> Several services even use the surreptitious data storage to reinstate traditional cookies that a user deleted, which is called 're-spawning' in homage to video games where zombies come back to life even after being 'killed,' the report found. So even if a user gets rid of a website's tracking cookie, that cookie's unique ID will be assigned back to a new cookie again using the Flash data as the 'backup.'[22]

There are three linked points to consider here, all of which have more general application than just for flash cookies. Firstly, legislation specifically covering HTML cookies would not cover flash cookies, so flash cookies could be used in place of HTML cookies and avoid that legislation. Secondly, technology itself can be used to avoid specific legislation. In this case, if legislation required an HTML cookie to expire after a certain

---

[21] See Chapter 6, Sections 4 and 5.
[22] See Schneier's blog at www.schneier.com/blog/archives/2009/08/flash_cookies.html.

time or after a particular event (such as logging out of a service), a flash cookie could be used to reinstate that cookie, again avoiding the legislation. Thirdly, technology can also be used to avoid technological controls. In this case, the flash cookie avoids the privacy controls (and in particular the privacy settings on browsers) used to govern HTML cookies.

The starting point for dealing with all three of these points could be looking at the process from a rights-based perspective. The rights establish the principles, and the legislation could (and should) follow the principles that have been established. As technology develops, specific pieces of legislation will require amendment, updating or replacing, but if the principles are set out in terms of rights, those amendments will be easier to establish and to understand, and, potentially at least, easier to put through legal systems. Flash cookies are only one example, but they demonstrate the problem that emerging and developing technologies can provide for the law.

(c)   HTML5 and future web technology

Another pertinent example is the ongoing development of the next generation of HTML (HyperText Markup Language), the technical language in which web pages are written. The newest version, HTML5, is currently under development, and is expected to improve many aspects of the ways in which the web works, integrating multimedia more effectively. It may also make it easier for individuals surfing the web to be tracked. As reported in *The New York Times* in October 2010:

> The new Web language and its additional features present more tracking opportunities because the technology uses a process in which large amounts of data can be collected and stored on the user's hard drive while online. Because of that process, advertisers and others could, experts say, see weeks or even months of personal data. That could include a user's location, time zone, photographs, text from blogs, shopping cart contents, e-mails and a history of the Web pages visited.[23]

As commentators have pointed out,[24] and as the examples described elsewhere in this book have shown, much of this has been possible with existing technology – indeed, much of it has already been done with existing technology. Importantly, incorporating the technology directly into HTML5 could make tracking both easier to do and more 'mainstream'.

---

[23] www.nytimes.com/2010/10/11/business/media/11privacy.html?_r=1&adxnnl =1&adxnnlx=1286794927-imUlp74yLiTLxFEIpNQWmA.

[24] For example, see blogger Space Ninja's comments at http://spaceninja.com/2010/10/ html5-nyt-privacy/.

Indeed, if it is built into the standards through which websites are created, full-scale detailed tracking could become the default position.

The development of HTML5 is close to completion. Parts of it have already been implemented, but full implementation is likely to take a number of years. The W3C, who have been developing the specification, issued their 'Last Call document', summarising the final issues remaining to be resolved, in May 2011,[25] with a ten-week initial review to follow,[26] but even two years later the problems had not been fully resolved.

How long it takes to become a de facto standard is yet to be seen. What is clear is that web technology is moving forward, and part of that move forward may have significant impacts on privacy and autonomy. Those who are concerned about privacy and autonomy need to find a way to have their voices heard and taken into account in the development of this technology. This is where rights can make a difference. They can add to the strength and in particular the coherence of the voices making claims about the need for privacy and autonomy. Putting rights in place (using the autonomy by design approach) could help find more appropriate uses for technologies such as flash cookies and could, if accepted and understood, shape the development of technologies such as HTML5 and in particular its successor technologies.

3.2 Rights, business models and jurisdictional issues

More importantly, if clear and well-understood rights can be established, they can play a key part in helping businesses to develop more positive business models. They can provide clear guidance to businesses that some ideas that they might be considering would be inappropriate and ultimately both illegal and unsustainable. The case of Phorm is one of the most obvious: if clearer, more explicit rights had been established and set out beforehand, the people who supported Phorm might have had a much better idea that Phorm would ultimately fail, and been able to avoid the whole farrago, with all its damaging implications.

As the concept of the Symbiotic Web suggests, the business model issue is crucial. To a great extent business models are what drive the development of the internet and all the commensurate benefits and technological

[25] See http://lists.w3.org/Archives/Public/public-html/2011May/0162.html.
[26] The first draft edition of HTML5 for web authors was issued in August 2011, see www.w3.org/News/2011#entry-9169, but in June 2013 agreement had still not been reached: see www.guardian.co.uk/technology/2013/jun/06/html5-drm-w3c-open-web.

advances that follow from it. Google and Facebook are perhaps the most obvious and dramatic recent examples. Their ways of doing business have transformed the internet. Future developments are likely to be similarly inspired and shaped: if the future of the internet is to be more 'privacy-friendly' it will be through the development of privacy-friendly business models. Coherent, well-established rights could be a key tool to help businesses to develop those models.

Another advantage of this approach is that it has the potential to overcome, at least to an extent, the issue of jurisdiction. Chapter 5 provided a prime example of how this works, discussing the way in which Google changed its policies on data retention in response to pressure applied by the EU Article 29 Working Party.[27] Google, considering itself a global organisation and preferring global policies and practices, made those changes worldwide. The impact of this is that though US users (for example) of Google do not have the benefit of European data protection, they have benefited from much reduced retention of their search data. Google is just one example, albeit probably the largest. In the internet, as it is currently developing, global businesses are increasingly prevalent, from fields such as search (Google) or social networking (Facebook) to those that create the software with which people browse the internet or even create the web pages that make up the internet. Influencing the practices of those global businesses is perhaps the most effective way to influence the environment of the internet itself.

Moreover, developments at most levels of the internet are essentially global: the standards set for the protocols and languages used in creating websites are global, the hardware used for PCs at least to some extent follow global standards (as do the operating systems) or are even made by companies marketing the same products worldwide, the software used to browse the web is generally the same the world over. If those products are built or written to work in places where there are high standards and requirements for privacy and autonomy (for example in the EU) then those high standards for privacy and autonomy will effectively benefit the users of the relevant software and hardware worldwide.

3.3   Real rights and underlying issues

Ultimately, however, a rights-based approach is appropriate because the rights proposed in this book really do constitute 'rights'. They are rights

---

[27] For detailed analysis see Chapter 5.

that people consider to be appropriate in the world as it has developed, as evidenced by the public actions over the events discussed above. The facts that more than 30,000 German citizens signed up to legal action against the implementation of the Data Retention Directive,[28] and that public uproar was critical in the collapse of Phorm's Webwise, are just two examples of how the public feel about this.

Each of the rights emerges from real wishes and needs. If the internet is a 'place' that is in effect an extension of the 'real' world, then the idea that people should have a right to roam that place with a reasonable expectation of privacy is sensible. Where surveillance occurs, it is reasonable that this surveillance is held in balance, and is accountable, so the right to monitor the monitors matches with real expectations. In the UK, for example, where CCTV is in operation, there is an expectation that there are warnings about that CCTV, signs indicating where it is in place, and legal controls about how and when it is used.[29] The right to monitor the monitors takes the idea a step further, but a step that fits with the different (and in some ways even more intrusive and pervasive) nature of internet surveillance. Finally, the idea that people should have control over the data that others hold on them is inherent in the data protection regime: the right to delete that data is in a sense a logical extension of that concept, a necessary extension if control over personal data is to be properly effective.

Meeting the real needs and desires of individuals is the point, as are helping to establish the nature of those real needs and desires and finding ways to communicate them. Throughout the case studies, most notably those of Google and Phorm, the battle over 'hearts and minds' has been crucial. Here too, following on from Gearty's suggestion that it is 'the intellectuals, the workers and the streets'[30] that matter, rights play a critical part. For the public to become engaged and to have their voices heard, they need a language to use, and they need the support of people who can help them to articulate their concerns, needs and desires. In this context, support can be particularly important. When the concept of privacy is difficult to pin down, define and explain, and where technical and technological language is complex and opaque, it is hard for ordinary people to explain why they are concerned. Furthermore, a basis of rights

---

[28] Chapter 4, Section 3.1

[29] ICO CCTV Code of Practice, online at www.ico.gov.uk/upload/documents/library/data_protection/detailed_specialist_guides/ico_cctvfinal_2301.pdf.

[30] Quoted in his talk 'The Rights' Future', see www2.lse.ac.uk/publicEvents/events/2010/20101006t1830vSZT.aspx.

can support a symbiotic regulation approach to bringing about change, one that in this situation is the most likely to succeed.

The three rights should be seen as a whole, and as underpinning a more basic right: the right to use and enjoy the internet with freedom. That, in turn, as discussed from the outset, arises from the idea that rights should be in place to enable people to flourish and fully enjoy and fully participate in society. If, therefore, people in our modern society have the right to use and enjoy the internet with the same kind of freedom and rights as they enjoy in the 'real' world, then these are exactly the kinds of rights that are required.

That, then, leads back to the privacy paradigm shift. It is this paradigm shift that is the basis of all the rights suggested. Freedom should be the assumption, the default, and surveillance and control the exception. The question should not be when individuals should be able to roam freely, unfettered and unmonitored, but when and why they should *not* be able to roam free. Similarly, the question should not be when individuals should have access to (and more importantly control over) data about them, but when they should *not* have such access and control. Businesses and governments should need to justify the gathering, utilising and holding of data, rather than individuals being obliged to challenge their actions.

4   Rights and symbiotic regulation

Chapter 6 looked at the Phorm saga through the lens of symbiotic regulation, and it was argued that the fall of Phorm was to a large extent due to its failure to understand the complexity or the nature of the regulatory matrix in which it operated. Further, it was argued that coherent and comprehensible rights could have helped Phorm and its backers to better understand that regulatory matrix, and to realise earlier in the affair the problems that were inherent in its business plan and its approach. Specifically, if it had understood why people would be concerned about the way they were being monitored and tracked by Phorm, and that the people who were concerned would have the ability to make that concern known – through working with advocacy groups, through their influence on other related commercial interests, through political lobbying, through legal challenges and so forth – then it would have been in a position to modify its business model to better meet the concerns of the community.

4.1   Extending the argument

These arguments extend to the other examples and scenarios examined in this book, and indeed to almost any related situation. In all cases the regulatory matrices are complex and multifaceted. In all cases there are many related and interested parties that have influence and effect. There are commercial organisations that both compete with and cooperate with each other in different contexts. Google, for example, cooperates closely with Apple in the integration of Google applications and services onto Apple's iPhone and iPad, but competes with it in that Google's Android operating system is used on smartphones competing directly with Apple's iPhone. Similarly, government and other regulatory bodies both cooperate and compete for jurisdiction and influence. The relationships between the UK government and various European bodies show this on a regular basis, with the EC's legal action against the UK over the implementation of its various directives in relation to Phorm a case in point.

Individuals have relationships with all those organisations and bodies, in various different ways: as customers of the commercial organisations, as voters for the various governments, as members of pressure groups or advocacy organisations, and so forth. The analysis of the Phorm farrago shows this in detail, but the same is true for Google in relation to its struggle with the Working Party over data retention periods, and even for the UK government in terms of its adoption or rejection of an ID card database. None of these situations is straightforward, and in all cases negotiating the complex regulatory matrix has proved far from simple.

That is another key reason to push for the use of a rights-based approach. Rights, if appropriately expressed, can help to clarify the complex regulatory matrix and help those who wish to negotiate it to a particular end to find a better way to do so. Those who opposed Phorm's Webwise were better able than Phorm's supporters to do this, as the eventual result of the saga demonstrated, but only after a long and painful struggle, one that could have been shorter and less painful had the relevant rights been clearer and better understood. Similarly, the struggle between Google and the Article 29 Working Party was long and drawn out, and to an extent continues to this day. The Working Party has the backing (and is formed from) the various information commissioners and their equivalents throughout the EU, but from the outside its mandate, backing and effectiveness are not as clear as they might be if the rights that it is effectively attempting to enforce were better understood and accepted. Well-presented and supported rights could have assisted the Working Party and perhaps brought about a more positive resolution to its struggle more quickly and more clearly. Similarly, working within the UK, properly expressed rights could support the work of the ICO, which to a great extent at the moment works with one hand tied behind its back, having to function through a softly-softly approach of coaxing and suggestion, only occasionally resorting to big threats, and even then such threats are rarely realised, as businesses know very well.

4.2   Empowering individuals

Most importantly, well-expressed rights could support and empower individuals themselves and help them to find ways to get their concerns across. It could help them to know which commercial services to choose, for example, if they are able to understand which are doing better in terms of supporting and satisfying their rights. In the Phorm story, Tim Berners-Lee said that he would change his ISP if it introduced a system such as Webwise;[31] if more people had known and appreciated their rights they could have been in a position to make similar decisions. What is more, the commercial organisations themselves would know that and would be more likely to set their policies accordingly. This would be symbiotic regulation in practice: rights having a ripple effect through the regulatory matrix, ultimately influencing the businesses that create the environment itself. If advocates wish for a privacy-friendly, or even an 'autonomy-friendly' internet, then rights can be the first step in bringing it about.

One further benefit of a rights-based, symbiotic regulatory approach in this field is that it has a chance of overcoming, at least to an extent, the differences of both political culture and legal systems between Europe and the United States. By working through rights to influence business models and to stimulate 'customer' attitudes and activity, it might be able to manoeuvre its way through the market-based systems that are both prevalent and preferred in the United States, while by providing backup and support for legislators such as the Article 29 Working Party it can help bolster the positive aspects of the more interventionist and legalistic systems of the European Union. That, together with the cross-jurisdictional issues discussed above – if a global internet entity changes its policies in one jurisdiction the benefits of those changes can apply worldwide – give this approach a chance of having more of a global impact.

---

[31] See Chapter 6, Section 4.1.

4.3 A self-balancing system?

The struggle through which privacy is gaining prominence and perhaps more acceptance may well be one that is happening anyway, without the need for the assertion of rights. In some of the case studies discussed in this book – most notably that of Phorm (and of Beacon) and to an extent that of the Google data retention periods – the outcome has at least in some senses been a 'privacy-friendly' one. Over the last few years the profile of the whole subject of privacy has risen, and more attention is paid to it by the internet industry than in the past.

That does not mean that there is no need for the assertion or establishment of rights. The purpose of the rights, and of their assertion, is not to start or impose a solution, but to support and help shape a process that has some momentum of its own, for if the rights are real rights, they would not need to be imposed, but would instead fit with something that people already want or need. Moreover, there are still challenges to the movement towards privacy and autonomy. Data retention is still very much in place. Behavioural targeting, despite the setbacks of Phorm and the growing willingness to legislate on both sides of the Atlantic, is still flavour of the month in the internet advertising industry, used by most of the big players including Google, Microsoft and Yahoo! News stories of data loss and debatable data privacy practices are arriving on a near daily basis and in a seemingly never-ending stream.

The trend in terms of privacy is far from clear, which makes the benefit of rights even more apparent. What is more, the rights proposed should also empower those who are losing (or have already lost) their autonomy. There have been many victims in this process, and there will almost certainly be many more. Indeed, part of the overall effect of the changes in the internet has been to further widen one aspect of the digital divide, the 'savvy' and the 'non-savvy': 'savvy' people have a better idea of what the problems are and how to avoid them. That is one of the most important aspects of the idea of promoting the rights suggested: to address the issue of this digital divide. It is the 'non-savvy' whose autonomy is most under threat and who are at the most risk.

Through these rights a better, more sustainable, more autonomous, more egalitarian, and less divided and divisive internet could develop in the future, one in which the digital divide between those in the know and the rest has less impact. That future, how it might look, and how the changes in it might address some of the problems inherent in the current situation, is one of the principal subjects of Chapters 9 and 10.

9

Privacy and identity

1 Online identity

The concepts of privacy, autonomy and identity are closely and inextricably linked. That linkage is played out very directly on the internet. In some ways, privacy on the internet is primarily about protecting identities, and autonomy is about control over identity. Conversely, control over identity can be seen as a way of protecting privacy and protecting autonomy. A rights-based approach can help clarify the links between them and help protect individuals' autonomy. In particular a right to online identity should be recognised, a right with three components: the right to *create* an online identity, the right to *assert* that online identity and the right to *protect* that online identity.

Online identity is more than a matter of authentication of a link from an online actor to a real person. Online identities are complex, multifaceted and constantly developing, and with both similarities and significant differences from 'real-world' identities. In order to understand how online identity should be treated, that complexity and those similarities and differences need to be better understood and taken properly into account.

1.1 Online identity in a maturing internet

If online life is now an intrinsic component of contemporary life, then to function fully in that life an individual needs to be able to assert an online identity, as a recognised online identity is necessary for much of what happens online. There are times and places both offline and online when the assertion (and certification) of identity can be required, and others where it can be of significant help, where finance is concerned, for example, or when dealing with e-Government. The recently launched UK Government Digital Service intends to use 'digital by default' as a basis for a wide spectrum of government services, and to close down non-digital versions.[1] As these services generally require some kind of authentication system, the need for a verifiable online identity will become crucial. People also need to be able to do business online, to enter into contracts and to buy goods and services, and as goods and services are increasingly available on better terms online, those unable to access those goods and services online will be increasingly disadvantaged.

In the original form of the internet – what may be loosely termed 'Web 1.0' – where the internet was essentially little more than an information resource that surfers tapped into, accessing the information and downloading data, there was little need for an online identity. As users browsed the web they left little trace and had little need to identify themselves. As the web has evolved into a more interactive form, where users supply their own content to the internet using such systems as wikis, blogs, social networking services, and media systems such as YouTube, Flickr and so forth, the need for an online identity has grown significantly. To properly utilise this version of the internet, an identity is crucial: it is part of the way that most of these 'Web 2.0 applications' function.

This interactive form of the internet has become mainstream. As previously noted, Facebook now has more than one billion active users around the world, while Twitter is estimated to have more than 500 million.[2] These numbers are significant; the interactive internet is maturing. With that maturity different habits are becoming normal. Where in the past an online identity might have been an ephemeral thing, generally created and abandoned at will, that has already become something of a misconception, and will increasingly be so. By mid-2013 Facebook was nine years old, Twitter seven, and some identities created on those sites and others have taken years to develop. Opportunities to develop online reputations are already greater than people who do not spend much time online may realise: the need to consider the nature of online identity and the rights associated with it is increasingly important.

1.2   Identity and anonymity

The primary contention of this chapter is of a positive right to online identity. There is, however, another side to the identity issue, one that needs to be considered if the idea of a right to online identity is to be seen in context: anonymity. Anonymity can be seen as the converse of identity – an

[1] The Government Digital Service can be found at http://digital.cabinetoffice.gov.uk/ and its Digital by Default policy can be found at http://digital.cabinetoffice.gov.uk/about/.
[2] See for example www.mediabistro.com/alltwitter/500-million-registered-users_b18842.

absence of identity – and just as there are times and places where identity is required, there may be times and places where anonymity is required and should be guaranteed: a limited 'right to anonymity'. UNESCO, in its 2012 *Global Survey on Internet Privacy and Freedom of Expression* views protection of privacy and of anonymity as being intrinsically linked, and to be supported.[3] Frank La Rue, UN Special Rapporteur on the Promotion and Protection of the Right to Freedom of Opinion and Expression, in his report to the Human Rights Council, said:

> restrictions on anonymity have a chilling effect, dissuading the free expression of information and ideas. They can also result in individuals' de facto exclusion from vital social spheres, undermining their rights to expression and information, and exacerbating social inequalities. (La Rue, 2013, para. 49)

Online anonymity, however, is not merely the absence of an identity. It can perhaps be more accurately portrayed as having an indiscernible identity. With this kind of anonymity, someone can browse the internet and interact with the internet (and other individuals on the internet) without leaving a trail or a trace, and without being able to be tracked down. This is a powerful concept, and any right to this kind of anonymity needs to be treated with a great deal of care.

A key element of online identity is the idea of pseudonymity, that is, an online identity not immediately linkable with the offline identity. Added to this are complications such as the possibilities of multiple online identities and shared online identities: these are discussed briefly at the conclusion of this chapter. They complicate the issues surrounding the recognition of a right to an online identity but at the same time emphasise its importance.

1.3   A rights-based perspective on online identity

Online identities are not the same as offline identities. There are some ways in which they are similar, others in which they are different. The multifaceted right suggested here reflects this. Some aspects of the right are effectively transpositions of existing rights from the 'real' world into the online world, while other aspects are designed specifically to deal with the differences. The threats to identity posed in and by the online world are different from those in the 'real' world, but there are also different

---

[3] See Mendel, Puddephatt, Wagner, Hawtin and Torres, 2012, particularly Section 4.

opportunities in relation to creating, asserting and protecting identities afforded by the technology and by the nature of the internet.

The human rights perspective attaches rights to individual humans. That is the position advocated here: the rights attach to individual people in the 'real' world, not to the 'entities' that they create to operate online. Nonetheless, it may sometimes appear that these 'entities' have rights because, as shall be discussed, perhaps the most important aspect of the right to an online identity is the right to protect the link between the 'real' person and the online identity. Protecting that link, and preventing that link from being revealed against the wishes of the person concerned, can and should mean in certain circumstances that what is dealt with is the online identity. That may make it appear as though the online identity has rights, but the difference should be clear. There are some online 'identities', such as corporate identities and 'bots', that have no direct connections to individual humans. Any rights attached to those kinds of identities are qualitatively different.

2   The privacy, identity, anonymity model

The previous chapter began the process of looking at how a privacy-friendly internet might look, examining how the three internet privacy rights considered so far fit together and how businesses might function in better compliance with these rights. The next step is to look at this from the perspective of identity. If the default position were to be one of privacy, what would this look like in relation to identity? Control over the links between the online and offline identities may be the most important aspect of the rights suggested: with this in place, the ideas of when and where identities need to be verified can become clearer and more appropriate. That means an internet where the paradigm is one of privacy – and sometimes anonymity – but with sophisticated and reliable systems for the verification of identity in appropriate circumstances.

2.1   A sea of privacy with islands of identity and anonymity

This privacy-friendly internet can be seen as a sea of privacy with islands where identity is required and others where 'true' anonymity is possible. The default position is privacy, and there must be good reasons to require identity or to allow full anonymity. In this sea of privacy, identity could be requested where needed and appropriate, or, from the perspective of the individual, could be asserted. When online shopping, for example, browsing could be private, without any need for proof of identity, but once the decision is made to make a purchase, the online identity could be asserted. If a user wants to use their identity to browse, to receive tailored content, tailored search results, links and so forth, they could choose to do so, making a conscious and consensual bargain between privacy and convenience.

This idea of a default position of privacy also provides part of the answer to the question of how 'public' the internet is. The sea of privacy can be viewed as the 'public' internet in which people are free to roam, but with an underlying level of responsibility. Rules about what is and is not acceptable in this public space would be relatively clear: general and universal monitoring would not be expected, for example, but the possibility of individual and targeted monitoring or localised surveillance would be known and understood. The islands of anonymity or identity could be seen as the 'private spaces' on the internet, where different rules apply – in either direction.

As with many ideas in this area there are risks: risks of function creep, risks that islands demanding identification could grow in inappropriate or disproportionate circumstances and merge into great continents that could fill the 'sea of privacy'. Coherent and understood rights can help, underlining the paradigm shift. By establishing that the default position is privacy, the onus is put upon those who want to breach that privacy to establish systems that are appropriate, proportionate and consensual.

2.2 'Strong' and 'weak' anonymity

Different 'levels' of anonymity are possible, some being stronger, more complete and harder to 'break' than others. The kind of anonymity represented by the mantra 'on the internet no one knows you're a dog', the kind of anonymity provided by the possibility of leaving 'anonymous' comments on people's blogs or creating pseudonymous twitter accounts, is a very weak form. It can be relatively easily broken using a wide variety of techniques and only gives an appearance of anonymity: it is close to useless in situations where anonymity is both genuinely useful and justifiable.

What can be termed 'strong' anonymity, the anonymity that really leaves no trace and makes tracking down effectively impossible, is much harder to achieve and much harder to justify. This is the kind of anonymity needed by dissidents struggling to resist an oppressive regime, abused spouses hiding from their abusers or whistle-blowers uncovering corporate malpractice. How this might be achieved from a technological perspective has been touched upon in earlier chapters. It is important to understand, however, that while there are situations where it is highly desirable that this kind of anonymity can be achieved, or at least closely approximated, at the same time the need for it is relatively rare. That means that the development of technology to make it possible should not be prevented – indeed it should be encouraged – and the infrastructure should not be designed in such a way as to make it all but impossible. There are powerful groups, from governments to corporate lobbyists, who would like the latter to become reality. Those groups should be strongly resisted.

2.3   The privacy, identity, anonymity model in the real world

Imagine someone going on a shopping trip. When they visit a shop, they window shop a little, browse a little, try on a few things and eventually decide to buy something. For the vast majority of the trip there is no need for the shops to know the identity of the shopper, not when they are window shopping, not when they are in the shop looking at the goods, not even when they are trying things on. Even when the shopper wants to buy something, the shop only needs to know that the shopper can pay. If the shopper is paying by cash, the shop has no reason to know the identity of the shopper at all; if the shopper pays by credit card, the shop only needs to have the credit card authorised, through a secure and limited system. There is no longer a need to provide a name and address or another form of ID as used to be the case to pay by cheque or card. Technology can support greater privacy, at least to an extent.

At any point in the shop, the shopper may ask for help, and the shop assistant may ask what the person is looking for and why, and may offer advice or suggestions. Similarly, the web user should be allowed (and invited) to tailor their web page according to their personal data. If people thought that just to enter a shop – or even to look in the window – they would be required to give all their personal details, they might be justifiably affronted.

In special situations, people might be asked for further information. For example, if they wished to purchase alcohol or tobacco they might be asked to prove their age, and if they wished to buy firearms they would be asked a lot more. In a similar way, more identity disclosure might be needed for particular sites on the internet.

At the same time as this, shoppers in the UK in particular accept that they might be recorded on CCTV (though there are privacy issues involved in relation to CCTV), but that CCTV is generally intended (and believed) to be specifically used for the purpose of crime prevention, and not looked at unless there is a particular need, triggered by a particular event. At least at present, CCTV is not (and in general should not be) used by shops in order to profile those shopping so as to be able to sell them more, let alone to be able to sell those profiles to other shops.[4]

All of this applies for the commercial areas that proliferate on the internet, but people would not accept the idea that the government should install CCTV in all other places more conventionally private, from their own homes to hotel rooms to the rooms used for Alcoholics Anonymous meetings. There are places where full, strong privacy needs to apply.

3   The concept and creation of identity

Identity encompasses a vast number of different aspects and has been investigated by a wide variety of different academic disciplines, from psychology and biological sciences, to anthropology, history, political science and philosophy. Even within these disciplines the idea of identity is one that is difficult to pin down. As Fearon (1999) puts it:

> Our present idea of 'identity' is a fairly recent social construct, and a rather complicated one at that. Even though everyone knows how to use the word properly in everyday discourse, it proves quite difficult to give a short and adequate summary statement that captures the range of its present meanings. (Fearon, 1999, p. 2)

Fearon goes on to list fourteen different academic attempts over the previous fifty years or so to provide succinct and precise definitions of identity from different perspectives, some conflicting, some complementary, some seemingly simple, some extremely abstruse. The primary conclusion to draw from the work of Fearon and others is that the concept is one that has many aspects and one that cannot be easily or precisely defined. From a legal perspective, this is both problematic and challenging, but not insurmountable. Just as with the concept of privacy, pinning down identity is complex, and indeed it may be counterproductive. Instead, the approach here is to look at certain aspects of the concept and then, rather

---

[4] It should be noted that in November 2013, Tesco's announced that it would be introducing a face-scanning system in its petrol station forecourts in order to target advertising. That announcement was regarded as controversial. See for example www.theguardian.com/technology/2013/nov/05/face-scanning-surveillance-society-tesco-quividi.

than attempt to fully define the *term* identity, to look at examining and defining the concept of a *right* to an online identity.

Identity can be looked at from two very different perspectives: as a social concept, a consideration of the position of an individual in relation to society, and as a personal concept, a consideration of an individual's internal construction of meaning and personality.[5] The social aspect considers things such as classifications within different categories, such as whether someone is younger than some, older than others, a member of this or that social, cultural, ethnic, racial, political or national group, and so forth. The personal aspect looks at personal choices, traits, wishes, desires, tastes, personality and so forth. The two aspects are in most ways inextricably interlinked and intertwined, but when identity, and in particular a *right* to identity is considered, both aspects need to be taken into account.

One particular philosophical perspective is to view identity as a narrative. As Gomes de Andrade puts it,

> Identity is not looked at as a sum of different elements, representative of one's identity and subject of being misrepresented and falsified, but as a narrative, an individual inner story that each person needs to build, develop and rewrite over time in order to define the meaning of their lives. (Gomes de Andrade, 2010, p. 432)

This perspective can be viewed as combining the social and personal aspects of personality referred to above. Cohen suggests a related narrative perspective, bringing in the many different dimensions of the developed identity and personality. As she puts it:

> Experienced selfhood is more accurately described as evolving subjectivity, formed and re-formed out of productive tensions between intake and outflow, performance and reflection, contact and separation. (Cohen, 2012, p. 131)

3.1   The creation of online identities

This 'narrative' approach is particularly relevant to online identities. The process of creating, establishing, asserting and protecting an online identity is something that happens in a similar way in many online communities. In these communities, which come in a wide variety of forms from

---

[5] What is described here as the 'personal aspect' can be seen as akin to what philosopher Paul Ricoeur called the 'ipse' identity, the social aspect to the 'idem' identity (see for example Ricoeur, 2005). De Hert, 2008, summarised the concept of 'ipse' identity as the 'irreducible sense of self of a human person', and the 'idem' identity as 'the objectification of the self that stems from comparative categorisation'.

message boards to virtual worlds such as Second Life or games such as World of Warcraft, identity is taken very seriously, and built up over time through a mix of creative and interactive processes. It can be argued that the personalities and identities created and used online have little connection with those of the people creating them, but the conception of identity put forward by Gomes de Andrade and others suggests that the development of 'real' personalities and identities follows very similar patterns. The online identity could therefore be viewed more as an 'extension' of the offline identity and personality of the individual concerned.

The blurring of boundaries between online and offline selves suggested in Turkle's pioneering work (1996) may have begun to be the norm. Turkle, referring to one of the most interactive activities then available on the internet, Multi User Dungeons (MUDs), suggested: 'In sum, MUDs blur the boundaries between self and game, self and role, self and simulation' (1996, p. 192). Turkle was referring to identities and activities in games, but In the internet of today the argument holds true in a wider context, encompassing almost all activities.

3.2   Real names and nymwars

There are some very different views about the relationship between online and offline identities, views that have particularly come into play in the so-called 'nymwars'.[6] Essentially, the nymwars represent the conflict over whether online identities should be based precisely on (and be linkable to) 'real' identities – something most directly shown by Facebook's 'real-names' policy. As described in Facebook's policy page:

> Facebook is a community where people use their real identities. We require everyone to provide their real names, so you always know who you're connecting with.[7]

When Google+ initially used a similar policy,[8] there was a strong adverse reaction from the online community, and eventually Google announced that it would be supporting the use of pseudonyms in the future.[9] Their current policy is slightly less strong than a 'real-names' policy: it requires what they call a 'common name'. As they describe it:

---

[6] See for example the Electronic Frontier Foundation analysis of nymwars at www.eff.org/deeplinks/2011/12/2011-review-nymwars.
[7] See the Facebook Help Center at www.facebook.com/help/?page=121104481304395.
[8] See http://support.google.com/plus/bin/answer.py?hl=en&answer=1228271.
[9] See for example http://mashable.com/2011/10/19/google-to-support-pseudonyms/.

> Your common name is the name your friends, family or coworkers usu-
> ally call you. For example, if your legal name is Charles Jones Jr. but
> you normally use Chuck Jones or Junior Jones, any of these would be
> acceptable.[10]

Precisely how this might be enforced remains unclear, but the key to
both Facebook's 'real-names' and Google+'s 'current-names' policies is
that they retain the right to delete or disable accounts where they know
or suspect that the user is not using their real or current name.[11] As
Google puts it:

> If we challenge the name you intend to use, you will be asked to submit
> proof that this is an established identity with a meaningful following. You
> can do so by providing links to other social networking sites, news art-
> icles, or official documents in which you are referred to by this name.[12]

The issues connected with real names played out most dramatically
in the case of the author Salman Rushdie in November 2011. Rushdie
found to his surprise that his Facebook account had been disabled, apparently because Facebook did not believe that the account was really his,
but might have either been a spoof account or an impersonator. Rushdie
complained, and was asked to produce his passport as proof of his identity. When he did so, they reinstated his account – but under the name of
'Ahmed Rushdie', because that was the name on his passport. Salman is a
middle name, but has been the one that Rushdie has used for many years,
and is the name by which he is internationally famous. That, initially, was
not enough for Facebook, who insisted that he be known by the name in
his passport, his 'real' name. Rushdie, however, understood the power of
social media and used Twitter to raise a storm of protest that proved successful in a matter of hours. As Rushdie put it in a tweet:

> Victory! #Facebook has buckled! I'm Salman Rushdie again. I feel SO
> much better. An identity crisis at my age is no fun. Thank you Twitter![13]

The Rushdie affair has implications for the creation and use of an online
identity. As *The New York Times* reported it, it asks the question of who

---

[10] See http://support.google.com/plus/bin/answer.py?hl=en&answer=1228271 (accessed
11 January 2013).

[11] Facebook's real name policy is under legal challenge in Germany, as there is a right to use
online pseudonyms in German law. See www.datenschutzzentrum.de/presse/20121217-
facebook-real-names.htm.

[12] See http://support.google.com/plus/bin/answer.py?hl=en&answer=1228271 (accessed
11 January 2013)

[13] http://twitter.com/#!/SalmanRushdie/status/136141997038776321.

determines the name by which you are known online.[14] It asks whether people have the right to 'create' their own identity – including the name by which they are known – both online and offline. Rushdie had chosen the name by which he was known in the real world – why should he have fewer and weaker rights over the name by which he was known online?[15]

While it is true that this initially impacted only on one aspect of Salman Rushdie's online identity – his identity on Facebook – there are broader implications for the future. Firstly, as noted earlier, Facebook is becoming close to ubiquitous, with more than a billion users worldwide. Secondly, where Facebook goes, other services follow, so if the idea of a 'real-name' policy is established and supported by Facebook, it may become an internet-wide norm. Thirdly, an integrated online identity could work better with linkage between the elements: people might wish the name by which they are known on one platform to be the same as that on another. To put it another way, one might *not* always wish to compartmentalise the online identity. Control over when and where to compartmentalise is a crucial part of control over online identity.

Many others, particularly those active in the online world, have challenged the whole idea of fixing online identities as direct parallels to 'real' identities. Chris Poole, one of the founders of the online forum 4chan, in a speech to the Web 2.0 summit in September 2011, challenged the assumptions of Facebook and Google. Poole suggested that they had fundamentally misunderstood the nature of online interaction. As he put it:

> It's not the audience, it's your context within that audience. It's not who you share with, but who you share as ... Google and Facebook would have you believe that you are a mirror, that there's one reflection that you have; one idea of self. What you see in that mirror is what everybody else sees. But in fact, we're more like diamonds: you can look at people from any angle and see something totally different.[16]

Poole's speech was well received and widely reported, particularly in the online world. Many of those who have 'operated' online for a significant

---

[14] See for example www.nytimes.com/2011/11/15/technology/hiding-or-using-your-name-online-and-who-decides.html?_r=1&hpw.

[15] There is evidence to suggest that more people are changing their names in the 'real' world. The BBC reported in October 2011 that an estimated 58,000 people in the UK would change their names by deed poll in 2011, compared to only 5,000 people a decade earlier. www.bbc.co.uk/news/magazine-15333140.

[16] The speech can be viewed online at www.youtube.com/watch?feature=player_embedded&v=e3Zs74IH0mc# and reports from it can be found for example at www.informationweek.com/news/231900986.

time have been using 'handles' rather than real names, have been creating 'images' for themselves and portraying themselves in ways that may bear little relationship either to their 'real' identities or personalities, or indeed to *any* conventional identities as understood by those unfamiliar with the online world. Enforcing a 'real-names' policy on the internet as a whole would be anathema to that community.

Whether that matters is another question. Does the 'mainstreaming' of the internet mean that the 'old' internet should be allowed to wither on the vine? The deeper question about the rights that people have over their own identity, and its use in the real world, remains. The need to have control over when and how that identity is used (whether by assertion or in answer to a demand), and the need to protect both that identity and links between the online identity and the real person imply that the idea of an enforced 'real-name' policy for the internet as a whole is deeply problematic and should be avoided. The risks associated with it, as well as the rights infringed by it, appear sufficiently strong to override the potential benefits.

It is not just online businesses such as Facebook and Google that are pushing for 'real names' as a general policy and practice on the internet, but governments too. The Chinese government has passed a law requiring real names before obtaining an account with an ISP,[17] while in both the UK and Ireland politicians have been exploring similar ideas.[18] In all these cases, the logic is about making users 'accountable' for their actions online, making privacy and anonymity subservient to that accountability. The risks that arise as a result seem inevitable. As danah boyd puts it:

> 'Real names' policies aren't empowering; they're an authoritarian assertion of power over vulnerable people.[19]

3.3   The complexity of creating online identities

A key component of the online identity is the name used when operating online – whether that name is the 'real' name (in Rushdie's case Ahmed Rushdie), the 'usual' name (in Rushdie's case Salman Rushdie) or some kind of 'handle' ('Oldlegalacademic' might be used as a Twitter name,

[17] See http://thenextweb.com/asia/2012/12/28/china-approves-regulations-that-introduce-real-name-registration-for-all-internet-users/.
[18] See for example www.bbc.co.uk/news/uk-politics-20082493 and www.tjmcintyre.com/2013/01/legislation-is-not-answer-to-abuse-on.html.
[19] See www.zephoria.org/thoughts/archives/2011/08/04/real-names.html.

for example). The name is often all that those who encounter you online see and can be argued to play a stronger role online than names play in the 'real' world. There is more to an online identity than a name, however, particularly when looked at from a narrative perspective, and those other aspects of the identity are all part of the identity creation process and also need to be considered carefully when looking at the protection of the identity.

First of all, there are images and related data associated with the name, known as 'avatars', which in some systems are how the identity appears. Some people use photographs of themselves, some use cartoons, some use pictures associated with the image that the user is trying to create – law books for a lawyer, perhaps, or a judge's wig. For many users the avatar says almost as much about them as the name. In some systems, the images associated with an identity may be far more complex, or may not even exist at all. In a sophisticated virtual world such as Second Life, the avatar is a fully rendered three-dimensional 'person', while on a message board there may be nothing except the name.

Further information may supplement the image of the avatar: a brief biography, description or similar that appears with the avatar as part of the 'public image' of the individual. The extent and nature of that additional information varies from system to system but it is another area that is often used to signify or individualise an online identity. It is a creative process, and neither the avatar nor the associated information is static. People change either or both on a regular basis, sometimes to reflect real personal changes, at others to change the image presented, and sometimes because they understand a little more about how they might appear to the outside (online) world. This is reflective of similar changes and developments of how people present themselves in the real world. The creation process online is more explicit and direct than that in the real world, but to a great extent they are the same processes.

Some of these developments are conscious but others arise naturally out of the process of interacting in the online world. As well as the 'presented' history of a person, an 'interactive' history is built up as a person navigates the online world, leaving footprints in cyberspace: messages left on message boards, sign-ups for services, interactions with other individuals and so forth. That history is also part of the identity and part of how the individual may be perceived. Once again, this is effectively the same process as in the real world. It includes such things as memberships of various services (current and past) and relationships with other actors online (again both current and past). It also includes links between the online and 'real-world' identity – from requirements to provide real names and other identifying details, credit cards or bank details, to information about employment (to enter websites set up for particular professionals, for example). It is a complex mixture of the controlled and the uncontrolled, the intentional and the unintentional, all building to create the overall online identity. The implications of the complexity of the ways in which individuals interact in a networked world are only beginning to be explored: as noted above, Cohen (2012) demonstrates the extent and importance of these interactions and the complexity of, as she puts it, 'locating the networked self'.

Looked at in this way, the creation and continued development of online identity is intrinsic to full involvement in the activities and functions of the interactive form of the internet that currently exists. If people are to involve themselves fully in this internet, then they will go through all those processes, and will, whether they realise it or not, be creating and developing online identities.

3.4 The right to create an online identity

The consequence is that the right to create an online identity is fundamental to proper functioning in the online world. As has been argued, full functioning in the real world now requires the full use of the online world, so for effective, efficient and fulfilling lives in the *real* world, people must have the right to create an online identity. Further, if the implications of the Rushdie affair are considered, and the needs and wishes of the online community are taken into account, control over that creation should be in the hands of the individual rather than determined by a specific authority, whether governmental or corporate. A right to create an online identity, however, is only the starting point for an online identity and needs to be understood in relation first of all to how the identity may be used, and then to how it can be protected.

4 The assertion of identity

There are two principal perspectives from which to look at the way that identity is used online: it can be demanded *from* an individual or it can be asserted *by* an individual. From the perspective of the service provider, an identity can be demanded of someone: the service will not be available unless the user proves who they are through some kind of authentication process. This generally includes the provision of certain information via a 'sign-in' process, followed by the allocation or choice of a username and password. Precisely what information needs to be provided in order for the user to complete this authentication system currently varies enormously and depends not only on the type of service involved but on the specific policies and business model of the provider of that service. On some occasions, from the perspective of the user it is hard to understand why certain information is requested or required, while on others it may seem as though almost nothing is required. To an extent this is inevitable – some services need more information than others, some need more certainty in terms of the identity of the person accessing their services than others.

What is lacking is consistency or understanding of what is needed and what the implications of the different approaches can be. Looking at it from the perspective of rights, shifting the angle so that an authentication process is a question of the user asserting their identity, rather than the service provider demanding that identity, can help to bring about that consistency and understanding.

4.1   Assertion of identity and disclosure minimisation

From the perspective of a service being provided, the 'requirement' for identity can be seen as meaning that you cannot do something *unless* you prove your identity. From the perspective of the user, however, it can be seen as meaning that the *assertion* of your identity *enables* you to do something. That change in perspective can help to shift the nature of the discussion of identity towards the rights associated with identity, and a shift in power into the hands of the user.

Once assertion is placed more in the hands of the user, it can help determine the requirements for information and for authentication. The guiding principle should be that to assert the right to use a service a user should only need to provide the information necessary to use that service. Following the pattern set by the data protection concept of data minimisation, this could be labelled '*disclosure minimisation*'.[20]

Requirements for disclosure would be adapted in accordance with the service concerned. If a service is age-restricted – available, for example, for over 18s only – then a user should need to prove only their age and

---

[20] 'Minimal disclosure for a constrained use' is the second of software engineer Kim Cameron's 'Laws of Identity', which set out from the perspective of software designers how identity should function on the internet. See www.identityblog.com/?p=354.

not be required to supply other information. If a service (for example an e-government service) is restricted to citizens of a particular country only, then the user should be required to prove their citizenship alone. If a service, site or location, for appropriate reasons, is restricted to one particular sex, the user should need to only prove that they are that sex and give no other information. There are technological solutions being developed that should make this kind of approach more practical and consistent,[21] but making the principle clear that only the minimum information should be required is important even before such solutions become fully developed and accepted. From a European legal perspective, this approach should already be practised: it is implied by the data protection's data minimisation principle.

4.2   Identity compartmentalisation and the right to assert

Related to this concept of disclosure minimisation, and following on from the idea that identity should be under the control of the individual, is the concept of identity compartmentalisation. From both a philosophical and a practical perspective, as suggested by Chris Poole, an identity has many different facets. Behind each facet lies a different narrative – if the narrative approach to identity is considered – and there are different disclosure implications. I, the author of this book, for example, am an academic lawyer and a lecturer at a UK university, but also a husband and father, a keen supporter of a particular football club, a lover of fine food, a fan of folk-punk music and a player of cards. When I am acting in my capacity as an academic, does it matter which football club I support? When I am performing my role as a parent, does it matter what kind of music I listen to?

Online, I might maintain a number of compartmentalised identities for use in different circumstances: to debate on an online football forum, to use Twitter for either personal or work reasons, to access information about food or music, or to play cards online. Those different identities are all 'me', but is it not my right to keep them separate, distinct from each other? This is not a matter of secrecy, it is a matter of choice. Arguments against such a right to compartmentalise include the idea that such compartmentalisation is effectively 'hiding' parts of yourself – another recasting of the 'if you've got nothing to hide, you've got nothing to fear' argument.

---

[21] See Section 6.1 below.

Ideas related to this are being explored in relation to different aspects of the online world, in Tene's work (2013), for example. Tene looks at the implications of the role of private systems such as Facebook in the practical management of identity on the internet, as demonstrated in the Salman Rushdie affair discussed in above. Tene's concept of disaggregated identity is closely related to the idea of identity compartmentalisation suggested here. Identity compartmentalisation itself fits closely with the idea of disclosure minimisation: if the latter is taken seriously, the former will be easier to achieve. Conversely, if identity compartmentalisation is supported it will require some form of disclosure minimisation.

A right to assert – one that includes the concept of disclosure minimisation – has an effect on a number of key issues in the way that the internet functions at present. The implications for e-government are clear and should encourage governments to continue the trend of putting more information and services online in ways that are more easily accessed. Properly implemented disclosure minimisation, backed up with appropriately designed authentication software, should support better development of ways to restrict access on the basis of age, gender and so forth without the need for extreme levels of privacy intrusion, levels that are not just objectionable in themselves, but which, as shall be set out below, present some significant risks.

The assertion of identity online could facilitate an updated, direct right of subject access under data protection regimes. Immediate, online access could become not just possible but required, potentially even allowing immediate deletion of data depending on how any right to be forgotten or right to delete becomes implemented.[22] Assertion of identity could also provide a means by which individuals could assert their own intellectual property rights online; the starting point for claiming such rights is asserting that you are who you say you are. Well-organised and rights-backed identity assertion systems could also streamline and support systems for entering into contracts online – and indeed other forms of business – without the need for formal contracts, electronic or otherwise.

5   The protection of online identity

The third key part of the right to an online identity is the right to protect that online identity. It is perhaps the most familiar part of the right, recognisable in relation to a number of generally known though not

---

[22] See Chapter 7

always understood risks, from defamation to so-called 'identity theft' to the question of whether there is a right to anonymity – or the opposite, a right for authorities to track down those who do 'bad things' online, from downloading illegal content, such as 'pirated' music, movies or games, to making inappropriate comments on online forums.

These issues and questions are very important in the internet as it currently exists, but there is more to the protection of online identity. Protecting an online identity means protecting it from a range of different risks: some old, some new, some well known, some known and understood only by those already very familiar with the nuances of online life. Protection of an online identity is very closely connected with the idea of privacy in the online world: it can be argued that online privacy is *primarily* concerned with the protection of an online identity.

There are three broad categories of protection required by an online identity: protection from harm or damage to that identity, protection from impersonation and protection of the links between online and offline identities.

5.1 Protecting the online identity from 'harm'

Some of the harms that an online identity can suffer are qualitatively different from those suffered offline. In one way, however, online identities can suffer harm almost identically to offline: damage to reputation. An online identity can be defamed in just the same way as a 'real' identity; and a right to protect the online identity should include protection from such damage in just the same way as a 'real' identity receives such protection. The key point, however, is that this should mean specifically protecting the online identity from that defamation rather than protecting the owner/user of that online identity from being defamed as a result of damage to their online identity.

Why does this matter? As noted earlier, part of the key to protection of online identity is protecting the links between the online and offline identities, so if the online identity can only get protection from defamation by revealing those links, it could end up as no protection at all. Though the harm, ultimately, is done to the 'real' person, effective protection of that real person may only be possible by protecting the online identity. There are clear difficulties with this idea, from the legal status of the online identity to the forum in which potential claims might be made. Some kind of online dispute resolution system could be developed in order to deal with this and other disputes relating to 'online-only' problems. Ultimately, should the dispute require it, the forum could move offline, with links revealed and more conventional law brought into play.

The second form of harm that an online identity can suffer is *exclusion*: where the identity is either prevented from being used in a particular forum or, having previously functioned in that forum, is subsequently banned from that forum. Users of Twitter, Facebook or a game such as World of Warcraft, for instance, will be banned for breaking the terms and conditions of those services, for example by harassing other users, or by using their identity for 'spamming' or otherwise behaving inappropriately. Indeed, the ability to ban users from many services is crucial to their effective functioning. The idea of providing users a right against this kind of banning is one that would have to be carefully balanced to ensure that it is not misused, but protection from arbitrary or malicious exclusion from services on the internet is nonetheless a key part of providing protection for an online identity.

The third, related form of harm – the most extreme form of harm – is that of *deletion* of the online identity. As in the case of exclusion, it is arbitrary or malicious deletion of an online identity that needs to be protected against.

5.2   Online impersonation

Where online 'communities' are moderated or regulated there are generally rules against impersonating someone else's identity, whether for malicious purposes or otherwise, because such practices are relatively common.[23] Such issues have parallels in more 'conventional' online situations: the 'Blaney's Blarney' case, most often noted as the case in which an injunction was permitted to be served via Twitter, revolved around this kind of deception, where the defendant served was effectively impersonating blogger Donal Blaney's online identity on Twitter.[24] In the 'Blaney's Blarney' case the link between the online and real-world identities was direct, intentional and explicit, but it may not be too great a leap from this kind of case to make purely online impersonation similarly illegal.[25]

---

[23] Twitter, for example, has an 'Impersonation Policy': 'Twitter accounts portraying another person in a confusing or deceptive manner may be permanently suspended under the Twitter Impersonation Policy.' See https://support.twitter.com/articles/18366-impersonation-policy.

[24] See www.griffinlaw.co.uk/2009/10/01/griffin-law-makes-law-by-serving-via-twitter/.

[25] Another relevant case is *Applause Store Productions Limited, Matthew Firsht* v. *Grant Raphael* [2008] EWHC 1781 (QB), relating to a form of impersonation on Facebook, resulting in defamation.

This fits well with the concept of an underlying right to protect an online identity.

Purely online impersonation can be qualitatively different from the form of impersonation perpetrated in the 'Blaney's Blarney' case, and the motivations behind it can be very varied. It can relate to some form of identity theft, where a person passes themselves off as another person, generally in order to gain some kind of financial advantage, enter into credit agreements, purchase goods and services, and so forth, taking the benefit and passing the risk or liability onto the original person. That is clearly fraudulent and illegal, and the problems with it, though undoubtedly of great significance, lie more with the detection, enforcement and proof than in the understanding or establishment of law. Nonetheless, an idea of a right to protect an online identity can bring additional force to the struggle against it.

Online impersonation, however, can take other, very different forms – forms common enough that a whole set of terms have arisen in different parts of the online world to describe them. One of the most obvious is 'clone' – an identity whose name or form is set up to deliberately look and sound like another user's identity. In a text-based system, that might be done by a slight change to a name, adding a letter here or there, changing the capitalisation, or misspelling a word, for instance. Cloned forms of the name 'Oldlegalacademic', for example, might be:

OldLegalAcademic
Oldlegalacedemic
Oldlegalaccademic

These identities might be used to confuse, to undermine a reputation or damage relationships, to make it look as though an individual's views were other than they were. They might, on the other hand, be used to tease or amuse – some names are chosen to make that more obvious. In this case, for example, an affectionate 'parody' name might be 'Oddlegalacademic'.

Another alternative form of potential impersonation is to use the name (and related data) that another person has used in one situation in another. For example, if one person had the Twitter name 'oldlegalacademic' but didn't use the alternative micro-blogging site Tumblr,[26] another could go onto Tumblr and give themselves the Tumblr name 'oldlegalacademic'. People using both forums might assume that the same 'real' identity lay behind both online identities – so material posted on Tumblr by the

---

[26] www.tumblr.com/.

second person might be assumed to have been written by the first, caus-ing confusion at best and potentially damage once more to reputation or relationships. Usernames on any system are generally allocated on a first-come-first-served basis, checking only whether the desired name has already been 'taken'. This kind of 'cloning' is not limited to names: it can apply to the avatars used and other data associated with an identity. If the name is similar, the avatar identical, the biographical details supplied consistent and so forth, the impersonation can be even more convincing.

Online impersonation can have many different purposes. 'WUMs' ('wind-up-merchants'), whose identities are designed to antagonise others, and 'griefers' in virtual worlds and online games, who just irritate and harass, are familiar to regular users of those systems. Most services have terms and conditions that forbid those sorts of activity, but they still go on as detection of inappropriate use and enforcement of the terms and conditions are rarely faultless, and there is a grey area between annoy-ance and harassment. There are similarly grey areas between affectionate parody, 'innocent' but annoying 'tributes' and malicious stalking.

There is an additional impersonation issue on the internet: the possi-bility of 'automated' impersonation. Writer, journalist and documentary film-maker Jon Ronson[27] discovered that there was 'another' Jon Ronson on Twitter, using his face as its avatar, and tweeting as though it were him – though in fairly random and disconcerting ways. He investigated and discovered that it was a form of 'bot': a computer-generated identity that tweets and responds to tweets automatically. He tracked down the creators, who explained that this bot was created by an algorithm that trawled over Jon Ronson's Wikipedia entry and used that to generate a 'personality' that functioned on Twitter.[28] Ronson himself confronted its creators and wanted them to remove the bot from Twitter. They refused, suggesting that he had no rights to make them delete it.[29] This form of automated impersonation has many implications, and the possibilities for this kind of thing are only just beginning to be explored. They need to be understood: should we have a right not to be impersonated, what-ever the motives? It was hard in Ronson's case to suggest that the intent

---

[27] Author of *The Men Who Stare at Goats*, amongst others.

[28] The creators call this a 'weavr'. In their words, '(s)tarting from interests given to them by their designers, Weavrs learn new emotions and grow to empathically reflect the inter-ests of those around them'. See www.weavrs.com/find/.

[29] See Jon Ronson's interview with the creators of his 'spam-bot' impersonator, online at www.youtube.com/watch?v=mPUjvP-4Xaw&feature=youtu.be.

was malicious, but should that matter? Automated parodies could be both entertaining and illuminating, but where should the line be drawn?

There can be no simple solution to protecting an online identity against impersonation. As suggested for harm, a solution might lie in the use of online dispute resolution, with legal solutions as a backup. The kind of resolution that is appropriate should depend on both intent and effect, and the law online should reflect equivalent laws offline. The argument for a 'parody' exception in the same way that in many jurisdictions there is a parody exception against copyright, is a compelling one when the nature of current interactions on the internet is considered. Parody or 'spoof' identities are part of the lifeblood of many parts of the internet – one might meet such figures as @SirIanBlair (modelled after the former Chief Constable of the Metropolitan Police) on Twitter, whose identity is clearly marked as a spoof account, and whose tweets on policing matters are poignant and amusing.

The Ronson case is clearly different, firstly because there is no attempt in the case of @SirIanBlair to pass the identity off as the real Sir Ian Blair, and secondly because there is no specific individual behind the fake Jon Ronson. Any protection given to a 'bot' is very different from the kind of protection that creators of parodies might need or deserve.

In relation to impersonation two things are important: that the idea that impersonating an online identity with malicious intent or with damaging effect is illegal, and that it is the online identity that is protected rather than just the real person behind it. It should not be necessary to sacrifice the advantages of protecting the links between the online and offline identities in order to protect the former. If this is not understood, the potential for using harm or impersonation in order to force an online identity to reveal itself is significant and, as will be noted below, this is potentially very damaging.

5.3   Protection of links between online and offline identities

The protection of the links between online and offline identities is the crux of the issue of whether online identities need or are entitled to protection at all. Though in many 'normal' situations these links may not seem important, there are also many circumstances where they can be crucially important, sometimes even a matter of life and death. Those apparently extreme situations need to be taken very seriously and the 'double-edged-sword' nature of the internet needs to be understood, in that it provides opportunities and threats at the same time. If a route, either technological or legal, is provided through which links between an online and 'real' identity can be 'proved' for a justifiable reason (such as tracking down the sources of defamatory comments on the net, or identifying individuals downloading copyrighted material illegally) then that route might be used for unjustifiable reasons or worse, such as oppressive governments tracking down dissidents or criminal gangs locating whistle-blowers.

One notable example of this issue came with the unmasking of the police blogger known as NightJack, in *The Times*. NightJack's blog, an 'insider' account of police life, was much admired, winning the prestigious Orwell Prize for blogging in April 2009.[30] As reported in *The Guardian*:

> According to the judges, the pronouncements of "NightJack – An English Detective" provided a perfect example of the medium's power and importance.[31]

Soon after the award journalists began to be interested in uncovering the identity of the author. After an article in *The Independent* confirmed that the author was a serving police officer who did not wish to be identified, *Times'* uncovered his name and told him they were going to publish. The blogger sought an injunction to prevent publication, but lost.[32] Mr Justice Eady, responding to the suggestion that many 'anonymous' bloggers would be 'horrified to think that the law would do nothing to protect their anonymity', suggested that though this might be true, the claimant's counsel would have to 'demonstrate that there would be a legally enforceable right to maintain anonymity, in the absence of a genuine breach of confidence'.

That legal right does not currently exist: one of the implications of the rights suggested here is that it should. There are many other issues surrounding the unmasking of the NightJack blogger, not least that it appears to have come about primarily as a result of illegal computer hacking by *a Times'* journalist, but if the right suggested in this paper was in existence it would not have mattered. The NightJack blogger's identity would have been protected, legally at least.[33]

The ultimate result of the unmasking by *The Times* of the NightJack blogger was that the blog itself ceased to exist – and a valuable and much

---

[30] See http://theorwellprize.co.uk/events/awards-ceremony-2009/.
[31] See www.guardian.co.uk/books/2009/apr/24/orwell-prize-jack-night-winner-blog.
[32] *The Author of A Blog* v. *Times Newspapers Ltd* [2009] EWHC 1358 (QB) (16 June 2009).
[33] For further details of the NightJack case and in particular the email hacking issue, see the work of David Allen Green in the *New Statesman* at www.newstatesman.com/blogs/media/2012/04/times-nightjack-hack-leveson.

respected source of important information was lost – but the blogger is still a serving police officer. Others whose online identities have been unmasked have suffered far worse fates, including the brutal killings and decapitations of Mexican bloggers by drugs cartels. By November 2011 there had been at least four instances of this practice.[34] There are many other examples: the tracking down of Chinese dissidents through the use of Yahoo! email accounts, with the cooperation of Yahoo!,[35] and the attempted hack of Gmail accounts again in China, apparently in order to locate other Chinese dissidents[36] are politically based examples, while the need for abused women not to be located by their abusive spouses and so forth is equally strong.

The implications of all of this are significant. First of all, it means that 'infrastructural' solutions to 'security' issues, such as building tracking and tracing systems into the technical infrastructure of the internet, are highly undesirable and should be strongly resisted. If 'back doors' are built into the system, they will be exploited for the wrong reasons as well as the 'right'. The best way to protect against this is to ensure that the back doors are not built to start with – and part of the function of a right such as the right to protect the links between online and offline identities is to guide those designing and implementing changes to infrastructure as to what should be possible. Secondly, it means that any decision to reveal the links between online and offline identities should not be taken lightly, and the balancing of rights in coming to any decision to do so should be weighted heavily in favour of not revealing the links.

If action needs to be taken against an online identity, the first option should be to take that action without revealing the links. Once again the use of online dispute resolution systems could come into play, as well as the possibility of redress in an online or 'anonymised' form being provided before enforcement is made upon the real person. This should, however, be a balancing act, and the revelation of the links between the online and offline should and would be appropriate where the harm is sufficiently significant.

---

[34] See for example www.englishpen.org/writersinprison/wipcnews/mexicoanother-bloggermurderedanddecapitated/.

[35] See for example www.nytimes.com/2007/11/07/business/worldbusiness/07iht-yahoo.1.8226586.html.

[36] See for example http://mashable.com/2010/01/12/google-china-attack/.

5.4   Rights to pseudonymity and anonymity

One more direct consequence of having the right to protect the links between the online and offline identities is that it implies a right to pseudonymity.[37] That is, a right to use a name other than your real name in your functioning on the internet, as discussed above. Real-name policies can automatically provide links between the online and offline identity, when combined with other publicly available data. This right matches closely with current practice in large parts of the internet, and its advantages, set out well by Chris Poole in the speech referred to above, are manifold. The idea of a right to anonymity is another matter, as has already been discussed.

There are, however, many complications with the use of pseudonymity online. Some issues will remain unresolved, and can only be managed. Some of these represent real fears, such as the use of fake, effectively fraudulent identities. Two noted examples of these have occurred in the last few years. One was the revelation that a noted Syrian blogger, supposedly a young lesbian woman struggling against the oppressive regime, was in fact the creation of a man called Tom MacMaster.[38] MacMaster claimed to have created the identity as a way of illustrating real issues, and that the whole thing had got out of hand. The unmasking of MacMaster was greeted with great dismay, and could have done significant damage both to people involved in the 'resistance' in Syria and to the credibility of genuine bloggers. The second was the use by journalist Johann Hari of a fake identity, David Rose, to smear opponents, to provide support for Hari himself and so forth. Hari has also admitted to plagiarism, modifying Wikipedia pages inappropriately and faking interviews. The fake identity of David Rose needs to be viewed in that context.

Both cases illustrate the risks of accepting an online identity as genuine and the problems with allowing people to create and use pseudonyms. Neither, however, should be used to undermine the idea that online identity separate from an offline identity is something that can and should be supported. There are rogues in all fields, and attempts will be made to bend rules, avoid laws and behave unethically in any situation. What they do illustrate, however, is the need for there to be appropriate checks and balances, and for there to be the possibility of authentication where

---

[37] As noted above, a right to use a pseudonym online exists in German law. See for example www.datenschutzzentrum.de/presse/20121217-facebook-real-names.htm.

[38] See www.guardian.co.uk/world/2011/jun/13/syrian-lesbian-blogger-tom-macmaster.

needed. There are other kinds of fakes that need to be 'unmaskable' – identities that are just automated programs ('bots' like the Jon Ronson bot) are perhaps the most obvious. As technology develops, the possibility of making these bots behave in ways that make them more convincing and less easily detected is growing.

'Astroturfing' is another concept that needs to be taken into account. It refers to the idea of establishing a 'fake' grass-roots movement by using fake identities to suggest a groundswell of opinion. The tobacco industry in the United States is reported to have used the technique, and there are risks that it will expand.[39] As for the MacMaster and Hari cases, these are problems that need to be understood and acknowledged, and where vigilance is required.

6   Identity in a privacy-friendly internet

Taking the issue of identity seriously is crucial if anything resembling a privacy-friendly internet is to become reality. Understanding how identity functions – and how it should function – on the internet is both highly complex and contentious. There are issues that are likely to remain unresolved and issues that will remain in tension. The first of these relates to the development of technology.

6.1   Identity and technology

There are two opposing movements in the development of identity-based technology. One, to a great extent driven by governments, is the movement towards stronger authentication systems. In the UK, for example, the government has an 'Identity Assurance Programme'[40] that 'could transform the way individuals prove they are who they say they are when dealing with organisations'.[41] The other, working from the opposite direction and driven to an extent by the opposite kinds of people – the hacker community – is the movement towards better systems to allow anonymity and to evade the increasing threat posed by electronic surveillance. The motivation behind some of the groups is the idea that the internet can be

---

[39] See for example www.guardian.co.uk/environment/georgemonbiot/2011/feb/23/need-to-protect-internet-from-astroturfing.

[40] See www.gov.uk/government/publications/identity-assurance-enabling-trusted-transactions.

[41] Quoted in http://ctrl-shift.co.uk/about_us/news/2011/07/11/the-uk-government-identity-assurance-programme.

a defender of human rights and a supporter of those who are oppressed, particularly in despotic regimes.[42]

There are close parallels between these tensions and those surrounding the development of privacy-friendly search engines[43] and anti-tracking systems.[44] It is a tension that exists in relation to many different aspects of the internet. When looked at from the perspective of the 'privacy, identity, anonymity' model, these two technological movements are not contradictory but complementary. As Vint Cerf puts it:

> We should preserve our ability to be anonymous or pseudonymous ... but we also need strong authentication tools.[45]

Both movements provide key components of an internet that can support the right to identity as well as the duty. Looking first at the movement towards stronger authentication systems, in the UK at least there is a recognition of the need for decentralised systems, learnt from some of the reasons for the dramatic failure of the ID card system that the Blair/Brown Labour government attempted to implement.[46] Some of the proposals for the UK system do incorporate a form of disclosure minimisation: the briefing from one of the parties involved, Ctrl-Shift, talks about 'attribute providers' being envisaged to verify 'particular attributes' such as age or driving licence.[47]

Looking from the other direction, the work of those seeking better protection for anonymity has come much more to the fore as a result of the role of technology in the Arab Spring. The 'despotic' rulers of Arab states, from those who fell (e.g. in Tunisia) to those who are still in power at the date of writing (e.g. in Syria), have been seen to use electronic surveillance on a significant scale,[48] and hackers seeking to oppose them have found ways to subvert that surveillance. In Tunisia, for example, one of the last moves of the old regime was to hack into the Facebook and Twitter log-in

---

[42] An example is the Liberation Technology Program run out of Stanford University – see http://liberationtechnology.stanford.edu/.

[43] See Chapter 5, Section 3.2.

[44] See Chapter 6, Section 6.2.

[45] From an interview in 'Cloudbeat', 14 November 2011, online at http://venturebeat.com/2011/11/14/vint-cerf/#.TsGmctgvSD8.twitter.

[46] See for example the interview with Edgar Whitley, 'Why It Failed in U.K.', at http://bas-antipurtimes.blogspot.com/2011/11/cover-story-why-it-failed-in-uk-r.html.

[47] See the Ctrl-Shift Identity Assurance briefing, p. 2. Downloadable from http://ctrl-shift.co.uk/shop/product/55.

[48] Evidence has been growing that Western companies have been heavily involved in selling electronic surveillance technology to these countries. See the work of 'Big Brother Inc.' in uncovering this industry, at www.privacyinternational.org/big-brother-incorporated.

pages that people accessing their systems in Tunisia would see, setting it up so that usernames and passwords were diverted to the authorities, who could then log into people's systems and monitor their activities.[49] This, however, was rapidly discovered by the hacker community in the United States, who 'hacked back', first of all correcting the log-in pages and then attacking the Tunisian government systems, knocking them out of action.[50]

Technology developed by these groups has been given some support by governments. One of the best known, Tor,[51] which attempts to provide anonymity by 'bouncing your communications around a distributed network of relays run by volunteers all around the world' receives funding from the US government. This is something that has been viewed with suspicion by some of the hacker community. The situation and motivations are not as clear-cut as they might seem, however, as the US authorities might like people to have effective anonymity when operating in other countries, for example. It should be possible to make the tension that exists between authorities and those seeking 'freedom' into a productive rather than a destructive tension. Ultimately, both sides recognise that for progress there needs to be a degree of trust, which means that people need both privacy and the ability to prove who they are, but on their terms. That needs both sides of the technology to be supported, but with appropriate checks and balances.

6.2   Multiple identities

Identity compartmentalising can (and should) be viewed as something positive, and something that people have the right to do, but should there be a limit on how many identities someone can have? Three? Ten? A hundred? Should all these identities have the same level of protection, the same rights? From a practical perspective, different people will need different numbers, and different people will be capable of 'running' different numbers of identities. It is probably not possible to set a hard-and-fast rule as to what is appropriate. The key should be the motivation and the use of the identities. If the motivations are appropriate and arguable, and

---

[49] E.g. www.theatlantic.com/technology/archive/2011/01/the-inside-story-of-how-facebook-responded-to-tunisian-hacks/70044/.

[50] E.g. www.thetechherald.com/articles/Anonymous-offers-support-to-Tunisian-protestors-(Update-2).

[51] www.torproject.org/.

the uses are appropriate and not malicious, then the identity should be afforded the relevant rights.

Perhaps the most complex issues in relation to online identity arise when the link between online and offline identities is not simple and one-to-one. An online identity may be shared by several 'real' people – for example a group of young gamers who can only afford one subscription to an online game and take turns in playing it. What about an identity that is transferred from one person to another? Should that be possible? And what should happen to an established online identity when the person who has been 'running' it die? Should that mean that the identity and all the things associated with it also die? In some cases the answers to these questions are clear, but in others they might not be. The expression 'The king is dead – long live the king!' could apply to certain forms of online identity.

There is a further, perhaps even more important consideration: what happens *online* has implications *offline*. As our online and offline lives become more intrinsically and inextricably intertwined, what we do with our online identities may be reflected in our offline activities. What becomes established as an online norm might become an offline norm. For example, if we are expected to go only by our 'real names', and provide some kind of identity certification wherever we go online, we might start to expect to do the same offline. The resistance to the idea that authorities have no right to demand to know who you are unless they have reasonable grounds for suspicion could be broken down without our realising how and why it is happening. Conversely, as noted above, there is an indication that more people are changing their names by deed poll now than a decade ago. Could the ease with which names may be changed online influence people to realise that they can change their names in the 'real' world too?

What we do online, and protection of our privacy online, is becoming more important to our 'real', offline existence. That means that if we believe that privacy has any importance in the real world, we need to find a way to bring about a privacy-friendly future for the internet. What that future might look like, and how it might be brought about, is the subject of the final chapter.

10

A privacy-friendly future?

1 A need for internet privacy rights?

The primary argument set out in this book is that we need internet privacy rights – and that we are increasingly demanding them – to address the threats to our autonomy that arise through privacy-related problems on the internet. The starting point in making this argument has been to demonstrate that these threats do exist: that has been a significant part of the work of the previous chapters. Some of the threats are clear and direct, some far more insidious, but deficiencies in the way our privacy is protected play a key role in all of them.

1.1 Deficiencies in privacy protection

Some of the problems are systematic and what might be described as 'intentional' – where the privacy issue is intentionally avoided, subverted or confused. These include: the way that consent is generally dealt with at best superficially; the lack of transparency in the way that search engines function; and the basic nature of monitoring systems such as the behavioural targeting systems. They also include the lack of transparency about governments' internet surveillance, exemplified dramatically in the summer of 2013 with the PRISM leaks by Edward Snowden. These systematic and intentional deficiencies in data privacy, all of which have both direct and indirect impacts upon our autonomy, represent the essential reality of the internet as it currently exists: the basic paradigm is that surveillance, monitoring and data gathering is the norm, and privacy the exception. It is this paradigm that needs changing.

These systematic and intentional deficiencies in data privacy are compounded by the various forms of data vulnerability set out in Chapter 7. These vulnerabilities in themselves represent privacy deficiencies and threats to autonomy, but the combination of the intentional and systematic deficiencies and the various vulnerabilities is even more significant.

Data gathered systematically then becomes vulnerable, and vulnerable in ways not initially envisaged by those gathering the data. Those gathering the data and invading people's privacy are often not doing so for any kind of malignant intent, or even particularly manipulative purposes. Even if they work without real consent and even without the *intention* of gaining consent, their motivations are frequently purely pecuniary or even based on the desire to develop interesting ideas or projects. Many things are just developed because 'they're cool' – the people creating and developing ideas may do so out of sheer enjoyment in the creative process. The implications of their ideas – and the ways in which their ideas may be used by others – are often more significant than they envisage. Once data gathered for benign purposes gets into the hands of others with less positive motivations, whether they be criminal, governmental or simply less than scrupulous businesses, that data may find very different uses than the neutral or benign ones initially envisaged. The WikiLeaks phenomenon, which exploded onto the public consciousness in 2010, provides just one example of how the data genie, once released, is very hard to get back into the bottle, while the PRISM saga, which emerged equally spectacularly in 2013, demonstrates how systems designed for one purpose (e.g. social networking) can easily be manipulated into use for another, quite different one (intelligence gathering by the authorities).

Some of these data privacy deficiencies appear to be currently legal in most jurisdictions, while some are clearly illegal. Many, however, seem to be somewhere between the two: Phorm, for example, claimed compliance with the relevant legislation, but that compliance was challenged in a number of ways at both national and European levels. The continuing discussions between Google and the European authorities suggest that the legality of the more mainstream activities of the largest operators on the internet may also not be as clear-cut as they might seem,[1] while the furore over PRISM and related surveillance challenges the legality of government actions in relation to the internet in many ways.

Moreover, as the legal landscape is complex, constantly shifting and to a great extent opaque,[2] there is scope for doubt not only as to what is acceptable but also as to what is actually legal. Again the Phorm saga provides a good example of how this kind of problem results in further confusion, the Cookies Directive being far from a paragon of clarity.

---

[1] Phorm is discussed in Chapter 6, the Google v. Article 29 Working Party dispute in Chapter 5.
[2] See Chapter 4.

There are more problems too: issues of jurisdiction, of enforcement, conflicts between different areas of law and conflicts of interest within governments. Governments, charged with the enforcement of privacy law, also have an interest in encouraging the gathering of personal data: Google demonstrated the conflict between data retention and data protection law; Phorm showed the conflict of interest for governments between supporting businesses and supporting privacy, while PRISM makes it entirely clear that authorities see huge potential advantages to be gained from the data gathered by social networks and others. All these issues and conflicts can and do result in further, deeper deficiencies in privacy.

1.2 Threats to autonomy

The form of autonomy used here, starting from Raz's concept of an autonomous person being the (part) author of their own life, is intended to be both broad and a real reflection of how we live. It includes the freedom to be irrational and the idea of autonomy in a social context. It serves to reflect some of the real issues in relation to informational privacy on the internet: those, for example, that arise from the advertising industry, which uses emotional and subliminal manipulation rather than purely rational or coercive methods of control. It addresses the increasingly social nature of the internet; social networking services such as Facebook and Twitter are just one aspect of this. It is also useful because, as will be discussed in more depth below, a broad definition of autonomy addresses some of the key criticisms of a more traditional privacy/autonomy approach, particularly the feminist and communitarian critiques, and also certain key aspects of the crucial transparency critiques and challenges.

The key case studies of this book – in particular Google and Phorm – address this kind of autonomy directly and demonstrate that threats to autonomy do arise through the deficiencies in privacy. Some of these threats to autonomy are inherent in the current commercial set-up of the internet. The conceptual model, the Symbiotic Web, sets out the nature and impact of these inherent threats to autonomy, emerging amongst other things from the commercial pressures building as a result of the symbiotic dependence of enterprises on the gathering and utilisation of personal data.

The case studies also reveal specific threats to autonomy in particular situations. Search engines are the key current tools for those using the internet to find what they want and to do what they want, so the ways in which search results are determined are fundamental to internet autonomy. That search engines do not currently operate with much transparency, that they have the potential to be 'tailored' without the knowledge or understanding of the user, that they could conceivably be set out to favour particular sites, services or providers all restrict the autonomy of the user.

Behavioural advertising uses private and personal data and surveillance in order to impact upon individuals' autonomy, controlling what they see and experience online. What is more, though it was initially intended to work in an advertising context, Phorm, the behavioural advertiser most analysed here, explicitly intended to extend its service to the tailoring of content as well as advertising, which could potentially have a significant impact upon autonomy, particularly when done without transparency or consent. Furthermore, as for search engines, this tailoring has the potential to be set in favour of the commercial interests of those doing the tailoring rather than in the interests of the user. While there is often a considerable overlap between the two, as most people may well prefer relevant advertising and content, that overlap is *not* complete.

In both the search engine and the behavioural advertising contexts, a key element of the processes used is profiling or its equivalents, and that in itself has a very direct impact upon autonomy. What is more, profiling means even apparently inconsequential data can become highly sensitive, and that kind of data is likely to be particularly vulnerable. There is attention to security – and an addressing of security by better management, technological security methods and so on – but that attention is focussed almost entirely on the most directly and obviously sensitive data. Profiling, and particularly the use of 'non-sensitive' data to infer sensitive information, can bypass that security.

Autonomy is threatened both by 'true' data and by false data, by both *accurate* suppositions and predictions and by *inaccurate* suppositions and predictions, and by both accurate and inaccurate profiling. A targeted advertisement, for example, based upon an assumption that an individual is gay could cause different kinds of damage to an individual if it was true or if it was false, but damage could be done either way. Autonomy and privacy include the right to keep certain things secret and private, even if they are true, while having decisions made about oneself based on false assumptions derived from infringements of privacy is self-evidently damaging and potentially unfair.

1.3 Profiling, the internet and politics

The question of whether much of this matters if its prime concern is advertising has been addressed,[3] but there is a further angle to consider. Imagine, for example, tailored advertisements created for individual 'swing voters' (selected automatically through profiling), pointing out a party's positive steps in the policy areas that are most likely to interest them (also selected automatically), omitting those areas where party policy does not fit, and couching it in a language appropriate to the individual's ethnic, educational, cultural and linguistic background, illustrated with a few appropriate TV news clips, and playing background music exactly to the individual's taste and voiced over by an actor that profiling reveals that individual likes? The reverse, of course, could also be sent about the political party's opponents: negative campaigning and personal attacks taken to an extreme level. This could be extended from tailored advertisements to whole 'news' pages where the 'news' provider has a particular political agenda, and also (and more simply) to individual automated emails.

The nature of the internet and the data gathering and utilisation processes suggest that a system that is already contentious could become worse and more persuasive than ever before. Much of this activity will by its very nature remain hidden. The extent of monitoring and the technologies used and developed for this purpose are naturally difficult to assess, but it is important neither to overestimate what is happening nor to ignore either the possibilities or realities of what is going on. With every new example it becomes clearer that those with a desire to profile and control, and indeed to take action, are aware of the potential. Recent developments – starting, for example, with the 2011 protest-led regime changes in Tunisia and Egypt, but continuing dramatically in 2013 with the PRISM revelations – have shown that communications technology in general, and the internet in particular, are having a growing political impact, and that the authorities are acutely aware of that impact and wish to use it to *their* advantage, rather than to the people's advantage.

When all of this is examined together, it is clear that autonomy *is* threatened through the kinds of deficiencies in privacy examined here. There are potential reductions in choices, selections of choices and inappropriate prioritisation of choices. What is more, autonomy is affected both by actual threats and by perceived threats – choices made depend on

---

[3] See Chapter 6, Section 2.

both – and by threats by both corporate and government bodies. It also appears that people are becoming more aware of the potential threats to their privacy and hence their autonomy, and they increasingly care about these threats.

1.4   Internet privacy rights

The possibility of addressing these threats through internet privacy rights is the central theme of this book. That rights have already been seen to be effective is borne out by the realisation that rights played a key part in the outcomes to the two principal case studies in Chapters 5 and 6, outcomes that were at least partially positive from the perspective of privacy. In the case of Google, it was the Article 29 Working Party's insistence that Google's data retention period breached the Working Party's understanding of users' rights that helped bring about the changes in Google's policies, while in the case of Phorm, it can be argued that the whole conflict was brought about by a realisation and assertion that what Phorm was doing was in breach of users' rights to privacy, almost in spite of how those rights were regarded in law.

These positive outcomes happened without the clearly expressed, coherent and acknowledged rights suggested here: rather, it is suggested that rights expressed and understood in this way would support the processes that bring about these kinds of positive outcomes. They could make those processes less painful for all concerned, with less 'collateral damage' and with less loss of trust. They could help prevent similar problems in the future, to the benefit of not only individuals but also of the businesses whose ideas would otherwise be likely to fail or at the very least be less successful and less profitable. In effect, they could support the beneficial aspect of the Symbiotic Web.

The rights would provide support and stimulus for the various mechanisms through which changes can and do actually take place. This is what is meant by the suggestion that the rights would work through symbiotic regulation. The rights could support the activities of bodies such as the Article 29 Working Party in their negotiations with Google, providing backup for their arguments and helping in their attempts to win the public battles for hearts and minds. The rights could help the advocacy groups and others make their points about business ideas such as Phorm's Webwise, and they could help businesses themselves realise that ideas such as Phorm are unlikely to succeed, either legally or as a business.

2 An internet with rights

What would the idea of a right-based approach mean for the internet as a whole? What is being suggested here is the idea that if human rights exist in the real world, then they should be extended to activities in the online world. This has significance well beyond what has so far been considered.

2.1 Rights to protect and support autonomy

The privacy rights that have been discussed so far relate directly to personal autonomy. They are not, however, the only rights in relation to autonomy that would arise once the general concept of an internet with rights is accepted.

Perhaps the most important right to consider in relation to the internet is a right to free expression. The internet is to a great extent a communications medium, and much of the current use of the internet relates to the expression of ideas, particularly in relation to what might loosely be described as the Web 2.0 applications: blogs, wikis, social networking and related services. Free expression is another aspect of autonomy; indeed, the privacy-related threats to autonomy have a significant impact on freedom of expression, not just directly (for example where a dissident blogger is tracked down and arrested as a result of breaches of privacy) but through the chilling effect – an 'internet panopticon' effect – that the knowledge of the potential privacy-related risks can produce.

There are also aspects to the issue of free expression that go beyond issues of privacy. One particularly direct aspect relates to the functioning of search engines and other navigation methods through the internet. The idea of neutrality of search is generally understood from the perspective of the searcher,[4] but in terms of a right to free expression, the neutrality of search from the perspective of the site is what matters. Does the creator of a website have a 'right to be found'? To be more precise, a 'right to be found if you want to be found'? That kind of right would not mean that a site could demand special treatment from a search engine, but that the site should be able to be sure that it would not receive especially *unfair* treatment, and that a search engine should treat it on its merits, according to the principles that are known and understood. The implementation of a right such as this would have particular difficulties in relation to the rights of the search engines themselves to trade secrets insofar as their

[4] See Chapter 5, particularly Section 1.

search algorithms are concerned, but companies and the EC have already bitten the bullet sufficiently to take Google on in terms of possible biasing of search results in the 'Foundem' case,[5] and this kind of right would relate directly to this kind of bias: bias in favour of something is by its very nature bias against something else. Google has responded to this accusation in relation to Foundem by saying (amongst other things) 'We built Google for users, not websites,'[6] but in an increasingly personal internet, where users are becoming publishers, is that a sufficiently strong argument? If free expression is to be taken seriously, it may not be.

A *right to be found* would be intended to prevent both bias and censorship – of the kind exercised by authoritarian regimes, for example – and would also have direct implications on filtering or blocking mechanisms such as BT's Cleanfeed, requiring them to be properly transparent and accountable, something that currently is questionable.[7] A *right to be found* could change the way that this kind of mechanism is looked at. As for the other rights discussed in this book, the aim would be to change the paradigm, to make individual rights and freedoms the starting point from which things proceed. This subject is one of significance and debate, and warrants further research.

There are other key rights and freedoms whose proper functioning on the internet needs to be considered. Freedom of assembly and association, guaranteed under the Universal Declaration of Human Rights (UDHR) and the European Convention on Human Rights (ECHR), are of very direct relevance to the internet, both in terms of gathering and associating online and in the way that the internet can help association and assembly offline. Privacy rights are crucial to enable this. As noted before, the authorities know this, which is one of the key reasons that more authoritarian regimes clamp down on privacy and engage in as much surveillance as they can. Social networks play an obvious part in the exercise of

---

[5] The European Commission opened an antitrust investigation into Google, which 'follows complaints by search service providers about unfavourable treatment of their services in Google's unpaid and sponsored search results coupled with an alleged preferential placement of Google's own services'. See EC press release at http://europa.eu/rapid/pressReleasesAction.do?reference=IP/10/1624&format=HTML&aged=0&language=EN&guiLanguage=en.

[6] Quoted for example in www.pcpro.co.uk/news/363244/google-faces-eu-probe-over-doped-search-results.

[7] See for example McIntyre and Scott (2008). McIntyre and Scott argue that 'where it is not clear what is being blocked, why or by whom, the operation of mechanisms of accountability – whether by way of judicial review, media scrutiny or otherwise – is greatly reduced'.

these freedoms, including their use for organising events or protests and finding people with common views or interests. Again, authorities know this: witness the UK government monitoring Twitter to try to manage possible protests about the 2013 'badger cull'.[8]

The role of rights in relation to social networks is another evolving area – and a full discussion of it is beyond the scope of this book – but a whole panoply of rights apply, from privacy and free expression onwards. In the broadest terms, in can be argued that there should be an effective 'right to social network', which would include the right to join and participate, the right for governments not to interfere and the right to expect social network providers to fully respect rights (rather than just their own internal rules) in the way that they operate. As noted in Chapter 9, that would mean, for example, that the idea of a 'real-names policy' is highly likely to be inappropriate.

2.2   A declaration of rights?

The rights envisaged here are not intended as simple legal rights, implemented through legal means, but something more fundamental, having effect through a process of symbiotic regulation. Communication and dissemination of the rights is a key part of this process, and looking at it from both a historical and a practical perspective, a 'declaration of rights' would be a particularly appropriate method of such communication.

As Gearty put it in his web project 'The Rights' Future': 'Proclaiming something is not enough to make it true, but it is a necessary preliminary in the struggle for its realisation.'[9] This could be particularly true in relation to online rights. There are many different groups with both interest in and influence over rights on the internet: states, corporations, programmers and hackers, community groups both online and offline, NGOs, pressure groups and lobbyists, as well as all the individuals who inhabit or could in future inhabit the online world. The huge differences between these groups in form, practices and histories make communication and mutual understanding both difficult and complex. Something like a declaration of rights could help bridge these gaps and underpin the more specific and precise agreements, rules and laws that are needed to enforce and protect these rights.

---

[8]   See www.bbc.co.uk/news/uk-politics-22984367.
[9]   In his online web project, 'The Rights' Future', Track 3, at http://therightsfuture.com/t3-making-truth/.

Such a declaration would not follow the lines of John Perry Barlow's famous 'Declaration of the Independence of Cyberspace' in 1996,[10] nor its 2010 YouTube successor by the now notorious hacker group Anonymous.[11] The suggestion here is to develop such a declaration by working with governments rather than confronting them as the Barlow and Anonymous initiatives did. It would not attempt to deny their jurisdiction or ability to regulate, but instead aim to guide, influence and shape the regulation that they can and do provide. The declaration would recognise that the essence of a successful Internet is one of mutual support and cooperation. It would in effect be an acknowledgement of the symbiotic nature of the web, with the benefits and dependencies that result from it.

As awareness of the issues has spread, the idea of a 'Bill of Rights for the internet' has begun to be talked and written about recently. Andrew Murray suggested something along these lines in his blog in October 2010,[12] analysing and developing two working suggestions, one based in Brazil by the country's Ministry of Justice, in partnership with the Centre for Technology and Society from Fundação Getúlio Vargas,[13] the other under the auspices of the Internet Rights and Principles Coalition.[14] Also in October 2010, UK Conservative MP Robert Halfon made the suggestion of an Internet Bill of Rights to the Backbench Business Committee of the House of Commons:[15]

> It should be up to the internet companies to respect the rights of the individual, not the other way around. I am calling for an internet bill of rights, a proper inquiry and an Information Commissioner who genuinely acts to safeguard our liberties. I hope that hon. Members and the Government will be able to support that.

In 2011, the Obama administration in the United States suggested something similar, confirming that it would support any congress proposal for

[10] https://projects.eff.org/~barlow/Declaration-Final.html.
[11] On video at www.youtube.com/watch?v=gbqC8BnvVHQ.
[12] See http://theitlawyer.blogspot.com/2010/10/bill-of-rights-for-internet.html.
[13] See http://portal.fgv.br/. Note that this page is in Portuguese. Murray's blog referred to above describes and analyses the key elements of this page in English.
[14] See http://internetrightsandprinciples.org/. The Internet Rights and Principles Coalition brings together people from academia, civil society, governmental institutions and the private sector, and has 'set out to make Rights on the Internet and their related duties, specified from the point of view of individual users, a central theme of the Internet Governance debate held in the IGF context'.
[15] See www.theyworkforyou.com/whall/?id=2010–10–28a.143.0.

a 'privacy bill of rights',[16] though what is suggested and envisaged is very limited and focusses entirely on the commercial use of data (and in particular behavioural advertising), rather than on any broader issues, treating people very much as *consumers* rather than *citizens*, let alone treating the rights as *human* rights. There are many reasons for this limitation: as the level of surveillance that the National Security Agency (NSA) has engaged in has become clearer as a result of Edward Snowden's whistle-blowing on PRISM and other programmes, it would have been difficult for Obama to make clear pronouncements about citizens having strong rights over government surveillance.

Furthermore, as the case studies throughout the book have demonstrated, the actions, tactics and approaches of governments and businesses are inextricably intertwined and effectively inseparable. The PRISM saga, which amongst other things suggested that authorities might have 'direct' access to the servers of the big internet companies, makes this point even more relevant. Corporate and governmental invasions of privacy and infringements on human rights need to be considered together. A declaration or bill of rights or similar would need to cover both, and, indeed, that should be one of the primary strengths of a rights-based approach, for by focussing on the rights of the individual, the actions of all those who infringe those rights, be they governmental agents or commercial actors, can be scrutinised, assessed and where appropriate opposed both politically and legally.

The Global Network Initiative (GNI) works towards somewhat similar goals. The GNI is a non-profit organisation bringing together ICT companies with civil society groups, academics and investors, with the principal aim of helping companies find ways to 'respect and protect the freedom of expression and privacy rights of users in responding to government demands, laws and regulations'.[17] Though the GNI has strengths, it also has weaknesses, and has not yet been able to produce much in the way of results. Important players in the field signed up to it from the start: some of the biggest ICT companies (specifically Google, Microsoft and

---

[16] White House spokesman, Commerce Department Assistant Secretary Lawrence Strickling, announced this in testimony before the Senate Committee on Commerce, Science & Transportation. See http://commerce.senate.gov/public/index.cfm?p=Hearings&ContentRecord_id=e018f33b-d047-4fba-b727-5513c66a6887&ContentType_id=14f995b9-dfa5-407a-9d35-56cc7152a7ed&Group_id=b06c39af-e033-4cba-9221-de668ca1978a. For further discussion see for example in *The Wall Street Journal*, http://blogs.wsj.com/law/2011/03/16/obama-to-push-privacy-bill-of-rights/.

[17] See www.globalnetworkinitiative.org.

Yahoo!), the best of civil society (including the Center for Democracy & Technology, the Electronic Frontier Foundation and Human Rights Watch) and some highly respected academic organisations (including the Berkman Center for Internet and Society at Harvard University). This breadth of membership may be the key to its problems; it appears to have moved slowly since its foundation in 2008. It has gained no additional corporate technology members since that foundation, and has not actually performed any of the reviews that were stated as one of its principal activities.[18] It has also faced criticism from groups such as Amnesty International, who withdrew cooperation prior to the initial launch, citing weakness in responding to human rights concerns,[19] and from bloggers such as Larry Downes in *Forbes*.[20]

An analysis of the problems faced by the GNI is beyond the scope of this book, but though it shows some promise, it does not appear, at least as yet, that it has the kind of strength to influence either corporations or governments sufficiently to make a real difference. It may be that in time it will be in a position to do so and that the work that it has done will go on to lay the groundwork for real progress, but so long as it is driven to a great degree by the industry, rather than informed by a properly supported, popular vision of rights, it is hard to see that its impact will be significant.

That, in many ways, is the key. It is the groundswell of community understanding that must underpin change: the rights suggested in this book are intended to represent and support *real* rights as needed and desired by people. Those must come first: declarations of rights are statements of what is already there in hearts and minds, not something imposed upon people from above.

2.3   The role of law

Rights understood and 'declared' can be seen as effectively arising from the community, but to make rights meaningful more is needed than community agitation and international declarations. As can be seen from the case studies throughout this book, the law itself, on many different levels, has a significant part to play.

---

[18] See for example www.nytimes.com/2011/03/07/technology/07rights.html?_r=1.
[19] See www.guardian.co.uk/technology/2008/oct/30/amnesty-global-network-initiative.
[20] See http://blogs.forbes.com/larrydownes/2011/03/30/why-no-one-will-join-the-global-network-initiative/.

In the Google v. EU case study, the lobbying of the Article 29 Working Party needed the backing of European Law. The combination of the existence of the Data Protection Directive (DPD) and the history of European action and substantial fines to the likes of Microsoft supported the Working Party's intervention. In the Phorm case study, the law was invoked both at a national level in relation to the Data Protection Act (DPA), Regulation of Investigatory Powers Act (RIPA), and the Fraud Act, and by bringing in the European angle in terms of the UK's implementation of the European Directives on Data Protection and e-Privacy. Again, the law was needed to back up the actions, and pressure brought to bear by the privacy advocacy groups and others in conflict with Phorm. In a slightly different way, the two *SABAM* cases in 2011 and 2012[21] have emphasised the role that European Law can play in supporting individual privacy rights against the competing right of intellectual property. Law can and does help keep the balance between the various competing rights.

That is the next key stage of the process: putting the laws into place that support and enforce these rights. The existence and coherent expression of rights can help in the processes through which the laws emerge. Declarations of rights can lead to international conventions, which can lead to regional and then local laws, laws that are more coherent and more in harmony with one another as they have a common basis. As Reed's concept of the 'cyberspace fallacy' made clear, human actors in cyberspace are accountable to local laws as they have a physical existence in a particular locale.[22] However, as he has subsequently argued, excessive use of local laws in cyberspace can lead to many problems, from conflict of law to the law itself having less effect and thus being less respected.[23] Having more harmonious laws governing activities in cyberspace could ameliorate those problems. Coherent rights could help speed up and simplify the kind of legal convergence that Reed argues can be beneficial, part of the strength of the rights-based approach.

Existing local laws can be brought more into line with common standards, and new laws brought in where required. With convergent laws, there would be less need for supranational courts or dispute resolution systems: rather, competent local courts in relevant jurisdictions should be

---

[21] *Scarlet* v. *SABAM* in November 2011 and *SABAM* v. *Netlog* in February 2012, discussed in Chapter 8, Section 1.4.

[22] See Reed, 2004, Chapter 7.

[23] See Reed, 2010. Reed argues that as states attempt to apply their own national laws to 'foreign' cyberspace actors, they can 'reduce the normative force of law as a whole and create the risk that otherwise respectable cyberspace actors become deliberate lawbreakers'.

able to deal with the key issues. There will continue to be issues and complications that need to be dealt with: to an extent it is likely to be through the resolution of these issues and complications that appropriate systems will arise. Through these processes appropriate laws will be developed, and greater levels of expertise and understanding of the complexities of both the technologies and how they are used will be built up. Expertise can be developed and communicated, and with the backing of coherent rights can give assistance to both legislatures and courts in navigating their way through the new and unfamiliar territory.

Law is not the starting point for the process of making rights real. Compared to the development of privacy- and autonomy-friendly business models it plays a relatively small part, and in addition is likely to be difficult and lengthy. It is, however, a key element of the regulatory matrix and a vital part of the process.

2.4   Security, monitoring and interception

The PRISM saga brought the role of the authorities in internet monitoring and surveillance starkly into focus for many people. Governments have many duties towards their citizens – to keep them secure, to protect the country from enemies, from terrorists and so forth – and those duties can require the monitoring and interception of communications. In the past, that has meant activities such as wiretapping: in the current era, it means some degree of monitoring and surveillance of the internet. To suggest that the authorities should not be entitled to engage in such surveillance (as Barlow's 1996 'Declaration of the Independence of Cyberspace'[24] might be said to suggest) is naïve in the current environment and inappropriate given the way in which the internet is now an intrinsic part of life for most people. The questions, therefore, are not whether governments should engage in this kind of surveillance but to what extent, how, and with what limitations, checks and balances? As La Rue's report to the UN General Assembly in 2013 makes clear, communications surveillance should only take place under legislative control, and 'must only occur under the most exceptional circumstances and exclusively under the supervision of an independent judicial authority' (La Rue, 2013, para. 81).

Amongst other things, understanding this would mean that the kind of surveillance envisaged in the Communications Data Bill, CISPA and

---

[24]   Online at https://projects.eff.org/~barlow/Declaration-Final.html.

its equivalents[25] would be essentially incompatible with a privacy-friendly internet: an internet with rights. This kind of surveillance, based on a 'gather all data, filter on access' methodology, with warrants either unneeded or needed only at the filtering stage, is fundamentally flawed when considered from the perspective of privacy. Two flaws are particularly significant: the vulnerability of the gathered data and the susceptibility to function creep. All data, however held, is vulnerable in a wide variety of ways.[26] Gathering data on all communications, particularly in a sortable and accessible form, would be particularly vulnerable. Moreover, the systems and laws would be especially susceptible to function creep, made only too clear by the experience with RIPA.[27]

What is more, the idea of universal surveillance, even with proper warranting at the filter stage, brings its own chilling effect that can accurately be labelled a panopticon chill. If people know that their communications – not just their phone calls and emails but their web browsing and other activities – are being monitored, their speech will be chilled and they will access less information, feel less free to associate and assemble, and so forth. In an internet with rights, that is fundamentally unacceptable.

What that means, ultimately, is that in an internet with rights the approach to surveillance and monitoring should be targeted, limited, and require warrants and controls. In La Rue's words, it should only occur in the most exceptional of circumstances. 'Surveillance minimisation', following the lines of 'data minimisation' and 'disclosure minimisation',[28] would be an appropriate way to describe this approach. Surveillance in an internet with rights would happen only when it is absolutely necessary. In the context of counterterrorism, for example, if a suspect has been identified, they may be monitored. If a website has been identified as being connected with terrorist activities, it may be monitored, as may those who visit it. In all cases, however, this monitoring must be with proper checks and balances, and with appropriate judicial oversight, warrants and so forth. These checks must take place at the data gathering stage, not at the data access stage – the idea of gathering on a broad or even universal basis and putting controls in at the access stage is anathema to a privacy-friendly internet.

The PRISM affair has made it clear that the scale of surveillance of internet activities by authorities is massive, and that the overall approach taken is the 'universal' approach. The most significant implication of this

---

[25] See Chapter 4, Section 3.2.   [26] See Chapter 7.
[27] See Chapter 4, Section 3.2.   [28] See Chapter 9, Section 4.

is that it will be very hard to bring about anything even slightly resembling 'surveillance minimisation'. It may indeed be the hardest part of creating an internet with rights – but that does not make it any less important.

3 The internet of the future and addressing critiques

The key test of the effectiveness of a rights-based approach to this issue is how it would pan out in reality. Rights in theory are only really worthwhile if they produce positive results. A sketch of how the internet might look if these rights were introduced – and how that form of internet might meet the criticisms that the ideas of privacy and autonomy face – was begun in the previous chapter. Filling in this sketch now can serve to demonstrate how the rights suggested in this book might address the critiques to the suggested approach discussed in Chapter 2.

3.1   Communitarian critiques

From a communitarian perspective it can be argued that an emphasis on the importance of privacy and individual autonomy tends to prioritise the individual over the community and/or misunderstands the essentially social nature of humanity. The broader definition of autonomy used here begins the process of addressing this, but the way that an internet with these rights in place would support the building and functioning of safe and effective communities plays a much more important part in meeting the critique.

The rights suggested here would specifically support those human rights that are far from individualist in character: freedom of association and freedom of assembly. The right to roam the internet with privacy combined with the right to monitor the monitors are particularly crucial in this, allowing online assembly and association with far less likelihood of that assembly and association being monitored, disrupted or prevented, as those who oppose that assembly and association would have their abilities to monitor and control curtailed. Similarly, the use of communications technologies to organise and support 'real-world' assembly and association, the importance of which was graphically demonstrated in the uprisings in Egypt and Tunisia in January and February 2011,[29] would be harder to disrupt.

---

[29] While headlines such as 'Tweeting Tyrants Out of Tunisia' in *Wired* (www.wired.com/threatlevel/2011/01/tunisia/) were somewhat hyperbolic, it does appear that the internet

The privacy, identity, anonymity model introduced in Chapter 9 would directly support these rights, and indeed the communities that the rights themselves support. Privacy for most activities, anonymity in times and places of trouble, and the technology and ability to verify identity when needed – for example to root out spies or infiltrators working for those wishing to disrupt the communities – is the kind of combination that is needed.

The risks of communities fracturing through 'backdoor Balkanisation', one of the side effects of the Symbiotic Web,[30] would be reduced by this kind of rights model, though the risks of the more deliberate form of fracturing, as set out in Sunstein's *Republic.com 2.0* (2007), remain. Indeed, if there is excessive use of anonymity, this risk might be increased: a private, unmonitored internet could allow further polarisation without the means to govern or control. Privacy, rather than anonymity, is the key here, privacy that can be overturned where necessary. Perhaps more importantly, one of the purposes of the rights suggested here is that they are intended to help build trust, a trust that the current deficiencies in privacy are putting at risk. Trust of business, trust of government and trust of other individuals are all crucial for community building. The rights suggested here are intended to help to rebuild that trust.

3.2   Feminist critiques

From a feminist perspective, the first and perhaps most important thing to note is that the internet has huge potential for women. It has the capacity to reduce both deliberate and 'automatic' discrimination – removing both the face-to-face problems and those that are triggered by indicators such as names. It can be a key enabler for women in many ways, supporting working from home and other forms of flexible working, for example. It can allow access to information and services, to democracy, communication and more to those previously isolated in homes. This needs to be acknowledged and supported: the internet can be a key tool for liberation and empowerment.

The privacy, identity, anonymity model could provide even more potential for women: it would allow people to disclose their sex only when

---

in general and social media in particular played a role in the organisation of the uprisings. Those whose power was under threat seemed to believe so, trying either to hack into those systems or, in Egypt's case, attempting to shut off the internet in total in their country in order to deny their opponents the opportunity to use those systems.

[30] See Chapter 3, Section 3.2.

they wanted to, and might even allow some kind of voluntary 'proof' of sex in certain circumstances. This is delicate and contentious ground, but something that might be effective if the rights and controls are in place. It takes some of the developments in terms of monitoring and profiling that might have been used in a negative way and turns them into something positive, from the instant tracking/tailoring of Phorm to the detailed profiling systems being developed throughout the advertising industry. As noted above when looking at freedoms of association and assembly, spotting 'imposters' has some valid applications, in particular areas and as the exception rather than the rule. The existence of a rule – in this case the default of privacy – can help enable the exception.

There are also specific risks associated with the Symbiotic Web that have a particular relevance to feminist critiques: automated discrimination, including price, service and access discrimination, for example, needs to be prevented. The 'whites-only websites' noted as a nightmare vision in Chapter 3 could just as easily be 'men-only' or 'women-only' websites, and while there are sometimes positive justifications for such kinds of exclusivity (at least on a gender basis), to be able to do so surreptitiously and automatically is something that needs to be done with care and control. Again, the privacy, identity, anonymity model could be the key here: if a website is intended to filter entry in ways other than by membership, it would have to demonstrate the need for that kind of filtration and openly acknowledge that it is taking place.

Having said all of this, there are still strong arguments against the excessive use of privacy and anonymity from a feminist perspective. Privacy has historically often been used to protect the powerful; from perpetrators of domestic violence to Catholic priests accused of child abuse, and that kind of privacy should not be prioritised or protected. As Allen (2003, pp. 195–6) puts it, it should be possible to:

> Rip down the doors of 'private' citizens in 'private' homes and 'private' institutions as needed to protect the vital interests of vulnerable people.

This is one of the reasons why the focus here is on privacy as a protector of a balanced, broadened form of autonomy, rather than privacy per se, and also why an unlimited right to anonymity is not suggested. The 'sea of privacy' is one in which people have general privacy, but that privacy can be 'overturned' when needed. Indeed, that is one of the principles behind the paradigm shift that underlies the rights. The shift is a shift in defaults. It is a shift from the general to the specific, from the all-encompassing to the targeted.

Taking this further, general surveillance and monitoring are unlikely in practice to provide the kind of protection 'in the private sphere' that the feminist critique would require. Those engaged in counterterrorism have huge resources and often think on a huge scale, hence the approach of data retention and universal surveillance. They have access to databases and the cooperation (at least to a degree) of similar organisations around the world, as the PRISM revelations suggested graphically. From the perspective of those who, in Allen's terms, wish to rip down the doors of private citizens in private homes, focussed, intelligent, targeted approaches – approaches based on surveillance minimisation – are more appropriate and more likely to be effective. Once again, having a default of privacy could encourage the development of the technologies and systems to provide those focussed, targeted systems.

3.3   The security challenge

The security challenge is one of the hardest challenges to engage with in a detailed and specific fashion. The very nature of the challenge makes it hard to examine: those engaged in counterterrorism are loathe to reveal their tactics and techniques, for understandable reasons. Nonetheless, the universalist approach that has led to concepts such as data retention has been coming under increasing pressure in recent years, most notably after the PRISM revelations. In December 2010 Peter Hustinx, the European Data Protection Supervisor, called for a European Commission review of the Data Retention Directive (DRD) to prove that it had achieved results or otherwise repeal it.[31] Further, Ian Brown (2010) argued that the DRD is not proportionate to the harm it seeks to remedy. Both Hustinx and Brown stress the serious level of intrusiveness of data retention. Such intrusion needs a great deal to justify it. Is the threat to security posed by terrorism sufficient, and even if it is, does data retention really work?

On the other hand, Walker wrote that 'Communications data retention and interception have become a non-negotiable fact of modern life' (Walker, 2009, p. 333). Indeed, calls in the United States for the institution of mandatory data retention have been growing. In January 2011 the US Department of Justice put their position to the House Crime

---

[31] Hustinx's speech can be found at www.edps.europa.eu/EDPSWEB/webdav/site /mySite/shared/Documents/EDPS/Publications/Speeches/2010/10–12–03 _Data_retention_speech_PH_EN.pdf.

Subcommittee: 'Data retention is fundamental to the department's work in investigating and prosecuting almost every type of crime.'[32] The issue remains highly contentious and, as suggested in Chapter 4, it is likely to remain so in the short term at least.

There are, however, pragmatic arguments against current practices in relation to security – to start with because what can be used for 'good' security can be used for 'bad' security. Technologies and practices developed by governments or other authorities that might be viewed as 'benevolent' or 'in favour' of human rights (which in itself is a complex and contentious question) can equally be employed by the malevolent or oppressive. Susan Landau, an expert in encryption and surveillance, has suggested that embedding eavesdropping mechanisms into communication technology itself builds tools that can be turned against those who wish to be protected.[33] A version of this may have already happened in the case of the Chinese hack of Google,[34] where it has been suggested that the hackers took advantage of a 'back door' created on the effective instructions of the American intelligence services. This case has not been proven, but even the existence of the rumour suggests that this kind of practice is being considered. It also highlights a fundamental problem with this kind of approach. As Schneier puts it:

> It's bad civic hygiene to build technologies that could someday be used to facilitate a police state. No matter what the eavesdroppers say, these systems cost too much and put us all at greater risk.[35]

In a similar way, when considering particularly the nature of data retention, data vulnerability in itself undermines the security challenge. Even those who might be expected to keep their data most securely, from the MOD and HMRC to the banks in Switzerland and Liechtenstein, have found their data vulnerable in one way or another.[36] The operations of WikiLeaks have been shown to take these vulnerabilities to another level again and have highlighted the fundamental problem with the gathering and accumulation of data. As Roger Smith, Director of Justice, wrote about 'Cablegate' in the *Law Society Gazette*: '[c]reate a database of fascinating information that is accessible to over three million people and the

---

[32] See for example http://news.cnet.com/8301-31921_3-20029423-281.html#ixzz1C4s-Ueyy4%3Cbr%20/%3E.

[33] This is one of the principal messages of her most recent book, Landau, 2011.

[34] See Chapter 7, Section 2.4.

[35] See Schneier's blog at www.schneier.com/blog/archives/2010/09/wiretapping_the.html.

[36] See Chapter 7, particularly Section 2.

only issue is how long you wait for the first leak'.[37] The argument can be widened to cover the whole of the internet. Governments have been made acutely aware of their own need for privacy; in the end, they may perhaps realise that a more privacy-friendly internet could be in their interests too. Murray (2004) has asked whether states should have a right to privacy. This is something that would become much more possible in an internet where privacy is the default rather than the exception.

The most important argument against the security challenge, however, is one that has run throughout this book. It is an argument of principle, and one that echoes Gearty's call in 'The Rights' Future': 'In taming counter-terrorism law, human rights can forge a soul.'[38] The underlying question here is what kind of a vision for the internet is to prevail, and beyond that, what kind of vision for society as a whole is to prevail, for the internet is a reflection and an extension of the 'real' world, intrinsically intertwined with it. As Benjamin Franklin wrote:

> They who can give up essential liberty to obtain a little temporary safety,
> deserve neither liberty nor safety.[39]

This book has attempted to show how essential the liberties that are at stake here can be: as Brown (2010), Hustinx and others have suggested, whether the safety being obtained is anything but little and temporary has yet to be shown.

4   A transparent society or a privacy-friendly future?

In many ways the 'transparency critique' is the most fundamental critique of the whole idea of privacy, not only on the internet but in society as a whole. It represents a challenge of critical importance, a challenge that must be met if privacy is to be taken at all seriously.

4.1   The transparency critique

There are three principal variants to the transparency critique:

---

[37] In 'WikiLeaks Take Us into a Legal – and Moral – Maze', *Law Society Gazette*, 16 December 2010, at www.lawgazette.co.uk/opinion/rights-and-wrongs/wikileaks-take-us-a-legal-and-moral-maze.

[38] See http://therightsfuture.com/t14-triumph-through-adversity/.

[39] This much quoted (and varied) phrase can be found in Franklin and Franklin, 1818, p. 270.

1. That the struggle for privacy is already lost – as epitomised by McNealy's suggestion that 'You have zero privacy anyway, get over it.'[40]
2. That the struggle for privacy is outdated – as implied for example by Facebook founder Mark Zuckerberg.[41]
3. That the struggle for privacy is 'wrong'. The virtues of a 'transparent society' have been written about by Brin (1998) and more recently by Bell and Gemmell (2009), amongst others.

The case studies and analysis throughout this book provide strong responses to all three of these variants. The principal case studies in Chapters 5 to 7 all argue against them. The strength of the public responses to Phorm and Beacon, the massive outcry and concern over the various data leaks from the HMRC disk loss onwards, and most recently the furore over the PRISM revelations all indicate that people do care about privacy. This suggestion has been emphasised by the continual struggles that Facebook has had in terms of its privacy policies; there have been at least three episodes in this saga over the last few years. Each time Facebook has introduced something reductive of privacy, after an outcry it has had to change it.[42]

There are more arguments against the idea that privacy is an outdated concept. First and foremost, there is little other than anecdotal evidence in its support. Indeed, research tends to suggest the opposite. Research such as the Turow *et al.* report (2009) on behavioural advertising is relatively limited in scope, but the evidence that it provides suggests that people do care about privacy. The same is true for the Ovum and Big Brother Watch's surveys in 2013: all indicate a significant level of current concern for privacy.[43] Secondly, the focus of Zuckerberg and others on young people's attitudes is limited in many ways: it is not only young people who matter, and young people grow up, while a lack of privacy,

---

[40] Quoted for example in *Wired*, at www.wired.com/politics/law/news/1999/01/17538.
[41] As noted in Chapter 2, Zuckerberg has made related statements to various elements of the media on the subject, from 2010 onwards. See for example Chris Matyszczyk's blog on CNET, at http://news.cnet.com/8301–17852_3–10431741–71.html.
[42] There have been outcries against Facebook's privacy policies and practices at various times since Facebook was founded. The Electronic Privacy Information Centre, for example, keeps a documented list of issues at http://epic.org/privacy/facebook/, while the Electronic Frontier Foundation keeps a record of the developments on Facebook's privacy policies at www.eff.org/deeplinks/2010/04/facebook-timeline/.
[43] See http://ovum.com/press_releases/ovum-predicts-turbulence-for-the-internet-economy-as-more-than-two-thirds-of-consumers-say-no-to-internet-tracking/ and www.bigbrotherwatch.org.uk/home/2013/06/new-research-global-attitudes-to-privacy-online.html respectively.

particularly on the internet, can last forever.[44] Solove's strong arguments about common misconceptions of privacy and its importance undermine the idea further.[45] The relationship between privacy and autonomy adds to these arguments: and even if the suggestion that people do not care about privacy was true, it would be hard to argue that people do not care about autonomy either.

As has already been briefly discussed,[46] Mayer-Schönberger (2009) has argued strongly against many aspects of the transparent society, suggesting not only that it is unrealisable but also that in many ways it goes against human nature, effectively subverting the crucial human ability to forget. As Mayer-Schönberger suggests, it would be evolutionarily very difficult, even if it were desirable, for humans to make the shift to living without forgetting. Some of his arguments go directly towards autonomy. As he puts it '[w]ithout our ability to forget, whenever faced with a decision we would always recall all our past decisions, resulting in potential indecision' (2009, p. 117). The arguments he sets out are complex, compelling and multifaceted.

The suggestion that the struggle for privacy is already lost is also challenged by the case studies. In many of the cases, it can be argued that privacy 'won', from Google's decision to reduce its data retention periods to the failure of Phorm, Facebook's abandonment of Beacon and the inability of the UK government to push through the Communications Data Bill. The toughening up of the Information Commissioner's Office (ICO), whether it ends up in being effective or not, suggests that the UK government has not given up the idea of privacy. Neither has the judiciary, a notable but somewhat Pyrrhic example being the Ryan Giggs case, where judges would not accept that either Twitter or Parliamentary privilege should be allowed to override privacy.[47] Other examples, such as the fact that in Germany, when given the option, almost 250,000 citizens opted to have the pictures of their houses 'blurred out' of Google Street View,[48] and the strength of the current movement in the United States for 'Do Not Track' options in internet browsing, suggest once more that people do care about privacy and that the delivery of options such as these can achieve results.

---

[44] Mayer-Schönberger's ideas on data having limited lifespans look at exactly this: see Mayer-Schönberger, 2009.
[45] Particularly in Solove, 2007.   [46] In Chapter 7, Section 4.
[47] The case is *CTB* v. *News Group Newspapers* [2011] EWHC 1232 (QB).
[48] See www.bbc.co.uk/news/technology-11595495.

Even when and where transparency is desired or desirable, should that transparency not be two-way? At the moment the transparency is all from the individuals: those gathering data, both in business and in government, are conspicuously opaque both in their practices and policies. As Mayer-Schönberger suggests, this may be an inevitable result of the relative imbalance in power between individuals and those gathering their data.[49] This suggestion is borne out in the case studies. The nature of Google search makes its data gathering activities far from clear, while the whole approach of Phorm was one where transparency was conspicuous by its absence. Facebook's privacy policies have been vehemently criticised for their complexity and opaqueness; its policy change in December 2010 was intended to address this issue,[50] though its success in achieving a greater degree of clarity is questionable,[51] and a new proposal was on the table only a few months later.[52] The strong reactions by governments and others to the WikiLeaks and PRISM sagas suggest that the idea of a fully transparent society is something that governments and businesses are far from enthusiastic about. As Murray has argued,[53] they may have good reasons for this attitude. Transparency needs limits.

The need for limited, two-way transparency rather than an open 'free-for-all' can be seen as another example of the web symbiosis, and of how it can function at its best. Individuals, businesses and governments all have needs for privacy and duties for transparency, and can get benefits from both. Both privacy and transparency are in themselves two-way issues: privacy is privacy *from*, while transparency is transparency *to*. The rights presented here should be a positive step towards reaching suitable levels

---

[49] See Mayer-Schönberger, 2009, particularly pp. 107–8.

[50] See for example the MSNBC blog on the subject 'Facebook Dumbs Down Privacy Policy (In A Good Way)': http://technolog.msnbc.msn.com/_news/2011/02/25/6133609-facebook-dumbs-down-privacy-policy-in-a-good-way.

[51] See for example ZDNet blogger Adrian Kingsley-Hughes, commenting in 2011 that 'Facebook Privacy Settings are Garbage' at www.zdnet.com/blog/hardware/facebook-privacy-settings-are-garbage/11029.

[52] In February 2011, Facebook put forward a proposal for 'A Privacy Policy Re-imagined For Users Like You', opening a consultation process with users in order to make their privacy policy more accessible and comprehensible. See www.facebook.com/note.php?note_id=10150434660350301&id=69178204322 and www.facebook.com/note.php?note_id=10150434652940301.

[53] In his blog at http://theitlawyer.blogspot.com/2011/02/freedom-of-information-in-wikileaks-era.html. Murray has taken this argument a stage further, noting that not only governments and businesses but WikiLeaks itself understands that transparency needs limits – for WikiLeaks is far from transparent about its own operations. See his article, Murray, 2011.

of transparency – two-way transparency, limited in both directions in appropriate ways. Ultimately, they could be key tools in developing a more positive version of transparency, as they could encourage more trust, and from trust comes transparency.

4.2   The rapidly developing internet

When this research began in 2007 the internet was a very different place. Much of what is now considered central to it was either very new or had not even been launched. Twitter was barely a year old,[54] the iPhone had been launched a matter of months before, just in the United States, and the Kindle had not been released at all.[55] The iPad was not even available until 2010.

Facebook, a relative veteran at three years old, had what looked like an impressive 50 million users, but by October 2012 it had passed one billion.[56] By the end of 2010, Amazon was reporting that Kindle e-books had outsold both hardbacks and paperbacks.[57] In the second quarter of 2013 alone, Apple sold more than 19 million iPads and 37 million iPhones;[58] the ways in which the internet is being accessed and the way in which it is being used have changed dramatically. The Apple 'App Store', through which applications for iPhones and iPads are sold, passed 50 billion app sales in May 2013.[59]

The growth in the quantity of the personal data that has been gathered and generated as part and parcel of these changes has been equally profound, and the changes in the nature of the data perhaps even more so, as new data types have emerged or grown in significance. One prominent new form is social data – who someone's 'friends' are and how they interact with each other – from social networking sites. Habitual data, which books people read or movies they watch, what sports they follow and so forth, has become far more significant as more people spend more of their time on the internet. Even more recently, information with deep significance for privacy, such as the geo-location data generated by smartphones

---

[54] Twitter was launched in July 2006.

[55] The Kindle was released in November 2007.

[56] See for example www.bbc.co.uk/news/technology-19816709#panel7.

[57] See   http://phx.corporate-ir.net/phoenix.zhtml?c=176060&p=irol-newsArticle&ID=1521090&highlight=.

[58] See www.apple.com/pr/library/2013/04/23Apple-Reports-Second-Quarter-Results.html.

[59] See www.apple.com/pr/library/2013/05/16Apples-App-Store-Marks-Historic-50-Billionth-Download.html.

and other devices, has emerged. Combining all of these different forms of data – and adding to it – is the profiling data that can ultimately be the most potent form of data of all, in terms of both commercial opportunities and impact on autonomy.

These changes have been accompanied by problems and issues relating to how this data is gathered, processed, used and held. What was already an important issue when this research began has become significantly more important. The scale and nature of these events, and the media coverage and public reactions to them, suggest three things: that significant events in the field are occurring with increasing regularity, that public interest in those events is growing and that the idea that people have rights concerning them is becoming more prevalent.

This is what makes the subject matter of this book important. The shape and form of the internet both mirror and impact upon the shape and form of society as a whole, not only in rich, Western countries but throughout the world. The role that the internet played in the uprisings in the Arab world in 2011 has been much debated, but it is clear that it did play a role, and that the challenged leaders of the countries concerned believed that this role mattered. The internet is no longer a luxury, it is no longer either just about information or just about leisure; it is a key part of the lives of a significant and growing proportion of the people of the world.

4.3   A creative tension over privacy

Given the internet's importance, it is crucial that the nature of the internet is given sufficient thought. If human rights and freedoms – and autonomy – are to be taken seriously in the world, they need also to be taken seriously in the online world. For that to happen, a lot of changes will need to take place. That, ultimately, is the aim of the paradigm shift and of the rights suggested in this book. If the human rights that are considered important are to be protected, fostered and supported, then privacy and autonomy need to become the default. Surveillance and breaches in privacy need to be the exception, and exist only when truly justified.

Is this kind of real change possible? The case studies suggest that it might be. There have been some very positive and quite radical changes in the policies and practices of some of the biggest players in the internet world. Where technology is concerned, changes can be implemented more quickly than in many fields, and in more radical ways. Whether or not it will happen in practice is another question. There are signs both ways and pressures both ways: indeed, it may be that both need to exist in a creative tension. The more that privacy is put under pressure, the more people care about it. The more technologies are developed that infringe on privacy, the more 'privacy-protective' technologies and techniques emerge in response, and vice versa.

Governments, and the US government in particular, seem conflicted or confused, or at very least capable of demonstrating distinct double standards or exceptionalism. On the same day in February 2011, for example, Hillary Clinton made a key speech on internet freedom[60] and the US Justice Department tried to subpoena the personal records on Twitter of some of those associated with WikiLeaks,[61] after having failed to prevent the disclosure of this fact via a gagging order. Just two days later the FBI requested more backdoor access into social networking services.[62] In Europe, there are similar tensions between the needs of privacy and security, as played out in the conflicts between advocates of data protection and data retention. Governments, however, are not the key to the development of the internet: to a great extent they are peripheral, piggybacking on the developments made by and the practices of businesses, even through such intrusive programmes as PRISM. A privacy-friendly internet, if it is to come to pass, is far more likely to be driven by the business sector than by government.

4.4   A privacy-friendly future?

The business sector is where what hope that there is appears to lie and where the rights suggested in this book could play their most important role. There are signs that businesses are starting to understand the importance of privacy and in particular how much people are beginning to show that they care about it. Some of the biggest players on the net are starting, at least on the surface, to embrace the idea of privacy. Microsoft, Mozilla and Google are all engaged in the 'Do Not Track' initiative for their respective browsers, and the first two have made very positive steps in that direction. Facebook have an avowed (if not entirely convincing) aim of making privacy simpler and more user-friendly, and more in the hands of its users. Twitter demonstrated commendable courage in challenging the gagging order placed upon it in the US government's attempt

---

[60] On 15 February 2011, see www.bbc.co.uk/news/world-us-canada-12475829.

[61] Also on 15 February 2011, see http://blogs.abcnews.com/politicalpunch/2011/02/doj-seeks-twitter-records-in-wikileaks-probe.html.

[62] See for example www.wired.com/epicenter/2011/02/fbi-backdoors/.

to subpoena personal data from particular individuals associated with WikiLeaks. Google has been taking steps in the direction of both privacy and autonomy: Alma Whitten, the then company's Director of Privacy, Product and Engineering, wrote a blog in February 2011 entitled 'The Freedom to Be Who You Want to Be...'[63] embracing the ideas of 'unidentified' and 'pseudonymous' uses of their services, and introducing ways to tell when and how Google is monitoring your activities, at least beginning to take on some of the concepts introduced in this book, from the right to roam with privacy to the right to monitor the monitors.

There are, however, distinct issues with these proposals. Google's idea of 'unidentified' is far from real anonymity, still retaining such information as IP addresses, and still posing risks to privacy, while Facebook's regular amendments to its privacy policies have often promised far more than they have delivered. All these companies with the exception of Twitter have been implicated to an extent in the PRISM project. Even so there are some reasons for optimism, not least from the growing sense of public concern over privacy. At the very least, Google, Facebook and Twitter have understood that there is a public desire for privacy and autonomy.

The work of privacy advocates, of the Article 29 Working Party and most importantly of the online community has played a key part in helping them to start along the path. If a privacy-friendly internet is to have any chance of becoming reality they need be supported and assisted along the way. That, ultimately, is the part that rights such as those put forward in this book can play. They can support businesses so that businesses can help to provide people with the kind of internet that they want and need. The symbiotic relationship between businesses and individuals has been hugely productive and substantially beneficial over the last few years; with the proposed rights in place it can continue to be so into the future.

Whether a privacy-friendly internet is a realistic possibility is very hard to say. Perhaps the best that can be said at this stage is that the argument that it is impossible is not completely convincing. The ideal of a privacy-friendly internet, however, is certainly worth fighting for.

---

[63] http://googlepublicpolicy.blogspot.com/2011/02/freedom-to-be-who-you-want-to-be. html.

BIBLIOGRAPHY

Academic and related sources

Agre, P. and Rotenberg, M. 1997. *Technology and Privacy: The New Landscape.* Cambridge, MA, MIT Press.

Allen, A. L. 2003. *Why Privacy Isn't Everything: Feminist Reflections on Personal Accountability.* Lanham, MD, Rowman & Littlefield.

Allen, A. L. and Mack, E. 1991. How Privacy Got Its Gender. *Northern Illinois Law Review* 10: 441–71.

Ayres, I. 2007. *Super Crunchers: How Anything Can Be Predicted.* London, John Murray.

Beales, H. 2009. *The Value of Behavioral Targeting.* Network Advertising Initiative. Available at www.networkadvertising.org/pdfs/Beales_NAI_Study.pdf.

Bell, C. G. and Gemmell, J. 2009. *Total Recall: How the E-Memory Revolution Will Change Everything.* New York, Dutton.

Bernal, P. 2010a. Collaborative Consent: Harnessing the Strengths of the Internet for Consent in the Online Environment. *International Review of Law, Computers & Technology* 24: 287–98.

2010b. Web 2.5: The Symbiotic Web. *International Review of Law, Computers & Technology* 24: 25–37.

2011a. A Right to Delete? *European Journal of Law and Technology* 2. Available at http://ejlt.org/article/view/75/144.

2011b. Rise and Phall: Lessons from the Phorm Saga, in S. Gutwirth, Y. Poullet, P. De Hert and R. Leenes (eds.) *Computers, Privacy and Data Protection: An Element of Choice.* Dordrecht, Springer: 269–83.

2014. The EU, the US and the Right to be Forgotten, in S. Gutwirth, P. De Hert and R. Leenes (eds.) *Computers, Privacy and Data Protection – Reloading Data Protection.* Dordrecht, Springer: 61–77.

Berners-Lee, T. and Fischetti, M. 2000. *Weaving the Web: The Original Design and Ultimate Destiny of the World Wide Web by its Inventor.* New York, HarperCollins Publishers.

Bohm, N. 2008. *The Phorm 'Webwise' System – A Legal Analysis.* Foundation for Information Policy Research. Available at www.fipr.org/080423-phormlegal.pdf.

291

Brin, D. 1998. *The Transparent Society: Will Technology Force Us to Choose Between Privacy and Freedom?* Reading, MA, Addison-Wesley.

Brown, I. 2010. Communications Data Retention in an Evolving Internet. *International Journal of Law and Information Technology* 19.

2012. Government Access to Private-Sector Data in the United Kingdom. *International Data Privacy Law* 2: 9.

Burghardt, T., Böhm, K., Buchmann, E., Kühling, J. and Sivridis, A. 2010. A Study on the Lack of Enforcement of Data Protection Acts, in A. B. Sideridis and C. Z. Patrikakis (eds.) *Next Generation Society. Technological and Legal Issues.* Berlin, Springer, pp. 3–12.

Burton, E. 2008. Report into the Loss of MOD Personal Data. MOD. Available at www.netconsent.com/NETconsent/media/Documents/Documentation/burton_review_rpt20080430.pdf.

Cate, F. H. 1997. *Privacy in the Information Age.* Washington, DC, Brookings Institution Press.

Clark, A. and Chalmers, D. J. 1998. The Extended Mind. *Analysis* 58: 10–23.

Clayton, R. 2008. The Phorm 'Webwise' System. Online at www.cl.cam.ac.uk/~rnc1/080518-phorm.pdf.

Cochrane, A. 2007. Animal Rights and Animal Experiments: An Interest-Based Approach. *Res Publica* 13: 26.

Cohen, J. E. 2012. *Configuring the Networked Self: Law, Code, and The Play of Everyday Practice.* New Haven, CT., Yale University Press.

Crisp, R. 1987. Persuasive Advertising, Autonomy, and the Creation of Desire. *Journal of Business Ethics* 6: 413–18.

Dahl, J. Y. and Sætnan, A. R. 2009. 'It All Happened So Slowly' – On Controlling Function Creep in Forensic DNA Databases. *International Journal of Law, Crime and Justice* 37: 83–103.

Davies, S. G. 1997. Re-engineering the Right to Privacy: How Privacy Has Been Transformed from a Right to a Commodity, in P. Agre and M. Rotenberg (eds.) *Technology and Privacy: The New Landscape.* Cambridge, MA, MIT Press, pp. 143–65.

De Hert, P. 2008. A Right to Identity to Face the Internet of Things? UNESCO. Available at http://portal.unesco.org/ci/fr/files/25857/12021328273de_Hert-Paul.pdf/de%2BHert-Paul.pdf.

Edwards, L. and Waelde, C. 2000. *Law and the Internet: A Framework for Electronic Commerce.* Oxford, Hart.

Fearon, J. D. 1999. *What is Identity (as We Now Use the Word)?* Mimeo, Inc., Stanford University.

Franklin, B. and Franklin, W. T. 1818. *Memoirs of the Life and Writings of Benjamin Franklin.* London, Henry Colburn.

Fura, E. and Klamberg, M. 2012. The Chilling Effect of Counter-Terrorism Measures: A Comparative Analysis of Electronic Surveillance Laws in Europe and the USA, in J. Casadevall, E. Myjer and M. O'Boyle (eds.) *Freedom of Expression – Essays in Honour of Nicolas Bratza – President of the European Court of Human Rights*. Oisterwijk, Wolf Legal Publishers, pp. 463–81.

Gandy, O. H. 1993. *The Panoptic Sort: A Political Economy of Personal Information*, Boulder, CO, Westview.

Gearty, C. A. 2006. *Can Human Rights Survive?* Cambridge University Press.

Gewirth, A. 1982. *Human Rights: Essays on Justification and Applications*. London, University of Chicago Press.

Ginsberg, J., Mohebbi, M. H., Patel, R. S., Brammer, L., Smolinski, M. S. and Brilliant, L. 2009. Detecting Influenza Epidemics Using Search Engine Query Data. *Nature* 457: 1012–14.

Gomes de Andrade, N. N. 2010, Human Genetic Manipulation and the Right to Identity: The Contradictions of Human Rights Law in Regulating the Human Genome, 7:3 *SCRIPTed* 429, www.law.ed.ac.uk/ahrc/script-ed/vol7-3/andrade.asp, p. 432.

Greenleaf, G. 2008. Function Creep – Defined and Still Dangerous in Australia's Revised ID Card Bill. *Computer Law & Security Report* 24: 56–65.

2013. Scheherezade and the 101 Data Privacy Laws: Origins, Significance and Global Trajectories. *Journal of Law, Information & Science*. Available at http://papers.ssrn.com/sol3/papers.cfm?abstract_id=2280877.

Hart, H. L. A. 1955. Are There Any Natural Rights? *Philosophical Review* 64: 175–91.

Hunter, D. 2001. Philippic.com. *California Law Review* 90: 70.

Jackson, E. 2001. *Regulating Reproduction: Law, Technology and Autonomy*. Oxford, Hart.

Kelly, P. J. 1990. *Utilitarianism and Distributive Justice: Jeremy Bentham and the Civil Law*. Oxford, Clarendon.

Klamberg, M. 2010. FRA and the European Convention on Human Rights – A Paradigm Shift in Swedish Electronic Surveillance Law, in D. W. Schartaum (ed.) *Nordic Yearbook of Law and Information Technology*. Bergen, Fagforlaget, pp. 96–134.

Klug, F. 2000. *Values for a Godless Age: The Story of the UK's New Bill of Rights*. London, Penguin.

Kosinski, M., Stillwell, D. and Graepel, T. 2013. Private Traits and Attributes Are Predictable from Digital Records of Human Behavior. *Proceedings of the National Academy of Sciences of the United States of America* 110: 5802–5. Available at www.pnas.org/content/early/2013/03/06/1218772110.full.pdf.

Kosta, E. 2013. The Way to Luxembourg: National Court Decisions on the Compatibility of the Data Retention Directive with the Rights to Privacy and Data Protection. *SCRIPTed* 10: 24.

La Rue, F. 2013. *Report of the Special Rapporteur on the Promotion and Protection of the Right to Freedom of Opinion and Expression*. New York, United

Nations. Available at www.ohchr.org/EN/Issues/FreedomOpinion/Pages/ Annual.aspx.

Landau, S. 2011. *Surveillance or Security? The Real Risks Posed by New Wiretapping Technologies*. Cambridge, MA, The MIT Press.

Lessig, L. 2006. *Code: Version 2.0*. New York, Basic Books.

MacIntyre, A. 1981. *After Virtue: A Study in Moral Theory*. London, Duckworth.

McIntyre, T. J. and Scott, C. D. 2008. Internet Filtering: Rhetoric, Legitimacy, Accountability and Responsibility, in R. Brownsword and K. Yeung (eds.) *Regulating Technologies*. Oxford, Hart Publishing, pp. 109–24.

Mayer-Schönberger, V. 2009. *Delete: The Virtue of Forgetting in the Digital Age*. Princeton University Press.

Mendel, T., Puddephatt, A., Wagner, B., Hawtin, D. and Torres, N. 2012. *Global Survey on Internet Privacy and Freedom of Expression. UNESCO Series on Internet Freedom*. Paris, UNESCO. Available at http://unesdoc.unesco.org/ images/0021/002182/218273e.pdf.

Mill, J. S. and Himmelfarb, G. 1982. *On Liberty*. Harmondsworth, Penguin.

Mossberger, K., Tolbert, C. J. and Stansbury, M. 2003. *Virtual Inequality: Beyond the Digital Divide*. Washington, DC, Georgetown University Press.

Murray, A. D. 2004. Should States Have a Right to Informational Privacy? In A. D. Murray and M. Klang (eds.) *Human Rights in the Digital Age*. London, The Glasshouse Press, pp. 191–202.

2006. *The Regulation of Cyberspace: Control in the Online Environment*, Milton Park, Abingdon, UK, and New York, Routledge-Cavendish.

2011. Transparency, Scrutiny and Responsiveness: Fashioning a Private Space. *Political Quarterly* 83: 509–14.

2013. *Information Technology Law: The Law and Society*, 2nd ed., Oxford University Press.

Narayanan, A. and Shmatikov, V. 2008. *Robust De-anonymization of Large Sparse Datasets*. IEEE Symposium on Security and Privacy.

Nissenbaum, H. F. 2010. *Privacy in Context: Technology, Policy, and the Integrity of Social Life*. Stanford, CA, Stanford Law Books.

Norris, P. 2001. *Digital Divide: Civic Engagement, Information Poverty, and the Internet Worldwide*. Cambridge University Press.

Ohm, P. 2010. Broken Promises of Privacy: Responding to the Surprising Failure of Anonymization. *UCLA Law Review* 57: 1701–78.

Paine, T. and Burke, E. 1791. *Rights of Man: Being an Answer to Mr. Burke's Attack on the French Revolution*. Dublin, *s.n.*

Pariser, E. 2011. *The Filter Bubble: What the Internet is Hiding From You*. London, Viking.

Posner, R. A. 1998. *Economic Analysis of Law*, Boston, MA, Aspen Law & Business.

Poynter, K. 2008. *Review of Information Security at HM Revenue and Customs*. London, HMSO.

Rawls, J. and Freeman, S. R. 1999. *Collected Papers*. Cambridge, MA, Harvard University Press.

Raz, J. 1986. *The Morality of Freedom*. Oxford, Clarendon.

Reed, C. 2004. *Internet Law: Text and Materials*. Cambridge University Press.

2010. *Think Global, Act Local: Extraterritoriality in Cyberspace*. Working Paper Series, Queen Mary University of London School of Law.

2012. *Making Laws for Cyberspace*. Oxford University Press.

Ricoeur, P. 2005. *The Course of Recognition*. Cambridge, MA, Harvard University Press.

Rorty, R. 1993. Human Rights, Rationality and Sentimentality, in S. Shute and S. L. Hurley (eds.) *On Human Rights: Oxford Amnesty Lectures*. Oxford: BasicBooks: 167–85.

Rosen, J. 2012. The Right to be Forgotten. *Stanford Law Review Online*, 64.

Samuelson, P. 2000. Privacy as Intellectual Property. *Stanford Law Review* 52: 1125–75.

Smartt, U. 2012. Safety First: the Ryan Giggs Superinjunction Part 2 of March 2012. *Communications Law* 17: 3.

Solove, D. J. 2007. 'I've Got Nothing to Hide' and Other Misunderstandings of Privacy. *San Diego Law Review* 44: 745–72.

2011. *Nothing to Hide: The False Tradeoff Between Privacy and Security*. New Haven, CT, Yale University Press.

Sunstein, C. R. 2007. *Republic.com 2.0*. Princeton University Press.

Sweeney, L. 1997. Weaving Technology and Policy Together To Maintain Confidentiality. *Journal of Law, Medicine and Ethics* 25: 98–110.

Taylor, C. 1992. *The Ethics of Authenticity*. Cambridge, MA, Harvard University Press.

Teff, H. 1994. *Reasonable Care: Legal Perspectives on the Doctor–Patient Relationship*. Oxford, Clarendon Press; New York, Oxford University Press.

Tene, O. 2013. Me, Myself and I: Aggregated and Disaggregated Identities on Social Networking Services. *Journal of International Commercial Law and Technology* 8: 118–33.

Tene, O. and Wolf, C. 2013. *The Draft EU General Data Protection Regulation: Costs and Paradoxes of Explicit Consent*. Washington, DC, Future of Privacy Forum.

Thomas, R. and Walport, M. 2008. *Data Sharing Review Report*. London, Ministry of Justice.

Thomas, T. 2008. The Sex Offender 'Register': A Case Study in Function Creep. *The Howard Journal* 47: 227–37.

Turkle, S. 1996. *Life on the Screen: Identity in the Age of the Internet*. London, Weidenfeld & Nicolson.

Turow, J., King, J., Hoofnagle, C. J., Bleakley, A. and Hennessy, M. 2009. *Americans Reject Tailored Advertising*. Annenberg, University of Pennsylvania.

Vaidhyanathan, S. 2011. *The Googlization of Everything: (And Why We Should Worry)*, Berkeley, University of California Press.

Van den Poel, D. and Buckinx, W. 2005. Predicting Online-Purchasing Behaviour. *European Journal of Operational Research* 166: 557–75.

Walker, C. 2009. Data Retention in the UK: Pragmatic and Proportionate, or a Step too Far? *Computer Law & Security Review* 25: 325–34.

Warren, S. and Brandeis, L. D. 1890. The Right to Privacy. *Harvard Law Review* 4: 193–220.

Other web-based sources and reports

All Party Parliamentary Communications Group Report into Internet Traffic, at www.apcomms.org.uk/uploads/apComms_Final_Report.pdf.

Amnesty International: Undermining Freedom of Expression in China. The Role of Yahoo!, Microsoft and Google, at www.amnesty.org/en/library/info/POL30/026/2006.

'Anonymous' Declaration of Intent 2010, at www.youtube.com/watch?v=gbqC8-BnvVHQ.

Attorney General Press Release on Identity Fraud, at www.attorneygeneral.gov.uk/nfa/whatarewesaying/newsrelease/pages/identity-fraud-costs-27billion.aspx.

Barlow, J. P. 1996. Declaration of the Independence of Cyberspace, at https://projects.eff.org/~barlow/Declaration-Final.html.

Big Brother Watch 2012: A Legacy of Suspicion: How RIPA Has Been Used by Local Authorities and Public Bodies, at www.bigbrotherwatch.org.uk/files/ripa/RIPA_Aug12_final.pdf.

Chinese Government White Paper, The Internet in China, at www.china.org.cn/government/whitepaper/node_7093508.htm.

Data Protection in the European Union, at http://eur-lex.europa.eu/LexUriServ/LexUriServ.do?uri=COM:2003:0265:FIN:EN:PDF.

Data Protection Directive – First Implementation Report, at http://eur-lex.europa.eu/LexUriServ/LexUriServ.do?uri=COM:2003:0265:FIN:EN:PDF.

Data Protection Laws of the World, DLA Piper, at http://information.dla.com/information/published/DPLaw_World_Handbook_2012.pdf.

Digital Britain, Interim Report, January 2009, at http://webarchive.nationalarchives.gov.uk/20100511084737/http://www.culture.gov.uk/images/publications/digital_britain_interimreportjan09.pdf.

Draft Communications Data Bill Joint Committee – First Report, at www.publications.parliament.uk/pa/jt201213/jtselect/jtdraftcomuni/79/7902.htm.

Dutch Data Protection Agency, Opinion on Data Retention, at www.dutchdpa.nl/downloads_adv/z2006–01542.pdf?refer=true&theme=purple.

E-Money Evaluation Report, at http://ec.europa.eu/internal_market/bank/docs/e-money/evaluation_en.pdf.

Fleischer, P., Letter to Peter Schaar, 10 June 2007, at http://64.233.179.110/blog_resources/Google_response_Working_Party_06_2007.pdf.

Gearty, C., The Rights' Future, at http://therightsfuture.com.

ICO CCTV Code of Practice, at www.ico.gov.uk/upload/documents/library/data_protection/detailed_specialist_guides/ico_cctvfinal_2301.pdf.

ICO Code of Practice for Privacy Notices, at www.ico.gov.uk/for_organisations/topic_specific_guides/privacy_notices.aspx.

ICO Guidance on Compliance with 'Cookies Directive', at www.ico.gov.uk/for_organisations/privacy_and_electronic_communications/~/media/documents/library/Privacy_and_electronic/Practical_application/advice_on_the_new_cookies_regulations.ashx.

ICO Press Release on Their Investigation into Street View, at www.ico.gov.uk/~/media/documnts/pressreleases/2010/google_inc_street_view_press_release_03112010.ashx.

ICO 'Specialist Guide' as to What Constitutes Personal Data, at http://ico.org.uk/~/media/documents/library/data_protection/detailed_specialist_guides/personal_data_flowchart_v1_with_preface001.ashx.

ICO 'Specialist Guide' to New Penalties for Data Breaches 2010, at http://ico.org.uk/enforcement/~/media/documents/library/Data_Protection/Detailed_specialist_guides/ico_guidance_on_monetary_penalties.pdf.

ICO 2008a. Privacy by Design Report. Available at http://ico.org.uk/for_organisations/data_protection/topic_guides/~/media/documents/pdb_report_html/PRIVACY_BY_DESIGN_REPORT_V2.ashx.

2008b. Taking Stock, Taking Action. London, Information Commissioner's Office.

2010. Response to the Ministry of Justice's Call for Evidence on the Current Data Protection Legislative Framework. London, Information Commissioner's Office.

IPCC Report on HMRC Data Loss 2008, at www.ipcc.gov.uk/sites/default/files/Documents/investigation_commissioner_reports/final_hmrc_report_25062008.pdf.

NFA Annual Fraud Indicator 2013, at www.gov.uk/government/uploads/system/uploads/attachment_data/file/206552/nfa-annual-fraud-indicator-2013.pdf.

OVUM Customer Insights Survey 2013, at www.ovum.com.

Pew Internet Research Report on 2008 Election Campaign, at http://people-press.org/report/384/internets-broader-role-in-campaign-2008.

Steiner, P. 1993. Cartoon, On the Internet Nobody Knows You're a Dog. In 2000, *The New York Times* published a piece entitled 'Cartoon Catches the Spirit of

the Internet'. www.nytimes.com/2000/12/14/technology/14DOGG.html?pa
gewanted=1&ei=5070&en=f0518aafeccf36fd&ex=1183089600.

UK Government Communications Plan 2013/14, at https://gcn.civilservice.gov.
uk/about/201314-government-communications-plan/.

Article 29 Data Protection Working Party opinions

Working Party Opinion 5/2002 (WP 64) on the Statement of the European Data
Protection Commissioners at the International Conference in Cardiff (9–11
September 2002) on mandatory systematic retention of telecommunication
traffic data. Available at http://ec.europa.eu/justice/policies/privacy/docs/
wpdocs/2002/wp64_en.pdf.

Working Party Opinion 9/2004 (WP 99) on a draft Framework Decision on the
storage of data processed and retained for the purpose of providing electronic public communications services or data available in public communications networks with a view to the prevention, investigation, detection
and prosecution of criminal acts, including terrorism. [Proposal presented
by France, Ireland, Sweden and Great Britain (Document of the Council
8958/04 of 28 April 2004)]. Available at http://ec.europa.eu/justice/policies/
privacy/docs/wpdocs/2004/wp99_en.pdf.

Working Party Opinion 4/2005 (WP 113) on the Proposal for a Directive of the
European Parliament and of the Council on the retention of data processed
in connection with the provision of public electronic communication services and Amending Directive. Available at http://ec.europa.eu/justice/
policies/privacy/workinggroup/wpdocs/2005_en.htm.

Working Party Opinion 3/2006 (WP 119) on the Directive 2006/24/EC of the
European Parliament and of the Council on the retention of data generated
or processed in connection with the provision of publicly available electronic communications services or of public communications networks and
Amending Directive 2002/58/EC. Available at http://ec.europa.eu/justice/
policies/privacy/workinggroup/wpdocs/2006_en.htm.

Working Party Opinion 1/2008 (WP 148) on data protection issues related to
search engines. Available at http://ec.europa.eu/justice/policies/privacy/
workinggroup/wpdocs/2008_en.htm.

Working Party Opinion 2/2010 (WP 171) on online behavioural advertising. Available at http://ec.europa.eu/justice/policies/privacy/docs/
wpdocs/2010/wp171_en.pdf.

Working Party Opinion 16/2011 (WP 181) on EASA/IAB Best Practice
Recommendation on online behavioural advertising. Available at http://
ec.europa.eu/justice/data-protection/article-29/documentation/opinion-
recommendation/files/2011/wp188_en.pdf.

Working Party Opinion 01/2012 (WP 191) on the data protection reform proposals. Available at http://ec.europa.eu/justice/data-protection/article-29/ documentation/opinion-recommendation/files/2012/wp191_en.pdf.

A note on web sources

Unless otherwise noted, all web links were last accessed on 30 July 2013. There are extensive additional links to websites included within the footnotes. These sources are not individually listed here as they relate principally to news stories or companies or services available over the web rather than to academic analysis.

INDEX

CAMBRIDGE INTELLECTUAL PROPERTY
AND INFORMATION LAW

Titles in the series (formerly known as Cambridge Studies
in Intellectual Property Rights)

Brad Sherman and Lionel Bently
The Making of Modern Intellectual Property Law
978 0 521 56363 5

Irini A. Stamatoudi
Copyright and Multimedia Products: A Comparative Analysis
978 0 521 80819 4

Pascal Kamina
Film Copyright in the European Union
978 0 521 77053 8

Huw Beverly-Smith
The Commercial Appropriation of Personality
978 0 521 80014 3

Mark J. Davison
The Legal Protection of Databases
978 0 521 80257 4

Robert Burrell and Allison Coleman
Copyright Exceptions: The Digital Impact
978 0 521 84726 1

Huw Beverly-Smith, Ansgar Ohly and Agnès Lucas-Schloetter
*Privacy, Property and Personality: Civil Law Perspectives on Commercial
Appropriation*
978 0 521 82080 6

Philip Leith
Software and Patents in Europe
978 0 521 86839 6

Lionel Bently, Jennifer Davis and Jane C. Ginsburg
Trade Marks and Brands: An Interdisciplinary Critique
978 0 521 88965 0

Geertrui Van Overwalle
Gene Patents and Clearing Models
978 0 521 89673 3

Jonathan Curci
The Protection of Biodiversity and Traditional Knowledge in International Law of Intellectual Property
978 0 521 19944 5

Lionel Bently, Jennifer Davis and Jane C. Ginsburg
Copyright and Piracy: An Interdisciplinary Critique
978 0 521 19343 6

Megan Richardson and Julian Thomas
Framing Intellectual Property: Legal Constructions of Creativity and Appropriation 1840–1940
978 0 521 76756 9

Dev Gangjee
Relocating the Law of Geographical Indications
978 0 521 19202 6

Andrew Kenyon, Megan Richardson and Ng-Loy Wee-Loon
The Law of Reputation and Brands in the Asia Pacific Region
978 1 107 01772 6

Annabelle Lever
New Frontiers in the Philosophy of Intellectual Property
978 1 107 00931 8

Sigrid Sterckx and Julian Cockbain
Exclusions from Patentability: How the European Patent Office is Eroding Boundaries
978 1 107 00694 2

Sebastian Haunss
Conflicts in the Knowledge Society: The Contentious Politics of Intellectual Property
978 1 107 03642 0

Helena R. Howe and Jonathan Griffiths
Concepts of Property in Intellectual Property Law
978 1 107 04182 0

Rochelle Cooper Dreyfuss and Jane C. Ginsburg
Intellectual Property at the Edge: The Contested Contours of IP
978 1 107 03400 6

Normann Witzleb, David Lindsay, Moira Paterson and Sharon Rodrick
Emerging Challenges in Privacy Law: Comparative Perspectives
978 1 107 04167 7

Paul Bernal
Internet Privacy Rights: Rights to Protect Autonomy
978 1 107 04273 5